GENERAL HIRAM MARTIN CHITTENDEN

THE AMERICAN
FUR TRADE OF
THE FAR WEST

« HIRAM MARTIN CHITTENDEN »

Foreword by William R. Swagerty

WITH INTRODUCTION AND NOTES BY
STALLO VINTON

AND SKETCH OF THE AUTHOR BY
DR. EDMOND S. MEANY

VOL. 2

University of Nebraska Press
Lincoln and London

First Bison Book printing: 1986

Library of Congress Cataloging-in-Publication Data
Chittenden, Hiram Martin, 1858–1917.
    The American fur trade of the Far West.
    "Bison."
    Reprint. Originally published: New York: Press of
the Pioneers, 1935.
    Includes index.
    1. Fur trade — West (U.S.) — History. 2. West (U.S.) —
Description and travel. 3. West (U.S.) — History.
I. Title.
HD9944.U 1986   381'.456753'0978   86-11227
ISBN 0-8032-6320-1 (v. 1: pbk.)
ISBN 0-8032-6321-X (v. 2: pbk.)

Volume 2 of the Bison Book edition reprints the last three parts and the appendix of
the 1935 edition published by the Press of the Pioneers in two volumes. In the latter
edition, however, Volume 2 begins with Chapter XXVII of Part II. A map and new
foreword have been added to this volume, as well as the frontispiece that appeared in
Volume 1 of the Press of the Pioneers edition. The comprehensive index in Volume 2
of that edition is here reduced to cover only this volume.

CONTENTS

ILLUSTRATIONS

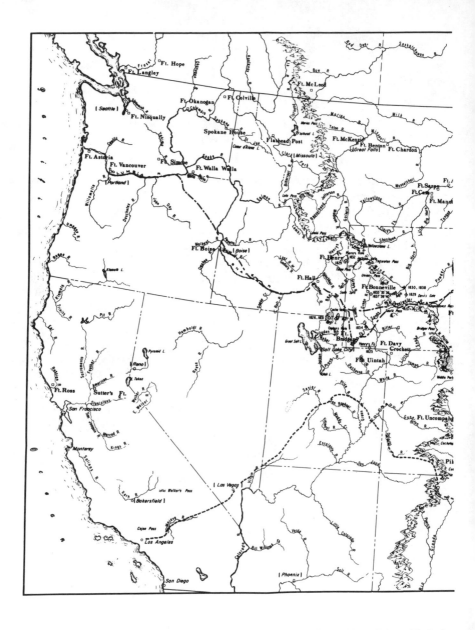

Reprinted by permission of the Arthur H. Clark Company from *The Mountain Men and the Fur Trade of the Far West,* edited by LeRoy R. Hafen, 10 vols (Glendale, Calif.: Arthur H. Clark, 1965–72).

heart of the trade on the Missouri River from the eighteenth century to the mid-nineteenth century. With the help of his wife, Nettie M. Parker-Chittenden, whose assistance speeded the project immensely, he dusted, sorted, and referenced package after package of documents in a stuffy little alcove at a St. Louis boardinghouse. The author recalled that these years of research required great personal sacrifice and were the most demanding in all of his writing efforts. Setting aside military uniform and gentleman's tie and putting on workman's overalls in order to commence "the appalling task of going through these records and extracting the fugitive gold from such masses of pure dross," Chittenden became the first researcher to thoroughly use the extensive papers of the most powerful and long-lived company on the upper Missouri.[6]

Unlike most modern researchers, accustomed to carefully indexed and well-organized archives, Chittenden faced a "half car-load or so of records . . . [that] were covered with at least three-fourths of the coal iron dust of St. Louis," and most of which required translation from French or Spanish in addition to sorting. His linguistic skills, acquired first at Cornell University, where he studied literature and history as well as foreign languages for two terms beginning in 1878, along with further training at West Point, enabled him to wade through several generations' intimate involvement in the Indian trade of the trans-Missouri West. Chittenden was so excited about his discoveries that he included several of these documents as appendixes to his two-volume interpretation. They are reproduced here in their entirety. The first is a letter dated April 10, 1810, from the Three Forks of the Missouri River, where Pierre Menard reported to Pierre Chouteau in St. Louis an incident that contributed to a long catalog of lethal confrontations between white trappers and Blackfeet warriors. Chittenden proved his skill at translation to would-be skeptics by printing the document in the original French, followed by a corrected French rendering and a final English translation. Readers interested in the types of primary sources available to Chittenden will appreciate the craft required to weave these into an interpretive framework.[7]

Beyond company records, Chittenden combed published sources and Missouri newspapers, as well as unpublished sources in the state historical societies of Missouri, Wisconsin, Kansas, Nebraska, Iowa, Minnesota, and Montana. Most topics that received chapter-length coverage in his *History* had not yet been reported in the literature. He readily acknowledged his predecessors in his Author's Preface, giving special credit to Washington Irving, Josiah Gregg, and Prince Maximilian, as well as numerous explorers, trappers, traders, and missionaries who left diaries and letters. Chittenden recognized that he had probably overlooked some sources in the writing of his *History* and he predicted that many other documents in "unexpected places" would eventually surface. Twentieth-century discoveries validate his prophecy. Critics who have subsequently charged Chittenden with oversights and deficiencies in his sources have a weak case, especially relative to the unparalleled contribution he made by locating and integrating entire collections of source materials. Those same critics and others have a better case for complaint in Chittenden's rather carefree system of annotation and bibliographic citation. However, given the relatively short amount of time devoted to the project and the limited number of researchers upon whom he could rely for advice and corroboration of data, most scholars agree that he did admirably well.[8]

The manuscript was accepted by Francis P. Harper of New York and was published in 1902. The association with Harper was gratifying, for that prestigious firm had published Elliott Coues's editions of the *History of the Lewis and Clark Expedition*

(1893) and the *Expeditions of Zebulon Montgomery Pike* (1895). An ornithologist and former military officer, Coues shared many interests with Chittenden and befriended him by frequent correspondence and by introducing him to editors at the New York publishing house. Even though they often disagreed on the motives of and relationship between Indians and whites during fur trade years, the two had common interests in the scientific and cartographic contributions of fur trade personnel as well as in the natural habitat of the trans-Mississippi West. With Coues's death in 1899, Chittenden became Harper's first twentieth-century "western" authority. Through his encouragement, Chittenden became interested in and incorporated much natural history in his *American Fur Trade*. Volume 2 may be viewed in part as a tribute to the extensive influence of Coues, a debt Chittenden was prompt to acknowledge.[9]

Another important reason the project succeeded was the author's authoritative acquaintance with the geography of the fur trade West, especially the upper Missouri and Rocky Mountain regions. His initial years in Yellowstone from 1891 to 1893 and a second tour of duty in the park beginning in 1899 provided a home base for exploring the intermountain West.

Even while based in St. Louis, Chittenden combined business with his avid devotion to research, fishing, and exploring, making three major western trips to assess the irrigation and reclamation potential of the arid West for the government in 1896 and 1897. He made numerous stops, by train, packhorse, and on foot, at historical fur trade post sites and scenes of trapper and trader activity. Like Herbert E. Bolton and other early-twentieth-century historians who advocated the necessity of retracing historic highways, Chittenden carefully mapped, photographed, and noted the places that would appear in his histories. Diary entries reveal his passionate appreciation of landscape and historic ruins as symbols of an era he admittedly romanticized. For example, in seeing the rubble of Fort Laramie for the first time in August of 1897, Chittenden rhapsodized: "As the sun fell behind the Laramie Hills and clothed the prairie landscape in a beautiful half light, there was a stillness everywhere around that was in keeping with this burial place of former activity. It was left for the imagination to fill up the void—to conjure up the far past when the seven returning Astorians passed by the mouth of the Laramie—when the early hunters under Ashley, Sublette and Campbell made their way to the distant mountains,—whence Bonneville and Wyeth and the Missionaries crossed the famous stream whose name Joseph Larémé in those early days gave and consecrated with his life. Then, what hardship, and suffering, of the long period of Californian emigration. Of the eventful period of military occupancy there are mementos, indeed, for the old garrison buildings are still there although now in ruins."[10]

All of Chittenden's work teems with minutiae enriching the historical geography essential to an understanding of the spatial arena of the fur trade. Often it is tucked between the pageantry and drama the author sought to recreate by lifting from obscurity or ensuring the remembrance of a gallery of traders and trappers from Manuel Lisa to Jim Bridger. Only recently has the American trade been fully understood as three interlocking but individual systems, two of which Chittenden understood well because of his experiences and his interest in the Rocky Mountain and upper Missouri trade.[11] Apart from the section on the Santa Fe Trade (attached to Volume 1 in the present edition), the southwestern trade system received much less attention than it deserved, a problem that led Stallo Vinton to undertake the editorship of the second edition, reproduced here. Vinton's appended "The Fur Trade of the Southwest" attempted to compensate for Chittenden's bias and lack of expertise in this area. It is but an outline of American activities in the trade of the Southwest and should be supplemented by more comprehensive work published since 1935. [12]

Part V, "The Country and Its Inhabitants," is a compilation of material used throughout earlier sections and could well be read independently of them, but it should not be. Here the West comes alive, the land taking on special meaning as the determinant in the human successes and failures in exploration, exploitation, and occupation that fill the previous pages of the two volumes. Chapter 9, "Native Tribes of the Missouri Basin," and Chapter 10, "Native Tribes of the Southwest and the Tra-Montane Country," are ethnographic documents in themselves and contain some errors, but do not contradict the interpretation given by the author in his narrative chapters. As period pieces, they postdate John Wesley Powell's 1891 linguistic survey of North American Indians and predate Frederick Webb Hodge's *Handbook of North American Indians* (1907, 1910) as well as most ethnographic casework among western tribes. These chapters should be viewed in that context, not as a definitive reference tool on tribes active in the trade during the first half of the nineteenth century. [13]

Less caution is necessary for the other sections in Volume 2, although Chittenden's choice of chronological parameters, from the opening of the Missouri River trade by Manuel Lisa and former members of the Lewis and Clark Expedition in 1807 to the completion of Fort Bridger in 1843 as an emigrant hostelry and service center, fall short on both ends of the true extent of the trade in all theaters of operation. That is especially true for the upper Missouri, where the American Fur Company remained active until 1865 and other business concerns continued the buffalo robe trade into the 1880s. [14]

Part III, "Contemporary Events Connected with the Fur Trade," is especially important for demonstrating the connection between government-sponsored surveys such as the Yellowstone Expeditions and the fur trade in the trans-Missouri West. Chapter V, "The Smallpox Scourge of 1837," was the first major discussion of the great pandemic that reduced northern plains tribes to a fraction of their former numbers and indicates Chittenden's awareness of the important role of disease in Indian-white relations throughout the West. Notes on explorers and missionaries give a rough framework of these groups' activities during the height of the Rocky Mountain trade, providing a glimpse of Chittenden's deep interest in those tribes such as the Flatheads who were largely cooperative with whites in the trade and who would be the subject of his superb edited work on Jesuit activities among northern plains and northern Rockies tribes. [15]

In Part IV, biographical vignettes and stories of human interest add color and action to preceding sections in Volume 1, which focus on business aspects of the trade. All of these men and events were special to the author and here he essentially shares his enthusiasm and findings with the reader. Those following the traps and trails of Ezekiel Williams, Henry Vanderburgh, Hugh Glass, Mike Fink, and John Colter will find the editor's notes useful, but should keep in mind that no sources were added after 1935. Much has since been learned about many of these fur trade participants, as reported by scholars in LeRoy R. Hafen's multivolume *Mountain Men and the Fur Trade of the Far West*. [16]

This is not to belittle the value of Chittenden's well-organized narrative in Volume 1 nor the potpourri contained in Volume 2. The corrective and supplemental notes by Stallo Vinton added much to the reliability of this edition, making it the best of the three heretofore published in cloth. Although Vinton was a lawyer, not a professional historian, he wrote minor works on such subjects as John Colter and Kit Carson, thus acquainting himself with much of the same source material available to Chittenden.[17] Used in tandem with more recent literature on the fur trade, Vinton's edition of Chittenden's pioneering work retains its place as an indispensable source.[18]

NOTES

1. Chittenden's publications and manuscripts are listed and analyzed in *H. M. Chittenden: A Western Epic; Being a Selection from His Unpublished Journals, Diaries and Reports,* edited with notes and introduction by Bruce Le Roy (Tacoma: Washington State Historical Society, 1961). A brief biography of the author by Edmond S. Meany is contained in Volume 1 of the present work, pp. xli–xliv.

2. The original edition of *The History of the American Fur Trade of the Far West* was printed in three volumes by Francis P. Harper in 1902. A second edition, reprinted here, with introduction and notes by Stallo Vinton and a sketch of the author by Dr. Edmond S. Meany, was printed in New York by Barnes and Noble and published by the Press of the Pioneers in 1935. A third edition, with an introduction by Grace Lee Nute, was released in two volumes by Academic Reprints of Stanford, California, in 1954 as number one in the American Culture and Economic Series.

The Yellowstone National Park: Historical and Descriptive (Cincinnati: Robert Clarke Co., 1895) was revised by Chittenden several times before his death in 1917; was adopted as the official guidebook to the park with additional revisions by his daughter, Eleanor Chittenden Cress; and was reissued, with Chittenden's final corrections from the 1917 edition, by Stanford University Press in 1933. In 1964 the University of Oklahoma Press published a useful edition by Richard A. Bartlett that has been available in paperback as well as cloth binding.

3. H. M. Chittenden, "Historical Work," September, 1917, four-page typescript published in *H. M. Chittenden,* ed. Bruce Le Roy, pp. 81–83.

4. Gordon B. Dodds, "The Fur Trade and Exploration," in *Historians and the American West,* ed. Michael P. Malone (Lincoln: Uni-

versity of Nebraska Press, 1983), p. 57. Also see Dodds, *Hiram Martin Chittenden: His Public Career* (Lexington: University of Kentucky Press, 1973).

5. For Chittenden's exalted place in the historiography of the West, see Grace Lee Nute's introduction to the third edition of *A History of the American Fur Trade of the Far West* (Stanford: Academic Reprints, 1954), 1:vii–xxi. Also see Dale L. Morgan, "The Fur Trade and Its Historians," *American West* 3 (1966): 28–35, 92–93, reprinted in *Aspects of the Fur Trade: Selected Papers of the 1965 North American Fur Trade Conference,* ed. Russell W. Fridley (St. Paul: Minnesota Historical Society, 1967), pp. 3–8; Dodds, "Fur Trade and Exploration," pp. 57–58; and Dodds, *Hiram Martin Chittenden,* pp. 72–102.

6. Chittenden, "Historical Work," 81–82. Grace Lee Nute became the second major researcher to use the American Fur Company records. She provided a calendar for future researchers and added to a general understanding of the collection in 1945 in the *Annual Report of the American Historial Association for the Year 1944,* vols. 2–3 (Washington: United States Government Printing Office, 1945).

7. See Appendices, pp. 878 ff. below.

8. See his Author's Preface in Volume 1, pp. xxvii–xxxix. Among the early reviewers, Frances Fuller Victor was most supportive. Chittenden frequently corresponded with Victor while writing his history, drawing upon her contributions to H. H. Bancroft's *History of the Pacific States of North America,* 34 vols. (1882–90) as well as her previous work, *The River of the West: Life and Adventures in the Rocky Mountains and Oregon* (Hartford, Conn.: R. W. Bliss Co., 1870). Her flattering review appeared in the *Oregon Historical Quarterly* 3 (1902): 260–70. On historians' criticisms of Chittenden's work, see Dodds, *Hiram Martin Chittenden,* pp. 78–84.

9. On Coues's influence on and importance in Chittenden's career, see "Historical Work," pp. 81–83. In addition to Coues's edition of the Lewis and Clark journals, Chittenden benefited from Coues's editing of *Forty Years a Fur Trader on the Upper Missouri by Charles Larpenteur* (New York: Francis P. Harper, 1898).

10. Chittenden, "Journal of a Trip to Jackson Hole and Idaho, Au-

gust 1897," in *H. M. Chittenden*, ed. Le Roy, pp. 52–53.

11. The best analysis of the two systems that Chittenden first unraveled is David J. Wishart, *The Fur Trade of the American West, 1807–1840* (Lincoln: University of Nebraska Press, 1979).

12. The most important works on the southwestern trade are Robert Glass Cleland, *This Reckless Breed of Men: The Trappers and Fur Traders of the Southwest* (New York: Alfred A. Knopf, 1950; reprinted, with an introduction by Harvey L. Carter, Albuquerque: University of New Mexico Press, 1976); David Lavender, *Bent's Fort: A Historical Account of the Adobe Empire That Shaped the Destiny of the American Southwest* (New York: Doubleday, 1954); Iris Higbie Wilson, *William Wolfskill, 1798–1866: Frontier Trapper to California Ranchero* (Glendale, Calif.: Arthur H. Clark Co., 1965); Charles L. Camp, ed., *George C. Yount and His Chronicles of the West* (Denver: Old West Publishing Co., 1966); David J. Weber, *The Taos Trappers: The Fur Trade in the Far Southwest, 1540–1846* (Norman: University of Oklahoma Press, 1971); and Janet Lecompte, *Pueblo, Hardscrabble, Greenhorn: The Upper Arkansas, 1832–1856* (Norman: University of Oklahoma Press, 1978).

13. The edition currently underway of the *Handbook of North American Indians*, edited by William C. Sturtevant, 20 vols. (Washington: Smithsonian Institution 1978–) will replace Frederick Webb Hodge's pioneering *Handbook*, published as *Bureau of American Ethnology Bulletin* 30 (2 pts. 1907, 1910).

14. For the limitations of Chittenden's chronological parameters, see Abraham Nasatir, ed., *Before Lewis and Clark: Documents Illustrating the History of the Missouri, 1785–1804*, 2 vols. (St. Louis: St. Louis Historical Documents Foundation, 1952); John E. Sunder, *The Fur Trade on the Upper Missouri, 1840–1865* (Norman: University of Oklahoma Press, 1965); Robert G. Athearn, *Forts of the Upper Missouri* (Lincoln: University of Nebraska Press, 1967); W. Raymond Wood and Thomas D. Thiessen, eds., *Early Fur Trade on the Northern Plains: Canadian Traders among the Mandan and Hidatsa Indians, 1738–1818* (Norman: University of Oklahoma Press, 1985).

15. On Chittenden's importance in assessing the impact of European diseases on the northern plains, see Clyde Dollar, "The High

Plains Smallpox Epidemic of 1837–38," *Western Historical Quarterly* 8 (1977): 15–16. Also see Chittenden and Richardson, eds., *Life, Letters and Travels of Father Jean-Pierre DeSmet, S.J., 1801–1873,* 1:188–89.

16. LeRoy R. Hafen, ed., *The Mountain Men and the Fur Trade of the Far West,* 10 vols. (Glendale, Calif.: Arthur H. Clark Co., 1965–72) is the most ambitious and complete collective biography in western American history. Most of the major subjects covered in Chittenden are surveyed by scholars in this important work.

17. Stallo Vinton was a New York City lawyer who published minor works on John Colter, Kit Carson, and Joseph Meek before editing the present volume at the age of fifty-eight in 1935. Vinton had a liberal arts education from Columbia University, having completed his bachelor's degree in 1898, a master's of arts in 1899, and a law degree in 1900. His notes are authoritative and beneficial in correcting minor errors made by Chittenden. Vinton died in 1946 (*New York Times,* Thursday, November 7, 1946, p. 31). His major publications were *John Colter, Discoverer of Yellowstone Park: An Account of His Exploration in 1807 and of His Further Adventures as Hunter, Trapper, Indian Fighter, Pathfinder and Member of the Lewis and Clark Expedition* (New York: E. Eberstadt, 1926) and *Overland with Kit Carson: A Narrative of the Old Spanish Trail in '48,* by George Douglas Brewerton, with an introduction and map by Stallo Vinton (New York: Coward-McCann, 1930).

18. Especially significant among the more recent studies are Frederick Merk, ed., *Fur Trade and Empire: George Simpson's Journal, 1824–1825* (Cambridge: Harvard University Press, 1931); Dale L. Morgan, ed., *The West of William H. Ashley* (Denver: Fred A. Rosenstock, Old West Publishing Co., 1964); Cleland, *This Reckless Breed of Men* (1950), E. E. Rich, *The History of the Hudson's Bay Company, 1670–1870,* vol. 2, *1763–1870,* Publications of the Hudson's Bay Record Society 22 (London: Hudson's Bay Record Society, 1959); LeRoy R. Hafen, "A Brief History of the Fur Trade of the Far West," in Hafen, ed., *The Mountain Men and the Fur Trade of the Far West,* 1 (1965): 20–176; Paul C. Phillips, with concluding chapters by J. W. Smurr, *The Fur Trade,* 2 vols (Norman: University of Oklahoma

Press, 1961); Richard E. Oglesby, *Manuel Lisa and the Opening of the Missouri Fur Trade* (Norman: University of Oklahoma Press, 1963); John E. Sunder, *The Fur Trade on the Upper Missouri, 1840–1865* (1965); Sunder, *Joshua Pilcher, Fur Trader and Indian Agent* (Norman: University of Oklahoma Press, 1968); Harvey L. Carter and Marcia C. Spencer, "Stereotypes of the Mountain Man," *Western Historical Quarterly* 6 (1975): 17–32; Carter, Introduction to *Mountain Men and the Fur Traders of the Far West: Eighteen Biographical Sketches,* ed. LeRoy R. Hafen (Lincoln: University of Nebraska Press, 1982); Janet Lecompte, *Pueblo, Hardscrabble, Greenhorn* (1978); Lewis O. Saum, *The Fur Trader and the Indian* (Seattle: University of Washington Press, 1965); David J. Weber, *The Taos Trappers* (1971); John C. Ewers, *Indian Life on the Upper Missouri* (Norman: University of Oklahoma Press, 1968); Ewers, "The Influence of the Fur Trade upon the Indians of the Northern Plains," in *People and Pelts: Selected Papers of the Second North American Fur Trade Conference,* ed. Malvina Bolus (Winnipeg: Peguis Publishers, 1972), pp. 1–26; David J. Wishart, *The Fur Trade of the American West* (1979); D. W. Meinig, *The Great Columbia Plain: A Historical Geography, 1805–1910* (Seattle: University of Washington Press, 1968); Gloria Griffen Cline, *Peter Skene Ogden and the Hudson's Bay Company* (Norman: University of Oklahoma Press, 1974); and Howard R. Lamar, *The Trader on the American Frontier: Myth's Victim* (College Station: Texas A&M University Press, 1977).

Additional context on Chittenden's enduring utility is provided by Dodds, "The Fur Trade and Exploration." His discussion, however, should be supplemented by the analysis of the limitations of the traditional white-centered approach as reviewed by Jacqueline Peterson and John Anfinson, "The Indian and the Fur Trade: A Review of Recent Literature," in *Scholars and the Indian Experience,* ed. W. R. Swagerty (Bloomington: Indiana University Press for the Newberry Library, 1984), pp. 223–57, and as emphasized by James P. Ronda in his preface to Volume 1 of the Bison Book edition of Chittenden's *American Fur Trade of the Far West* (Lincoln: University of Nebraska Press, 1986), pp. xiii–xxiii.

PART III. *Contemporary Events Connected with the Fur Trade*

Chapter I

THE WAR OF 1812

Effect of the wat on the Missouri Fur Trade—Influence upon the Indians—speech of Big Elk—The work of Manuel Lisa— Commission to treat with the Indians—The "One-eyed" Sioux —Lieutenant Kennedy's journey.

The war of 1812, so humiliating in many of its phases to American pride, affected the trans-Mississippi fur trade only on the Columbia and the Upper Missouri rivers. The irretrievable ruin which it wrought to American interests on the Pacific has been considered in another part of this work. Its effect on the Missouri trade was to curtail its volume in a large degree, both on account of the diminished territory in which it was carried on, and because of the fall of prices due to the uncertainty of the traffic. "Since the Declaration of War," wrote Charles Gratiot to Astor in 1813, "the traders will not receive any [skins] from the Indians, that article having fallen in price." And ten months later he wrote: "In former years, before the war, we could calculate on at least one thousand packs [of buffalo robes] at this time, besides beaver and other different sorts of furs. But from the unsettled situation of the Indians during the war, particularly the last winter, the scarcity of merchandise among them, the dislike the fur traders have to meddle with that article, the kind of monopoly injurious to the Indian trade carried on by the factories of the United States—all these reasons induce me to suppose that it will not be in my power to buy the quantity you want, nor perhaps one-half."

The second and most serious effect of the war was the general unrest of the tribes within reach of border influence, and the imminent danger that the frontier settlements of Missouri would suffer the horrors of an Indian war. There was great reason to fear a general uprising of the Upper Missouri tribes, similar to that which embarrassed our government on the headwaters of the Mississippi. British influence was strong among these tribes, and it was certain that no efforts would be spared to make the most of it, now that the two countries were at war. Long before the outbreak of hostilities British emissaries were evidently making ready for it. "Your excellency will remember," wrote Manuel Lisa to Governor Clark in 1817, "that more than a year before the war broke out I gave you intelligence that the wampum was carrying [being carried] by British influence along the banks of the Missouri, and that all the nations of this great river were incited to join the universal confederacy then setting on foot."

The conditions were particularly favorable for such a conspiracy. By an almost uninterrupted series of misfortunes the Missouri Fur Company, the only important American organization which had yet attempted to carry its business into the region of the Upper Missouri, had been practically driven from that field. It was impossible that this ill success, as compared with the progress of the British companies, should not draw upon the American traders the contempt of the Indians; and when the Americans finally withdrew altogether from the Missouri above Council Bluffs the British felt that their opportunity had arrived. How great was this danger may be inferred from an incident which occurred after the close of the war, at a general council of the chiefs of the Mississippi and Missouri tribes held at Portage des Sioux in the summer of 1815. Big Elk, the Omaha chief, made a speech on that occasion which left little doubt as to the character of the influence that had penetrated even so far as to that peaceful tribe. He said in part, addressing General Clark: "Last winter when you sent your word and presents by Captain Manuel Lisa, which he gave us from our Great Father, in the night one of the whites (he was once your son) wanted my young men to rise. He told them that their blankets were dung and the strouds rotten, and if they wanted good presents, to cross to the British for good clothing. This man was Baptiste Dorion. . . . When I was at the Pawnees, I wanted to bring some of them down, but the whites who live among them told them not to go, that no good would come from the Americans; good only came from across the neck of land—from the British. . . . I am willing to go to war against the Sacs on the Mississippi, but I had no guns only blunt arrows. The British put guns into the hands of all the Sacs. . . . I have little more to tell you. I have already told Captain Manuel to request you to keep those men [British emissaries] away from us. . . . Take care of the Sioux. They listen to too many. They are like a bird that lights upon the branch of a tree and knows not which way to turn. Take care, or they will fly from under your wing."

The Sioux indeed, and all the tribes above, were at the outbreak of the war practically in the power of the British. Trade was almost suspended and such reports as came down indicated the hostility of those tribes. Thus we read in the *Missouri Gazette* of June 5, 1813: "Arrived here a few days ago from the Mandan villages (Upper Missouri), Mr. M. Lisa, acting partner of the Missouri Fur Company. From Mr. Lisa we learn that the Arapahoes, Cheyennes, Aricaras, Gros Ventres, and Crows are, or may be, considered at war with the Americans. The British Northwest Company having a number of trading houses within a short distance of the Missouri, are enabled to embroil our people with the savages, who are constantly urged to cut them off."

This reference to the Northwest Company is suggestive. At this very moment they were straining every nerve to extirpate American influence on the Pacific and it was a part of the general purpose to make the most of the opportunities offered by the war to drive Americans from the entire field along their own territories.

That there were no serious outbreaks among the Missouri Indians must be attributed mainly to the influence of Manuel Lisa. Although a Spaniard by birth, he fully appreciated the advantages of a free government and accepted it loyally and earnestly. "I have suffered enough in person and property under a different government," he said, in a letter already quoted, "to know how to appreciate the one under which I now live." He took an active part in keeping the Missouri tribes at peace. Recognizing the value of his services Governor Clark appointed him sub-agent of the Upper Missouri tribes in the summer of 1814, and this office he held until he voluntarily relinquished it in 1817. We give his own statement of what he accomplished. "The Indians of the Missouri," he said to General Clark, on resigning his commission, "are to those of the Upper Missouri as four to one. Their weight would be great if thrown in the scale against us. They did not arm against the republic; on the contrary they armed against Great Britain and struck the Iowas, the allies of that power. When peace was proclaimed, more than forty chiefs had intelligence with me, and together we were to carry an expedition of several thousand warriors against the tribes of the Upper Mississippi, and silence them at once. These things are known to Your Excellency. To the end of the war, therefore, the Indians of the Missouri continued friends of the United States."

Immediately after the news of peace arrived, Lisa took to St. Louis a deputation of forty-three chiefs and head men of the several bands of the Sioux, also the chiefs of the Omaha and other tribes residing between the Missouri and Mississippi rivers. These chiefs represented nations who had offered their services to the government, and were about to start a campaign against the Indians of the Mississippi when the war came to an end—another example of belated preparations which, had the war continued longer, would have turned the tide of military success heavily in favor of the Americans.

Some of the Missouri tribes had actually gone to war against the tribes hostile to the United States, and were so engaged at the time of the treaty of peace, and it was one of the first cares of the government, after the ratification of the treaty, to put a stop to their operations. In the spring of 1815 a commission was appointed by President Monroe, consisting of Governor William Clark, Ninian Edwards, and Colonel Auguste Chouteau, for the purpose of informing the Indians who had lately been hostile to the United States of the terms of the treaty with Great Britain, and of entering into peaceful relations with them. The commission met large deputations of Indians from the Mississippi and Missouri rivers at a little place called Portage des Sioux on the narrow neck of land between the two streams. Among these Indians were those brought down by Manuel Lisa, and with them satisfactory treaties were made without difficulty. But with the Mississippi Indians the case was different. The Sacs of Rock river, Illinois, in particular, were bitterly hostile to the Americans, opposed to peace, and could not be induced to treat. The labors of the commission were protracted all summer owing to these difficulties, and their report discloses in the clearest light the powerful influence which British traders and emissaries still exercised on our own soil.

So far as events of the war were concerned, very few of a hostile character occurred on the Missouri. There were some destructive raids on the settlements in the vicinity of Boone's Lick, and also a few near St. Louis in the spring of 1815, but with these we have nothing to do. The two principal events which transpired wholly or in part in the valley of the Upper Missouri were the sending of messengers to the Indians of the Upper Mississippi. So hostile were the Sacs and Foxes that it was found well-nigh impossible to get messengers through their country. It accordingly became necessary to send by way of the Missouri, and thence, from some point above the Omahas, to St. Peter's river in Minnesota. The first of these messengers was sent by Governor Clark in the fall of 1814, with conciliatory messages to the Sioux tribes of the Upper Mississippi. He was the noted Sioux, L'Original Levé, Standing Moose, commonly called One-Eye, or the One-Eyed Sioux, owing to the absence of one of his eyes, lost by accident in boyhood. He was one of the few Upper Mississippi Sioux who sided with the Americans. He had formed a great friendship for General Pike when that officer passed through his country in 1805, and remained true to that attachment by adhering to the cause of Pike's country. When a party was organized under the leadership of Joseph Renville and Little Crow to make war on the Americans, One Eye went to St. Louis, offered his services to General Clark, who gave him a commission and engaged him to go on the dangerous errand of carrying messages to the upper tribes. The *Missouri Gazette* of June 13, 1815, referring to this event, says: "Four Sioux Indians arrived here on Thursday last from Prairie du Chien, among whom is the One-Eyed Sioux who came down in the gun-boat last year, and who distinguished himself so gallantly when the boat was attacked by British artillery and a host of Indians. This Sioux and another of his tribe left this place last autumn with Manuel Lisa, Esq., and ascended the Missouri to the river Jacques [James river, South Dakota] from whence he traveled across the country to Prairie du Chien." It appeared that on his arrival there, Dickson mal-treated him, threatened him with death, imprisoned him, and tried in every way to extract information, but the Indian remained firm and would disclose nothing. He was then lib-erated and made his way to the Sioux tribes, whence he re-turned to Prairie du Chien and remained until the British evacuated that place. He came back to St. Louis in June 1815. He had promised General Clark to visit the various tribes and he kept his word. He always retained his commission as a precious memento and several persons have left a record of having seen it (1).

When the commissioners for forming treaties of peace met at Portage des Sioux in the spring of 1815 they were still con-fronted with the impossibility of communicating with the Upper Missouri tribes. Some attempts were made, although it was a matter of the greatest difficulty to secure volunteers for so perilous an undertaking. Among those who did attempt it was Joseph La Barge, father of the late Captain Joseph La Barge, the noted Missouri river pilot. But it was impossible to get through the Sac and Fox country, and finally the com-mission had to send by way of the Missouri, as Governor Clark had done the year before. On this important and perilous mission Lieutenant Kennedy, "one of the disbanded officers [of the late war] equally distinguished by his bravery and enterprise," volunteered to go. He succeeded in making the journey, although, owing to the theft of his horses, he did not accomplish as much as he had hoped. He made his way up the Missouri and across to Prairie du Chien, whence he re-turned late in September or early in October to St. Louis. While among the Missouri Indians he received intelligence that the British had opened an establishment among the Mandan nation. There is no doubt that the Northwest Company hoped to gain a foothold in this quarter, but the treaty of peace defeated their expectations.

With the close of the labors of the peace commission and the rendition of their report, October 18, 1815, the incidents of the War of 1812, so far as they pertain to the Upper Missouri country, may be considered at an end.

AUTHOR'S NOTE

(1) For further details in the life of this distinguished Indian see Coues' *Expedition of Zebulon Montgomery Pike*, 1895, p. 87.

Chapter II

THE YELLOWSTONE EXPEDITION OF 1819-1820

Origin of the expedition—Great expectations—Expedition both military and scientific—The military force—The scientific party—Absurd scheme for moving the troops—The steamboat fiasco—Bad management of the expedition—Sickness at Camp Missouri—The "Western Engineer"—Progress of Major Long up the Missouri—Arrival at the Council Bluffs—Winter Cantonment—Major Long goes to Washington—Failure of the expedition—Organization of Long's expedition of 1820—Expedition arrives at the Pawnees—Reaches the base of the mountains —Pike's Peak—The Arkansas—Division of the party—Captain Bell's journey down the Arkansas—Major Long's journey down the Canadian—Arrival at Fort Smith—Arrival of party at Cape Girardeau—Itinerary of Long's expedition—Estimate of results—Canadian and Red rivers—Pike's Peak—Publication of report—Major Long's description of the country.

The expedition whose history forms the subject of this chapter was everywhere popularly known in its day as the Yellowstone Expedition. The enterprise was regarded as one of great possibilities for the public good, particularly in the West. The failure of Mr. Astor's project upon the Columbia; the disastrous fortunes of the Missouri Fur Company; the evidences of British influence with Indians residing in United States territory; and the necessity of protection to American trade in the more remote regions; these considerations had prevailed upon Congress to make a formidable showing of national authority along the upper course of the Missouri. Not a few hoped that the arms of the govment would be carried to the Columbia, and that American rights upon that river would be restored, as the Treaty of Ghent required, to the status existing before the War of 1812.

The enterprise was a popular one in all parts of the country and was a favorite measure of President Monroe, and of his Secretary of War, John C. Calhoun. In a letter to the Secretary during the progress of the enterprise, the President said: "The people of the whole Western country take a deep interest in the success of the contemplated establishment at the mouth of the Yellowstone river. They look upon it as a measure better calculated to preserve the peace of the frontier, to secure to us the fur trade and to break up the intercourse between the British traders and the Indians, than any other which has been taken by the government. I take myself very great interest in the success of the expedition, and am willing to take great responsibility to ensure it."

The object of the expedition is officially stated by Secretary Calhoun as follows: "The expedition ordered to the mouth of the Yellowstone, or rather to the Mandan village, is a part of a system of measures which has for its objects the protection of our northwestern frontier and the greater extension of our fur trade."

To the people of the West, and in fact of the whole country, the expedition promised results of which the official purpose above quoted was a very inadequate expression. Quotations might be given at great length from the press of the country and even of Europe, evincing the warmest interest in the enterprise; but it will suffice to notice a few from the Western press to show how great were the expectations of those most directly interested. In an editorial of April 21, 1819, the *Missouri Gazette* of St. Louis said: "The importance of the expedition has attracted the attention of the whole nation, and there is no measure which has been adopted by the present administration that has received such universal commendation. If the agents of the government who have charge of it fulfill the high expectations which have been raised, it will conspicuously add to the admiration with which the administration of James Monroe will hereafter be viewed. . . . In every point of view the Yellowstone Expedition will stand prominent. It will add to the security of the Western country, particularly the frontier settlements; it will keep in check the Indians and prevent their depredations; it will tend to destroy in some measure the influence that our British neighbors possess over the minds of the natives; it will throw additional light upon the geography of that noble river, the Missouri, and also the country on its banks now inhabited by the Indians; it will also encourage Western emigration; it will protect and encourage the the fur trade which is now productive of such important benefits to the country, and which can be made much more productive; it will conduce to open the communication which nature has ordained ought to exist between the Mississippi and the Pacific ocean. . . . If the expedition should succeed, as we fondly hope and expect, the time will not be far distant when another nation will inhabit west of the Mississippi, equal at least, if not superior, to those which the ancient remains still found in this country lead us to believe once flourished here: a nation indeed rendered more durable by the enjoyment of that great invention of American freemen—a Federal Republic.'' The article then went on to state some of the dangers of failure which might arise if unpractical men were put in charge. It gave wise advice in regard to the treatment of the Indians, and throughout displayed a knowledge of the conditions of success which might well have indicated the writer as a fitting individual to form part of the personnel of the expedition.

Niles' Register of October 17, 1818, quoting the *St. Louis Enquirer*, said: "The establishment of this post [at the mouth of the Yellowstone] will be an era in the history of the West. It will go to the source and root of the fatal British influence which has for many years armed the Indian nations against our Western frontier. It carries the arms and power of the United States to the ground which has hitherto been exclusively occupied by the British Northwest and Hudson Bay Companies, and which has been the true seat of British power over the Indian mind. Now the American arms and American policy will be displayed upon the same theater. The Northwest and Hudson Bay Companies will be shut out from the commerce of the Missouri and Mississippi Indians; the American traders will penetrate in safety the recesses of the Rocky mountains in search of its rich furs, a commerce yielding a million per annum will descend the Missouri, and the Indians, finding their wants supplied by the American traders, their domestic wars restrained by American policy, will learn to respect the American name.

"The name of the Yellowstone river will hereafter be familiar to the American ear" (1).

The high expectations which were built on the possibilities of this expedition are in no better way illustrated than in the exaggerations to which they gave rise. One enthusiast seriously avowed his opinion that the expedition would open a "safe and easy communication to China, which would give such a spur to commercial enterprise that ten years shall not pass away before we shall have the rich productions of that country transported from Canton to the Columbia, up that river to the mountains, over the mountains and down the Missouri and Mississippi, all the way (mountains and all) by the potent power of steam. These are not idle dreams, rely upon it; to me it seems much less difficult than it was universally considered when I first came here to navigate the Missouri with sailboats (2)." The writer of this letter was indeed a trifle "previous" in his forecast, but one can discern in his heated imagination a dim conception of the railroad yet to be. It was not to be for many years, but the time *has* come when the "potent power of steam" transports the goods of China over "mountains and all" to every mart where the needs of the people require them.

We can hardly realize now what visions of future greatness then filled the minds of our people. Steam had fairly entered upon its conquest of the navigable waters of the globe, and scarcely a day passed but that some new feat astonished the world and brushed aside another of the "impossibilities" of conservatism. All ranks of society felt the thrill of the new era, even men of sober experience were swept along in the current. The following views, expressed by a man of long and distinguished public service, reflect the general enthusiasm of the time. Speaking of the Yellowstone Expedition he said: "See those vessels, with the agency of steam, advancing against the powerful currents of the Mississippi and the Missouri! Their course is marked by volumes of smoke and fire, which the civilized man observes with admiration, and the savage with astonishment. Botanists, mineralogists, chemists, artisans, cultivators, scholars, soldiers; the love of peace, the capacity for war; philosophical apparatus and military supplies; telescopes and cannon, garden seeds and gunpowder; the arts of civil life and the force to defend them— all are seen aboard. The banner of freedom which waves over the whole proclaims the character and protective power of the United States."

We have given somewhat at length, and in their own language, the views of the people at the time upon this important expedition, because a full understanding is necessary in order to appreciate their deep disappointment at their non-fulfillment. Unfortunately the very magnitude of the enterprise and its unbounded possibilities led to an elaboration of the means for carrying it into effect which, by its cumbersomeness, proved fatal to the undertaking.

The expedition was to be both military and scientific in character. The movement of troops was planned on a scale wholly beyond the requirements of the occasion, and it was at one time contemplated to send upward of a thousand men. Congress had been led to believe that the movement would actually result in a saving to the military establishment of upwards of forty thousand dollars a year, owing mainly to the diminished cost of subsistence in a country where game was so abundant and grazing free. Troops were moved from Plattsburg, Philadelphia, Detroit, and Bellefontaine near St. Louis. The military expedition was under command of Colonel Henry Atkinson, and so far as he was unhampered in his operations he seems to have conducted it with the practical good sense for which that officer was distinguished. He adopted a device of his own for propelling keelboats, consisting of paddle wheels similar to those of a steamboat, but operated by soldiers who were on board. This arrangement worked well enough to justify its adoption in an expedition conducted by General Atkinson to the mouth of the Yellowstone in 1825. The movement of the troops began in the fall of 1818 and a considerable detachment under Captain Martin passed the winter near the mouth of the Kansas river at a

KENNETH McKENZIE

cantonment christened Camp Martin. The general advance took place in the following spring.

The scientific part of the expedition was under the direction of Major Stephen H. Long, of the Corps of Engineers, U.S.A., an officer of high professional reputation. He was assisted by Major Biddle, who kept the journal; Dr. Baldwin, botanist; Dr. Say, zoologist; Dr. Jessup, geologist; Mr. Peale, assistant naturalist; Mr. Seymour, painter and sketcher, and Lieutenant Graham and Cadet Swift, topographical assistants. The instructions of the Secretary of War to Major Long stated that "the object of the expedition is to acquire as thorough and accurate knowledge, as may be practicable, of a portion of the country which is daily becoming more interesting, but which is yet imperfectly known. You will ascertain the latitude and longitude of remarkable points, with all possible precision. You will, if possible, ascertain some point in the 49th parallel of latitude which separates our possessions from those of Great Britain. A knowledge of the extent of our limits will tend to prevent collision between our traders and theirs.

"You will enter into your journal everything interesting in relation to soil, face of country, water courses, and productions, whether animal, vegetable, or mineral.

"You will conciliate the Indians by kindness and presents, and will ascertain as far as practicable the number and character of the various tribes, with the extent of country claimed by each."

The instructions of President Jefferson to Captains Lewis and Clark were also cited for guidance.

Such were the fond expectations in regard to this great undertaking and such the elaborate preparations for carrying it into effect. But the magnitude of the conception was in no wise sustained by the skill of its execution. The arrangement for the transportation of the troops disclosed a degree of folly, if nothing worse, which is a disgrace to the military history of the government. The conditions of travel up the Missouri were thoroughly understood at the time, and it was known that by the aid of keelboats the march to the mouth of the Yellowstone could be easily accomplished in a single season. Such was evidently Colonel Atkinson's idea. But the officials in St. Louis having the matter of transportation in charge thought otherwise. So great an enterprise as the Yellowstone Expedition must be conducted with becoming state. No keelboat transportation would answer. The steamboat, that new power on the Western rivers, was alone appropriate to the occasion. Although no steamboat had yet entered the Missouri river, and although a little practical reflection must have shown that some experience would be required to develop and overcome the difficulties of navigating that unruly stream, and that the first efforts must be largely failures, still the government decided to rely mainly upon steamboats. In putting into effect this plan it committed the always disastrous mistake of trusting itself, bound hand and foot, to the tender mercies of a contractor. Of those connected with this expedition, one Colonel James Johnson, a contractor, emerges from its confused history with the glory of having accomplished all and more than he expected. Without competition he secured a contract, December 2, 1818, in which not only were the prices exorbitant, but some of them were left to future contingencies to be fixed by arbitration if agreement should fail between the principals. He was also to be allowed advances before services were performed, and that without adequate security to the government. Thus practically guaranteed against loss, the shrewd Colonel Johnson took little care to see that his equipment was of a character which should ensure a prompt fulfillment of the contract. He provided five steamboats, the *Jefferson*, *Expedition*, *Johnson*, *Calhoun*, and *Exchange*, There is no record that the last two were able to enter the Missouri at all. The *Jefferson* gave out and abandoned the trip thirty miles below Franklin. The *Expedition* and *Johnson* wintered at Cow Island, a little above the mouth of the Kansas, and returned to St. Louis in the following spring. In his entire arrangements Colonel Johnson failed to come up to the contract, and the expedition was thereby hopelessly delayed and its main purpose thwarted. In the disagreements that subsequently arose arbitrators had to be called in, and these sided with the contractor, allowing him over forty thousand dollars for loss occasioned by the very delays for which he alone was responsible. The matter was so scandalous that it led to an investigation by a committee of Congress, who reported against the justice and legality of the award, and recommended the institution of legal proceedings to recover the amount wrongfully paid (3).

The expedition had not proceeded far before it became evident that its management was hopelessly weak and that it must fall far short of its original purpose (4). The whole summer was spent on the lower river and it was September 26th before the troops reached Council Bluffs. All thought of going farther was abandoned for the time. A camp was established called Camp Missouri, and here the troops remained for the winter. It proved to be one of the most disastrous winter encampments in the history of the army. The troops suffered terribly from the scurvy. Over three hundred were attacked and of these about one hundred died. The disease prevailed to some extent all winter, and by spring the situation had become "truly deplorable." As soon as it was possible to navigate the river, many of the sick were sent to Fort Osage.

The steamboat craze on this expedition was not confined to the military portion, but extended to the scientific adjunct as well. For the use of Major Lang's party a special boat was constructed which appears in every way to have been a decided novelty. It was called the *Western Engineer*, and was probably the first stern-wheel steamboat ever built. It was launched in Pittsburg in the winter of 1818-19. The only description of this craft which has come to our notice is the following from the *Missouri Gazette* of May 26, 1819, and a letter written about a month later: "The *Western Engineer* is well armed and carries an elegant flag representing a white man and an Indian shaking hands, the calumet of peace and the sword. The boat is 75 feet long, 13 feet beam and draws 19 inches of water. The steam passes off through the mouth of a large figure-head (a serpent). . . . The wheels are placed in the stern." Omitting the absurd attempts at ornamentation, the boat was as much of a success as could have been expected at that early stage of steamboat experience. It was far better adapted to the navigation of the Missouri than were any of

Colonel Johnson's boats, and although it did not leave St. Louis until sometime after the rest of the expedition had gone, it passed them all before they reached the mouth of the Kansas, and was the only boat that went through to Council Bluffs.

How this unusual craft impressed the popular eye may be inferred from the following extract from a letter dated St. Louis June 19, 1819, ten days after its arrival at that city: "The bow of this vessel exhibits the form of a huge serpent, black and scaly, rising out of the water from under the boat, his head as high as the deck, darted forward, his mouth open, vomiting smoke, and apparently carrying the boat on his back. From under the boat at its stern issues a stream of foaming water, dashing violently along. All the machinery is hid. Three small brass field pieces mounted on wheel carriages stand on the deck. The boat is ascending the rapid stream at the rate of three miles an hour. Neither wind nor human hands are seen to help her, and, to the eye of ignorance, the illusion is complete, that a monster of the deep carries her on his back, smoking with fatigue, and lashing the waves with violent exertion. Her equipments are at once calculated to attract and to awe the savages. Objects pleasing and terrifying are at once placed before him—artillery, the flag of the Republic, portraits of the white man and the Indian shaking hands, the calumet of peace, a sword, then the apparent monster with a painted vessel on his back, the sides gaping with portholes and bristling with guns. Taken altogether, and without intelligence of her composition and design, it would require a daring savage to approach and accost her with Hamlet's speech: 'Be thou a spirit of health or goblin damned etc.' "

The *Western Engineer* left St. Louis on the 9th of June, 1819 and proceeded by very leisurely stages up the Missouri (5). The little boat seems to have done very well and to have experienced but few breakages of machinery. There were no incidents of special importance en route. At St. Charles four of the party left the boat for the purpose of exploring the country along there, but the experience was too rough for them and they were fain to seek the comforts of the boat before a week had passed. At Franklin a stop of a week was made. The people of this frontier town fairly outdid themselves in their extravagant celebrations, on the occasion of the visits of Colonel Atkinson and Major Long. Banquets were had and toasts proposed on a scale that would have done honor to the Capital or metropolis of the country. The record of these elaborate ceremonials may still be read in the files of the newspaper published in Franklin at the time.

Major Long was unfortunate in losing one of his party at Franklin. Dr. Baldwin who was in very ill health was left here and died on the 31st of August following. On the 19th of July four of the party left Franklin to go by land to Fort Osage and the boat left the next day. Fort Osage was reached on the 1st of August. On the 6th most of the party set out from this place by land with the intention of visiting the Kansas and Pawnee Indians and rejoining the expedition near Council Bluffs. The boat left Fort Osage on the 10th, and on the 18th arrived at Isle à la Vache, a few miles above the present site of Leavenworth, where Captain Martin had wintered with three companies of troops, expecting to proceed up the river early in the spring.

A delay of a week was made at Camp Martin for the purpose of treating with the Kansas Indians. The *Western Engineer* resumed her trip on the 25th of August, being accompanied by fifteen soldiers under a Lieutenant Field in the keelboat *General Smith*. Four days after their departure the land party, who were to have gone on to Council Bluffs, arrived at Isle à la Vache for the purpose of again availing themselves of the comforts of the boat. They had been pretty roughly handled by a small party of Pawnees and were satisfied with their taste of frontier experience. Two of them, Messrs. Say and Jessup, were quite ill. Finding the boat gone, the party, except the two sick men, set out by forced marches, and overhauled her on the 1st of September. No other incident of moment occurred until the 17th of September when the boat arrived at Fort Lisa, where it was received by the inmates of the fort with a salute of ordnance and a hospitable welcome. Although yet scarcely halfway to the mouth of the Yellowstone, the great objective point of the expedition, it was decided to go into winter quarters here. Major Long remained only two weeks when he set out for Washington.

The site for a camp for the scientific party was located "half a mile above Fort Lisa, five miles below Council Bluffs, and three miles above the mouth of the Boyer river." The place was christened the *Engineer Cantonment*.

The winter passed away pleasantly enough with the scientific party. They improved their time in securing information concerning the neighboring tribes and particularly the Omahas. They made a few short excursions into the surrounding country, obtained the latitude and longitude of their cantonment, and made some investigation into the geology and natural history of the Missouri valley.

The records of the expedition show that there were continuous and friendly relations subsisting between the military and the members of the Missouri Fur Company. Hospitalities were given and received. Manuel Lisa invited the officers to dinner at his house and the officers reciprocated in kind, and thus began the hospitable intercourse between the citizens of this locality and the officers of the army which has continued until the present day. There were two ladies present, one of them the wife of Lisa and daughter of Stephen Hempstead of St. Louis. The name of the other is not known, but these two women are presumed to be the first who had ascended the Missouri as far as to the present site of Omaha.

It must be apparent from the account just given of the operations of 1819 that the Yellowstone Expedition thus far had been an unqualified failure if not a huge fiasco. The whole enterprise had been smothered in elaboration of method. Although the troops could with ease have marched three times as far as the boats carried them, it was considered necessary to transport them in a manner becoming the dignity of so vast an enterprise. As a result it took an entire season to reach a point which ought to have been reached in two months at most, and the troops passed a frightful winter in a deadly situation where they might have been encamped in the salubrious country at the mouth of the Yellowstone.

The same spirit of absurd extravagance pervaded the scientific branch of the enterprise. If Major Long had been content with a sensible field equipment transported on pack mules, or on a keelboat while along the Missouri, he could have kept his party in the field for five years, and have explored the entire region east of the mountains, for less money than his actual operations cost in the year 1819 alone. The insignificant results of the first season's work and the scandal growing out of the transportation contract, disgusted Congress with the whole enterprise and that body declined to appropriate any further funds for it. The preface of Dr. James' report of the expedition says that the "state of the national finances during the year 1820 having called for retrenchments in all expenditures of a public nature—the means necessary for the further prosecution of the objects of the expedition were accordingly withheld."

The Yellowstone Expedition was thus cut off before it was half completed, and as a half-hearted apology to the public for its failure, a small side show was organized for the season of 1820 in the form of an expedition to the Rocky mountains. It was placed under charge of Major Long, who returned to the Engineer Cantonment on the 28th of May of that year. The extent to which the great enterprise of the previous year had forfeited public confidence may be inferred from the niggardly assistance which the government lent to the present expedition. The party of Major Long consisted, beside himself, of Captain John R. Bell, Lieutenant W. H. Swift, Thomas Say, Edwin James, T. R. Peale, Samuel Seymour, H. Dougherty, D. Adams, three engagés, one corporal and six private soldiers. Of the horses and mules required for the party the government furnished only six, while the members of the party furnished the remaining sixteen. The stock of merchandise wherewith to treat with the Indians was ridiculously small, and the whole equipment was justly styled by Dr. James a "very inadequate outfit."

The immediate object in view on this expedition was to go "to the source of the River Platte and thence by way of the Arkansas and Red rivers to the Mississippi." The expedition left winter quarters on the Missouri June 6, and arrived, with no occurrence worth mentioning, at the Pawnee villages on the Loup fork of the Platte, June 11. To what degree the size and equipment of this expedition were calculated to command the respect of the Indians may be seen in the fact that the chiefs of the Grand Pawnees not only did not welcome the visitors to their camp, but, when invited to appear before the party, declined on the ground that they were otherwise engaged. Nothing was accomplished here beyond an abortive attempt to introduce the process of vaccination among the tribe.

The party left the Loup villages June 13th and the following day reached the Platte about at the present site of Grand Island, Nebraska. Their progress up this river was devoid of incident. They ascended the north bank to the forks of the Platte, both of which they crossed just above the junction, and then ascended the south bank of the South fork. On the 30th of June they saw the mountains, and the peak which first attracted their attention now bears the name of Major Long. When they first saw it they thought it to be Pike's Peak. On the 5th of July they were encamped within or near the present limits of the city of Denver, and the next day they halted about noon at the point where the South Platte emerges from the mountains. Here the party encamped for the purpose of following the stream into the mountains. The 7th of July was spent in this work, but the small detachment who undertook it got into the foothills only five or six miles, far enough, however, so that some of them saw the junction of the two forks of the South Platte. Finding mountain climbing a pretty exhausting business they returned to camp. Thus terminated that part of the official instructions directing an exploration of the Platte to its source, and the famous Bayou Salade, or South Park, from which the river flows, remained unknown, except to the hunter, for more than twenty years thereafter.

On the 9th of July the party resumed its journey and on the 12th encamped on Fountain creek about twenty-five miles from the summit of Pike's Peak. Here some definite results were accomplished in the ascent of Pike's Peak and the measurement of its altitude. Dr. James with two men made the ascent, arriving at the summit at 4 P.M. on the 14th, and were presumably the first white men to perform that now popular feat. They remained only an hour, made part of the descent that night, and reached camp after dark on the 15th. Lieutenant Swift, in the meanwhile, had measured the height of the peak by a system of horizontal and vertical triangles, and had found its altitude above the plain where the measurement was made to be 8,507 feet. Major Long erroneously estimated the elevation of the plain at only 3,000 feet above sea level. His estimate was arrived at from assumed slopes of the Mississippi, Missouri and Platte rivers, and was naturally liable to great error. The actual elevation of the plain, where the measurement of the altitude of the peak was made, is probably about 5,700 feet, which would give 14,200 feet as the altitude of the peak, as against Long's recorded estimate of 11,507 feet. The trigonometric work seems therefore to have been very accurate.

The party resumed its march on the 16th and arrived that day at the Arkansas near the mouth of Turkey creek. Here another excursion was made to the mountains, very much like that on the Platte. Captain Bell and Dr. James ascended the river one day's march to the cañon of the Arkansas and returned next day to camp. Although it was yet only the middle of July, no further attempt was made to explore the source of either of these rivers, and on the morning of the 12th the party took up its march for the settlements. It arrived in the vicinity of the present town of La Junta, Colorado, on the 21st and spent the next two days in arranging a division of the party and plans for the homeward journey. It was decided that Captain Bell, Lieutenant Swift, three Frenchmen and five soldiers, with most of the horses and baggage, should descend the Arkansas, while Major Long, Dr. James, Mr. Peale, and seven men should proceed to the sources of the Red river and follow that stream to the settlements. A rendezvous was appointed at Fort Smith on the Arkansas. Both parties took up their respective journeys on the 24th of July, 1820.

There is almost nothing in these two journeys that need detain us. Captain Bell's party encountered several small bands of Indians, but had no trouble of moment with any of them. On the 7th of August, two days before arriving at the Great Bend of the Arkansas, two French interpreters who had been hired at the Pawnee villages, terminated their engagements and set out alone to return. These men had given very satisfactory service. On the night of August 30th Captain Bell's party suffered a genuine catastrophe in the loss of much of their camp property, including nearly all the notes and records of the expedition. They were stolen by three men who deserted that night. Captain Bell arrived at Fort Smith on the 9th of September after a march in which the greatest cause of suffering was the excessive heat.

Major Long's party took a course slightly east of south until they reached the valley of Purgatory creek, probably a little below Bent's Cañon. They ascended a fork of this stream which joined the main stream from the east a little above the canon and made their way to the high land at the head of the stream. Continuing south across several of the sources of the Cimarron, they at length came to a valley which, from its general direction and appearance, they believed to be tributary to Red river, and they resolved to follow it. This was July 30th. The course for the next four days was southeast down the valley of this stream, until they came to its junction with the main Canadian, which they supposed to be the Red river.

The route from the time the party left the South Platte until they arrived at the Canadian is extremely difficult to follow except along the Arkansas. It would be scarcely possible to find in any narrative of western history so careless an itinerary, and in a scientific report like that of Dr. James it is quite inexcusable. Those who care to follow the route may do so by aid of the footnote below, where it has been worked out as fully as the deficient record will permit.

From the camp of August 4th on the Canadian the party descended that stream without any remarkable experience except considerable suffering from the heat and lack of food. On the 10th of September they arrived at the Arkansas and found for the first time that they had been following the Canadian Fork of that stream and had not been on the Red river at all. On the 13th of September the party arrived at Fort Smith.

September 21st the re-united party left Fort Smith for Cape Girardeau. A portion of their number visited the noted hot springs of the Washita on the way, and all finally assembled at Cape Girardeau on the 12th of October. Major Long set out at once for St. Louis on the *Western Engineer*, which had arrived a few days before (6).

In reviewing this expedition and comparing its actual results with what it proposed and what the public expected, the impression left is one of disappointment. In scarcely any respect did it accomplish its purpose. In the movement up the Missouri the point reached was but little more than one-third of the distance to the mouth of the Yellowstone, the intended destination. The whole purpose of carrying the power of the United States to those remote regions and of rendering American trade secure there, fell to the ground. The cherished idea that the expedition might open the way to a resumption of the lost business on the Columbia received not the slightest encouragement.

The net result of the military expedition was to establish a post near the present site of Omaha. The position was occupied but a few years when the garrison was withdrawn to the new Fort Leavenworth near the mouth of the Kansas river. Even as to those Indians who visited Fort Lisa or who lived in that vicinity, no intercourse of importance was had with any of the tribes and the influence of the expedition upon the Indian question was very small. It should be said, however, that the position near Council Bluffs became the base of operations against the Aricaras in 1823 and of the expedition to the Yellowstone under Atkinson and O'Fallon in 1825.

The expedition of 1820, which was the insignificant finale of the great enterprise, was scarcely more satisfactory than the other operations had been. The party was wretchedly equipped, and as a consequence kept almost continuously on the move in order to avoid starvation until they could get back to the settlements, and they spent at the most but five or six days in exploration of the mountains. The only permanent addition which they made to geographical knowledge was in discovering the great western extent of the Canadian river. This stream, which takes its rise near the mountains east of Santa Fe and flows east, had heretofore been supposed to be the head of Red river. Major Long's expedition showed this not to be the case. He did not, however, descend the main stream in the vicinity of the mountains, but a branch farther east, that formed a junction with the main stream more than a hundred miles from its source; but he saw enough to show that all of the watershed in that section was tributary to the Canadian.

The ascent of Pike's Peak by Dr. James and his companion is supposed to have been the first performance of that feat; and Lieutenant Swift's very excellent measurement of its altitude above the plain where his observations were made is likewise the first attempt in that line. His determination has been but slightly modified by later and more accurate measurements. Major Long named the peak James, but posterity has decreed that the name of its discoverer shall stand.

Captain Bell's expedition down the Arkansas, so far as it has been given us is almost of no geographical consequence. So important a tributary as the Cimarron he missed entirely, and identified the small stream Squaw creek, as that river. He made other similar errors, although traveling in a country which even then was no longer unknown.

Major Long's description of the country, which appears as an appendix to Dr. James' work, is on the whole an accurate one. His astronomical determinations of latitude were correct within an error of five or six miles; his longitudes were too great by from thirty to fifty miles.

By some consideration which had weight in the earlier history of our government the results of this expedition were not published as an official report under the authorship of its leader. Major Long did not write the narrative of his own travels. The work was published under a private copyright by Dr. Edwin James, with an elaborate dedicatory to the Secretary of War which reminds one of the obsequious grovelings to royalty so characteristic of early English writers. The report is interesting and valuable. Its accounts of the Indian tribes and of the native fauna are among the best we possess. Many incidents of historic importance have also been preserved.

To the public, however, the work was a disappointment. They had looked to it for information relating to the great questions of Western progress then agitating men's minds. It was not a geological survey that they wanted, but a comprehensive view of the country from a practical standpoint. Long disquisitions upon the evidence found in the mounds about St. Louis, tending to show that our Indian races were of Asiatic origin, might be very interesting to the cause of science, but they did not satisfy the public who were seeking the wealth of the Rocky mountains and a route to the distant Pacific. The report, in short, was not fitted to its purpose; it belonged to the scientific explorations of later times.

Nothing is clearer than that the managers of this enterprise utterly failed to grasp the spirit of its conception; and if this were not bad enough, Major Long added in his report the strongest possible negation to the hope that good could ever flow from such a country. Read the summary of his views upon that region which has honored his name by fixing it upon those magnificent mountains, and has given the world an accession of wealth such as the followers of Cortez never dreamed of: "In regard to this extensive section of country, we do not hesitate in giving the opinion, that it is almost wholly unfit for cultivation, and of course uninhabitable by a people depending upon agriculture for their subsistence. Although tracts of fertile land, considerably extensive, are occasionally to be met with, yet the scarcity of wood and water, almost uniformly prevalent, will prove an insuperable obstacle in the way of settling the country. This objection rests not only against the immediate section under consideration, but applies with equal propriety to a much larger portion of the country. Agreeably to the best intelligence that can be had, concerning the country northward and southward of the section, and especially to the references deducible from the account given by Lewis and Clark, of the country situated between the Missouri and the Rocky Mountains, above the river Platte, the vast region commencing near the sources of the Sabine, Trinity, Brazos, and Colorado, and extending northwardly to the forty-ninth degree of latitude, by which the United States territory is limited in that direction, is throughout, of a similar character. The whole of this region seems peculiarly adapted as a range for buffaloes, wild goats, and other wild game, incalculable multitudes of which find ample pasturage and subsistence upon it.

"This region, however, viewed as a frontier, may prove of infinite importance to the United States, inasmuch as it is calculated to serve as a barrier to prevent too great an extension of our population westward, and secure us against the machinations or incursions of an enemy that might otherwise be disposed to annoy us in that quarter."

Here is an essay in prophecy that would have done credit to that great man, Daniel Webster, who could with difficulty see anything of national greatness beyond the Mississippi. Did Major Long perceive no inconsistency in declaring in one breath that the country he had traversed was "uninhabitable by a people depending upon agriculture for their subsistence" and in the next that "incalculable multitudes" of grazing animals could "find ample pasturage and subsistence upon it"? And he did not confine his views to the region under his immediate observation, but applied them to the entire sweep of country from the Spanish to the British possessions and westward from the meridian of Council Bluffs to and beyond the mountains—a country where now are several large cities, towns and villages without number, and a population of more than six million people. In that section which he traversed at the base of the Rocky Mountains where he said "the scarcity of wood and water" would "prove an insuperable obstacle in the way of settling the country" is now found some of the best agricultural land in the United States, from which products are annually exported to distant parts of the country.

It is hard for us to comprehend today how an officer of such signal ability and long experience should have seen in this country nothing better than a fortunate frontier "calculated to serve as a barrier to prevent too great an extension of our population westward, and to secure us against the machinations or incursions of an enemy that might otherwise be disposed to annoy us in that quarter." It is true that at that time there had been cause enough to apprehend annoyance from our traditional enemy in the Southwest, and Major Long is certainly not to be criticized for not foreseeing the expulsion of that enemy from the greater part of the territory west of our own; but his fear of undue expansion of our population was no more justifiable than have been, and are still, the phantom fears of certain minds at every effort of their country to put off the vestments of infancy for the more appropriate clothing of maturer years.

And so it resulted that Major Long's report proved a veritable stumbling-block in the way of a just appreciation of the importance of our western interests. Whenever any measure was urged in Congress looking to the more immediate occupation of that country, this report was a sufficient answer. Why waste the public treasure in establishing possession of a region which could never become the abode of civilized man? Here was an official government report, prepared by an able officer sent out for the express purpose of spying out the land. Surely the statements of irresponsible adventurers and uninformed enthusiasts were not to stand against it? It thus became one of the most powerful weapons which men of the Webster type made use of whenever they felt called upon to resist "too great an extension of our population westward."

Thus the people of the West, who had hoped from this expedition to enlist government aid in the reclamation of a remote region, found themselves in a worse plight than before. Instead of the government becoming enthused with their own faith, its doubts were strengthened. But the people themselves did not lose faith. They continued to penetrate farther and even farther—even to the shores of the Pacific—through the unknown places of that illimitable country. Government was finally compelled to follow where it had refused to lead, and within another generation it was glad enough to be the fortunate possessor of those regions which were at this time not considered worth having.

AUTHOR'S NOTES

(1) Little did the writer imagine the causes which would yet make the name *Yellowstone* familiar throughout the world.

(2) Letter from Fort Osage to Editor *Niles Register*, May 17, 1819. Published in issue of July 3, 1819.

(3) "The estimated cost for transportation in this favorite project, as reported to Congress at the last session was $162,994. The sum claimed by Colonel Johnson, and, he [the speaker] was told, actually paid is $256,818.15." Speech of Mr. Cooke of Tennessee in H. R., Dec. 1, 1820.

(4) "Our great Yellowstone Expedition, about which you have seen so much in the papers, has not yet got above this place, except a detachment of 260 men which passed here last fall, and are now about 80 miles above waiting for the rest. Five or six hundred are expected here every day. When they arrive this fort will be broke up and I shall be left here pretty much alone. The expedition is very badly managed, and will, I fear, fall very far short of the public expectations. The steamboats expected to accompany it are not found to answer very well, and will very probably be abandoned. There is no doubt that the Missouri can be easily navigated by steamboats, but they must be of peculiar construction, and have greater power than those used elsewhere." Letter from G. C. Sibley, July 10, 1819. Fort Osage.

(5) The following is an extract from the log of the *Western Engineer:* "Average running time five hours per day. Average leisure time for examining the country ten hours per day."

(6) ITINERARY OF MAJOR LONG'S ROUTE BETWEEN JULY 9TH ON THE SOUTH PLATTE AND AUGUST 4TH ON THE CANADIAN

July 7th and 8th the party were encamped in the valley of the South Platte near where Wheatland, Colorado, now stands.

July 9.—The party set out on their journey, first ascending to its source a small tributary of the Platte, and then crossing the dividing ridge into the valley of Defile [Plum?] creek. This stream they "ascended to the place where its principal branch descends from the mountains," and there encamped. "In the evening a favorable opportunity, the first for several days, presented, and observations for latitude were taken." The table of latitudes and longitudes in the Appendix to Dr. James' book gives the 8th as the day when the observations were taken and the place as the "Camp at the base of the Rocky mountains." The latitude was computed as 39 degrees 23 minutes 40 seconds, which corresponds more nearly with the probable location of the first camp after leaving the Platte. These considerations indicate that the record may have slipped a day at this point.

July 10.—This day's journey is wholly indefinite. The most that can be made of the description is that the main party ascended Plum or Defile creek for a distance, and then crossed a sandstone ridge about 1,000 feet high to another stream, the valley of which was about a mile wide. From the top of the ridge the bearing of Pike's Peak was S. 50 degrees W.

July 11.—The record of this day is equally unsatisfactory, but the course was probably southeast in the direction of the valley of Squirrel creek. The party, with amazing innocence of their where-abouts, kept on, and "towards evening our guide discovered that we had already passed considerably beyond the base of the Peak, near which it had been our intention to halt." Having performed the remarkable feat of passing the base of Pike's Peak without knowing it, the party "thought it advisable to encamp for the night." Where their camp was is largely a matter of conjecture, but from the course of the following day, and the place where the party then went into camp, we think that it was probably about 20 miles east-southeast of the present site of Colorado Springs.

July 12.—The party retraced their route of the 11th for a distance and then crossed a ridge and descended into the valley of the Fontaine qui Bouit [now Fountain] Creek, at a point about 25 miles from the Peak. They arrived here not later than noon. This camp seems to have been at least 15 miles and perhaps more, from Manitou Springs, and was therefore probably a few miles above the present site of Fountain, Colorado.

July 13.—In the morning Dr. James, Lieut. Swift, and five men set out before sunrise up the valley of Fountain creek. Lieutenant Swift was to find a suitable base from which to measure the altitude of the Peak, and Dr. James with two men was to ascend the Peak.

July 14–15.—These days were consumed in ascent of Pike's Peak and in measuring its altitude. Dr. James reached the summit of the Peak about 4 P.M. of the 14th; remained there one hour; pursued his way back until dark; reached Manitou Springs about noon of the 15th; and the main camp a little after dark on the same day. Lieutenant Swift finished his measurements on the 14th. The altitude of the Peak was found to be 8,507 feet above the plain where the measurements were made.

July 16.—The party set out for Arkansas. They move "in a south-western direction" for 28 miles, which they accomplish in ten hours without dismounting. The soil along the line of march was of

"incurable barrenness," and the scenery "dreary and disgusting."
The first camp on the Arkansas is not described at all, but from the
course and distance of the day's march and those of the following
days we think the position was about 12 to 15 miles above the present site of Pueblo. The party searched for Pike's old redoubt, but of
course did not find it where they were. When they descended the
Arkansas it was along the north shore and they did not pass by the
position at all.

July 17-18.—Captain Bell and Dr. James made an ascent of the
Arkansas to the cañon just above the present site of Cañon City.
They called the distance 30 miles. They returned on the following
day. Latitude of camp 38 degrees 18 minutes 19 seconds. Longitude
105 degrees 39 minutes 45 seconds.

July 19.—The party started down the Arkansas along the left
bank. They must have crossed Fountain creek about noon, but they
made no mention of it. They passed the mouth of the St. Charles
from the south in the afternoon. Traveled 25 miles, latitude of camp
38 degrees 14 minutes 18 seconds.

July 20.—The party set out at 5 A.M. and "soon afterwards"
passed the mouth of the Huerfano from the south. Made 26 miles.

July 21.—Set out at 5 A.M. Having traveled about 6 miles they
met an Indian and his squaw who conducted them down to the ford
of the Arkansas, where they arrived about 10 A.M.

July 22-23.—These days were spent in preparation for the homeward march. The party was divided. Captain Bell, Lieutenant Swift,
three Frenchmen and five soldiers, with most of the horses and baggage, were to descend the Arkansas. Major Long, Dr. James, Mr.
Peale and seven men were to descend the Red river.

July 24.—Major Long's party crossed the Arkansas and set off
"a little to the east of south nearly at right angles to the Arkansas."
Distance 27 miles. The valley of "a considerable stream" [Las Animas or Purgatory] is visible "eight or ten miles" to the southeast.

July 25.—Major Long's party strike the Purgatory a little below
Bent's Cañon, although they thought they were only on a tributary.
A little after noon they began ascending a small tributary from the
east. This is presumably Chaquaqua creek. The party progressed with
great difficulty, making only 15 miles.

July 26.—Major Long's party continue up stream, the real distance being estimated at 15 miles, eliminating windings. Halted at
4 P.M. at head of stream.

July 27.—Major Long's party proceed under great difficulties
and at length emerge from the valley of the stream which they had

been ascending. After reaching the open plain they make some obser-vations. "James [Pike's] Peak bore N. 71 degrees W.; and the West Spanish Peak S. 87 degrees W.; magnetic variation 13½ degrees east." Halted at 5 P.M., "having traveled about ten miles nearly due south from the point where we had left the valley of the creek." Total distance for the day could not have been over 15 miles.

July 28.—Major Long's route was "south" and "a little east of south." The party cross several extensive valleys, the upper courses of the Cimarron, and finally descend into a valley, where they find running water, and encamp there. No distance is given. Probably about 20 miles.

July 29.—Major Long's party leave the valley of the creek where they were, and keep on to the south and possibly a little east of south. They encounter a severe storm from the northeast, and the horses refuse to move except with the wind, "so rather than suffer ourselves to be carried from our course," they await the subsidence of the storm. No distance stated—say 20 miles.

July 30.—Major Long's party cross a wide plain and descend into the valley of a creek about noon. This they resolve to follow as one of the probable sources of Red river, and therefore decide to abandon their further "journey to the southwest." No distance given—say 20 miles. This stream has received the name of Major Long's creek.

July 31.—Major Long's party continue down the valley in which they encamped the night before. No distance given—say 20 miles. Camp at the mouth of a tributary from the east, probably Leon creek.

August 1.—Major Long's party remain in camp all day.

August 2.—Major Long's party continue down the valley. S. 80 degrees E. Distance about 25 miles.

August 3.—Major Long's party continue down the valley. No distance stated—say 20 miles.

August 4.—Major Long's party continue down the valley, mak-ing 16 miles before noon. "General direction . . . still toward the southeast." The stream was believed to be "one of the most con-siderable of the upper tributaries of the Red river." Confirming this opinion was the presence of a large Indian trail, of some twenty paths, which here entered the valley from the west and passed down the left bank. The distance traveled this day may have been 28 miles. The point where the great trail came in was undoubtedly at the junction of Long Creek with the main Canadian and the trail led directly from the Mexican settlements.

Chapter III

THE ARICARA CAMPAIGN OF 1823

*Col. Leavenworth organizes an expedition against the Aricaras
—Joshua Pilcher made sub-Indian agent—Loss of a keelboat—
Organization of troops and allies at Fort Recovery—March resumed—Strength of opposing forces—Beginning of the attack—
Result of first day's fight—Second day's operations—Disaffec-
tion among the Sioux—Charge abandoned—Result of second
day's fight—Attempts to treat with the Indians—Pilcher's disap-
proval—Third day's operations—Treaty of Peace—Pilcher and
Vanderburgh refuse to participate—Failure of Aricaras to com-
ply with treaty—Charge contemplated but abandoned—Aricaras
abandon their village—Attempts to get them back—Expedition
starts down the river—Losses of the campaign—Successful
operation until villages are reached—Vacillating conduct before
the villages—Effect upon the Aricaras—Colonel Leavenworth's
motives—Quarrel between Leavenworth and Pilcher.*

This important campaign was the first ever conducted by
the army against the Indians west of the Mississippi and it
was the precursor of that long series of operations in which
so many American soldiers lost their lives and which cul-
minated only a decade since in the conquest of the West.
The campaign, therefore, deserves something more than a
passing notice.

It will be remembered that General Ashley, after his
disaster before the Aricara villages, June 2, 1823, dropped
down the river to a safe distance, threw up a defensive work
on an island, dispatched J. S. Smith to notify Henry on the
Yellowstone, and sent a message to Benjamin O'Fallon,
Indian agent near the old Council Bluffs, detailing his misfortune. Colonel Henry Leavenworth, in command of the
troops at that point, acted with commendable promptness.

The message was shown to him on the 18th of June and he at once decided to march against the Aricaras without waiting to communicate with the Department at St. Louis. The necessary preparations were made as rapidly as possible, and on the 22nd the troops set out, partly by boat and partly on foot, Colonel Leavenworth commanding in person. The force amounted to two hundred and twenty men and comprised six companies of the 6th U. S. Infantry. They carried two six-pounder cannons and several small swivels. The supplies were transported in three keelboats.

Joshua Pilcher, president of the Missouri Fur Company, who had just suffered an even greater disaster than that of Ashley in the destruction of his party under Immel and Jones on the Yellowstone, was eager to lend such assistance as he could in the campaign. He was at old Fort Lisa at the time, and was made special sub-agent for the Sioux tribes by O'Fallon during the operations against the Indians. He equipped two boats, took on a 5½ inch howizter from Fort Atkinson, and overtook Colonel Leavenworth on the 27th. Pilcher was of much assistance to Leavenworth, who repeatedly acknowledges his indebtedness to him.

The expedition proceeded continuously although slowly on account of the difficulties of river navigation. On the 3rd of July a distressing accident occurred in the wrecking of Lieutenant Wickliffe's boat and the loss of Sergeant Stackpole, a brave and experienced veteran of the War of 1812, with six privates, seventy muskets, and a large quantity of supplies. This misfortune caused greater loss than all the rest of the campaign.

Ashley was on his way down the river from the point where he had left his men when he heard of the approach of the United States troops. He immediately turned about and made haste to his camp, one hundred and twenty miles above, where he made preparations to join Leavenworth with his entire party. Henry, who had arrived from the Yellowstone some time before, augmented Ashley's force to about eighty men. The entire party seems to have then gone down to meet Leavenworth. Pilcher also had hastened on in advance of the troops and had gotten his own party in readiness, numbering about forty men under the immediate command of Henry Vanderburgh. He also succeeded in collecting Indian auxiliaries numbering some four or five hundred Yanktons and Sioux. The point where Pilcher and Ashley were waiting is called Fort Recovery (1) in Colonel Leavenworth's reports. Fort Brasseaux, mentioned by Ashley, seems to have been in this vicinity.

Colonel Leavenworth arrived at Fort Recovery on the 19th of July at 10 A.M. Several days were now spent in organizing the troops and allies. Two additional officers here joined the command. They were Major Wooley and Brevet-Major Ketchum, who had not reached Fort Atkinson before Leavenworth's departure, but had at once set out to overtake the troops (2). In the re-organization the companies of regulars were reduced to five in number, and arms distributed accordingly, ten rifles being borrowed from Pilcher and thirty from Ashley to help make up for those lost in the keel-boat wreck. Ashley's and Pilcher's auxiliaries were accepted.

"General Ashley," says Leavenworth in his report, "nominated his officers and their appointments were confirmed in orders. They were as follows: Jedediah Smith for Captain, Hiram Scott, do; Hiram Allen, Lieutenant; George C. [David?] Jackson, do; Charles Cunningham, Ensign; Edward Rose, do; ——— Fleming, Surgeon; T. Fitzpatrick, quartermaster; William Sublette, Sergeant Major.

"Mr. Pilcher, as acting member of the Missouri Fur Company, for himself and party offered me the services of forty men. These were formed into one company. Mr. Pilcher was assigned to the command of the Indians, with the nominal rank of Major. He nominated his officers and their appointment was confirmed in orders. They were as follows: Henry Vanderburgh, Captain; Angus McDonald as Captain of the Indian Command; [Moses B.] Carson, 1st Lieutenant; [William] Gordon, 2nd do;

"These appointments were merely nominal, and intended only to confer the same privileges and respect on them as were paid to our own officers of the same grade. No nominal rank was conferred on General Ashley as he was then a

Brigadier General in the militia of the State of Missouri, and Lieutenant Governor of the same.

"The forces thus organized, including regular troops, mountaineers, voyageurs and Indians, were styled the 'Missouri Legion!' and numbered altogether about eight hundred fighting men."

As soon as the re-organization was complete the march was resumed and the command arrived before the Aricara villages on the 9th of August, having made the distance from Council Bluffs, 640 miles, in forty-eight days, including the time spent in re-organization at Fort Recovery. On the previous day, August 8th, the command left the boats at a point about twenty-five miles below the villages. The flotilla was placed in charge of Major Wooley and ten men to each boat, with instructions to move it up the river after the troops. The advance from this point was made in the following order: A scouting party of Sioux under Pilcher's direction went ahead, the better to conceal the character of the attacking force. These were followed by Captain Riley with a company of riflemen, after whom came General Ashley with his two companies of mountaineers followed by the rest of the command, except Pilcher's men, who kept on with their boats. Before the attack began about three hundred and fifty additional Indian recruits joined the command, making a total force before the Aricara villages of about eleven hundred men. Opposed to this force there were between six and eight hundred warriors in the two Aricara villages, and between three and four thousand individuals all told, men, women and children. The attacking force was amply sufficient for the work in hand, notwithstanding that the Aricaras were to some extent sheltered in their dirt villages and had erected some rude palisades. The Aricaras do not seem to have had any expectation of this formidable attack and had made no especial preparations to resist it. Thus far, therefore, the campaign had progressed most favorably and there was no reason to doubt its early and successful termination.

The command had passed the night of the 8th some eight or nine miles below the villages, and early the next morning moved out to the attack. Pilcher was ordered to advance with

his Indian auxiliaries and surround the villages so as to prevent escape, and give battle if the Aricaras came out. The
Sioux moved to the front with great impetuosity and were met
by the Aricaras at the termination of the plain on which the
villages stood, and about half a mile below them. Here ensued
a sharp struggle in which the valor of the Sioux was met with
equal valor on the part of the Aricaras. Thirteen of the latter
were left dead on the ground (A). Whether any of the dead
were removed, or what was the number of wounded, is not
known. The Sioux lost two killed and seven wounded, but
failed to drive back the enemy.

Alarmed at the prospect of a repulse, and finding that the
troops were not yet in supporting distance, Pilcher hastened
to the rear for reinforcements. The whole line was then advanced rapidly in the following order: Ashley's two companies were on the right, resting on the river; next were the
five companies of the 6th Regiment, and on the left were
Major Riley's riflemen, who seem to have been a picked company formed when the number of regular companies was reduced to five. The Sioux still being engaged in front, it was
not possible to open fire on the Aricaras until they were passed.
When the Aricaras saw the whites approaching they broke
and fled to their villages and the troops followed to within
three or four hundred yards, where they halted to await the
arrival of the boats with the artillery. It would hardly seem
that the hour could have been later than noon, although
Pilcher says that "the day was already far spent." The artillery did not arrive until sundown, and further attack was delayed until next day. After the Aricaras left the field the Sioux
withdrew to the cornfields of their enemies and bore no further
part in the operations.

The attack for the following day, August 10th, was
planned to take place simultaneously against both villages.
Two companies under Major Riley were sent to the upper
village where they secured a good position within one hundred
yards of the palisades. Major Vanderburgh, with the Missouri
Fur Company contingent, was also stationed at this point, and
hither was sent one of the six-pounders under Sergeant
Perkins. General Ashley, as on the day before, held the ex-

treme right of the line below the lower village, and on his left was Lieutenant Morris, with the other six-pounder and the howitzer. The rest of the troops were disposed along the front of the lower village, except one company under Major Ketchum, which was ordered at 8 a.m. to reinforce the line at the upper village. The attack was opened by Lieutenant Morris with the artillery. His first shot killed the chief, Gray Eyes, and his second cut down the medicine flag staff. Vanderburgh's artillery was posted at too high an elevation and the shot passed over the village into the river. He was ordered down into the plain and his firing then had more effect. Meanwhile the infantry advanced to within three hundred yards and fired one volley to discharge their guns, which had been loaded for a long time (3).

It soon became evident that the artillery was not going to accomplish its purpose of driving the Indians from their lodges, and that it would be necessary to storm the works if they were to be taken. Colonel Leavenworth now began to investigate the strength of the position. He was told by those who had been in the villages that the palisades were strong, with a trench on the inside. One man who had wintered at the Aricara villages advised the Colonel that they could be taken only by "sapping and mining": that the Indians had full confidence in their ability to hold the town, and that every squaw would "count her coup" rather than yield. This was not the kind of resistance that Colonel Leavenworth had expected, but in order to test its real strength, he ordered preparations for an assault upon the "acute angle" at the upper village. Ashley in the meanwhile was ordered to make a diversion at the lower village. He took possession of a ravine within "20 paces" of the village, from which he opened a brisk fire. Pilcher was instructed to notify the Sioux of the approaching attack and to bring them in to co-operate. He cautioned the Colonel not to rely upon them for this work, for they would probably wait until the Aricaras were driven out, when they could be attacked in the open. Nevertheless an attempt was made to secure their aid, but not very successfully, and owing to their lack of co-operation the charge was abandoned. The cannonade was continued until midday.

After the charge was declared off, Colonel Leavenworth, with a subordinate officer, went around to view the river side of the towns, where he heard that the Indians were escaping. Learning the falsity of this report he returned, and on his way back saw some Aricaras who had gotten into a ravine and were pouring a "galling fire" upon the troops. Major Ketchum was sent to dislodge them.

Leavenworth then went to the upper village. Pilcher, whom he found there, told him that he could no longer vouch for the assistance of the Sioux unless some decisive action were taken. The impetuous and fickle nature of the Indians was not suited to the tedium of a siege, and they could be held to work only by the excitement of actual combat. Leavenworth replied that he was meditating a general assault, but thought that he would first try a strategem, and asked Pilcher's opinion. Pilcher thought that stratagem was justifiable toward such a people. Leavenworth then said that "he had thought of sending Simeneau, the Aricara interpreter, to hail the Indians and tell them that they were fools that they did not come out and speak with the whites." If they would do this, it would give "an opportunity to examine the works." Pilcher thought that this stratagem "could do no harm, at any rate." The effort failed in due course and Leavenworth repaired to the lower village, where Lieutenant Morris was still working away with his six-pounder. Finding that there were but thirteen shot left the Colonel ordered the artillery to cease firing. He then sent word to the Sioux that he had decided to withdraw the forces from the upper village and advised them to leave the cornfields in order to "save their stragglers from the tomahawks of the Aricaras."

The forces were then withdrawn from the upper village and the whole command was moved back about half a mile to a camp opposite the boats. By this time it was after 3 p.m. "Orders were given to senior officers of corps to have their men obtain some refreshment as soon as possible, and then form their corps and march to the enemy's cornfield to obtain some corn for the subsistence of our men, several of whom, and particularly General Ashley's men, had not had any provisions for two days." Colonel Leavenworth then withdrew to his cabin on the boat.

Such were the inglorious proceedings of the 10th of August, for nothing else was attempted during that day. Their effect upon the Sioux had been to discourage them and arouse their contempt for the whites. They had joined the expedition with the expectation of plundering the Aricara villages. They had made the only real fight, so far, and had since been the spectators of the futile efforts of the whites. They now lost all heart in the campaign, and having laden themselves with Aricara corn, withdrew from further co-operation.

Presently Colonel Leavenworth came out of his boat and had interviews with General Ashley and with Pilcher. His plan was now to secure a supply of provisions and renew the attack next day. At this time a Sioux Indian and an Aricara were observed holding a parley and it was learned that the Aricaras were suing for pity on their women and children. They said that the man who had caused all the trouble was dead and the rest of the people wanted peace. Leavenworth sent the Indian back to tell the Aricaras to send out their chiefs at once if they wanted peace. He then returned to his boat and soon ten or twelve Indians were seen approaching. The senior officers advanced to meet them. The Indians appeared much frightened and begged the whites not to fire any more at them for they were "all in tears." Leavenworth told them that they must restore Ashley's property as a condition of peace, promise to behave well in the future and surrender five men as hostages. They promised to restore all the property that they had, but said that the horses had mostly all been killed or stolen. Leavenworth then told them of the great power of the Americans, which they had yet scarcely felt, and assured them that while his people desired to live on terms of friendship with them, they must conduct themselves differently or they would be punished more severely than they had yet been. They all made fair promises. Colonel Leavenworth adds: "Considering my small force, the strange and unaccountable conduct of the Sioux, and even the great probability of their joining the Aricaras against us—and also considering the importance of saving to our country the expense and trouble of a long Indian war, and the importance of securing the Indian trade, I thought it proper to accept the terms.''

The pipe of peace was brought forth and passed the rounds until it reached Pilcher, who refused to smoke or even shake hands, and got up and walked back and forth in great agitation, telling the Indians they could look out for him on the morrow. He finally consented to smoke, as it was Colonel Leavenworth's wishes but he refused his assent to the rest of the proceedings. His manner produced a bad effect on the Indians, who had been told by Colin Campbell that Pilcher was the most important man among the whites. After smoking Leavenworth picked out five principal Indians as hostages, and with a present of twelve robes from the Indians, made ready to depart. But at the instigation of Colin Campbell, as Colonel Leavenworth thought, and also at the sight of the dead body of one of their nation who had been killed by the Sioux on the day before, the Indians became frightened and refused to go. Some shots were exchanged, but no harm was done; and thus ended the first attempt at negotiations for peace.

Colonel Leavenworth now learned that the disgusted Sioux had turned enemy to a certain extent and had stolen six government mules and seven of Ashley's horses (B). Fearing that they had conspired with the Aricaras to destroy the whites, he ordered his command to entrench for the night. There was indeed some ground for this fear. The operations for the day had given the Sioux a lively contempt for the Americans. One of the chiefs, Fire Heart, had been acting a mysterious and equivocal part for a day or two back, and he had now retired to the hills with a large party, where he was most likely waiting to see which side would come out victorious.

The night, however, passed without incident, and on the morning of the 11th the Aricara chief, Little Soldier, came out. He said that his people had been much alarmed at the incident of the night before. Leavenworth tried to explain it away, whereupon Little Soldier said that he would get some of the chiefs to come out, and he wished that some of the white chiefs would visit the village. In particular he wanted

NATHANIEL J. WYETH

to know if Pilcher would make peace, and Leavenworth replied that he would have to. Edward Rose, one of the interpreters, was now sent in and soon returned with the information that the Indians were completely humbled. Doctor Gale and Lieutenant Morris also went in and returned with similar information. They found that the fortifications were much weaker than they had supposed; "that the pickets were very frail, and that they had but slight ditches on the inside." Major Ketchum then went in and confirmed the report of the humbled feeling of the Indians. Their attitude was further evidenced by their offer to give the whites a load of provisions if they would send a boat up.

They were now ordered to send out their chiefs, but they evasively sent out irresponsible men. Finally some of the principal men came out. Leavenworth then called upon Sub-Agent Pilcher to draft a treaty, but Pilcher declined. A similar request to Major Vanderburgh, also a sub-agent, was similarly declined. Leavenworth then drew up the treaty himself. It was signed by eleven Indians (although, according to Pilcher, by no chief of authority) and by six army officers. General Ashley, at whose request the expedition had been undertaken, was the only other person who signed it.

The treaty contained four articles. In the first the Aricaras agreed to restore the property taken from Ashley. By the second they stipulated not to molest the traders in the future. Articles 3rd and 4th were mutual promises that the United States and the Aricaras should henceforth live at peace.

Immediately upon the conclusion of the treaty unrestrained intercourse opened between the whites and the Indians. In carrying out the first article of the treaty, the Aricaras surrendered three rifles, one horse and sixteen robes. They were told that this would not do. Late in the afternoon Chief Little Soldier, who seems to have been a coward and a traitor to his own people, and evidently very little esteemed by them, although the first one to sign the treaty, came to Leavenworth's boat and said that it was impossible for the Indians to do more than they had done. The upper village, which had no part in the attack on Ashley, refused to contribute anything. He said that Grey Eyes, the principal agitator, was dead, and that for himself he had always been friendly to the whites, and had sent warning to Ashley at the time of the Aricara attack, the previous June. He begged that he might come over to the side of the whites in case of a renewal of the attack. He gave the interesting advice that the artillery should fire *low*, and he pointed out the best place for the attack. Such was the craven individual for whose welfare Colonel Leavenworth showed so much solicitude.

It now became a question of accepting the failure of the Indians to restore Ashley's property or of renewing the attack. The latter alternative was the choice of the army officers and the auxiliaries. Lieutenant Morris had found more shot for the cannon and every one was confident of success if the charge were made. But for some unaccountable reason Colonel Leavenworth could not bring himself to take the decisive step. He has described the conflict of his own thoughts, which clearly shows that, while he was actuated by the purest motives, he lacked the firmness which the occasion demanded. "I felt that my situation was a disagreeable and unpleasant one. It appeared to me that my reputation and the honor and success of the expedition required that I should gratify my troops and make the charge. But I also thought that sound policy and the interests of my country required that I should not.

"For my own part I felt confident that the Indians had been sufficiently humbled, fully to convince them of our ability to punish them for any injury which they might do us, and that they would behave well in the future."

The responsibility of the situation Colonel Leavenworth evaded for the present by postponing the attack until the next day, August 12th. He did this at the request of Little Soldier, in order to permit that shifty savage to escape with his family; and also because it was so nearly night that to attack them would leave the wounded to be cared for after dark. Rose, the interpreter, then went into the villages and got the Indians to send out a few more robes, which they said was the utmost they could do. He assured Colonel Leavenworth that the Indians were preparing to leave and that they would certainly escape that night; but in spite of all these proofs of their insincerity the Colonel sent word to them that he would waive further compliance with Article 1, and urged them not to leave. No precautions were taken to prevent escape, and when the command awoke on the morning of the 12th the villages were deserted except by one woman, the aged and decrepit mother of the fallen chief, Grey Eyes. The next two days were spent in a futile attempt to find the Aricaras and induce them to return to their villages; and at 10 A.M. on the morning of August 15th, the command embarked for the return journey, leaving the aged mother of Grey Eyes with plenty of provisions in peaceable possession of the villages. Scarcely were the boats under way when the villages were discovered to be on fire and are presumed to have been destroyed.

In the operations before the Aricara villages the whites lost none in killed and but two slightly wounded. The Sioux lost two killed and seven wounded in the attack of the 9th. The loss of the keelboat with its property and crew on the way up the river was the one serious disaster of the expedition —a very serious one indeed—but, so far as is known, wholly accidental. Colonel Leavenworth thought that the Aricara loss amounted to fifty, but Pilcher was positive that it would not exceed thirty, including women and children, and of these thirteen had been killed by the Sioux. The bombardment caused very few casualties, for it is evident from the hint dropped by Little Soldier that the Indians lay on the ground and that most of the shot passed over them. The effect of the shot on the mud huts was inappreciable. These were all the material results of the campaign under Leavenworth's immediate command, to which may be added the looting of the Aricara cornfields by the Sioux and the burning of the villages by unknown hands. The cost of the expedition was only about two thousand dollars, and the time consumed about seventy-five days. The experience of the troops on the long march and the knowledge it gave them of the country were among its most valuable results.

Colonel Leavenworth's prompt and energetic action, when he received the news of Ashley's disaster, was most creditable. It was a serious responsibility to take—that of ordering an expedition over six hundred miles away without previous authority from his superior. But Colonel Leavenworth rightly judged that it was not a time to wait several weeks for communication with St. Louis, and he decided to go at once.

The co-operation of General Ashley and Major Pilcher was hearty and energetic. The latter succeeded in getting a large auxiliary force from the Sioux on the strength of a prospect of plundering the Aricara villages. With both gentlemen Colonel Leavenworth was highly pleased at first, although he had a serious falling out with Pilcher before he got through.

Excepting the loss of a keelboat everything went well until the arrival before the villages. The opening attack by the Sioux was vigorous and determined. But from this point on the conduct of Colonel Leavenworth was so vaccillating and ineffectual, and apparently governed by such an undue estimate of the obstacles in his way, and such a dread of incurring any loss, that he disgusted the Indian allies, forfeited their friendship and co-operation, and excited the contempt and amazement of the trappers and mountaineers. There is no reason to suppose than an assault on the towns would not have been successful, and from every point of view it was imperative upon Colonel Leavenworth to attempt it. Why had he come this great distance if it was not to inflict summary punishment upon these people? Instead of doing so he fairly begged them for peace, and after having completed a treaty, which he was compelled to write himself because the duly constituted officers of the government flatly refused to participate in it, he next waived fulfillment of its one essential article.

The whole conduct of the fight, if such it can be called, had only served to detract from the credit of the national arms. How little effort was actually made to reduce the villages is apparent from the lack of casualties. It is, of course, no proof of bad management that an officer brings his men out of action without loss of life—rather quite the reverse, if he has accomplished his purpose. But when a whole day's attack upon a fortified town held by six hundred able-bodied warriors results in only wounding two of the assailants, it is evident that the attack could not have been very efficient. Such a result is scarcely compatible with Colonel Leavenworth's account of the "galling fire" to which his command was, on at least one occasion, subjected.

In regard to the Aricaras, Colonel Leavenworth's impression that they were "completely humbled" was wholly erroneous. Even while the treaty was going on, and immediately afterward, proof of their bad faith was patent to every one. They failed to carry out the principal article of the treaty and virtually repudiated the whole compact by deserting their villages in the very presence of the troops. In "Orders" issued to the regiment August 29th upon the return of the expedition to Fort Atkinson, Colonel Leavenworth said: "The blood of our countrymen has been honorably avenged, the Aricaras humbled, and in such manner as will teach them and other Indian tribes to respect the American name and character." Such was not the opinion of those conversant with the facts. The affair was then considered a complete fiasco and its fame as such persisted in tradition until the details were wholly forgotten. Ten years afterward Maximilian thus referred to it: "The inhabitants of the banks of the Missouri affirm that this enterprise was conducted with very little energy; they retired from the enemy's villages without destroying them or doing much injury to the inhabitants, at which the allied Indians especially were much dissatisfied. The Aricaras, on the other hand, became extremely arrogant, and henceforth murdered all white men who were so unfortunate as to fall in their way."

Scarcely had Leavenworth read his orders to the troops at Fort Atkinson when several trappers were massacred by these Indians near the Mandan villages. In the following winter several were killed by them in the valley of the Platte, and similar outrages were of frequent occurrence for many years thereafter. It is true that General Atkinson in 1825 found them humble and peaceably inclined, but his visit was in company with a formidable military force. The history of the twenty years following this affair, far from justifying the hopeful predictions of Colonel Leavenworth, were rather a literal fulfillment of the despondent prophecy of Major Pilcher in a letter to Benjamin O'Fallon within a week after the troops left the Aricara villages. "It is my sincere and candid opinion" he wrote, "that the expedition against the Aricaras, from

which so much service might have been rendered to this
dwindling and bleeding commerce, will rather tend to increase, than diminish, the evil; that the situation of affairs is
worsted materially; that instead of raising the American
character in the estimation of its inhabitants and impressing
them with the power and spirit of our government, the contrary effect has been produced; and that the outrages of the
Indians will increase in consequence. That a most unfavorable
impression has been left upon the minds of our Indian allies
is a fact that I am sorry to communicate."

It is difficult to fathom the motives which actuated
Colonel Leavenworth in this campaign. It was not lack of
courage, for his excellent record was evidence against any
such theory. It is probable he felt alarmed at the responsibility
that he had voluntarily assumed. He might reasonably doubt
that his superiors would approve of his action in taking so
large a command to so great a distance simply to punish an
outrage against a party of traders and trappers. The lamentable accident in the wreck of the keelboat doubtless increased
his anxiety and made him doubly anxious to achieve the object of the expedition without further loss. Finally he may
have distrusted his Indian allies and even the trappers and
mountaineers, and have feared that a successful assault of the
villages might have ended in a massacre of its inhabitants. He
was well aware that such a result would have raised a storm
back in the States where the circumstances would be imperfectly understood. It is only from considerations of this character that it is possible to explain his conduct at the Aricara
towns, and his deliberate choice of a course which could not
fail to tarnish his reputation and bring down the contempt of
the Indians upon the American arms.

One of the most regrettable features of the whole affair was
the feeling of bitter animosity that was engendered between
Colonel Leavenworth and Joshua Pilcher. Both were men of
high character and unblemished reputation. Colonel Leavenworth had already won enviable distinction in his country's
service, particularly in the battles of Chippewa and Niagara
Falls in the War of 1812. He was a true soldier and a good
officer and whatever may have been his error of judgment in

the present case, there was no suspicion that he acted from any but the most disinterested motives.

Mr. Pilcher was one of the ablest of the traders, and had succeeded Manuel Lisa in the presidency of the Missouri Fur Company. His character was above reproach; he was well informed, and his opinion on matters relating to the Indian trade were more than once sought for by the government. He had apparently joined the expedition purely from a desire to help punish the Aricaras, for as he had now withdrawn all his establishments above the Sioux, he was not protecting his own interests to the same extent that Ashley was. Leavenworth was highly pleased with him up to the time when he began his negotiations for peace. He says in one of his reports: "Allow me to say that up to this time I had been very well pleased with Mr. Pilcher in every respect, particularly as sub-agent. He has neglected no opportunity to be serviceable to the expedition and had done everything in his power to ensure its success."

Colonel Leavenworth's decision to negotiate peace without a victory excited the indignation of Pilcher, who had just seen his Sioux auxiliaries draw off in disgust at the failure to accomplish anything. He refused to be a party to the treaty and probably did all that he could to cause this part of the proceedings to fail. His conduct naturally aroused the ire of Colonel Leavenworth, who considered him bound to obey orders as long as he was attached to the command. The burning of the villages after the troops had left was at once attributed by Colonel Leavenworth to Pilcher, but it was probably one of Pilcher's men, William Gordon. Pilcher positively denied being a party to the act, and disclaimed any knowledge of who the guilty party was, at the same time intimating that in his opinion the act was altogether justifiable.

Colonel Leavenworth added fuel to the flame of discord by issuing an order on the day of departure from the Aricara towns, in which he directly charged the Missouri Fur Company with the destruction of the villages, and declared that "with such men he would have no further intercourse." From this ban of displeasure he excepted Major Henry Vanderburgh and Moses B. Carson. But these gentlemen would not accept the Colonel's indulgence, and wrote to Pilcher on the day following that they felt "extremely mortified at having been selected as the object of his [Leavenworth's] approbation and praise." Pilcher himself was enraged at Leavenworth's order, and permitted his indignation to get the better of his judgment entirely. On the 23rd of August, at Fort Recovery, he addressed a letter to Colonel Leavenworth, which, whatever truth it might contain, was couched in such violent and abusive language as to produce the opposite effect upon the public from what was intended. His provocation was indeed great, and he was not a man given to the mincing of words, but he ought at least to have refrained from personal abuse. He closed his letter with the following passage, in which, it must be acknowledged, there was more truth than the partisans of Colonel Leavenworth would have been willing to admit: "I am well aware," he wrote, "that humanity and philanthropy are mighty shields for you against those who are entirely ignorant of the disposition and character of Indians, but with those who have experienced the fatal and ruinous consequences of their treachery and barbarity these considerations will avail nothing. You came to restore peace and tranquillity to the country, and to leave an impression which would insure its continuance. Your operations have been such as to produce the contrary effect, and to impress the different Indian tribes with the greatest possible contempt for the American character. You came (to use your own language) to 'open and make good this great road;' instead of which you have, by the imbecility of your conduct and operations, created and left impassable barriers" (4).

MILITARY RECORD OF COLONEL LEAVENWORTH
Powell's *List of Officers of the U. S. Army.*

"LEAVENWORTH, HENRY. (Born in Conn. Appointed from New York.) Capt. 25th U.S. Inf., 25 April, 1812. Maj. 9th Inf., 15 Aug., 1813. Trans. to 6th Inf. 1st Oct., 1821. Col. 3rd Inf., 16 Dec., 1825, Died 21 July, 1834. Bvt. Lieut. Col., 15 July, 1814, for distinguished and meritorious service at the Battle of Chippewa. Bvt. Col. 25 July, 1814, for distinguished service at Niagara Falls. Bvt. Brig. Gen. 25 July, 1824, for ten years' faithful service in one grade."

AUTHOR'S NOTES

(1) "Arrived at a trading establishment called by the Indian traders Fort Recovery and sometimes Cedar Fort." Fort Kiowa was "eight or ten miles above where we lay." Leavenworth.

(2) The roll of officers who accompanied the expedition included the following: Colonel Leavenworth, Major Wooley, Brevet-Major Ketchum, Captains Riley and Armstrong, Lieutenants Bradley, Cruger, Wickliffe, Moore, Noel, and Doctor Gale.

(3) Leavenworth's report.

(4) My authorities for the foregoing account of the campaign against the Aricaras are the orders, reports, and correspondence of Ashley and Pilcher; and various items of information gleaned from the newspapers of the time printed in St. Louis and Franklin, Missouri.

EDITOR'S NOTES

(A) The *Missouri Intelligencer*, September 9, 1823 says fifteen; Leavenworth in his *Report* says ten; and the casualty list furnished by Smith, Jackson and Sublette says fourteen. See Dale, *Ashley-Smith Explorations*, page 80 note.

(B) The *Missouri Intelligencer* says, "All the horses belonging to the United States troops and ten of those belonging to General Ashley's company."

Chapter IV

THE YELLOWSTONE EXPEDITION OF 1825

Purpose of the expedition—Keelboat transportation—Progress of the expedition—Treaty with the Poncas—Arrival at Fort Kiowa—Treaties with the Sioux—Buffalo hunt—Treaties with Cheyennes and Ogallalahs—Indian feast—Footprints in the rocks—Treaty with the Aricaras—Arrival at the Mandans —Trouble with the Crows—Mosquitoes—Arrival at the Yellowstone—Meeting with General Ashley—Excursion to find the Assiniboines—Return to the mouth of the Yellowstone—Return journey—Arrival at Council Bluffs—More treaties with the Indians—Arrival at St. Louis—Report of the expedition.

This expedition, like that of Lewis and Clark a score of years before, is one which can be reviewed with great satisfaction, because it was conducted in an eminently sensible and practical way, and because it fully accomplished its purpose. The restlessness of the Missouri tribes ever since the War of 1812, and their frequent acts of hostility to the whites, culminating in the Blackfoot and Aricara outrages of 1823, caused the government to adopt more effective measures for their reduction and pacification. In 1824 Congress passed an act authorizing treaties to be formed with the Missouri tribes, and the President appointed General Henry Atkinson of the army, and Major Benjamin O'Fallon, Indian agent, commissioners to visit and conclude the treaties.

The appointments were made too late in the year 1824 to permit the accomplishment of the work during that season, but measures were taken to carry it promptly into effect with the opening of spring. The commissioners left St. Louis about the 20th of March, 1825, and arrived at Council Bluffs on the 19th of April. The last invoice of their goods arrived on the 13th of May, and preparations were completed for the departure of the expedition on the following day. The transports consisted of eight keelboats, which had, in addition to the usual appliances of sails, cordelles, poles, etc., a set of paddle wheels operated by hand power. The boats were named after the furbearing animals most commonly met in the Missouri river trade—*Beaver, Buffalo, Elk, Mink, Muskrat, Otter, Raccoon,* and *White Bear.* As animals of these varieties were constantly encountered along the route, an amusing confusing of names occurs now and then in the journal; as for instance: "Two elk were killed by Lieutenant Swearinger and a man of the *Muskrat* crew";' 'an antelope was killed this morning by a hunter from the transport *Elk*"; "the *Mink* and *Beaver* halted and sent out to bring in a buffalo"; "the whole flotilla, *Bear; Buffalo, Elk, Mink,* etc., stopped at Elk Island to secure three buffalo found there"; the *Muskrat* halted and took in two elk, three white bears and one deer that our hunters had killed"; General Ashley's beaver were "shipped on board the *Mink, Muskrat,* and *Raccoon.*"

The commission set out from Council Bluffs with an escort of 476 men, of whom forty were mounted and went by land, keeping always within reach of the boats. Among the officers of the expedition besides General Atkinson were Colonel Leavenworth, Majors Kearney, Langham and Ketchum, Captains Armstrong, Riley, Mason, Gaunt, Pentland, Kennedy, and Culbertson; Lieutenants Harris, Swearinger, Wragg, Greyson, Waters, Holmes, and Doctor Gale.

The expedition proceeded without serious accident, although with much disarrangement of the machinery, and arrived at the Ponca village on the 8th of June. Captain Armstrong with the mounted troops and with Edward Rose, the interpreter, arrived thirteen days before the force landed and went into camp just below the mouth of Paint creek, and arrangements were made to hold a council and form a treaty with the Indians on the following day. Here a military display was given, which, with the considerable force of the troops present, made an excellent impression on the Indians. The ceremony is thus recorded in the journal: "The troops were paraded in brigade in uniform at nine this morning, and were reviewed by General Atkinson in the rear of the Ponca village. They appeared extremely well and excited great curiosity in

the Indians, the whole tribe, men, women and children,
leaving the village to witness the scene." Following immediately upon the review a council was held with the Indians at
which nearly the whole tribe was present. The desired treaty
was unanimously approved and the business was concluded
with present-making, all in the most satisfactory manner."

The necessary repairs to the boats delayed departure until
1 P.M. of the 10th, when the expedition resumed its course
and camped that night a little above the Niobrara (L' Eau qui
Court). Hither the Indians followed and entertained the
expedition with native dances. The party then made its way
without notable incident to Fort Kiowa, at this time in
charge of a Mr. Wilson, trader of the American Fur Company.

Some runners were dispatched to bring in the Tetons,
Yanktons, and Yanktonais, while Rose, the interpreter, was
sent to tell the Cheyennes to meet the commission at the
Aricara villages. After some delay the Indians arrived, and on
the 20th military ceremonies were again gone through with.
The brigade was reviewed by General Atkinson and staff on
horseback. "The display was very fine, the troops being in
fine order," and the impression on the Indians was excellent.
The council was then organized and the credentials of the
chiefs examined. At this time there was delivered to the
Yanktons a girl of their tribe who had been a prisoner among
the Otoes, and whom the expedition had taken up the river.
That night the Indians were treated to a display of rockets,
which greatly impressed them.

The next day the treaty was concluded with these tribes,
and presents were distributed among them, including one gun
for each chief. If the military made a good impression upon the
Indians, the Indians made no less favorable an impression upon
the whites. "These tribes deport themselves with gravity and
dignity," says the journal, "while they displayed a great
quality of taste in their dress, which did great credit to their
untutored view of things."

The expedition resumed its journey on the 22nd, and on
the following day reached the Great Bend of the Missouri.
Here a portion of the passengers, as generally happens in
navigating the river, crossed the narrow neck of land while

the boats passed around. They left the flotilla on the 24th and were taken up on the boats on the 26th. At Elk Island the party had their first real excitement in buffalo hunting. Majors O'Fallon and Ketchum were walking along the shore when they descried three buffalo on the island. One of them remained to watch the animals while the other went to notify the party. It being about noon the flotilla halted for dinner, while a small party under Major Ketchum crossed to the island to get the buffalo. "The party landed and went into pursuit, but their design was partly frustrated by the imprudence of Lieutenant Wragg, who crossed over to the island shortly after, and ran forward and fired upon the buffalo." This frightened the animals, and they immediately leaped into the water. One swam toward the boats, was shot, but sank into the river, and did not rise. The remaining two came back to the island, where one was killed, and the other escaped in a wounded condition. The troops being in want of fresh meat, Lieutenant Wragg's performance on this occasion did not redound much to his credit in their eyes.

On the 30th of June the expedition arrived at the mouth of the Teton river about two and a half miles above which the American Fur Company at this date had a trading establishment. Here the party waited until the Sioux, Cheyennes and Ogallalahs could be brought in. On the first day of the arrival a party under Lieutenant Waters secured six buffalo. The journal says that "Rose, an interpreter, one of the party, we understand, covered himself with bushes and crawled into the gang of eleven bulls, and shot down the six on the same ground before the others ran off." The six buffalo weighed, dressed, 3,300 pounds.

While waiting for the arrival of all the Indians the commissioners were treated to a feast by the Ogallalahs, of which the following account is given in the journal: "It consisted of the flesh of thirteen dogs boiled in plain water in seven kettles, much done. Our drink was water from the Missouri brought up in the paunches of buffalo, which gave it a disagreeable taste. . . ./We were occupied about an hour and a half at the feast, when ourselves and the officers returned to camp and sat down and partook of wine and fruit at a table provided by the camp." The journal is here provokingly silent in not informing us how, after such a feast, the surfeited guests could have found an immediate appetite for such ordinary viands as wine and fruit. This banquet was part of the celebration of July 4th, 1825.

The Indians having been finally gathered together, the usual review took place on the 5th, with the added feature of a mounted artillery drill, by which "the Indians were struck with great awe." On the 6th the council and treaties took place, and presents were given and received. "This evening," the journal says, "Lieutenant Holmes threw six shells from the howitzer in the presence of the Indians. They exploded handsomely and made a deep impression upon the savages."

The expedition set out about 9 A.M. on the 7th. "The exhibition was beautiful. The wind being fair, the boats put off in regular succession, under sail and under the wheels, and ran up a stretch of 19½ miles in view of more than three thousand Indians who lined the shore." This day the cavalry horses were mostly sent back to Council Bluffs, only enough horses being retained to pack in the game, and to flank the river. The party arrived at Hidden creek on the 11th of July, and here, on the following day, after the usual military ceremonies, a treaty was made with a band of Sioux called the Fire Hearts, numbering about 150 souls. From one of the young men Major O'Fallon took a British medal.

The journal notes the following occurrence at this place. "Major O'Fallon and General Atkinson obtained two Indian horses and rode three-quarters of a mile back to see the hills in rear of our position at the impression of footsteps on a rock. We found the impression of three tracks of the foot of a common-sized man. The first, near the upper edge of the rock, is made by the right foot, and is about an inch deep, making a full impression of the whole track, with the full impression of five toes ¼″ deep. The next trap is of the the left foot, about 3½ feet from the first—impression full and deep as the first. The next footprint of the right foot is not visible, but at about six feet from the second track an impression is again made by the left foot as large and plain as the others. This is near the lower edge of the rock which of itself is about 11 feet long by 9, lying at an angle of about 30 degrees of elevation" (A).

The expedition arrived at the Aricara village on the 15th of July, where treaties were made with these Indians and the Hunkpapas, after the usual ceremonies. The journey was resumed on the 18th. No incidents of special importance occurred from this point to the Mandan villages, where the expedition arrived on the 26th of July. Here it was expected to make treaties with the Mandans, Minnetarees and Crows. The latter tribe was some distance off, and seemed reluctant to come in, for although repeatedly sent for they did not arrive until the 3rd of August. In the meanwhile treaties were made with the other tribes and a large amount of buffalo hunting was indulged in. After the arrival of the Crows the usual military ceremonies were gone through with and a treaty was made with that nation. At this time there ensued an occurrence that has passed into nearly all the narrative literature of that period. It is thus related in the journal: "Two Iroquois prisoners were demanded of the Crows. From this or some other cause unknown to me, the Crows became very hostile in their conduct, and from their attempting to take the presents before they were told to do so, Major O'Fallon struck three or four of the chiefs over the head with his pistol. About this time General Atkinson, who had been absent from the council to get his dinner, on returning to the council saw the commotion and ordered the troops under arms. This probably saved bloodshed."

The occurrence as it has found its place in literature is best stated by Irving in *Captain Bonneville*, from which it appears that Rose had a hand in the affair. Irving's narrative runs thus: "The last anecdote we have of Rose is from an Indian trader. When General Atkinson made his military expedition up the Missouri, in 1825, to protect the fur trade, he held a conference with the Crow nation at which Rose figured as Indian dignitary and Crow interpreter. The military were stationed at some little distance from the scene of the 'big talk.' While the General and the chiefs were smoking pipes and making speeches, the officers, supposing that all was friendly, left the troops and drew near the scene of ceremonial. Some of the more knowing Crows, perceiving this, stole quietly to the camp, and, unobserved, contrived to stop the touch-holes of the field pieces with dirt. Shortly after a misunderstanding occurred in the conference; some of the Indians, knowing the cannon to be useless, became insolent. A tumult arose. In the confusion Colonel O'Fallon snapped a pistol in the face of a brave and knocked him down with the butt end. The Crows were all in a fury. A chance medley fight was on the point of taking place, when Rose, his natural sympathies as a white man suddenly recurring, broke the stock of his fusee over the head of a Crow warrior, and laid so vigorously about him with the barrel that he soon put the whole throng to flight. Luckily, as no lives had been lost, this sturdy ribroasting calmed the fury of the Crows and the tumult ended without serious consequences."

The expedition left the Mandan villages on the 6th of August and reached the mouth of the Yellowstone on the 17th without special incident. Game everywhere abounded and there was plenty of hunting. We find in the journal of the 10th a reference to that pest which has disturbed the peace of every traveler on the Missouri. "The hunters are too much annoyed by mosquitoes," it says, "to remain in the bottoms for any length of time. The insects are more numerous on this river from the Poncas up, indeed on the plains and on the largest hills, than I have witnessed them anywhere else in my travels. They make no singing noise, but strike you as soon as they come up, and penetrate the skin at once."

After passing the mouth of the Yellowstone, the expedition "came to Ashley's old fort, a mile above the mouth of that river, on the bank of the Missouri. This position is the most beautiful spot we have seen on the river, being a tongue of land between the two rivers, a perfectly level plain, elevated above high water, and extending back two miles to a gentle ascent that rises, at the distance of two miles, 100 feet. Three sides of the fort, or picket work remain intact. The west side has been burned down. One house is standing, and three appear to have been burnt, as also the gate of the work."

While still at this place the party were agreeably surprised by the arrival of a band of hunters descending the Yellowstone in boats with a cargo of furs. It was no other than

General Ashley, who had just arrived from Salt Lake valley with a party of twenty-four men and with one hundred packs of beaver. General Atkinson offered him transportation for his party and property if he would await the return of his troops from an excursion farther up the river. This he readily assented to, as it gave him protection the rest of the way to the settlements.

From such information as General Ashley could give it was thought that the Blackfeet must be above the Falls of the Missouri, and that therefore there was no prospect of seeing them. But it was thought that they might run across the Assiniboines. Accordingly a part of the force set out on the 20th accompanied by General Ashley, and ascended the river about one hundred and twenty miles. Finding no indication of the presence of the Indians they turned about on the 24th and arrived at the mouth of the Yellowstone on the 26th. The next day the whole party commenced the descent of the Missouri, "at forty minutes past five A.M.," "having embarked the horses on board of the *Buffalo, Elk, Otter*, and *Beaver*," with Ashley's beaver "on board the *Mink, Muskrat*, and *Raccoon*" (B).

No incident worthy of mention occurred on the way down, except the wrecking of the *Muskrat* on a snag three miles above the mouth of the James river. The boat was repaired and General Ashley's fur was saved. The expedition arrived at Council Bluffs on the 19th of September. Here councils were held and treaties signed with the Otoes September 26th, with the Pawnees September 30th, and with the Omahas October 6th. General Ashley left St. Louis on the 22nd of September. On the 7th of October at 4 P.M., General Atkinson, Major O Fallon, and three officers, with eight effective men and the invalids, set out in the transport *Antelope* for St. Louis, where they arrived at 5 P.M. on the 20th of October, just seven months after their departure.

On the 7th of November the commissioner forwarded the treaties which they had concluded to Washington with a comprehensive report upon the expedition. They were able to give the gratifying statement that they had found all the tribes they had hoped to except two; that they had everywhere

formed satisfactory treaties; that they had left a strong impression among the Indians of the friendship, and at the same
time of the power, of the United States; and that on the whole
expedition "not a boat or man was lost, nor did any accident
occur of any sort of consequence." The report gives a succinct
account of the conditions of the tribes at that time and makes
recommendations in regard to them. The commissioners found
no evidence that the British interfered in the least with any of
the tribes whom they saw.

On the 23rd of November General Atkinson transmitted
from the headquarters of the Western Department at Louis-
ville, Kentucky, to General Brown, commanding the Army of
the United States, a copy of the above report, with some additional comments of importance. He discussed the propriety of
establishing a military post higher up the river than Council
Bluffs, and thought that it was not a necessary measure. If one
were to be established, however, he thought that it ought to
be at the mouth of the Yellowstone, with a dependent post
near the Great Falls. But he believed that better results would
follow from an occasional display of military force such as had
just taken place, than from the permanent presence of troops
among the Indians. His advice was followed.

General Atkinson referred to the valuable geographical
and other information which he had derived from General
Ashley and J. S. Smith pertaining to routes, the location of the
South Pass, the extent of British trade on the Columbia, and
other matters. He stated that General Ashley had in preparation a topographical sketch of the country that he had visited
and that this would be forwarded as soon as received. It is to
be hoped that this sketch was made and that it will yet
come to light (C).

On the whole the expedition was a distinct success. It had
undertaken to accomplish a definite thing and had accomplished it promptly and thoroughly. It was a conspicuous exception among the various enterprises with which we are here
called upon to deal.

MILITARY RECORD OF GENERAL ATKINSON

Powell's *List of Officers of the U. S. Army.*

"ATKINSON, HENRY. (Born in N. C. Appointed from N. C.)
Capt., 3rd Inf., 1 July, 1808. Col. I. G. 25 April, 1813. Col.
4th Inf., 15 April, 1814. Trans. to 37th Inf. 22nd April, 1814.
Trans. to 6th Inf., 17 May, 1815. Brig. Gen. 13 May, 1820.
Col. A. G., 1 June, 1821, which he declined, and on 16 Aug.,
1821, was assigned as Col. 6th Inf. Retired as Col., 21 Aug.,
[1821] with Bvt. rank of Brig. Gen., 13 May, 1820. Died 14
June, 1842."

EDITOR'S NOTES

(A) This is Medicine Rock, a well known land mark near
Cheyenne Agency, South Dakota.

(B) Beckwourth gives some picturesque details. Bonner, *Beckwourth*, page 7.

(C) Dale says, page 117, that all searches in the War Department
for this map have proved fruitless.

Chapter V

THE SMALLPOX SCOURGE OF 1837

Effects of vice and disease upon the Indian—The smallpox—
Origin of the plague of 1837—Action of the American Fur Com-
pany—The disease among the Mandans—Terrible scenes—The
Aricaras attacked—Smallpox at Fort Union—Horrible ex-
pedient—Disastrous results—Disease spreads among the As-
siniboines—Brazeau and Larpenteur—The Blackfeet and Crows
attacked—Effect upon the various tribes—Effect upon the trade
—Morality among the various tribes.

The vices and diseases that came to the Indian with the
white man well-nigh resulted in the extermination of the race.
The wars among the tribes, the wars between the tribes and
whites, were the merest bagatelle in comparison with these
desolating influences which sapped the vitality of the people.

The proportionate destructiveness of these various agencies
of ruin is not easy to determine. The effects of alcohol and
immoral diseases were vast and universal, but not of a character to be reached by statistics. But that they corrupted the
life of the people, enervated their physical force, poisoned
their ambitions, rendered them an easy prey to the hard environment of their lives, and in the aggregate reduced the
native population at an alarming rate, the testimony of contemporary observers conclusively proves. It is only the arrest
of these influences in recent times by the better control now
exercised on the reservations, that has turned the tide and has
again placed the native population upon a basis of increase.

While there are no precise data as to the destructiveness of
the influences just noted, there was one plague that was so
rapid and complete that its effects are known with considerable accuracy. This was the smallpox scourge of 1837. This
terrible pestilence had visited the western tribes before, spreading destruction and terror in its path. The first great epidemic

occurred about the year 1800, when it swept over the country to the Pacific and destroyed the power of several tribes. Less terrible visitations occurred from time to time, but the most destructive of all was in 1837. So deadly was the pestilence at this time that many thought it must be something more terrible than smallpox, for it seemed to outdo any previous record of that disease.

The ravages of the scourge were practically confined to the upper Missouri river. The information relating to it, in the form of letters of eye-witnesses, is so graphic and complete that the story will be told mainly in their language (1).

The plague was introduced through the annual steamboat *St. Peters*, of the American Fur Company, which according to Larpenteur, arrived at Fort Union on the 24th of June, 1837. Some accounts say that there was but a single case on board, but it appears certain that there were several. The course of the American Fur Company on this occasion was in many respects culpable, for, knowing the terrible effects of the disease, it should not have permitted the infected boat to visit the tribes. The situation, however, was a very difficult one to deal with. The Indians expected the boat and knew that it had many goods for them, and if it failed to arrive they could never have been made to understand that it was not because of an attempt to rob them. Moreover, to have returned and sent up another steamboat would have been impossible, for the river would have been too low by that time. As the company would be the greatest sufferer from an epidemic among the Indians, they cannot be accused of any selfish motives in the course they pursued. Nevertheless that course was very ill-advised. It would have been better to have put the goods on shore, and fumigated them, and then to have taken them up in keelboats. Such, however, was not the decision. Although the disease had broken out before the boat reached Pierre, and had several victims before it reached the Mandans, it pursued its way clear through to Union, carrying with it one of the most awful scourges that ever befell any people.

The company's officers tried to avert the calamity by the impossible expedient of keeping the Indians away from the boat. But the Indians could not be restrained. They knew that the boat had goods for them, and suspected that it was all a ruse to cheat them. It was in vain to expostulate, implore and explain. They were deaf to all entreaty. When the boat arrived at Fort Clark a Mandan chief stole the blanket of a watchman upon the boat who was dying of the disease. Mr. Chardon made every effort for the immediate return of the blanket, promised pardon for the theft, and new blankets in its place, but all to no purpose. He sent messengers warning the people to keep away, and used every argument in his power, but the whole village came down to the river.

The disease broke out among the Mandans about June 15, and continued as long as there was any one left to attack. It raged with a virulence never before known. Deaths were almost instantaneous. The victim was seized with pains in the head and back, and in a few hours was dead. The body immediately turned black and swelled to thrice its size. Nearly everyone who was attacked died.

When the Indians found that the warnings of the whites were true, and realized the character of the calamity that was upon them, it produced the most profound effect upon their feelings. Some were for taking summary vengeance upon the whites, but before they could carry out their purpose the hand of death was upon them. Others who saw it felt that the Great Spirit had stricken them for attempting to injure their friends. They would then supplicate the whites to defend them. But the whites were now powerless. The disease spread rapidly. Hundreds died daily. It was impossible to bury them, and the bodies were thrown in heaps over a cliff and the terrible stench infected the air for miles around.

In the presence of this disaster, without power to stay or avert it, the Indians became desperate. Many committed suicide by shooting, stabbing, or drowning. One chief, before he was stricken, but feeling that he soon would be, commanded his wife to dig his grave. Sorrowfully she obeyed his command, and when the work was done her warrior threw himself into it, and seizing his knife, stabbed himself to death. His broken-hearted squaw went back to her tent and child, where both were to meet a more terrible fate ere another sun should pass over their heads. Two young men just stricken with the disease conferred with each other as to the best way to end their existence, and having agreed on the method, fearlessly carried it into execution. Every day was crowded with these pathetic and soul-stirring incidents as the pestilence carried away victim after victim. Tenderness and compassion at last became blurred in the presence of this terrible calamity. The Indians sought to avoid each other by wandering singly upon the prairie, and finding subsistence wherever they could.

Thus the great tribe of the Mandans was literally led to slaughter. Only about thirty persons remained, and these were mostly boys and old men. "No language can picture" says one writer, "the scene of desolation which the country presents. In whatever direction we go we see nothing but melancholy wrecks of human life. The tents are still standing on every hill, but no rising smoke announces the presence of human beings, and no sounds, but the croaking of the raven and the howling of the wolf, interrupt the fearful silence."

Of all the tribes the Mandans suffered the most severely, and came very near actual extermination. A band of the Aricaras was encamped near by, and for some unaccountable reason escaped the disease until after it had wrought terrific ravages among the Mandans. The latter were suspicious of this, and thought that the whites were in league with the Aricaras. But they were soon undeceived, for the pestilence broke out among them later, and nearly annihilated that tribe as well. It also made great inroads among the Minnetarees.

The introduction of smallpox at Fort Union would seem to have been as certain as any sublunary sequence of cause and effect, but no adequate measures were taken to prevent it. Besides the infected cargo which had to be unloaded, one of the passengers, Jacob Halsey, well known on the river as clerk and partner of the Upper Missouri Outfit, was already sick when he arrived, but nevertheless took up his residence at the fort. Halsey had been vaccinated and the disease was not malignant in his case, although it was a severe shock to a constitution naturally not strong and further weakened by habitual dissipation. As Halsey's was the only case, it was thought that the spread of the disease could be circumvented. But Mr. E. T. Denig, another well-known clerk of the company, had it, though not fatally, and then a squaw was carried off with it. The only Indians at the post at the time were some thirty squaws, and now as the spread of the infection was hopelessly certain, "prompt measures were adopted," in the language of Larpenteur, "to prevent an epidemic." These measures were no other than the vaccination of all the squaws with the smallpox virus itself, there being no regular vaccine matter at the fort. The poor squaws knew no better, and meekly submitted to the operation. "Their systems" were "prepared according to Dr. Thomas' Medical Book," and they were vaccinated from Halsey himself. This course was adopted, Larpenteur assures us, with cynical coolness, "with a view to have it all over and everything cleaned up before any Indian should come in, on their fall trade, which commenced early in September." Such is the astonishing confession of one of the American Fur Company's servants, and such was the desperate length to which the traders would go when the interests of their business could be promoted. Thirty squaws, imprisoned within the palisades, were deliberately sacrificed to one of the most loathsome pests in nature, in order "to have it all over and everything cleaned up" before the company's trade should be injured.

But this heroic purpose utterly miscarried. Larpenteur says that the mistake was made in not vaccinating from a person of sound physical constitution which Halsey did not have, as if a disease which was at that moment raging farther down the river with unprecedented power could be much intensified by being communicated from an unsound constitution! The result of this culpable oversight was, in the terse and unsentimental language of Larpenteur, that "the operation proved fatal to most of our patients" (2). It seems never to have occurred to him that he and his abettors were red-handed violators of the Sixth Commandment. He goes on to say: "About 15 days afterward there was such a stench in the fort that it could be smelt at a distance of 300 yards. It was awful—the scene in the fort, where some went crazy, and others were half eaten by maggots before they died." This was during the hottest part of the summer.

As if fate were bent on making the worst of a bad situation, the Indians began coming in to trade while the epidemic was at its height. Halsey says that the fort was absolutely closed to them and they were entreated to keep away, but that probably the "air was infected" with the disease "for a half a mile without the pickets" Larpenteur says that they did open the door to a celebrated chief, "but on showing him a little boy who had not recovered, and whose face was one solid scab, by holding him over the pickets, the Indians finally concluded to leave." Whatever the facts, the fearful truth is that the pestilence got abroad. It first spread among the Assiniboines, who were the Indians that had come to the fort, and it raged among them until winter. Halsey, who left Union in October, says that at that time it was "raging with the greatest destructiveness imaginable—at least ten out of twelve die with it."

At Fort Union in these trying times one John Brazeau, a familiar name in those days on the upper rivers, was undertaker, and seemed to take a fiendish satisfaction in his new occupation. "How many?" Larpenteur would ask him of a morning now and then. "Only three, sir, but according to appearances at the hospital, I think I shall have a full load tomorrow or next day." These two worthies missed their opportunity in life by coming upon the stage at the wrong time and place. They would have found a more congenial atmosphere among the gruesome scenes around the French guillotines of Ninety-Three (A).

In spite of the destructive ravages of the disease among the Assiniboines they still came to trade, and the business did not fall off as much as had been expected. Larpenteur says that when the Indians were asked how it was under the circumstances, that "there were so many robes brought in, they would say laughingly that they expected to die soon and wanted to have a frolic till the end came."

The pestilence reached the Blackfeet through another most culpable act of negligence on the part of the company's officers. An Indian of that nation was permitted to get on the *St. Peters* at the mouth of the Little Missouri and then to go to his people before it was known whether he had taken the disease or not. The Crow post, Van Buren, was also infected, most likely through other acts of negligence. The disease ran the usual course there, but the Crows at the time were on Wind river, and escaped until later in the fall. But before the end of the year all the tribes of the Missouri valley above the Sioux had been stricken and the extent of the calamity was well-nigh appalling.

The effect upon the tribes was various. The Assiniboines were for open hostility to the whites, to whom they rightly attributed the direful visitation. They did not, however, come to any overt act. The Blackfeet, on the other hand, were completely humbled. One band had been on the point of making war on the whites, and the smallpox appealed to them as the judgment of Heaven for thus attempting to injure their friends. For the most part all the tribes behaved remarkably well, and the trade did not suffer so much as had been expected. In the following winter it began to fall off, and although buffalo were more plenty than had been known for years, there were few Indians to hunt them.

It was a severe blow to the traders. In a letter of February 25, 1838, from Pratte, Chouteau and Company to Mr. Pierre Chouteau, Jr., one of the firm, then on his way to New York, we read: "Late last evening Provost arrived, and this morning (Sunday) we have all been perusing the melancholy details of plague, pestilence and devastation, ruined hopes and blasted expectations." It then recounts the loss of the various tribes, and the prospects for the ensuing year. And in an earlier communication to Halsey on the Upper Missouri, the company said that the calamity was "calculated to fill us with dismay as regards the trade of the Missouri for some years to come. We can only view it as a visitation of Providence with which, though it be vain for us to contend, it behooves us to make the best of existing circumstances; to put forth all our energies; and by pursuing a course of strict economy in our expenditures, with kind and conciliatory conduct to the Indians who have escaped this dreadful pestilence, endeavor, by prudence, fortitude, and perseverance, to support ourselves under the melancholy scourge."

The real mortality during this memorable plague has been variously estimated. Audubon, upon the authority of Mitchell, places it at 150,000, an impossible figure, for it would have meant the total annihilation of all the tribes where it prevailed. Another estimate was 60,000. This also seems impossible. Judging from detailed estimates, gleaned from various sources, it seems hardly probable that the total mortality of the Missouri tribes amounted to more than 15,000. But considering the population of these several tribes—Blackfeet, Crows, Mandans, Minnetarees, and Aricaras—even this diminished estimate makes a mortality almost without parallel in the history of plagues. It fully justifies the powerful word picture which is given in the letter already quoted from the works of Maximilian: "The destroying angel has visited the unfortunate sons of the wilderness with terrors never before known, and has converted the extensive hunting grounds, as well as the peaceful settlements of these tribes, into desolate and boundless cemeteries. . . . The warlike spirit which but lately animated the several Indian tribes. and but a few months ago gave reason to apprehend the breaking out of a sanguinary war, is broken. The mighty warriors are now the prey of the greedy wolves, and the few survivors, in utter despair, throw themselves on the pity of the whites, who, however, can do little for them. The vast preparations for the protection of the western frontier are superfluous; another arm has undertaken the defense of the white inhabitants of the frontier; and the funeral torch, that lights the red man to his dreary grave, has become the auspicious star of the advancing settler and the roving trader of the white race."

AUTHOR'S NOTES

(1) My authorities are principally letters from the American Fur Company's posts at Union, Pierre, and Clark. In the preface of Maximilian's work, English edition, 1843, there is a powerful pen picture in the form of a letter written the following year, June 6, 1838, from New Orleans. In Audubon's Missouri Journals there is an account of the scourge among the Mandans, received from Francis A. Chardon, in charge of Fort Clark at the time. Like most history which is furnished by individual traders, the attempt to magnify the narrator's part in the events related robs the narrative of much of its reliability. Charles Larpenteur, who was at Union at the time, gives

some valuable data concerning the commencement of the plague. See *Forty Years a Fur Trader*, Coues, 1898.

(2) Halsey's own evidence as written some five months later, is different. He says: "A few days afterward there were 27 persons ill with it, out of which number 4 proved fatal." But Halsey had good reason to conceal the true results of the desperate act for which he, as in charge of the fort, was responsible.

EDITOR'S NOTE

(A) Chittenden's judgment of Larpenteur seems entirely too harsh. He represents him as delighting in the numerous deaths and prospects of more. Yet Larpenteur's own account does not sustain this criticism. In Coues' *Larpenteur*, page 134, he gives the same colloquy with Brazeau (Brazo he calls him). But Chittenden fails to quote Larpenteur's comment that it seemed to be fun for Brazeau but not for himself. Then too, Chittenden in telling of the innoculation of the squaws, by the use of the expressions "cynical coolness" and "astonishing confession" gives a sinister meaning to Larpenteur's acts that is wholly unfair. In the absence of regular vaccine, Larpenteur was doing the best he could, and his practice was in accordance with a medical book he had. He evidently was attempting to avoid a general epidemic and not create one. That he had no evil intentions toward the Indians is shown by the fact that at the same time and in the same way he innoculated some of the white men at the fort.

Chapter VI

MILITARY OCCUPATION

Early military expeditions—Question of advanced military occupation—Post at Council Bluffs—Founding of Fort Leavenworth— Colonel Dodge's expedition from Fort Gibson—Deadly malaria—Colonel Dodge's expedition of 1835—Summary of military occupation.

As early as the year 1807 the armed forces of the United States had ascended the whole course of the Missouri river, had crossed to the Pacific, had ascended the Arkansas river nearly to its source and had penetrated to the gates of Santa Fe. But these expeditions were chiefly in the nature of explorations, and were not intended to be followed up by immediate military occupation.

In 1807 a small detachment of troops was sent up the Missouri to conduct back to his home the Mandan chief whom Lewis and Clark had brought down the previous year. This expedition met with disaster at the Aricara villages and was forced to return. No permanent occupation of any advanced point was intended in this case. There was at this time no post west of the immediate vicinity of the Mississippi in the valley of the Missouri.

In 1808 Fort Osage, or Fort Clark, as it was also called, was founded and garrisoned with a small force. Here also was established the only government factory for the Indian trade west of the Mississippi River. The post was not occupied continuously and was abandoned altogether upon the founding of Fort Leavenworth (1).

In 1819 took place the important military expedition under General Atkinson known as the Yellowstone Expedition. It resulted in the establishment of a post of eight years' duration near the present site of Omaha, Nebraska. The post was known successively under the names of Camp Missouri, Fort Atkinson, and Fort Calhoun, the last name having descended to the present day.

The next important military move was the campaign against the Aricaras under Colonel Leavenworth in 1823. It resulted in no permanent advance.

In 1825 General Atkinson and Major O'Fallon, commissioned to conclude treaties with the Missouri Indians, proceeded with a formidable military escort from Fort Atkinson to a point one hundred and twenty miles above the mouth of the Yellowstone. The expedition resulted in permanent occupation of none of the country passed through.

The Yellowstone expeditions had their origin in a desire on the part of the Government, created largely by the agitation of the frontier settlements, to overawe the tribes of the Missouri by acquainting them with the military power of the United States, to counteract British influence along the frontier, and to establish a line of posts leading to the headwaters of the Missouri and possibly beyond. Estimates had been prepared by the War Department showing the cost of carrying such a movement across the continent. But the plan never succeeded. General Atkinson upon his return in 1825 set at rest the rumors of British intrigue along the borders, for he had not succeeded in finding any evidence of it. He advised against the necessity of military posts in that quarter, but recommended the mouth of the Yellowstone if one were decided on. For protection of the traders he rightly considered the Three Forks of the Missouri as the most important location; but even here he considered that the benefits would fall short of the sacrifice. Acting upon General Atkinson's advice, the government did not advance beyond Council Bluffs.

Fort Atkinson was occupied until 1827, mostly by the 6th Infantry; but the unhealthiness of the place, and other considerations, led to its abandonment, which took place on June 27th of that year, the regiment returning to Jefferson Barracks.

Fort Leavenworth was established in pursuance of orders from the headquarters of the Army, dated March 7, 1827, directing Colonel Leavenworth to select a site within twenty miles above or below the mouth of the Little Platte river. On the 17th of April four companies of the Third Regiment, U.S.

Infantry, left Jefferson Barracks under the immediate command of Captain W. G. Belknap for the purpose of establishing and garrisoning the post. Colonel Leavenworth was unable to find a suitable location on the east bank, and finally chose the site where Fort Leavenworth now stands. The choice was a fortunate one and does credit to the officer whose name was given to the fort. The selection was reported on May 8th to the War Department and was duly approved there. Major Ketchum, in the meanwhile, arrived from Council Bluffs, May 4th, with the public property from that place and the transfer from old Fort Atkinson to new Fort Leavenworth was thus accomplished.

The establishment of this post was mainly due to the growing importance of the locality near the mouth of the Kansas river as a starting point for parties bound for the mountains and for Santa Fe. Experience had shown the need of a post here rather than at Council Bluffs. The distance of twenty miles above or below the mouth of the Little Platte embraced the territory where Kansas City now stands, really a more commanding situation for the protection and control of the trade, but Colonel Leavenworth does not seem to have approved of it.

Fort Leavenworth played an exceedingly important rôle in the history of the fur trade, not so much on account of its military character as from its relation to the regulations governing the Indian trade. In particular it was charged with the inspection of cargoes, the examination of licenses, and a strict enforcement of the rules against introducing liquor into the Indian country. No military operations of importance were conducted from it during the period covered by our present work except on two occasions when military escorts accompanied the Santa Fe caravans—in 1829 and in 1834. These have been described in our Santa Fe chapters.

In 1834 Colonel Dodge conducted a military expedition from Fort Gibson westward for the purpose of reducing the Indians along the Santa Fe route to submission. The expedition left Fort Gibson June 15, 1834, and encountered several villages of Indians about July 22nd. Three days later it started back and reached Fort Gibson August 15th. George Catlin was with this expedition.

This movement, which was ordered from Washington, seems to have been very ill-advised, and it resulted most disastrously. It took place during the heat of summer and a deadly malaria prevailed all the time. Several officers, including Colonel Leavenworth and his aide and many enlisted men, died. Catlin very nearly lost his life. The following graphic description of this unfortunate expedition is from the pen of of one of the officers who accompanied it:

"It is painful to dwell upon this subject. Nature would seem to have conspired with an imbecile military administration for the destruction of the regiment. On, on they marched, over the parched plains whence all moisture had shrunk, as from the touch of fire; their martial pomp and show dwindled to a dusty speck in the midst of a boundless plain; disease and death struck them as they moved; with the false mirage ever in view, with glassy eyes, and parched tongues, they seemed upon a sea of fire. They marched on, leaving three-fourths of their number stretched by disease in many sick camps; there, not only destitute of every comfort, but exposed with burning fever to the horrors of the unnatural heat—it was the death of hope. The horses too were lost by scores. In one sick camp, they were in danger of massacre by a horde of Comanche Indians, who had established themselves near by; and were in all probability only saved by the judgment and determination of the officer in command, the lamented Izard; and he was fortunately indebted to his experience on the Santa Fe expedition. In the face of the overwhelming numbers, he kept every man who could possibly bear arms on constant guard; and opposed at the point of the bayonet the passage of a single Indian over their slight breastwork. He knew the influence of dauntless boldness over the Indians, who dread every loss, and seek the attainment of their ends by cunning and management; thus on friendly pretenses they sought admittance singly with a view gradually to obtain the power to crush the small force at a blow.

"General Leavenworth and his aide stopped. They both lost their lives. Colonel Dodge with 150 of the hardiest constitutions, persevered and overcame every obstacle; they reached the Tow-e-ash village, in a picturesque valley, amid mountainous precipices and rocks; such he discovered to be the name of a numerous tribe who altogether with the Comanches, Kiowas, and Arapahoes had hitherto been confounded under the name of Pawnees.

"There, perhaps within the boundary of Mexico, was made the first though feeble demonstration of the power and ubiquity of the white man. Some breath was expended in an effort to mediate peace between these wandering savage robbers and their red neighbors of our border; as availing as it would be to attempt to establish a truce between the howling wolf of the prairie and his prey" (2).

In 1835 Colonel Dodge made another expedition into the prairie, this time from Fort Leavenworth. His route lay upon the Platte and South Platte rivers to the mountains; thence south to the Arkansas; and home by the Santa Fe Trail. The expedition is said to have been set on foot for the purpose of putting a stop to outrages by the Aricara Indians in the upper valley of the Platte.

It will thus be seen that, prior to 1843, actual military occupation of the Western country did not extend beyond Fort Leavenworth. The various expeditions into the interior, however, had served to give the military authorities a fairly accurate knowledge of the entire region. The extensive operations of the traders contributed to the same end and in later years some of them were always present with the troops in the capacity of guides wherever movements were made into new parts of the country. The government was therefore well prepared for the great military problems with which it was soon to be called upon to deal.

AUTHOR'S NOTES

(1) The following references indicate the unsettled state of this post.

Letter from George C. Sibley, government factor at Fort Osage, September 25, 1813: "I will therefore briefly tell you now that early in last June Fort Osage was evacuated and the factory broken up."

Letter from Sibley, July 10, 1819: "When they (the Yellowstone Expedition) arrive this fort will be broken up, and I shall be left here pretty much alone."

The fort was as good as abandoned in 1822, for Jacob Fowler, who passed there in July of that year, informs us that "the garrison at this time was commanded by one officer of the United States armey—Having two men under Command Both of them having disarted a few days ago and Carreyed off all his amenition."— *Journal of Jacob Fowler*, p. 173.

(2) *Scenes and Adventures in the United States Army*, by P. St. G. Cooke, Colonel Second Dragoons U.S.A., Philadelphia, 1859.

PETER SKENE OGDEN

Chapter VII

GEOGRAPHICAL AND SCIENTIFIC EXPLORATIONS

Lewis and Clark and Pike—Bradbury—Nuttall—Townsend— Brackenridge—Prince Paul of Wurtemburg—Catlin—Maximilian—Nicollet—Wislizenus—Other explorers.

The field of official exploration was but slightly developed during the period from 1807 to 1843. The expeditions of Lewis and Clark and of Pike were in the true sense exploring expeditions, and their results were of the highest importance. Though by profession soldiers, these officers were also accurate observers, and not unworthy pioneers in the field of scientific investigation which at a later date, was so thoroughly occupied by men of more specific qualifications. Their reports upon the geology, fauna, flora, and the native tribes, were in general sound and discriminating, and justly entitled to high standing in the history of scientific research in the Western country.

In the years 1809-11 John Bradbury the English naturalist did much important work in the valleys of the Missouri and Mississippi. Bradbury was a remarkable man—one has only to read the journal of his voyage up the Missouri in 1811 to see that. His devotion to his pursuits was the wonder of all who observed them. There was no hardship too severe for him to undergo. One can but shiver to read of his stripping and swimming unbridged and unfordable streams of the upper country in March, carrying his clothes on a stick, and then dressing and proceeding as if nothing had happened. The simple-minded voyageurs could never comprehend him, and the practical trader was constantly put to his wit's end to restrain him from dangerous excursions into the country beyond the boat's protection.

An amusing example of Bradbury's devotion to his studies is afforded in his record of his journey down the Missouri after parting with Hunt and Lisa in 1811. Henry M. Brackenridge was with him. One day a terrible storm swept down upon them almost without warning. It caught them on the leeward side of the river against high abrupt banks where no landing could be found. Their case seemed desperate, but finally they found a solitary shrub that promised strength to moor the boat to, and here they made fast and awaited in imminent peril the abating of the storm. But great as was the danger it did not deter the naturalist from examining the friendly bush, and he gives us its full botanical name in the narrative.

Bradbury's well-known book, *Travels in North America*, is one of the most useful works of this period, and one which the careful student of Louisiana history never fails to consult. It is the best existing authority on many points, and on some the only one. Irving drew largely upon it in his narrative of Hunt's voyage up the Missouri.

Thomas Nuttall, Bradbury's traveling companion on the Missouri voyage, rivaled him in his close devotion to his studies. Nuttall is the individual about whom Brackenridge relates a story that more than offsets the incident above related about Bradbury: "The day after passing the Sioux," says Brackenridge, "they met, as I have before mentioned, three hundred Aricara Indians; these were so delighted to see them that a number rushed into the river, to swim or wade to the boats; the party supposing them to be inimical, was on the point of firing; while every one was in momentary expectation that this would take place. Nuttall, who appeared to have been examining them very attentively, turned to Miller. 'Sir,' said he, 'don't you think these Indians much fatter, and more robust than those of yesterday?' "

"To the ignorant Canadian boatmen," as Brackenridge elsewhere says, "it affords a subject of merriment. *Le fou*, the fool, is the name by which he is commonly known. No sooner does the boat touch the shore than he leaps out, and when his attention is arrested by a plant or flower everything else is forgotten. The inquiry is sometimes made '*Ou est le fou?*' (Where is the fool?) '*Il est après rammasser des racines.*' (He is gathering roots.)"

In 1834 Nuttall and J. K. Townsend crossed the continent with the missionaries Jason and Daniel Lee. They went under the protection of Nathaniel J. Wyeth as far as to the Snake river. Both of these gentlemen published the results of their observations, and Townsend's book in particular is full of intelligent references to the events of the mountains. It is thus of historic as well as scientific value.

Henry M. Brackenridge ascended the Missouri with Lisa in 1811, and he and Bradbury were the peacemakers in the celebrated quarrel between Lisa and Hunt. Brackenridge was a young man of good education, very observing, and a promising young writer. His *View of Louisiana*, and his journal of his voyage up the Missouri, like Bradbury's *Travels*, are among our most reliable early authorities.

After 1811 no scientific parties or individuals penetrated the fur countries until 1819-20 when Major Long and his corps of scientists made their expeditions. The published results of this expedition have already been noticed.

In 1823 an individual referred to in the Chouteau correspondence as Prince Paul of Wurtemburg, went up the river and passed the winter. He returned to New Orleans in the summer of 1824. In 1829 he again went up and was found among the Mandans April 22, 1830 by Joshua Pilcher, who was then returning from his tour of the Hudson Bay Company posts. The purpose of his journey, as stated in the correspondence, was the "pursuit of knowledge." He left Fort Tecumseh in August, 1830, and was in St. Louis in October of that year. In reference to this last visit a local paper under date of January 29, 1830, had the following; "Paul William of Wurtemburg, a nephew of the King of England, arrived at New Orleans the 1st inst., from Europe. About six years ago he spent some time exploring the upper regions of the Missouri, but business requiring his return to Europe, he has revisited the American hemisphere and will, in the prosecution of his former plan cross the Rocky mountains and visit the continent on the Pacific. He is in his 33rd year." He does not seem to have crossed the continent at this time for he was back in St. Louis in the fall of 1830. There is no record of his making any other trip up the Missouri.

In 1832 George Catlin, the well-known Indian painter, ascended the Missouri to Fort Union on the first steamer that ever reached that point. He descended by skiff in the fall, having made a large number of sketches of scenes in the upper country, and many portraits of the Indians and traders. Subsequently Catlin visited other portions of Western America, and even of South America and Europe. His paintings and sketches, as well as his published works, are well known. He undoubtedly did a great work in preserving in pictorial form a condition of life that no longer exists except in history. He was a true and passionate friend of the Indian and an ardent worshiper of everything pertaining to the aboriginal customs and life. His works, like those of Maximilian, will always be resorted to by students of the native races and early conditions of the Missouri valley. The contrast between the methods of these two men, however, was most marked. Maximilian was a scientist—discriminating and accurate in his observations and careful and conservative in recording his impressions. Catlin was a visionary enthusiast upon a single theme, the American Indian. He saw everything pertaining to the natives through highly colored glasses, and, as if that were not enough, he recklessly exaggerated his impressions when he attempted to record them with his pen or pencil. He was distrusted by those who knew him in the West and was more than once taken to task by his contemporaries. Audubon for example flatly insinuates that he was dishonest. Parkman characterizes him as a "garrulous and windy writer." It is regretable that one who did so much of real worth should have marred it by a characteristic which throws doubt upon the accuracy of it all.

In the year 1833 Maximilian, Prince of Wied, ascended the river, visiting Forts Union, McKenzie and Clark, and wintering at the latter post. He traveled at this time under the name of Baron of Brausenberg (A), and is always so referred to in the correspondence. He passed a most miserable winter at Fort Clark, owing to a scarcity of provisions that amounted almost to a famine, and to insufficient shelter and a very severe winter. He was so ill at one time that his life was despaired of. He was accompanied by a small party among whom was a skilful artist by the name of Bodmer (B). The Prince, upon his return to Europe, published the results of his labors in the most complete and elaborate work ever prepared upon this region. It is much to be regretted that it is so inaccessible to the public (C). The most convenient edition to American readers is: *Travelers in The Interior of North America* by Maximilian, Prince of Wied, with Numerous Engravings on Wood and a Large Map Translated from The German by H. Evans Lloyd. To Accompany the Original Series of Eighty-one Elaborately Colored Plates, Size, Imperial Folio. London, Ackerman & Co., 96 Strand, MDCCCXLIII. The work covers a great variety of subjects—narrative, anecdote, history, ethnology, geology, natural history—and omitting a few errors, it is exceedingly accurate, discriminating and judicious in all its scope. It ranks with *Astoria, Bonneville,* and the *Commerce of the Prairies,* as a descriptive work, while it is far ahead of the others in the elaborate character of its illustrations. In this respect it has no competitor, or only a feeble one in Catlin.

Between 1836 and 1840 J. N. Nicollet carried on several valuable explorations in the valleys of the Mississippi and Missouri rivers. In 1839 he ascended the Missouri as far as to Fort Pierre and then crossed the country by way of James river, Devil's Lake, Red river and the St. Peter's to the Mississippi. John C. Fremont served his apprenticeship on these expeditions. Nicollet was one of the most industrious, indefatigable, earnest, and accurate of the American explorers, and the map which embodied the results of his labors was, in the opinion of General G. K. Warren, "one of the greatest contributions ever made to American geography."

In 1839 Dr. F. A. Wislizenus of St. Louis made an expedition to the Rocky Mountains and in the following year published the result of his observations in a little volume printed in German and now rarely seen (D). It is an exceedingly important contribution to our knowledge of the period and an interesting and ably written work.

The work of Father De Smet is considered in the next chapter.

In 1842 the government entered in earnest upon its long and important work of official exploration of the country west of the Mississippi. This was the year of Fremont's first expedition to the Rocky Mountains. His work pertains entirely to the period following that here considered, and it is referred to in this connection as an interesting link between the two.

EDITOR'S NOTES

(A) Error for Braunsberg.

(B) Karl Bodmer, 1809-1893, born in Zurich, had a long and distinguished career. He specialized in landscapes and animal pictures. Besides the Maximilian illustrations, he issued a volume of *Indian Costumes and Chiefs*, 1836.

(C) Coues, in his *Larpenteur*, page 142, says he knows of only two perfect copies.

Maximilian's book has since been re-printed, in 1906, in Thwaite's *Early Western Travels*.

(D) Dr. Wislezenus' books has since been published in English by the Missouri Historical Society, 1912, under the title of "*A Journey to the Rocky Mountains in the Year 1839.*"

Chapter VIII

MISSIONARY WORK

*Early missionary effort—The Nez Perce or Flathead deputation
—The popular version—The true version—The sensation caused
by the deputation—The Protestant missions—Catholic missions—Father De Smet.*

In the Far West, as in every other field which the genius
of the explorer has made known to the world, the followers
of the Cross have zealously proclaimed to the native races
the tidings of the Christian religion. The real work of the
missionaries west of the Missouri belongs to a later period
than 1843, and only the foundations were laid prior to this
time. Most of the Protestant denominations, and the Catholics as well, had missions along the lower tribes of the
Missouri; but in only two or three instances were any important advancements made into the country beyond. Such
as there were relate to the Oregon missionaries whose field
of labor lay beyond the territory, and extended beyond the
period, embraced in this work. The present consideration of
this subject will therefore be limited to an inquiry into the
origin of these missions and a reference to the early pilgrim-
ages across the plains.

The inception of the Oregon missions, both Protestant and
Catholic, is connected with an event which has about it an
air of inspiring romance, well calculated to arouse the ardor
of those devoted to the propagation of the Christian faith.
In its orthodox form, as set forth by the latest biographer of
Marcus Whitman (1), the story is as follows: In the summer
of 1832 four Nez Perce Indians (2) made their way to St. Louis
for the avowed purpose of getting some one to go and preach
to their people the white man's religion of which they had
heard through the Catholic voyageurs from Canada. They
were entertained by General Clark, who did all in his power
to interest them, showing them whatever was worth seeing,

and giving them the best of accommodations. They were fêted and feasted to such an extent that it made them sick, and two of their number died during the winter. As spring approached the other two prepared to return home and decided to go by way of the American Fur Company's steamer as far as they could. Before their departure General Clark gave them a banquet and at this banquet one of the Indians made a speech which has now become celebrated in the annals of missionary work among the Western Indians. The Indian is reported to have said:

"I come to you over the trail of many moons from the setting sun. You were friends of my fathers, who have all gone the long way. I came with an eye partly open for my people who sit in darkness. I go back with both eyes closed. How can I go blind, to my blind people? I made my way to you with strong arms through many enemies and strange lands that I might carry back much to them. I go back with both arms broken and empty. Two fathers came with us, they were the braves of many winters and wars. We leave them asleep here by your great waters and wigwams. They were tired in many moons and their moccasins wore out.

"My people sent me to get the 'White Man's Book of Heaven.' You took me to where you allow your women to dance as we do not ours, and the book was not there. You took me to where they worship the Great Spirit with candles and the book was not there. You showed me images of the good spirits and the picture of the good land beyond, but the book was not among them to tell us the way. I am going back the long and sad trail to my people in the dark land. You make my feet heavy with gifts and my moccasins will grow old carrying them, yet the book is not among them. When I tell my poor blind people, after one more snow, in the big council, that I did not bring the book, no word will be spoken by our old men or by our young braves. One by one they will rise up and go out in silence. My people will die in darkness, and they will go a long path to other hunting grounds. No white man will go with them, and no White Man's Book to make the way plain. I have no more words."

The day after the delivery of the speech they set out on the steamboat. George Catlin claims to have been a passenger on this same boat, and to have painted the portraits of these Indians without knowing their identity or the singular purpose of their long journey. Afterward, upon learning the truth he was delighted at his good fortune in having accidentally procured two portraits which could hardly fail to become of historic interest. They now constitute numbers 207 and 208 in his collection.

"When this speech was translated," says Dr. Nixon, "and sent East, it was published in the *Christian Advocate* in March, 1833, with a ringing editorial from President Fisk of Wilbraham College. 'Who will respond to go beyond the Rocky mountains and carry the Book of Heaven?' It made a profound impression. It was a Macedonian cry of 'Come over and help us,' not to be resisted. Old men and women who read this call, and attended the meetings at this time, are still living, and can attest to its power. It stirred the Church as it has seldom been stirred into activity."

The result of the spiritual agitation set on foot by the news of this deputation of Indians was that the Church in the East seriously took hold of the question of sending missionaries into this new field, and as soon as the necessary preparations could be made, parties were sent out. Jason and Daniel Lee with several co-workers went out for the Methodists in 1834. Marcus Whitman and Samuel Parker for the Presbyterians followed in 1835 and 1836. The Catholics under De Smet followed in 1840.

Returning now to the romance of the Flathead Indians, the actual facts, so far as they can be discovered, will be stated. The Nez Perce and Flathead Indians were the most religious of all the Western tribes, observing regularly their ceremonial rites, and evincing the greatest piety and fervency in their worship. They had heard of the white man's religion through employes of the British traders and were anxious to learn more of it. It was not an uncommon thing for them to send deputations to St. Louis, nor was it so difficult a matter as one might suppose. The Rocky Mountain Fur Company went annually to the very borders of their country and they could accompany the outgoing and incoming caravans with perfect safety. The Catholic records in St. Louis show the arrival of three such deputations prior to 1840. One of these, consisting of a single Indian, arrived in the fall of 1831, but he died shortly after his arrival (3). A second deputation, consisting of a father and his two sons, arrived in 1835, and a third, consisting of two Indians in 1839. The year following the Catholics sent out De Smet to establish a mission among them.

The Catholics make no record of the deputation of 1832, but of the fact that one was sent there is the clearest proof. There is still extant a letter by one who saw these Indians and received from General Clark the purpose of their visit. His name was William Walker, a member of the Wyandotte nation with whom he served as interpreter. His letter shows that he was a man of intelligence. In November, 1832, he went as representative of the Wyandottes to examine certain lands in Western Missouri which the government proposed to give those Indians in exchange for their lands in Ohio. On his way through St. Louis Mr. Walker called upon General Clark and the latter directed his attention to the three Flathead chiefs who were sick in the adjoining room, a fourth having died a few days before. After looking at the Indians he returned to General Clark's room and heard from him the circumstances of their visit. Mr. Walker wrote the following account of the incident to G. P. Disoway, which was published in the *Christian Advocate*, March 1, 1833: "It appeared that some white man had penetrated into their country, and happened to be a spectator at one of their religious ceremonies, which they scrupulously perform at stated periods. He informed them that their mode of worshiping the Supreme Being was radically wrong, and instead of being acceptable and pleasing, it was displeasing to Him; he also informed them that the white people away toward the rising of the sun had been put in possession of the true mode of worshipping the Great Spirit. They had a book containing directions how to conduct themselves in order to enjoy his favor and hold converse with Him; and with this guide, no one need go astray, but every one that would follow the directions laid down there could enjoy, in this life, His favor, and after death would be received into the country where the Great Spirit resides, and live forever with Him (A).

"Upon receiving this information they called a national council to take this subject into consideration. Some said, if this be true, it is certainly high time we were put into possession of this mode, and if our mode of worshipping be wrong and displeasing to the Great Spirit, it is time we laid it aside. We must know something more about this; it is a matter that can not be put off; the sooner we know it the better. They accordingly deputed four of their chiefs to proceed to St. Louis to see their Great Father, General Clark, to inquire of him, having no doubt that he would tell them the whole truth about it.

"They arrived at St. Louis and presented themselves to General Clark. The latter was somewhat puzzled, being sensible of the responsibility that rested upon him; he, however, proceeded by informing them that what they had been told by the white man in their country was true; then went into a succinct history of man from his creation down to the advent of the Savior, His life, precepts, His death, resurrection, ascension, and the relation He now stands to man as a mediator—that he will judge the world, etc.

"Poor fellows, they were not permitted to return home to their people with the intelligence. Two died in St. Louis, and the remaining two, though somewhat indisposed, set out for their native land. Whether they reached home or not is not known. The change of climate and diet operated very severely upon their health. Their diet when at home is chiefly vegetables and fish."

The paper containing this letter found its way to St. Louis, and elicited correcpondence from several parties, including General Clark, Robert Campbell, E. W. Sehon, and others. Mr. Sehon's letter, dated at St. Louis April 16, 1833, was published in the *Advocate* on the 10th of May following and throws additional light upon the origin of the Flathead visit. It says: "General Clark informed me that the publication which had appeared in the *Advocate* was correct. Of the return of the two Indians nothing is known. He informed me that the cause of their visit was the following: Two of their number had received an education at the Jesuitical school in Montreal, Canada, had returned to their tribe, and had endeavored as far as possible to instruct their brethren how the white man approached the Great Spirit. The consequence was a spirit of inquiry was aroused, a deputation was appointed, and a tedious journey of over three thousand miles performed, to learn for themselves of Jesus and Him crucified."

President Fisk published in the *Advocate* of March 22nd the following call which is probably the "ringing editorial" referred to by Dr. Nixon:

"Here! Hear! Who will respond to the call from beyond the Rocky Mountains? The communication of Brother G. P. Disoway, including one from the Wyandotte agent, on the subject of the deputation of the Flathead Indians to General Clark, has excited in many in this section intense interest. And to be short about it, we are for having a mission established there at once. I have proposed the following plan: Let two suitable men, unencumbered with families, and possessing the spirit of martyrs, throw themselves into the nation; live with them—learn their language—preach Christ to them—and as the way opens, introduce schools, agriculture, and the arts of civilized life. The means for these improvements can be introduced through the fur traders, and by the reinforcements with which from time to time we can strengthen the mission. Money shall be forthcoming. I will be bondsman for the Church. All we want is men. Who will go? Who? I know of one young man who I think will go; and of whom I can say, I know of none like him for the enterprise. If he will go (and we have written to him on the subject) we will only want another, and the mission will be commenced the coming season. . . . Were I young, healthy, and unencumbered, how joyfully would I go! But this honor is reserved for another. Bright will be his crown, glorious his reward " (4).

The quotations above given make possible a very complete separation of truth from fiction in this noted incident. There *was* a deputation of four Flathead chiefs to St. Louis in the fall of 1832. Two of them died while in St. Louis. The other two departed before the end of the year, but how they returned is unknown. The story that they were fêted and shown all the sights of the town is pure fiction. There was no banquet upon their departure. The famous oration was not made by one of their number but was a composition of later date by some individual whose identity has not yet been established. It did not appear in the *Christian Advocate*. George Catlin did not paint the portrait of these Indians. His own trip up the Missouri river was in the *spring* of 1832; and furthermore, these Indians did not return by boat at all.

It is not to be supposed, however, that the fictitious romance which time has built up from this simple story is necessary to account for the results which it produced. The fact was that these Indians had traveled upward of two thousand miles to find instruction in the Christian religion, and the churches felt that it was nothing less than a merited rebuke for their own activity and lack of religious zeal. Steps were at once taken to answer the call. In the year following that in which these publications were made the Methodists sent a strong delegation under Jason and Daniel Lee, who accompanied Wyeth's expedition as far as the Snake river and made the rest of the way under different escort. In the following year the famous expedition of Marcus Whitman and Samuel Parker went out. Both of these enterprises bore fruit in Oregon. The Methodist missions prospered. Whitman seems to have studied quite as thoroughly the temporal aspect of affairs in this new country as he did the spiritual. He did not make the journey clear through in 1836 but returned from Green river and went out the following year with important reinforcements, among whom were the Rev. H. H. Spalding and bride. Whitman himself married just before starting on his second trip (5).

In 1842 Whitman returned to the United States, some say for the express purpose of urging the government to take some action in regard to Oregon, which he considered too valuable a territory to lose. Others say that his journey related solely to personal affairs and to matters connected with the American Board of Foreign Missions. Whatever it was, the business was urgent; otherwise he would not have taken the journey in the dead of winter. He took the southern route by way of Santa Fe. While East he visited Washington and there is little doubt that he improved the opportunity to urge the claims of Oregon upon those who were near the Government. That he was given an audience by President Tyler and Secretary Webster may well be doubted, and it is certainly an extravagant claim, though put forward with great persistency in these later days, to say that "Marcus Whitman saved Oregon."

The history of the Catholic missions in the Rocky mountains is little more than a record of the work of Father P. J. De Smet, S. J., one of the most interesting and noteworthy characters in the annals of the West. Father De Smet came to St. Louis from Belgium in 1820, and was engaged in the mission work in the lower country for several years. In 1829 he became connected with the University of St. Louis and in 1932 visited his home in Belgium for his health. After a sojourn of several years he returned to St. Louis in 1837. In the following year he commenced his career as a missionary among the Indians, taking up his residence among the Pottawatomies near Council Bluffs. Finally in response to the repeated calls of the Flathead Indians it was decided to send Father De Smet to that tribe. He accordingly set out in 1840 and thus commenced that famous series of journeys throughout the West which made his name well known on both sides of the Atlantic.

Father De Smet was a zealous and devout religious teacher, but he was far more. He was a careful and discriminating observer and a fluent and interesting writer. During all his journeys he kept up correspondence with friends in Europe. His letters were meant to be something more than friendly epistles and were doubtless intended for publication. They abound in descriptions of the country, its fauna, flora, the Indian tribes, anecdotes of wilderness life, and a multitude of cognate subjects. Altogether they form one of the most comprehensive descriptions that we possess of the West as it was in the days of the fur trade.

Father De Smet traveled extensively among the Western tribes. He was loved and respected by the Indians, and never suffered harm at their hands. Many are the entertaining incidents connected with the visits of the "Black Robe" and his figure was always a welcome one in the wigwam of the Indians. His principal labors were among the Flathead Indians, for whom he conceived a most sincere and paternal affection, and in whose territory he founded his first mission (B).

AUTHOR'S NOTES

(1) *How Marcus Whitman Saved Oregon*, O. W. Nixon, Chicago, 1895.

(2) See Part V, Chapter X.

(3) The record of this Indian's burial is still in the archives of the St. Louis Cathedral, and is of interest, not only for the record itself, but as proof of the well-known confusion that prevailed at the time in regard to the identity of the Nez Perce and Flathead tribes. The Indian was buried October 31, 1831; his name was Keepeelele; and he was a *"ne Perce de la tribu des Choponeek, nation appellée Téte Plate."*

I am indebted to Father Walter J. Hill, S. J., of the University of St. Louis for the above interesting record.

(4) For these various letters, etc., see Appendix D.

(5) In tracing the progress of wheeled vehicles across the continent we have noted Bonneville's feat of taking wagons to Green river in 1832. Whitman succeeded in taking a cart as far as Fort Boise on Snake river where it was abandoned. Farnham saw it there in 1839.

EDITOR'S NOTE

(A) E. L. Sabin in his *Kit Carson Days*, page 140, has suggested that it might have been Jedediah S. Smith who sowed the seeds of Christianity among them.

However, it is much more likely that it was George Simpson of the Hudson's Bay Company. As early as 1824, he recorded in his journal (Merk, *Fur Trade and Empire*, page 106), "I do not know any part of North America where the natives could be civilized and instructed in morality and religion at such a moderate expence and with so much facility as on the banks of the Columbia River."

The next year, on April 8, (*op. cit.* page 135) says Simpson, "The Spokan and Flat Head Chiefs put a son each under my care to be educated at the Missionary Society School, Red River, and all the chiefs joined in a most earnest request that a missionary or religious instructor should be placed among them; I promised to communicate their request to the Great Chiefs on the other side of the water."

The two boys were accordingly sent to the school. One died and the other, after his return to his people, "relapsed into his original barbarism, taking to himself as many wives as he could get; and then becoming a gambler, he lost both all he had of his own and all that he could beg or borrow from others." *Op. cit.*, page 38.

(B) Chittenden himself, with Alfred Talbot Richardson, wrote the *Life Letters and Travels of Father Pierre-Jean De Smet, S.J.*, published in 1905.

PART IV. *Notable Incidents and Characters in the History of the Fur Trade*

Chapter I

"THE LOST TRAPPERS"

*"The Lost Trappers"—The story of Ezekiel Williams as re-
lated by himself—The story as told by David H. Coyner—
Comments.*

It would be extremely interesting to know the names of
those forty "Americans and expert riflemen" who escorted
the Mandan chief back to his nation in the summer of 1809.
Some of them figured again prominently in later events of
this period, and doubtless there were others who became
known in the annals of the West, but whose connection with
this expedition has been forgotten. Under the quoted title of
the present chapter will be narrated the adventure of a company who went up the river with the expedition of 1809.
Their leader and probably others, belonged to the Mandan
escort. Their experiences were the text of the completest
fabrication that was ever published under the guise of history
—*The Lost Trappers*, by David H. Coyner, 1859. The central
figure of the adventure, both in fact and fiction, was Ezekiel
Williams, a pioneer of Cooper county, Missouri, who, according to all the evidence that has come to light, was a thoroughly
respectable character. His name occurs frequently in the
chronicles of the time, and never in any questionable relation.
That he was *particeps criminis* in the wholesale fraud which Coyner perpetrated in his name, there is no reason to believe. His
experiences were bad enough on the plain basis of fact, and required no fictitious embellishment to add to their interest.

In 1809 Williams went up the river with the Missouri Fur
Company and remained there two years. In August, 1811,
with nineteen others, all independent hunters except two who
were in the employ of one of the party named Chaplain, he
set out on a hunting expedition to the south. They left Lisa's
fort "on the Missouri" and were assured by Lisa that he
would maintain until their return. They traveled south for

nearly two months when they found themselves on the Arkansas river and remained there unmolested until the following spring. The Indians then became troublesome, "robbing and harassing the company in every quarter." In June the party, then on the headquarters of the Platte, concluded to separate into smaller bands. Eight or ten crossed the mountains to the westward, and as many more, including Williams, and Chaplain, went south along the eastern base of the mountains until they again reached the Arkansas, where, through some means or other, they learned that Lisa's post on the Missouri had been broken up and that there was no use of their returning to that quarter.

Williams' party now separated again, four going to Santa Fe, while the rest, including Williams, Chaplain, and his two men, and two Frenchmen, struck out into the mountains to hunt. They spread about in small parties, and while thus separated three of the men were killed, leaving only Williams, Chaplain, and one Parteau. The three survivors then sought protection among the Arapaho Indians, the very ones who had slain their companions. The chief told them that their only safety was to remain under his protection, which they did, "and passed a wretched winter filled with despair of ever being able to return home." In the spring Chaplain and Parteau desired to continue with the Indians, who assured them that they would certainly be killed if they attempted to return home; but Williams determined to get away or lose his life in the attempt. His comrades helped him to make a canoe, and having cached his furs, he bade his companions farewell and set out down the river March 1st, 1813. The parting was a gloomy one. Chaplain shook hands with Williams, while Parteau turned away and wept. A number of Indians witnessed the scene. Chaplain and Parteau told Williams just as he was departing that they should also try to get away in about three days. Each promised to notify the friends of the others if he should get back first, and thus they parted, never to see one another again.

Williams descended the Arkansas about four hundred miles, trapping beaver on the way, until his canoe was stopped by the shallow water. The June rise enabled him to start again, but on the 23rd of June he was captured by the Kansas Indians, who bound him fast and took possession of all his property, consisting of the furs he had caught along the river. The Indians kept him prisoner until August 15th, when they restored part of his furs and set him free. He arrived at Boone's Lick, his home, about September 1st (A). The Indian sub-agent at Fort Osage, G. C. Sibley, to whom Williams reported the theft of his furs, caused the Indians to restore them (1).

Soon after his return home Williams went to St. Louis, and there saw Lisa, who related to him his misfortunes on the upper river, and predicted that Williams' companions were all killed if they had undertaken to return to the fort. In May, 1814, Williams, in company with Morris May, Braxton Cooper, and eighteen Frenchmen, called Phillebert's Company, set out for the mountains to bring in the furs cached there. They arrived safely at the Arapaho village, where they called a council of the chiefs and demanded to know what had become of Chaplain and Parteau. The Indians could give no satisfactory account of them except that, some time after William's departure, they had set out with eleven horses and their furs to try to reach the Missouri, and that two white men supposed to be they, had been found by the Crows, dead.

Failing in his inquiries, Williams hired Le Claire (or LeClerc) of Phillibert's Company, and with May and Cooper, uncached his furs and started home (2). After descending the Arkansas about five hundred miles they were stopped by low water, and Williams was again compelled to cache his furs and return home without them. In the course of the following winter he received information that Le Clair had told of the cache of furs, and that a company under his pilotage had started to find it. Williams with Joseph and William Cooper, brothers of Braxton, and all members of the noted pioneer family for whom Cooper county, Missouri, is named, made haste to forestall Le Clair in his scheme of robbery. They succeeded in reaching the furs first, and guarded the cache until spring, when they took advantage of high water and floated down to the settlements. It afterward came out that certain parties from St. Louis were back of Le Clair and his companions, and had promised them immunity even if they had to murder Williams to achieve their purpose. They hired a band of Indians to help them, but when the latter learned of the extreme business that they were called upon to do, they withdrew from their engagement and the whole scheme fell to pieces.

Such were the adventures of Ezekiel Williams which were made the basis of the romance of the "Lost Trappers." According to this work Williams was engaged to escort the Mandan chief back to his home. He set out on his mission April 25, 1807, with twenty men, himself included, traveling by land, west of the Missouri and far back from the stream. He reached the Mandans July 1. From this point the party, which included the noted character, Edward Rose, wandered all over the Western country from the Missouri to the Arkansas. Misfortune pursued them. Rose deserted to live with the Crows; Hamilton died from sickness, and ten men were killed in various encounters with the Indians, until "Captain Williams saw his party" (originally only twenty strong) "reduced to ten." Naturally enough, in these untoward circumstances, "the spirits of the men dropped and their hearts became sad," but through it all the redoubtable Captain Williams "wore a serene and cheerful contenance," and forwith proceeded to lead his party into fresh disaster. One after another they fell victims to the Indians, until there finally remained only three, Captain Williams, James Workman and David Spencer. In this plight they agreed to separate, Williams with the intention (which he carried out) of returning home, and the other two of going to Santa Fe. The latter did not succeed in their purpose, but after wandering a long time among the mountains, fell in with a party of Spaniards on their way to California. They joined this party and spent the winter of 1808-09 in California, returning to Santa Fe in 1810, where they remained for fifteen years, and finally returned home with a caravan bound for the States.

In all of this ingenious creation it is apparent that the author, Coyner, was chiefly a coiner of lies. In the first part of the narrative there is not a semblance of truth, and the details of the story are themselves physically impossible.

GENERAL B. L. E. BONNEVILLE

Bancroft, the historian of the West, has shown that the second part of the story, that of the adventure of Workman and Spencer, is also impossible, for no American had reached California over land at that early day (B). So crude a fabrication would not merit the notice here given it, were it not that high historical authority has commended it as most reliable data. Strange to say, Bancroft himself accepts it in the main and avers that Coyner tells his story "in a honely but truthful and direct way, which commands the reader's respect and confidence (C)" Less remarkable is the endorsement of the book by Colonel Inman, the compiler of the *Old Santa Fe Trail* and the *Salt Lake Trail* (D). Other authors refer to it favorably, and its false and spurious character seems generally to have escaped detection.

AUTHOR'S NOTES

(1) See official report of Sibley to Gen. Clark, dated Nov. 30, 1813, which is entirely confirmatory of Williams' account.

(2) Phillebert remained in the mountains. For further trace of him see page . . . .

EDITOR'S NOTES

(A) Dale, *Ashley-Smith Explorations*, page 36, discusses the various conflicting dates and facts.

(B) H. H. Bancroft, *History of California*, II, page 89.

(C) *Ibid*.

(D) The quisquillious Inman as Coues scornfully calls him in his *Garces*.

Chapter II

THE BATTLE OF PIERRE'S HOLE

Pierre's Hole—Rendezvous of 1832—The Grosventres—The Grosventre chief slain—The battle commences—The Blackfoot fort—Progress of the battle—Mistake of the interpreter—the siege raised—Indians escape during the night—Casualties— Affair in Jackson Hole—Ill fortune of the Indians—Godin murdered—The story of an Indian woman.

Pierre's Hole, as it was then called, or Teton Basin, its present name, is one of those valleys which are veritable oases in the desert of rugged mountains. Very few of these valleys exceed Pierre's Hole in beauty. It is overhung on the east by that noble range of mountains whose culminating peak is the Grand Teton. The valley extends in a direction from southeast to northwest. It is fully thirty miles long and from five to fifteen in breadth. It appears like a broad, flat prairie, almost destitute of trees except along its principal river and the various tributaries. These typical mountain streams descend mostly from the Teton range, where they are fed by perennial snows and almost daily summer rains. The course of these streams can be traced for great distances by the ribbons of verdure which cross the plains here and there and unite with a larger line of trees along the central stream. These riparian forests are more extensive than the observer from a distance would imagine. The more considerable cottonwood groves are often so filled with tangled growths of willows and creeping vines as to be almost impenetrable, and in many places it is a physical impossibility to get through them until the brush has been cut away.

In the summer of 1832 the Rocky Mountain and American Fur Companies had their rendezvous in the upper part of the valley of Pierre's Hole some twelve or fifteen miles from Teton Pass. With their accustomed alacrity of movement the managers of the Rocky Mountain Fur Company had excelled their rivals in reaching the rendezvous with their annual supplies. William L. Sublette arrived there with a party of about sixty men on the 6th of July. Wyeth was with him and so were the remnants of Blackwell and Gant's parties of the previous year whom Sublette had found on Laramie river. Vanderburgh and Drips, of the American Fur Company, were also present. Fontenelle, who was coming from Fort Union with supplies, was still far behind in the Bighorn valley. Captain Bonneville, likewise headed in the same direction, was still in the valley of the Platte.

In the valley of Pierre's Hole were also many hundreds of Indians, mostly of the Flathead and Nez Perce tribes. The Grosventres, ever hostile to the whites, were this year particularly troublesome around the headwaters of the Snake and Green rivers. Although a post had been built in the Blackfoot country scarcely a year before—Fort Piegan, at the mouth of the Marias—this fact seems not at all to have tempered the ferocity of the tribe. They were at this time returning home from a visit to their kindred, the Arapahoes. Sublette had had a sharp brush with them on the way to the rendezvous, and Fitzpatrick who had gone on ahead, was unhorsed and forced to secrete himself in the mountains, and wandered for five days without food, reaching the rendezvous more dead than alive.

When the business of the rendezvous was nearly completed, a party of trappers under Milton G. Sublette set out, July 17th, in the direction of the main Snake river toward the southeast. Wyeth embraced this opportunity to secure a good escort out of the Blackfoot country for the remnant of his party who had decided to continue on to the Pacific. The joint party proceeded but a short distance, six or eight miles, and encamped for the night. Just as they were setting out next morning they discovered a party of horsemen approaching. They were in doubt for a time whether it was white or Indian, but they soon found that it was a band of Grosventres. They were approaching in two parties, and numbered apparently about a hundred and fifty men. According to Leonard they carried a British flag which they had captured from a party of Hudson Bay trappers, whom they had lately defeated. Irving says that the Indians discovered the whites first, and came down into the valley with the most vociferous demonstrations. John B. Wyeth says that the trappers could not at first tell whether they were buffalo, white men or Indians. Finally, by the aid of Wyeth's glass, they discovered them to be Blackfeet, and Milton Sublette at once sent two men to the rendezvous for assistance (1).

In the meantime a tragedy of revenge had been enacting on the plain. The Blackfeet, discovering that the force before them was larger than they had supposed, made signs of peace, displaying, it is said, a white flag. But such was their general reputation for perfidy that no confidence was placed in their friendly advances. There were, moreover, in the white camp two men who cherished inextinguishable hatred toward the Blackfeet. One of these was Antoine Godin, whose father had been murdered by these Indians on Godin creek. The other was a Flathead chief whose nation had suffered untold wrongs from the tribe. These two men it was who advanced to meet the overtures of peace from the other side. A Blackfoot chief came forward to meet them. By a preconcerted arrangement between Antoine and the Flathead, the latter shot the Blackfoot dead at the instant when Antoine grasped his hand in friendship. Seizing the chief's scarlet robe, Antoine and his companion beat a hasty, though safe, retreat. "This was Joab with a vengeance!" remarks young Wyeth. "Art thou in health, my brother?"

The Indians now withdrew into some timber near by, surrounded by a copse of willows, and immediately intrenched themselves by digging holes in the ground, and building a breastwork of timber in front of their rifle pits. This work was mostly done by the women, the Indians maintaining a skirmish line in front of the fort. While the express was gone to the rendezvous for reinforcements, Milton Sublette's trappers held the Indians within the wood, and Wyeth fortified his own camp, where he ordered his men to remain.

William L. Sublette and Robert Campbell, upon receipt of the news of attack, immediately left the rendezvous and in short order arrived on the field with a large force of whites and Indians. Sublette assumed direction of the battle. He forbade Wyeth's men and his own raw recruits to engage in the fight, and used only the seasoned trappers and Indians. Wyeth himself, however, was present in the engagement part of the time. The Blackfeet, when they saw the overwhelming force with which they had to reckon, withdrew within their entrenchments, evidently determined to sell their lives dearly.

The whites and allied Indians promptly commenced the attack by random firing into the thicket. This accomplished nothing, but gave the Blackfeet a chance to do some effective work in return. It was apparent that other measures would have to be adopted to dislodge them, and Sublette proposed to storm the breastworks. His men thought it too dangerous, but Sublette insisted. About thirty of the whites and as many Indians joined him, and together they entered the willow thickets. Pushing their way cautiously through the tangled copses, Sublette, Campbell, and Sinclair of Arkansas led the besiegers toward the Indian fort. Sublette and Campbell and doubtless others had made their wills to each other in anticipation of the consequences that might ensue. After working their way on hands and knees through the dense line of willows they came to more open ground, and then saw the rude fortifications of the besieged. As they emerged into this open space they were more exposed to the fire of the Blackfeet. Sinclair was killed on the spot and Sublette was severely wounded. In the meanwhile Wyeth with some Indians had gained nearly the opposite side of the fort, and one Indian near him was killed by a chance shot from Sublette's party. The besieged evidently suffered but little at this time, for they were well protected, although completely overmatched in numbers.

The attack continued for the greater part of the day without any substantial progress, owing to the secure position of the enemy and the evident reluctance of the attackers to storm it. Finally Sublette decided to burn them out, although much against the wish of the Indians, who wanted to plunder the fort. A train of wood was laid and was about to be ignited, when an accident occurred which brought immediate relief to the beleaguered garrison. One of the friendly Indians who understood the Blackfoot language held some conversation with the besieged during the fight. They told him that they knew the whites could kill them, but that they had six or eight hundred warriors who would soon arrive and who would give them all the fighting they wanted. In the process of interpretation the Blackfoot was made to say that this force was then actually attacking the main rendezvous. Such an attack would have been disastrous in the absence of the fighting force, and the whites, without waiting to verify the news, hastened off pellmell. When the mistake was discovered it was too late to resume the attack. On the following morning the Blackfoot fort was found abandoned.

The casualties in this fight were, on the side of the whites, five killed, among whom was the partisan Sinclair, and six wounded, of whom William L. Sublette was one. The allied Indians lost seven killed and six wounded. The loss of the Blackfeet was never fully known. They left nine dead warriors in the fort together with twenty-five horses and nearly all their baggage. Irving says that the Blackfeet admitted to have lost twenty-six warriors. Evidently the blunder of the interpreter saved the band from annihilation. The survivors escaped during the night and effected a junction with the larger band.

The battle of Pierre's Hole was not without its important sequels. On the 25th of July, seven men of Wyeth's party, together with Alfred K. Stevens and four men, the joint party including a Mr. More of Boston, a Mr. Foy of Mississippi, and two grandsons of Daniel Boone, set out from the rendezvous to return East. They had intended to accompany William L. Sublette, but the latter's departure had been postponed ten days on account of his wound. Impatient of delay, these men set out to the eastward, and on the following day they were attacked in Jackson Hole by a band of some twenty Blackfeet. More and Foy were killed and Stephens was wounded. He, with the rest of the party, returned to the rendezvous, where he lingered until the 30th of July, when he died, just after starting for St. Louis in company with W. L. Sublette. His horses and traps were sold the same day, and his beaver fur was taken to St. Louis (2).

Sublette with his party of about sixty men and the returns of the past year left rendezvous on the 30th of July. The day after crossing Snake river, August 4th, they passed the large band of Blackfeet of whom they had been told by the Indian at the battle of Pierre's Hole. These Indians had been hovering in the vicinity of the camps of Fontenelle and Bonneville, but had not ventured to attack. In like manner their recent experience in Pierre's Hole made them hesitate about attacking Sublette's party, and he was suffered to pass unmolested. This band of Indians finally left the country by the way of the Wind river valley, where they were attacked and routed by some Crow Indians with a loss of forty killed. The remainder were scattered like fugitives throughout the Crow country.

It will be remembered that it was Antoine Godin who killed the Blackfoot chief at Pierre's Hole in revenge for the death of his father. But the account was not yet considered closed—at least on the part of the Blackfeet. At some time between September 1834 and September 1835, the exact date unknown, a party of Blackfeet appeared on the opposite bank of the Snake from Fort Hall. They were led by a desperado named Bird (3), a former employe of the Hudson Bay Company, who, having been made a prisoner by the Blackfeet, in a skirmish with some of that tribe, had remained with them and had become an influential chieftain. From the opposite side of the river Bird requested Godin to come across and buy their furs. Godin complied, not suspecting treachery. He sat down to smoke with the company, when Bird signaled to some Indians, who shot him in the back. While he was yet alive, Bird tore his scalp off and cut the letters "N. J. W.," Wyeth's initials, on his forehead. Thus ended the tragedy of Pierre's Hole.

Irving relates an incident which, whether true or not, has passed into the tradition of the battle. In their advance upon the Blackfoot redoubt some of the trappers saw an Indian woman leaning against a tree. Surprised that she should thus indifferently expose herself to certain death, they looked for the cause and found that she was standing beside the corpse of her dead warrior. The trappers would have saved her, but no sooner did the Indian allies see her than they fell upon and slew her (4) (A).

AUTHOR'S NOTES

(1) For an explanation of the confusion of names, Blackfeet and Grosventre, see Part V, Chapter IX.

(2) There is now in possession of M. L. Gray of St. Louis, a receipt by Sam Merry, administrator of the Stephen estate, for the proceeds of this sale and for the beaver fur.

(3) "A half Indian and treacherous, very dangerous man, who had great influence among the Blackfeet. He had formerly been in the service of the American Fur Company, had then gone over to the Hudson Bay Company, and had cheated both. He was a tall, strong man, with a brownish complexion, thick, black hair, spoke the language of the Blackfeet perfectly, and lived constantly among them. At present he was not in the service of either company, but lived by catching beaver and hunting on his own account." Maximilian, Prince of Wied; *Travels in North America*, p. 267.

(4) Our authorities for the battle of Pierre's Hole are numerous and reliable. Irving is the best, for he evidently digested his account from information derived from all available sources. The first published account is by an eye-witness and the principal actor in the battle, William L. Sublette. It is a letter to Ashley, written at Lexington, Mo., Sept. 21, 1832, while the writer was en route home. It may be seen in the old *Missouri Republican* of October 16, 1832, which republished it from the "last *Beacon*." There are also three other accounts by eye-witnesses extant—that of the elder Wyeth in his journal, and one by John B. Wyeth in his account of the expedition, and a third by W. A. Ferris.

Ferris' account, which is much less satisfactory than that of Sublette, nevertheless contributes a few items of interest. His record of the number killed was 3 whites, 5 friendly Indians, and 9 Blackfeet. There were many wounded on both sides, and 24 dead horses were found within the fort. Irving's story of the Indian woman is confirmed in the following paragraph: "Our Indians followed the route of the fugitives for several miles, and found their baggage which they had concealed in divers places, as well as the bodies of five more Indians, and two young women who were yet unhurt, though their heartless captors sent them to the shades in pursuit of their relations without the least remorse."

EDITOR'S NOTE

(A) Meek says that the woman was wounded and could not escape. Victor, *River of the West*, 117.

Chapter III

THE DEATH OF HENRY VANDERBURGH

Henry Vanderburgh—Competition in the mountain trade—Vanderburgh and Drips pursue Fitzpatrick and Bridger—Neck to neck game—Drips finally gives up—Starts up the Jefferson—Fitzpatrick and Bridger run onto Vanderburgh—Parties separate—Vanderburgh passes Alder Gulch—Alarm of Indians on the Stinkingwater—Reconnoitering party ambushed—Vanderburgh slain—Party moves to Beaverhead—Vanderburgh and Pillon buried—Meeting with Drips—Drips crosses the Divide to Snake River—Adventure of Bridger—Bridger wounded—The Loretto episode—Arrowhead extracted from Bridger's shoulder.

The fate of this unfortunate leader was a direct result of the extreme rivalry which prevailed among the fur companies of the mountains in 1832. Henry Vanderburgh, "one of the principal clerks attached to the American Fur Company," was an able, enterprising and indefatigable leader. He was the man upon whom the conduct of the mountain expeditions had hitherto mainly devolved, when Kenneth McKenzie found that the affairs at Fort Union would not give him the time to conduct them in person. With Vanderburgh were associated for a while Andrew Drips and Lucien Fontenelle, who, after Vanderburgh's death, carried on their operations from their post at Bellevue on the Missouri instead of from Fort Union. Vanderburgh had seen considerable service. Ten years before this, he was in the Missouri Fur Company. He was given the nominal rank of Captain in the affair of the Aricara villages in 1823, and seems always to have borne himself with the air and quality of a leader.

In 1832 the competition in trade in the mountains was at its height. The agents of the American Fur Company were still comparative strangers in the Rocky mountains, and were not yet a match for the experienced leaders of the Rocky Mountain Fur Company. Fitzpatrick and Bridger had fixed upon the headwaters of the Missouri as the field for their fall hunt. Vanderburgh and Drips had for some time been pursuing what must be pronounced a most exasperating, if not unprincipled, course. Being less familiar than their rivals with the good trapping country, their policy was to keep close on the trail of the latter and thus make these redoubtable partisans their unwilling guides to the rich beaver country. The Rocky Mountain Fur Company had recently tried to shake them off, and at the rendezvous at Pierre's Hole had proposed to divide the territory with them. The proposition was not accepted, but as the American Fur Company supplies had not arrived in time for the rendezvous, and as there was no immediate prospect of their arrival, Fitzpatrick and Bridger thought to get away before their persistent rivals should receive their equipment.

In the meantime Vanderburgh and Drips started in all haste for Green river to find out what had become of Fontenelle, who was to bring their supplies. They left Pierre's Hole August 2nd, and reached Green river August 8th, where they found Fontenelle in camp about four miles above Captain Bonneville. Four days were spent here transacting the necessary business of the annual rendezvous, when Fontenelle started with the returns of the year to Fort Union, and Vanderburgh and Drips set out to overtake Fitzpatrick and Bridger, whom they believed to be somewhere on the headwaters of the Missouri.

When the party reached Pierre's Hole on their return, W. A. Ferris was detached to make a circuit to the head of Salmon river to find the Flathead Indians, whence he was to rejoin his comrades in the valley of the Big Hole river, the principal tributary of Jefferson fork of the Missouri. In the meanwhile the two leaders would beat up the country on the sources of the Jefferson. They proceeded down that stream, and at Horse Prairie, the valley of a small tributary of the Jefferson, they cached such of their equipment as would encumber them in their pursuit of Fitzpatrick and Bridger. They had found the fresh trail of their rivals and knew that they could not be far away. Ferris rejoined them from the Flatheads on the 1st of September, and ten days later they succeeded in overtaking the party of the Rocky Mountain Fur Company. The records of the journey state that upon this day a man named Miller died in camp from a wound received in the battle of Pierre's Hole the previous July.

Fitzpatrick and Bridger were completely exasperated at finding themselves persistently followed by the partisans of the American Fur Company, and they resolved to lead them a chase which they would remember. In this they succeeded only too well. On the 17th of September they set out to the north down the valley of the Jefferson apparently for the Three Forks of the Missouri. Drips with a portion of his party followed hard after them, while Vanderburgh crossed over to the Madison to trap along the course of that stream. How far the rival parties pursued their course north is uncertain, but far enough for Drips to see that he was being made a dupe at his own game; for he had been led quite beyond the good trapping country. He accordingly resolved to give up the chase and turn back to the south. The parties separated about the 1st of October at the Three Forks, Drips starting up the Jefferson and Fitzpatrick and Bridger up the Gallatin. The latter party, after ascending the Gallatin for some distance, crossed over to the Madison, October 6th, where they quite unexpectedly came upon Vanderburgh and his party. It seemed impossible to keep out of the way of their resourceful opponents.

But this was the last encounter of the opposing parties during the fall hunt of 1832. On the 11th of October the Rocky Mountain Fur Company started off up the Madison to trap the sources of that stream. Vanderburgh did not move until October 12, when he went down the Madison about fifteen miles. The next day he crossed over in a northwest direction eighteen miles and encamped on a little stream, one of the sources of the Jefferson. This was probably Alder creek, a stream destined to world-wide fame in later years as the location of the famous placer of Alder Gulch; and the party most likely trampled over ground which was glistening with gold beneath their feet.

On the morning of the 14th the party moved down the stream to its junction with the Stinkingwater river, a tributary of the Jefferson to which Lewis and Clark gave the name Philanthropy. Here they became aware of the presence of Indians in the neighborhood. Ferris and a few others went out to reconnoiter and their worst fears were soon confirmed by finding the remains of a buffalo just butchered, from which the Indians had evidently fled on the approach of the whites. This discovery was at once reported to Vanderburgh. As the trappers could not be persuaded to work when danger was imminent, Vanderburgh and six others left the main party in camp and set out up the river where the Indians were supposed to be, determined to ascertain what the situation actually was. After traveling about three miles they found a fire still burning, a buffalo just killed, and the fresh tracks of the Indians. The small number of these tracks, and the fact that buffalo were grazing all about quite unalarmed, made them think that there could not be more than seven or eight Indians at most.

The little party therefore pushed on another three miles toward the only dense bunch of timber there was in the vicinity. Here it was felt certain that the Indians must be, for anywhere else they would be in sight unless they had fled to the mountains. With a sense of possible danger they approached the grove, watching with the utmost care for any evidence of life. At this point they came to an old channel of the river through which the water flowed in flood time, but which now interposed no greater obstacle than a small but deep ditch which a horse could leap over. They crossed the gully, but scarcely had they reached the other side when a volley from twenty or more firearms disclosed the presence of a body of Indians concealed along the banks, apparently to the number of about a hundred. Three of the party of hunters turned instantly and fled. Vanderburgh's horse was shot under him, but he calmly disengaged himself, aimed his gun at his assailants and called out to his men, "Boys, don't run." But there was no possibility of making a stand. Ferris and a Mr. R. C. Nelson turned their horses and vaulted the ditch, Ferris receiving at the same instant a severe wound in the left shoulder. Another man, Alexis Pillon, a French voyageur, was thrown from his horse, which broke away riderless toward camp. Pillon, thus left to the mercy of the savages, was almost instantly slain. Vanderburgh was now left alone without hope of succor. One of his men, Nelson, who had jumped the ditch with Ferris, was in despair at his leader's peril, and was about to turn back, when his horse received two shots in the neck and he was compelled to flee to save his own life. As the Indians approached Vanderburgh he killed the nearest one with a shot from his rifle, and was raising his pistol to fire again when he received a volley in the back, and fell a victim to his savage foes.

When the survivors returned to camp there was the greatest consternation and most of the party were for resorting to instant flight. But wiser counsels prevailed, and they withdrew to a point of timber on the river side, where they fortified themselves and passed a sleepless night. The next morning it was proposed to go back and bury their dead companions, but none of the party would undertake it. They accordingly packed up and started for the caches at Horse Prairie. Upon rounding the point of a mountain they came in sight of the Beaver Head, a famous landmark on the Jefferson river, now known as the Point of Rocks, some fifteen miles below Dillon, Montana. A large smoke was rising there, and fearing the presence of another party of Indians, they turned directly toward the Jefferson and made for a grove of cottonwoods, which they reached after a march of fifteen miles. Here another restless night was spent in a fortified camp.

Next day a reconnoitering party found to their great relief that the Indians at Beaver Head were Flatheads and Pend d' Oreilles, always firm friends of the whites, and the whole party at once moved to join them. On the 17th of October a burial party was sent back to the scene of the late attack. They found and buried Pillon, but could not find Vanderburgh. Ferris then sent some Flathead Indians to the place under promise of reward if they could discover the remains of their lamented leader. They succeeded in finding his bones, which the Indians had stripped of the flesh and thrown into the river. They buried these on the margin of the stream. The

Indians had, however, carried away the arms of the "White Chief," as they called him, and these were later exhibited as trophies of victory at Fort McKenzie on the Missouri.

The whole affair was one of the most lamentable tragedies that ever occurred in the mountains, for the principal victim was a man of chivalrous character, high standing, and universally beloved by those who knew him. Its most regrettable feature is the fact that it grew out of a bitter and unreasonable commercial strife in which Vanderburgh was a victim of his own zeal.

After a short stay at Beaver Head the party pushed on to the caches at Horse Prairie, where they found Drips, October 21, and acquainted him with the sad fate which had befallen his able associate (1). The united parties left Horse Prairie on the 24th for Snake river.

If Fitzpatrick and Bridger had led Vanderburgh to his death, they did not wholly escape themselves, although their great experience of Indian wiles saved them from ambuscade or surprise. One day they saw a body of Blackfeet in the open plain, though near some rocks which could be resorted to in case of need. They made pacific overtures, which were reciprocated by the whites. A few men advanced from each party. a circle was formed and the pipe of peace was smoked. It is related by Irving that while this ceremony was going on, a young Mexican named Loretto, a free trapper accompanying Bridger's band who had previously ransomed from the Crows a beautiful Blackfoot girl, and had made her his wife, was then present looking on. The girl recognized her brother among the Indians. Instantly leaving her infant with Loretto she rushed into her brother's arms and was received with the greatest warmth and affection.

Bridger now rode forward to where the peace ceremonies were enacting. His rifle lay across his saddle. The Blackfoot chief came forward to meet him. Through some apparent distrust Bridger cocked his piece as if about to fire. The chief seized the barrel and pushed it downward so that its contents were discharged into the ground. This precipitated a melee. Bridger received two arrow shots in his back, and the chief felled him to the earth with a blow from the gun which he had wrenched from Bridger's hand. The chief then leaped into Bridger's saddle, and the whole party made for the cover of the rocks, where a desultory fire was kept up for some time.

The Indian girl had been carried along with her people, and in spite of her pitiful entreaties, was not allowed to return. Loretto, witnessing her grief, seized the child and ran to her, greatly to the amazement of the Indians. He was cautioned to depart if he wanted to save his life, and at his wife's urgent insistence he did so. Some time afterward he closed his account with the Rocky Mountain Fur Company and rejoined his wife among her own people. It is said that he later was employed as an interpreter at the fort below the falls of the Missouri.

One of the arrowheads which Bridger received in his back on this occasion remained there for nearly three years, or until the middle of August, 1835. At that time Dr. Marcus Whitman was at the rendezvous on Green river en route to Oregon. Bridger was also there and Dr. Whitman extracted the arrow from his back. The operation was a difficult one "because the arrow head was hooked at the point by striking a large bone, and a cartilaginous substance had grown around it. The doctor pursued the operation with great self-possession and perseverance; and his patient manifested equal firmness. The Indians looked on meanwhile with countenances indicating wonder, and in their own peculiar manner expressed great astonishment when it was extracted." The arrow head was of iron and about three inches long.

AUTHOR'S NOTE

(1) The date of Vanderburgh's death, October 14, 1832, is confirmed by the records of the American Fur Comany.

"Dans ma dernière j'ai de vous informer qu'un exprès venant de la Roche Jaune nous a apporté la facheuse nouvelle que M. Vanderburgh a été tué par les Pieds-Noirs le 14 Octobre dernier sur une des trois fourches du Missouri appellée le Jefferson. Cet accident nous caisera un grand déficit dans cet équipement. La chasse fut aussitôt interrompu et le parti retraversa la montagne pour rejoindre M. Dripps et hiberner sur la rivière au Serpent. Il est à regretter que M. Fontenelle fut absent à cet époque." Chouteau to Astor, March 30, 1833. See also *Missouri Republican*, March 26th, 1833, and Fort Pierre Journal, Jan. 9th, 1833. For sketch of Vanderburgh's life see p. 390

Chapter IV

THE BATTLE OF FORT McKENZIE

The building of a fort in the Blackfoot country—Treaty of peace between the Blackfeet and the Assiniboines—Unexpected attack by the Assiniboines—Battle continues all day—Assiniboines driven off—Piegan valor.

No bolder or more courageous measure was ever accomplished in the history of the fur trade than the establishment of a trading post by the American Fur Company in the country of the Blackfeet. The implacable hostility of these Indians to the whites had been in evidence since the first appearance of white men among them. The expulsion of the traders from the headwaters of the Missouri in 1810 and the massacre of Jones and Immel and several of their followers in 1823 were still fresh in the minds of many then living. It was well known that the attitude of these people had not changed and that the trader who should venture into their territory did so at the imminent peril of his life.

The Blackfeet and Assiniboines were hostile to each other, and a preliminary step in the establishment of a post in the Blackfoot country was an attempt on the part of McKenzie at Fort Union to establish peace between these two tribes. This was accomplished in 1831. James Kipp built Fort Piegan at the mouth of the Marias in the fall of that year, and D. D. Mitchell built Fort McKenzie a few miles above, when Fort Piegan was abandoned the following year. Everything went well until the summer of 1833, when the Assiniboines, becoming tired of peace, and perhaps urged on by the British traders, concluded to attack the fort.

During the latter part of the month of August, 1833, the Indians had mostly withdrawn from the vicinity of Fort McKenzie, but there were still a few tents of Piegans encamped close to the fort. They had been singing and drinking most of the night and by morning had fallen into a state of stupid lethargic slumber from which it was not easy to arouse them. While in this condition they were attacked at day-break on the morning of August 28, by some six hundred Assiniboines and Crees. This was before the inmates of the fort had arisen, and their first intimation of trouble came from Doucette, one of the engagés, who rushed into the room where Prince Maximilian and Mr. Mitchell were, and called out: "*Levez vous, il nous faut battre.*"

The attack was so sudden and unexpected that consider-able damage had been done before any effective resistance was offered. The Assiniboines first fell upon the Piegan camp, tore their tents to pieces, killed several of the Indians, and threw the remainder into a panic. The employes of the fort made haste to let in the friendly Indians, but the women, by a fool-ish endeavor to save their property, encumbered themselves with saddles, etc., blocked the door of the fort, and several of them were massacred before they could get in. As fast as the Piegans got inside they mounted the palisades and opened fire. Many of the engagés had imprudently sold their ammuni-tion to the Indians, and were helpless until a supply could be issued to them.

In the meanwhile it transpired that the attack had been directed against the Blackfeet and not against the whites. Mr. Mitchell accordingly ordered his men to stop firing. The Blackfeet within the fort, however, could not be restrained, and even Doucette and Loretto persisted in firing. This Loretto, who is the same one that was with Bridger when he was wounded on Jefferson Fork, now went outside the fort and at close range slew the nephew of the principal chief of the Assiniboines. The Assiniboines then withdrew beyond the effective range of the fort.

A strange scene it must have been within the fort during this time. Happily we have two effective pictures of it, one from the pen of Maximilian, and the other from the hand of his artist, Bodmer. "While all this was passing," says the Prince, "the court yards of the fort presented a very strange scene. A number of wounded men, women and children were laid or placed against the walls; others in their deplorable condition, were pulled about by their relatives amid tears and lamentations. The White Buffalo, whom I have mentioned, and who had received a wound at the back of his head, was carried about in this manner, amid singing, howling, and crying. They rattled the schischikue in his ears, that the evil spirit might not overcome him, and gave him brandy to drink. He himself, though stupefied, sang without intermission and would not give himself up to the evil spirit. Otsequa-Stomik, an old man of our acquaintance, was wounded in the knee by a ball which a woman cut out with a pen knife, during which operation he did not betray the least symptom of pain. Natah-Otanee, a handsome young man with whom we became acquainted on our visit to Kutonapi, was suffering dreadfully from severe wounds. Several Indians, especially young women, were likewise wounded. We endeavored to assist the wounded and Mr. Mitchell distributed balsam and linen for bandages; but very little could be done; for instead of suffering the wounded, who were exhausted by the loss of blood, to take some rest, their relatives continually pulled them about, sounded large bells, and rattled their medicine or amulets, among which were the bear's paws which the White Buffalo wore on his breast. Only a spectator of this extraordinary scene could form any idea of the confusion and noise, which was increased by the loud report of the musketry, the moving backwards and forwards of the people carrying powder and ball, and the tumult occasioned by above twenty horses shut up in the fort." We imagine that the royal seeker for knowledge, who had forsaken the luxury of courts for the deprivations of the wilderness, felt that he was now getting more than he had bargained for.

From the beginning of the engagement the Blackfeet had reproached the whites for not coming out of the fort to fight the enemy, although there was no occasion to do so, for the attack was not directed against the whites. But the Blackfeet did not see it in that light, and were evidently getting the idea that the whites were not brave. This would not do, and accordingly Mr. Mitchell with some of his best men sallied out for the bluffs to which the Assiniboines had retreated. Early in the engagement runners had been dispatched to the Piegan camp ten miles away, for assistance, and parties were now beginning to arrive from that direction. "They came galloping in groups of from three to twenty together," says Maximilian, "their horses covered with foam, and they themselves in their finest apparel, with all kinds of ornaments and arms, bows and quivers on their backs, guns in their hands, furnished with their medicines, with feathers on their heads; some had splendid crowns of black and white eagle feathers, and a large hood of feathers hanging down behind, sitting on fine panther skins lined with red; the upper part of their bodies partly naked, with a long strip of wolf skin thrown across the shoulder, and carrying shields adorned with feathers and pieces of colored cloth. A truly original sight!"

The expedition of Mr. Mitchell and his followers to the bluffs had the effect of completely reinstating the whites in the confidence of the Blackfeet. They were always in advance, and Mr. Mitchell was finally compelled to taunt the Blackfeet themselves with cowardice. They certainly behaved with far less spirit than their enemies.

On the bluffs between the Missouri and the valley of the Marias the battle was continued for some time in a wild and desultory fashion. The Assiniboines were finally driven back across the Marias and here Mr. Mitchell's horse was shot under him, and he himself was slightly wounded. After dinner, Doucette, De Champ, and Berger rode over to the valley of the Marias, which was still occupied by the Assiniboines, and again came in contact with the enemy. Some Blackfeet who were with them came back boasting of their great exploits. The final result was that the Assiniboines, who had expended all their ammunition, retreated toward the Bear Paw mountains during the night.

The losses on the part of the Blackfeet occurred mostly in the first onset and fell principally on the noncombatants. Culbertson says that "during the day we lost seven killed and twenty wounded. It is impossible to tell how many of the enemy were killed, but their loss must have been greater than ours, as they had little ammunition, and at last none."

The result of this affair was to nullify the treaty of peace between the Blackfeet and the Assiniboines. It also showed that, as between the Piegan band of the Blackfeet and the Assiniboines, the latter were the better fighters. The whites were a good deal astonished at the feeble efforts of their allies and could with difficulty see anything to justify the terrible reputation of the Blackfeet. On the other hand, the Blackfeet estimate of the prowess of the whites was greatly exalted and the situation at Fort McKenzie was materially improved.

Chapter V

SMUGGLING LIQUOR UP THE MISSOURI

Steamboat trip of American Fur Company, 1843—Audubon on board—Arrival at Bellevue—Boat stopped by soldiers—Audubon visits Captain Burgwin—Inspection of the boat—Everything satisfactory—Voyage of 1844—Liquor casks put inside the flour barrels—Barrels rolled off at Bellevue—Inspector finds nothing—Barrels rolled on after dark—Boat leaves before daylight—Suspicions of Agent aroused—Discovers the fraud—Serious complications.

The annual outfit of the American Fur Company for the Upper Missouri for 1843 was sent up in the steamboat *Omega*, Captain Joseph A. Sire master, and Captain Joseph La Barge pilot. The boat carried as passenger the celebrated naturalist, Audubon, who was ascending the river with a small company in the interests of his scientific pursuits. There was on board the usual amount of liquor, which was gotten safely past Fort Leavenworth. The point of greatest danger was at that time Bellevue. It happened, however, on the present occasion that the agent was absent from the post when the boat arrived and accordingly there was no inspection. Elated at this unexpected good fortune Captain Sire lost no time in putting off the freight destined for this point and in getting on his way. He pursued his voyage until nine o'clock that evening, and doubtless felicitated himself that he was out of danger. But it appears that the agent had delegated the function of inspector during his absence to the commander of the United States troops in the vicinity. The boat left her mooring at daylight next morning, but had scarcely gotten under way when a couple of rifle shots were fired across her bow. She brought to at once and made for the shore. There they found a lieutenant in charge of a few dragoons who had come from the camp four miles distant. The young officer came on board and presented to Captain Sire a polite note from Captain Burgwin, who commanded the detachment of troops, stating that his orders required him to inspect the boat before letting her proceed.

This was like a dash of cold water on the buoyant spirits of Captain Sire and none the less so to Audubon, to whom, as well as to the company, the loss of the liquid portion of the cargo would have been irreparable. The naturalist had a permit from the government to carry with him a quantity of liquor for the use of himself and party, and upon showing his credentials to the young officer he was, to use his own words, "immediately settled comfortably." But in the moment of his good fortune he did not forget his companions who were not yet "settled comfortably." He understood that time was required for the crew to prepare for the approaching function, and he could at least help to secure this time by delaying inspection as long as possible. He accordingly expressed a desire to visit the camp, and the Lieutenant detailed a dragoon to accompany him. The great naturalist rode four miles to camp to call upon an obscure army officer whom he knew he could see in a short time by waiting at the boat. The officer was overwhelmed at the honor of the visit, and when Audubon offered to present his credentials he politely and gallantly replied that his name was too well known throughout the United States to require any letters. Audubon says of the occasion: "I was on excellent and friendly terms in less time than it has taken me to write this account of our meeting." Between his entertaining conversation and the shooting of some birds he contrived to detain the Captain for a good two hours before they returned to the boat.

The time had not been wasted by Captain Sire and his loyal crew. The shallow hold of the steamboat of those days was divided lengthwise into two compartments by a partition or bulkhead running the full length of the boat. A narrow-gauge tramway extended down each side of the hold its entire length, the two sides connecting with each other by a curve which passed under the hatchway in the forecastle. Small cars received the cargo let down through the hatchway, and carried it to its place in the hold or brought it out again when the boat was being unloaded. A car could pass from the stern of the boat on one side of the hold around the curve in the bow and to the stern of the boat on the other side. There being no windows in the hold, everything was buried in blackness a few feet from the hatchway. Workmen were lighted in their labors by means of candles.

During the absence of Audubon the crew loaded all the liquor upon the cars, and had run them down one side of the hold far enough from the hatchway to be entirely concealed in the darkness. They were carefully instructed in the part they had to play in the approaching comedy, and very likely were put through a preliminary rehearsal or two.

When Captain Burgwin arrived in Audubon's company he was received most hospitably and treated to a luncheon, in which was included, as a matter of course, a generous portion from the private store embraced in Audubon's "credentials." By this time the young Captain was in most excellent temper toward his hosts, and was quite disposed to forego the inspection altogether. But the virtuous Sire would not have it so. "I insisted, as it were," says the worthy navigator in his log of May 10th, "that he make the strictest possible search, but upon the condition that he do the same with the other traders" (1).

A proposition so eminently fair was at once agreed to by the inspector, whose mellow faculties were now in a most accommodating condition. The shrewd steamboat master, who never forgot to be sober when his company's interests were at stake, escorted the officer down the hatchway, and together they groped their way along the hold by the light of a not too brilliant candle. It may be imagined with what zeal the scrupulous Captain thrust the ineffectual flame into every nook and corner, and even insisted that the inspector move a box or a bale now and then to assure himself that everything was alright.

Arrived at the foot of the hold they passed through an opening in the partition and started back on the other side. The officer was doubtless too much absorbed with the effects of his recent collation to notice the glimmer of light under the hatchway at the other end of the boat, where a miniature

train with its suspicious cargo was creeping stealthily around
the curve and disappearing toward the side which they had
just left. The party finished their inspection and everything
was found quite as it should be. With many protestations of
good will the clever hosts and their delighted guest parted
company and the good Captain Sire went on his way rejoic-
ing. But woe to the luckless craft of some rival trader with no
Audubon in the cabin and no tramway in the hold!

In the year following that of the incident just related,
Captains Sire and La Barge were in charge of the company's
annual boat, this year the *Nimrod*. The same agent, a Mr.
Miller, still held the reins of authority at Bellevue. He was an
ex-Methodist minister, and as zealous in suppressing the
liquor traffic among the Indians as he had ever been in the
regular practice of his profession. It was his boast that no
liquor could pass his agency. He rummaged every boat from
stem to stern, broke open the packages, overturned the piles
of merchandise, and with a long, slender pointed rod pierced
the bales of blankets and clothing, lest kegs of alcohol might
be rolled up within. The persistent clergyman put the experienced agents of the company to their wits' end, and it
was much as ever that they succeeded in eluding his scrutiny.

The urgency of the problem, however, produced its own
solution. Captain Sire had the alcohol all packed inside
barrels of flour. But he knew that even this device would alone
not be enough, for the energetic agent would very likely have
the barrels burst open. The Captain therefore had them all
marked as if consigned to Peter A. Sarpy, the company's agent
at Bellevue, and they were labeled in large letters "P. A. S."
The moment the nose of the boat touched the landing at
Bellevue, the Captain, as was his custom, ordered the freight
for that point placed on shore, and the barrels were promptly
bowled out upon the bank and carried into the warehouse.
The agent, never suspecting this freight, went on board, and
after the most rigid search, found nothing. The boat was permitted to proceed, but contrary to its usual haste in getting
on its way as soon as the loading or unloading was complete,
it remained the rest of the day and gave out that it would not
sail until the following morning. The extraordinary good

character of the boat on this occasion, and the unusually long delay in departing, roused the suspicions of the agent, who stationed a man to watch the boat and to whistle if he saw anything wrong.

Everything remained quiet until some time after midnight, except that a full head of steam was kept up in the boilers. Presently there was great activity on the boat, although with an ominous silence about it all. The pilot, Captain La Barge, was quietly engineering the reloading of the barrels. He had spread tarpaulins on the deck and gang plank to deaden the noise, and the full crew of the boat were hurrying the barrels back in a most lively fashion. "What does this mean?" one of the deck hands asked of another. "We unloaded these barrels yesterday." "Why don't you see?" was the brilliant reply of another, "they're marked 'P A S'; they've got to pass."

The work was quickly over and every barrel was on board, when the agent's sleepy guard awoke to the fact that something was going on. He uttered his signal, and the agent made haste to turn out and see what was the matter. La Barge and Captain Sire, who knew full well what the whistle meant, did not linger to make explanations. Captain La Barge seized an axe and cut the line. "Get aboard, men!" he shouted, "The line has parted!" The boat instantly dropped into the current and then stood out into the river under her own steam. She was already too far from the bank to be reached when the reverend inspector appeared and wanted to know why they were off so early. It was about 3 A. M. "Oh, the line broke," replied Captain La Barge, "and it was so near time to start that it was not worth while to tie up again" (2).

This was a little too much for the agent, who could not understand how it happened that the boat was so thoroughly prepared for such an accident, with steam up, pilot at the wheel, crew at their places, and all at so early an hour. Next day he found that the barrels consigned to Sarpy were gone, and saw how completely he had been duped. Mortified and indignant, he reported the company to the authorities, and a long train of difficulties ensued, with ineffectual threats of cancelling the company's license. Meanwhile the alcohol found its intended destination in the stomachs of the Indians, and the company reaped the enormous profit which traffic in that article always yielded.

AUTHOR'S NOTES

(1) Log of Steamboat *Omega*, May 10, 1843.—Nous venons très bien jusqu'aux côtes à Hart où, à sept heures, nous sommes sommés, par un officer de dragoons de mettre à terre. Je recois une note polie du Capitaine Burgwin m'informant que son devoir l'oblige de faire visiter le bateau. Aussitôt nous nous mettons a l'ouvrage, et pendent ce temps M. Audubon va faire une visite au Capitaine. Ils reviennent ensemble deux heures après. Je force en quelque sorte l'officer à faire une recherche aussi stricte que possible, mis à la condition qu'il en sera de même avec les autres traiteurs."

(2) Captain Sire, in the log book of the *Nimrod*, Friday, May 10, 1844, says: "Il s'est passe encore longtemps avant que Messrs. les agents faisaient leur visie. Tout se trouvait satisfaisant. J'ai décidé de ne partir que demain matin, *et pour cause.*—May 10. Nous nous mettons en route avant le jour."

PIERRE (CADET) CHOUTEAU

Chapter VI

ROSE AND BECKWOURTH, THE CROW CHIEFS

Adoption of white men into the Indian tribes—Edward Rose—
His bad reputation—His service with Hunt—In Ashley's em-
ploy—Interpreter for Colonel Leavenworth in the Aricara cam-
paign—Interpreter for General Atkinson in 1825—Rose's
death—His grave—James P. Beckwourth—Youth—Enters
service of General Ashley—Adopted by the Crows—Comment on
his work.

It was a common thing among all the Indians to adopt
white men into the tribes and occasionally to make them
chiefs. They were sensible of the superiority of the white
man's intellectual power and the advantage which his knowledge gave him, and where they found one who would enter
with true spirit into their own manner of living, they were
always ready to honor him with authority. There were two
conspicuous examples of this in the history of the Crow tribe
during the period of the fur trade. Edward Rose and James P.
Beckwourth were recognized Crow leaders for many years.
Strange to say, both of these men were of mixed negro blood,
but except in this respect there was no similarity. Of Rose
nothing is known except what is reported by others. There is
no written word of his in existence nor any verbal expression
reported by others. Beckwourth, on the other hand, dictated
his biography, and it was duly published. Beckwourth did not
begin his career among the Crows until Rose was nearly done
with them, and there are certain noted exploits related by
Beckwourth in his autobiography which were probably performed by Rose.

EDWARD ROSE was the son of a white man, a trader among
the Cherokee Indians, and of a half-breed Cherokee and negro
woman. He was a man of powerful frame and in some of his
experiences had received a cut through the nose, which gave

him the nickname of *Nes Coupe*, or Cut Nose Rose. He was a
man of few words, rather inclined to be moody in disposition.
All in all, his appearance and habits may have justified the
description given by Irving, particularly if one did not like
him—" a dogged, sullen, silent fellow, with a sinister aspect
and more of the savage than the civilized man in his appearance." Irving gives the following additional facts in Rose's
early history: "Rose had formerly belonged to one of the
gangs of pirates who infested the islands of the Mississippi,
plundering boats as they went up and down the river, and who
sometimes shifted the scene of their robberies to the shore,
waylaying travelers as they returned by land from New Orleans with the products of their downward voyage, plundering them of their money and effects, and often perpetrating the
most atrocious murders.

"These hordes of villains being broken up and dispersed,
Rose had betaken himself to the wilderness, and associated
himself with the Crows, whose predatory habits were congenial to his own, had married a woman of the tribe, and, in
short, had identified himself with those vagrant savages."

In 1823 Joshua Pilcher referred to Rose in one of his letters
as "a celebrated outlaw who left this country in chains some
ten years ago." Colonel Leavenworth in an official report of
the same year, after commending the services of Rose as his
interpreter, says: "I have since heard that he was not of
good character."

It is apparent, therefore, that Rose bore a bad reputation,
but the singular thing is that everything definite that is
known of him is entirely to his credit. If judgment were to be
passed only on the record as it has come down to us, he
would stand as high as any character in the history of the
fur trade.

Rose first went up the river either in 1807 or 1809, and soon
after fell in with the Crow Indians, with whom he took up
his abode (A). He apparently remained there until the spring
of 1811, when he went over to the Missouri river. Meeting
Wilson P. Hunt with his party of Astorians, he engaged as
interpreter and guide through the Crow country, Hunt, dur-

ing the journey, became thoroughly panic-stricken because he imagined that Rose was planning to betray his party to the Crows. There is not the slightest evidence of any such intention, and Hunt's conduct which was the result of his inexperience, is little better than ridiculous. When the party passed the Crow country Rose was left with those Indians, much to Mr. Hunt's relief.

There is only one reference to Rose after this time and before the Aricara campaign. In 1812 he was in account with the Missouri Fur Company, apparently in the capacity of a free hunter, and a record of the account may be seen in one of the company books now in possession of the Kansas Historical Society. Rose probably remained with the Crows most of the time for the next eight or ten years, when he went to reside with the Aricaras, not later than 1820, and stayed with them for the next three years. With the revival of the trade under Pilcher and Ashley in the early twenties, Rose became useful as an interpreter. He acted in that capacity for Ashley when the latter met his disastrous defeat at the hands of the Aricaras in 1823. Rose had warned Ashley of this danger, for he had seen that something wrong was going on; but Ashley was deceived by the pretended friendship of the Indians and rejected the warning.

When Colonel Leavenworth came up the river a month later with his military force, Rose was engaged as interpreter, and was also given the nominal rank of ensign upon Ashley's recommendation. The report of Colonel Leavenworth shows that Rose took an active part in the operations before the villages, and it was upon him that the main reliance was placed for opening communications with the Aricaras. Rose gave Leavenworth notice of the intention of the Indians to evacuate the villages, but in this case, as in that of Ashley, his warning was not believed until it was too late. That Colonel Leavenworth placed a high value upon the services of Rose may be seen from the following reference contained in his official report to General Atkinson, dated October 20, 1923: "I had not found any one willing to go into those villages, except a man by the name of Rose, who had the nominal rank of ensign in General Ashley's volunteers. He appeared to be a brave and enterprising man, and was well acquainted with those Indians. He had resided for about three years with them; understood their language, and they were much attached to him. He was with General Ashley when he was attacked. The Indians at that time called to him to take care of himself, before they fired upon General Ashley's party. This was all that I knew of the man. I have since heard that he was not of good character. Everything he told us, however, was fully corroborated. He was perfectly willing to go into their villages, and did go in several times."

When General Atkinson and Major O'Fallon went up the Missouri with the military expedition of 1825, Rose was employed as interpreter. The record of the expedition mentions him frequently and it is clear that he was of great use to the commissioners.

From this time on very little is known of Rose. He is mentioned now and then in connections that show him still among the Crows. He was seen there in 1832 by Leonard, who gives a somewhat extended though inaccurate account of him. Leonard saw him again in 1834, when he was the hero of an exploit which Beckwourth claims as his own. In November of that year there was a terrible battle between the Blackfeet and the Crows in the country of the latter tribe. The Blackfeet, who were at a disadvantage in point of numbers, had fortified themselves on a hill, where they succeeded in standing off the attack. The Crows made several ineffectual charges, but did not dare to assault the fort. Finally "the old negro," as Leonard calls Rose, came to their aid. He upbraided them for their failure, exhorted them to show more spirit, and then himself led the charge. It was successful, and all the inmates of the fort were slain. It is not certain when or how Rose died, but one account says that it was near Fort Cass. With several companions he was surprised and surrounded by a band of Aricara Indians. They succeeded in holding them off for some time, but finally the Indians set fire to the prairie grass and the whites saw that the game was up with them. The fire would either burn them to death or force them to leave their cover, in which case they would fall an instant prey to the savages. What action they took can only be surmised, but a loud explosion was soon heard, and upon going to the spot it was found that all had been killed by the explosion of a keg of gunpowder. It is presumed that they ended their lives in this way rather than fall into the hands of the Indians.

Whether this story is true or not, the locality of the occurrence is most likely wrong, for Rose was buried on the banks of the Missouri nearly opposite to the mouth of the Milk River. On any of the old steamboat itineraries of the Missouri River may be seen among the names in that vicinity, "Rose's Grave."

The second of the Crow chiefs above referred to was JAMES P. BECKWOURTH. The name of this redoubtable prevaricator was not Beckwourth until his biography came to be written. In the days when he was a roustabout on Missouri River steamboats, or a wild savage among his adopted tribe, he was plain Jim Beckwith, and is so carried on the rolls of the American Fur Company, who employed him at various times.

According to his own account (a most questionable authority, but we have no other upon most of the matters relating to him), he was born in Fredericksburg, Virginia, April 26, 1798. At the age of seven or eight he was taken to St. Louis with his parents, who soon moved to the point of land between the Mississippi and Missouri rivers near old *Portage des Sioux*. At fourteen he was apprenticed to learn the blacksmith trade. After five years' service he fell out with his employer and hired out on a steamboat going up the Mississippi River. He remained in the vicinity of Galena for eighteen months. Returning to St. Louis he made a steamboat trip to New Orleans and caught the yellow fever on his way back. Surviving this attack he enlisted in Ashley's Rocky Mountain party of 1824. He did not get to the mountains that year, but was sent back by Ashley for horses, and in the following spring went through to Green River.

After Ashley had made his fortune and retired from the mountains, Beckwourth entered upon a series of experiences that filled every month of his life with more adventures than the average mountaineer could boast of in twice as many years. The most important event, however, was his induction into the Crow nation as a *bona fide* member of that rascally commonwealth. Whether Beckwourth or the Crows got the worst of the bargain it might be difficult to decide, but the way it came about has all the naïve ingenuity which characterizes the most elaborate of his yarns. Beckwourth was a mulatto or some other combination of white and African blood. The color of his skin, joined with other characteristics of physiognomy, made it quite possible to counterfeit a resemblance to the Indians which was hard to distinguish from the genuine article. One of his companions, by way of joke, told the Crows that Beckwourth actually belonged to their nation, having been separated from it in infancy, in some way or other. The Crows eagerly swallowed the story, and insisted on restoring Beckwourth to his long-lost place in a family of the tribe. Henceforth Beckwourth was a Crow, and the deeds of valor which he says he performed in the ensuing years exalted his name among his people and raised him to a high pre-eminence among the surrounding tribes.

It is idle to treat as reliable history the ingenious collection of heroic achievements which he has dignified under the style of "autobiography" (B). The whole work is replete with fable, and there is probably not a single statement in it that is correct as given. So far as can be determined, only a few positive facts stand out with definite clearness. There was a such a man as Beckwourth. He went to the mountains with Ashley. He somehow gained great influence with the Crows. He worked for the American Fur Company. He was never in government employ during this early period. He was seen now and then by parties who have recorded their journeys in this country, but he was certainly not a character of high standing or importance.

Knowing the slender basis of fact upon which his biography rests, it is at once accepted as fable and enjoyed as one of the richest assortment of yarns that has ever found a resting

KIT CARSON

place within the covers of a book. It is not without value, either, for it does unintentionally now and then furnish sidelights that assist in checking the statements of others. While it makes no pretension to be, what it is not, reliable history, it reflects, in its very exaggeration, a living picture of the times. Its lack of fidelity to facts is readily forgiven where it would be condemned in a book like the *Lost Trappers*, which pretends to be truthful history (1).

Beckwourth belonged to a class without which the history of those times would lose much of its spice and variety—he was one of those "charming liars," as some one has expressed it, who are delightful to listen to for the very enormity of their misstatements. The early West had many such characters, but few, like Beckwourth, have made for themselves a place in literature or history.

Although a man of the most ordinary importance, Beckwourth nevertheless stood fairly well with his fellows. He was employed by the American Fur Company, not at Beckwourth's alleged figure of $3,000 per year, but $800, a very good salary as wages then ran, and one that indicates good standing with the company. There are also references in the correspondence of the company that indicate as much.

AUTHOR'S NOTE

(1) The Life and Adventures of James P. Beckwourth, Mountaineer, Scout, Pioneer, and Chief of the Crow Nation of Indians. Written from his own dictation by T. D. Bonner. New Edition edited with preface by Charles G. Leland ("Hans Breitmann"), London and New York, 1892.

EDITOR'S NOTES

(A) Rose was apparently one of Ezekiel Williams' companions, and accordingly his early history is entangled in the same dubious chronology and geography. See Dale, *Ashley-Smith Explorations*, page 36.

(B) A side light on his *Life and Adventures* is given in Carl L. Wheat's note to Letter Eighth of the *Shirley Letters*, just re-printed. In 1851 Beckwourth was in California running a tavern for the accommodation of immigrants, and the *Life and Adventures* was in process. "Both worthies were fond of rum and the more they drank the more Indians 'Jim' would recall having slain, his eloquence increasing in inverse ratio to the diminishing rum supply, and at last he would slap the 'Squire' on the knee and chortle, 'Paint her up, Bonner! Paint her up!'"

Chapter VII

ALEXANDER HARVEY, DESPERADO

Early life—Enters the fur trade—Troublesome disposition—
Summoned to St. Louis—Makes winter journey—Re-employed
—Ascends the Missouri—Thrashes his personal enemies—
Kills Isodoro the Spaniard—Blackfoot massacre of 1843—
Atrocious murder of Indians—Attempted murder of Harvey—
Forms the opposition company of Harvey, Primeau and Company.

Alexander Harvey (1) was one of the boldest men and most
reckless desperadoes known to the fur trade. He was well
built physically, about six feet tall and weighed between one
hundred and sixty and one hundred and seventy pounds. He
was strongly knit, capable of great endurance, and wholly
devoid of physical fear. In ordinary intercourse, when not
under the influence of liquor or passion, he was disposed to be
fair and reasonable. But he had a perverse and unruly temper,
and when once his enmity was aroused he was relentless and
unforgiving.

He was born and reared in St. Louis, and was apprenticed
to learn the saddler's trade; but his headstrong disposition
got him into trouble with his employers and he left them.
Before he had passed his minority he had entered the employ
of the American Fur Company, and saw his first service at
Fort McKenzie, the most remote of the company's posts.
Here he remained for several years; but his wicked and in-
tolerant demeanor toward his associates made his presence a
constant source of irritation, and word was sent to St. Louis
that he would have to be gotten rid of in some way. Mr.
Chouteau accordingly sent him his discharge, and in order to
insure his early departure requested him to report in person
at St. Louis.

It was Christmas time before the discharge arrived, and at
that season of the year it was considered almost madness to

undertake a long journey, particularly if one were alone. But Harvey, in spite of all remonstrance (no doubt feigned in large part), made ready to start the next morning on the long journey of nearly two thousand five hundred miles through a desolate and dangerous country. "I will not let Mr. Chouteau wait long on me," he said. "I shall start in the morning; all I want for my journey is my rifle, and my dog to carry my bedding." He reached St. Louis early in March, and Mr. Chouteau was so much impressed with the hazard of the performance that he actually renewed Harvey's engagement.

It was now about time for the annual steamboat to start up the river, and Harvey made ready to return at once. On his way up he remarked to Larpenteur, who was also returning to Fort Union from St. Louis, that he had several settlements to make with the gentlemen who had caused him his long winter's tramp. "I never forget or forgive," he said; "it may not be for years, but they will all have to catch it." Accordingly he kept his eye out for those whom he suspected of any complicity in the movement against him. He found one of them at Fort Clark and gave him an unmerciful pounding, remarking when he was through, "That's number one." At Fort Union he found several more, and as fast as he could single them out from the sixty or more inmates of the fort, he would knock them down and administer a terrible drubbing.

Harvey kept on in the company's employ and served them well, but he had aroused the hatred of most of the other employes, and there were no doubt many plots to take his life. In 1841 he was sent down from Fort Union to Pierre with mackinaw boats laden with furs. He was to return on the spring steamboat from St. Louis. To assist him on the down voyage was one Isodoro, a Spaniard, and bitter personal enemy of Harvey. This singular action of the authorities at Union was believed by some to signify a plot to murder Harvey on the way. The trip, however, passed off all right and the two men returned with the boat to Fort Union.

Soon after their return Isodoro opened up hostilities in earnest, and started to parade around with his rifle, threatening to kill Harvey. The latter, thinking that he was drunk, kept out of his way and the day passed without further development. The next day all the clerks were ordered by Mr. Culbertson to go to the warehouse and make up the equipment for Fort McKenzie. Going there in a little while himself, Culbertson found that Isodoro had not put in appearance as directed. He and Harvey then went into the retail store, where they found the Spaniard standing behind the counter. Harvey asked him what he meant by his conduct of the day before and then challenged him to come out. The Spaniard did not stir and Harvey then "went back into the store and said, 'You won't fight me like a man, so take that!' and shot him through the head. After this he went into the middle of the fort, saying, "I, Alexander Harvey, have killed the Spaniard. If there are any of his friends that want to take it up, let them come on'; but no one dared to do so, and this was the last of the Spaniard."

Two years later Harvey was the principal actor in that diabolical tragedy at Fort McKenzie, the Blackfoot massacre of 1843. The trader in charge of the post was Francis A. Chardon, almost as desperate a character as Harvey himself. Through one of those chance misunderstandings which now and then occurred, the Blackfeet had killed a negro servant of Chardon. It happened that Chardon thought a good deal of the fellow and in his exasperation he resolved on a terrible revenge. He laid the matter before Harvey and the latter gladly agreed to carry out the details of Chardon's plan. This was to have the cannon of the bastion trained upon the door of the fort when the band next came in to trade. Two or three of the chiefs would then be admitted, and while the door was crowded with Indians the cannon would be discharged and the three chiefs massacred. It was expected that the rest of the Indians would be so panic-stricken that they would run, leaving their horses, furs, and equipments. The plan only partly succeeded, owing to failure to cooperate exactly. Chardon opened fire on the chiefs, but before Harvey could set off the cannon the Indians had begun to scatter. Only three Indians were killed and three wounded, including one of the chiefs. Harvey killed the wounded man with his knife and then made the squaws dance around the scalps of their fallen warriors. Chardon and Harvey secured very little of the booty which they had expected to obtain.

Another of Harvey's atrocious deeds while at Fort McKenzie has been preserved by Larpenteur. One day a party of five Indians undertook to steal some cattle belonging to the post. Harvey took some horses and started in pursuit of them. He soon overtook one Indian who had shot a cow, and firing at him, broke his thigh. The Indian fell to the ground and lay there, when Harvey came up and sat down beside him. The heartless fiend then "having lighted his pipe and made the poor Indian smoke . . . said: 'I am going to kill you, but I will give you a little time to take a good look at your country.' The Indian begged for his life, saying, 'Comrade, it is true I was a fool. I killed your cow, but now you have broken my thigh; this ought to make us even—spare my life!' 'No,' said Harvey; 'look well, for the last time, at those nice hills—at all those paths which lead to the fort, where you came with your parents to trade, playing with your sweet-hearts—look at that, will you, for the last time.' So saying with his gun pointed at the head of his victim, he pulled the trigger and the Indian was no more."

Harvey eventually became a very heavy burden to the American Fur Company, for although an able man and a good trader, his outrageous deeds were too much for his associates to endure. There was a strong undercurrent of feeling against him which was liable at any time to result in his murder. Harvey himself began to see that his life was in danger, and he was probably ready to relinquish the service as soon as he could decently do so. The matter came to a head in 1845, when an abortive attempt to murder him ended in his sever-ance of further connection with the company. Harvey was at this time in temporary charge of Fort Chardon, which had been built at the mouth of the Judith river after the abandon-ment of Fort McKenzie. Mr. Culbertson went up with the spring outfit from Fort Union to take charge and build a new post further up. Malcolm Clark, James Lee, and the old in-terpreter Berger were along. These three men were enemies of Harvey and concerted together to kill him. When Harvey heard of the approach of the boat he rode some twenty miles down stream to meet it. Leaving his horse with a man who had come with him, he went to the boat and entered the cabin. He offered to shake hands with Clark, but the latter replied that he would have nothing to do with such a man, and struck him over the head with a tomahawk. Berger also struck him with a rifle. Harvey grappled Clark and would have thrown him into the river had not Lee disabled him with a blow from his pistol across the hand. Harvey then escaped to shore, took his horse and fled to the fort. The employes took sides with him, and they placed the fort in a state of defense, refusing admission to any of the boat party. Finally after much hard pleading, Culbertson was admitted. He had always been friendly to Harvey and he now agreed, on condition that Harvey would surrender the fort, to give him a draft for all his wages and a letter of recommendation. Harvey then left the fort in a canoe with one man (2).

After stopping for two days at Fort Union he pursued his course down the river. Before leaving he said, "Never mind! You will see old Harvey here again." And sure enough, when he arrived at Fort Pierre he found several of the old employes of the American Fur Company who had become dissatisfied, banding together to form a new company. He joined them and became senior member of the new firm, which was called Harvey, Primeau and Company. It carried on quite an effective opposition to the American Fur Company for a number of years.

AUTHOR'S NOTES

(1) This sketch of Alexander Harvey is taken mainly from *Forty Years a Fur Trader*, by Charles Larpenteur.

(2) The foregoing statement is confirmed in the following letter from M. H. Harvey, Superintendent of Indian Affairs, St. Louis, to Andrew Drips, Indian Agent for the tribes of the Upper Missouri, dated St. Louis, March 13, 1846:

"It having been satisfactorily established by a recent investigation held at this office that Mr. Francis A. Chardon, one of the traders of P. Chouteau, Jr. & Co., has clearly violated the intercourse laws of the United States by directing the sale of spiritous liquors to Indians; and it having also been set forth *under oath* that three of the engagés of the said P. Chouteau, Jr. & Co., namely,

James Lee, Malcolm Clark, and Jacob Berger, have attempted the murder of an American citizen, Alex Harvey; you are hereby required to order the above named persons out of the Indian country forthwith. It is highly desirable that they should, if possible, be sent here, in order that they may be dealt with according to law."

Chapter VIII

MIRACULOUS ESCAPE OF HUGH GLASS

Biographical notes—Wounded in Aricara fight—Joins Henry's expedition to the Yellowstone—Attacked by a grizzly bear—Nearly killed—Left with two companions—His companions desert him—Crawls to Fort Kiowa—Ascends the river to find faithless companions—Arrives at Henry's fort on Bighorn river—Sets out for Fort Atkinson—Attacked by the Aricaras—Arrives at Fort Atkinson—Forgives his enemies—Continues in the fur trade—Finally killed by the Aricaras—Glass' Bluffs—Johnson Gardner avenges his death.

Among the anecdotes that have come down to us of wild life on the plains, none is better authenticated than that of the escape of Hugh Glass from the very portal of death at the hands of a grizzly bear. The story has survived in oral tradition and is well known by the older men of the mountains and plains who still live. It has thrice been embodied in written description (1). The following account is taken from the *Missouri Intelligencer*, which in turn borrowed it from the *Portfolio*. It is in all respects the most circumstantial extant and is evidently the most correct in its details. The incident is one of those which were so frequent in those early days, although it must have been considerably more noteworthy than the average or it would not have survived so long.

Hugh Glass was born in Pennsylvania—the only scrap of his early history that has come down to us. He was called an "old man" as early as 1824. Our first real knowledge of him is in 1823, when he is discovered to be one of Ashley and Henry's men. He received a wound in Ashley's fight before the Aricara towns.

After the Leavenworth campaign was over, Andrew Henry set out for the Yellowstone River and Glass was one of his party. (2). The route lay up Grand River through a country interspersed with thickets of brushwood, dwarf plum trees and other shrubs indigenous to this barren soil. As these nomadic parties usually drew their food, and to a large extent their raiment, from the country through which they were passing, it was necessary to keep one or two hunters ahead of the main party in search of game. Glass, having a high reputation as a hunter and a good shot, was often detailed upon this important duty. On the present occasion he was a short distance in advance of the party, forcing his way through a thicket, when he suddenly came upon a grizzly bear that had lain down in the sand. Before he could "set his triggers," or even turn to fly, the bear seized him by the throat and lifted him off the ground. Then flinging him down, the ferocious animal tore off a mouthful of flesh and turned and gave it to her cubs, which were near by. Glass now endeavored to escape, but the bear, followed by her cubs, pounced upon him again. She seized him by the shoulder and inflicted dangerous wounds in his hands and arms. His companion had by this time come up and was making war upon the cubs, but one of them drove him into the river, where standing waist deep in the water, he killed his pursuer with a shot from his rifle. The main body now arrived, having heard cries for succor, and after several shots from close at hand, slew the bear as she was standing over the prostrate body of her victim (3).

Although still alive, the condition of the unfortunate hunter seemed well-nigh hopeless. His whole body was in a mangled condition. He was utterly unable to stand and was suffering excruciating torment. There was no surgical aid to be had and it was impossible to move him. Delay of the party might bring disaster upon all, yet it was repugnant to the feelings of the men to leave the sufferer alone. In this predicament Major Henry succeeded, by offer of reward (4), in inducing two men to remain with Glass until he should expire, or until he should so far recover as to bear removal to some of the trading houses in that country. These men remained with Glass for five days, when, despairing of his recovery, and at the same time seeing no prospects of immediate death, they cruelly abandoned him, taking with them his rifle and all his accoutrements, so that he was left without means of defense, subsistence or shelter. The faithless wretches then set out on the trail of their employer, and when they overtook him, reported that Glass had died of his wounds and that they had buried him in the best manner possible. They produced his effects in confirmation and their story was readily accepted.

But Glass was *not* dead, and although the dread messenger had hovered for many days so near, yet the stricken sufferer would not receive him, but persistently motioned him away. When Glass realized the treachery of his companions, far from despairing on account of it, he felt a new determination to live, if for nothing else than to search out his base betrayers and call them to account. There was a spring near by and hither Glass drew himself. Over it hung a few bushes with wild cherries and near by were some buffalo berries that he could reach. Here he remained day after day, gradually nursing back his strength, until he felt that he could undertake to leave his lonesome and unhappy camping ground. He resolved to strike out for Fort Kiowa, a post on the Missouri River a hundred miles away. It required magnificent fortitude to set out on a journey like that, still unable to stand, and with hardly strength to drag one limb after the other; with no provisions nor means of securing any, and in a hostile country where he was at the absolute mercy of the most worthless renegade that might cross his path. But the deep purpose of revenge held him up, and a stroke of fortune came to his rescue.

He happened one day upon a spot where a pack of wolves had surrounded a buffalo calf and were harrying it to death. Glass lay low until the calf was dead, when he appeared upon the scene, put the wolves to flight, and took possession of the calf. Without knife or fire, it was not an easy thing to turn to account his good fortune, but hunger is not fastidious and Glass most likely took counsel of the wolves as to ways and means of devouring what he required. Taking what he could with him, he pursued his way, with inconceivable hardship and distress, and at last reached Fort Kiowa (5). After an experience like that through which he had just passed, it might be supposed that Glass would have been inclined to rest at the fort, at least until his wounds could get well. But he had not long been there when a party of trappers came along in a boat bound for the Yellowstone River. This was just the opportunity that he wanted, and he promptly joined them, bidding adieu to the protection of the fort.

When the party was nearing the Mandan villages, Glass thought to save a little time by going overland across a bend in the river to Tilton's Fort, a trading establishment in that vicinity. It proved to be a lucky move, for on the following day all of his companions were massacred by the Aricara Indians (6). Those always treacherous savages had but lately taken up their abode near the Mandan villages and the travelers were wholly ignorant of the snare into which they were running. As Glass was approaching the fort he saw two squaws whom he at once recognized as Aricaras (7). Alarmed at his danger he sought to conceal himself, but too late, for the squaws at once notified the warriors, who immediately began pursuit. Glass, still feeble from his wounds, made an ineffectual effort at flight. His enemies were almost within gun shot when two mounted Mandans rushed forward and seized him. Great was his surprise and joy at this unexpected deliverance, and it gave him increased faith that he should yet live to accomplish his mission of revenge.

The Indians carried Glass to Tilton's Fort, and the same night he left the fort alone and set out up the river. After traveling alone for thirty-eight days, all the way through hostile country, he at length arrived at Henry's Fort near the mouth of the Bighorn River. Here he was received as one risen from the dead, for no one had doubted the story of his companions. Glass was chagrined to find that his companions had gone to Fort Atkinson (8). Still intent on his purpose of revenge, he promptly accepted an offer of service as a messenger to carry a despatch to Fort Atkinson. Four men accompanied him and they left Henry's Fort on the 28th of February, 1824.

The route of the party lay eastward into the valley of Powder River, thence southward to the sources of that stream, and across into the valley of the Platte. Here they made some skin boats and floated down the river until they were out of the foothills, when, to their infinite dismay, they came upon a band of Aricaras, a part of Grey Eye's band, the chief who had been killed the previous summer by a shot from Leavenworth's artillery. The new chief's name was Elk Tongue. The warriors came down to the river and by many protestations of friendship induced the travelers to believe that they were sincere. Glass had at one time spent a whole winter with the chief, had joined him in the chase, had smoked his pipe, and had quaffed many a cup with him in the wigwam. When he alighted from his canoe the old chief embraced him as a brother. The whites were thrown off their guard and accepted an invitation to visit the chief's lodge. While partaking of the hospitable pipe a child was heard to utter a scream, and on looking around, Glass perceived some squaws carrying away their effects. The little party well understood what this meant, and springing at once to their feet fled with the utmost precipitation. Two of them were overtaken and put to death, one within a few yards of Glass, who had found concealment behind a point of rocks. Glass was thoroughly versed in the arts of Indian life and he succeeded in baffling their search until finally they abandoned it altogether. He had lost all his property except a knife and flint, and thus equipped he set out in a northeast direction to find Fort Kiowa (9).

The buffalo calves at this season were very young, and as the country abounded in buffalo, Glass had no difficulty in getting what meat he desired, while his flint enabled him to build a fire. He was fifteen days in reaching Fort Kiowa, and at the first opportunity went down the river to Fort Atkinson, where he arrived in June, 1824. Here he found his faithless companion (for he now cherished revenge only against one of the party), who had enlisted in the army. Thus under protection of law, Glass did not feel disposed to resort to extreme measures. The commanding officer ordered his property to be given up and provided him with new equipment. Thus appeased, he relinquished his scheme of revenge and contented himself with entertaining the people of the garrison with stories of his marvelous experiences.

In weighing the two principal authorities for this story we are inclined to think that Glass' sudden relinquishment of his purpose of revenge may have been due to a new light ob-

tained from the two men who deserted him. It was asking a
great deal for those two men to expose themselves to destruction for one whose life they doubtless believed was already as
good as lost, and whatever may have been the considerations
of humanity, it was only heroic indifference to personal safety
that could have induced them to stay. They should have
stayed, of course, but their failure to do so is not without its
justification.

In Colonel Cooke's account, the name of one of the men
left with Glass was Fitzgerald; the name of the other is not
given, but he is said to have been a mere youth of seventeen
and doubtless on his first trip to the mountains. Glass does not
seem to have cherished revenge against him, but to have
blamed Fitzgerald alone. Who the young man was is not
known, but the late Captain La Barge, who remembers the
tradition well, says that it was James Bridger (A). Bridger is
supposed to have been born in 1804 and this would indicate
1821 or 1822 as the year of the occurrence. The discrepancy is
not great enough to preclude the possibility of its being
Bridger, but there is no other proof of it than this intangible
tradition.

Glass turns up occasionally in the correspondence of those
early days and we know that he was at Fort Union about 1830.
He was at one time employed as hunter for the fort and used
to hunt for bighorns on the bluffs opposite the post. These
bluffs are still known as Glass' Bluffs (B).

Glass finally succumbed to his old enemies, the Aricaras,
in the winter of 1832-3. The circumstances of his death were
related (10) to Maximilian, Prince of Wied, who thus recorded them: "Old Glass, with two of his companions, had
gone from Fort Cass [winter of 1832-3] to hunt bears on the
Yellowstone, and as they were crossing the river on the ice
farther down, they were all three shot, scalped, and plundered
by a war party of thirty Aricaras who were concealed on the
opposite bank. These Indians, who are the most dangerous to
the whites, went then to the sources of the Powder River, and
it happened that Gardner with about twenty men and thirty
horses was in the neighborhood. As it was dark, when they
were seated about several fires, the Indians suddenly appeared,

addressed them in the Minnetaree language, surrounded the fire and dried their shoes. Gardner, being well acquainted with the character of the Indians, immediately took some precautions, which were the more necessary, as a Minnetaree woman who was with the party told him that the strangers were Aricaras. He gradually collected his people around one of the fires, with their arms in readiness to act. He was also afraid for his horses, which were scattered on the prairie, and some of which were actually missing, and he had already sent some of his men to erect in the neighborhood what is called a fort, of trunks of trees, for the night. The Indians are accustomed, when they intend to steal horses, suddenly to give a signal, on which all jump up, scatter the horses, and drive away with them. Gardner, aware of this, watched the enemy closely, and when, on the signal being given, they all withdrew, three of them were seized and bound. When the Aricaras perceived this, several of them came back, pretended to be innocent of the stealing of the horses, and begged for their captive comrades, but Gardner declared to them that if they did not immediately deliver up all the horses, the prisoners must die; one of them, however, had cut the bonds with which he was bound, and escaped. The Indians entreated for a long time but were refused. The others seeing that they must die, commenced their death song, related their exploits, and affirmed that they were distinguished warriors. One of them had old Glass' knife, and his rifle had also been seen in the possession of these Indians. The horses, however, were not brought, and the prisoners alleging a pressing necessity, were taken aside; but in the thick copse they attempted to escape, on which one of them was stabbed and several shots were fired at the other, who was then killed with a knife. They were both scalped and I received one of the scalps as a present, which was unfortunately lost in the fire on board the steamer. Gardner, by way of precaution, had all the fires put out and passed the night in the fort, which was now completed. They were not disturbed during the night, and found, in the morning, that the Indians had retired with their booty, leaving the prisoners to their fates. The Aricaras had begged for one in particular, who was a celebrated warrior, and had even brought back three horses which they tied up near at hand, to exchange them for the prisoners; but Gardner did not attend to their request.''

AUTHOR'S NOTES

(1) *Missouri Intelligencer*, June 18, 1825; *Scenes in the Rocky Mountains* (Sage) p. 117; *Scenes and Adventures in the United States Army* (Cooke), p. 135.

(2) According to Cooke, Henry had eighty men bound for the headwaters of the Yellowstone. The incident with the bear occurred on the fifth day out, near evening.

(3) Cooke's account is quite different, the essential particulars being that Glass was caught too suddenly to retreat and staked his all upon a single deliberate shot, which though it was ultimately fatal, was not immediately so. The bear rushed upon Glass with such speed and ferocity that escape was impossible. She overtook him, crushed him to the earth, and mangled him so terribly that it seemed as if he must have been killed. She then started after the other hunters, who barely escaped with their lives before the bear succumbed to the effects of Glass' shot.

(4) Cooke says that a purse of eighty dollars was made up by the men as a present to any two who would stay with Glass.

(5) Cooke says that Glass' razor was left; that in the incident of the wolves and the buffalo calf he waited until the wolves had eaten enough to satisfy their hunger before he drove them off lest they should attack him. He further says that Glass went first to the Aricara villages, which he found deserted except by some dogs, and that he spent two days taming these before they would come near enough for him to get hold of them. This is, however, not probable, for Glass would not have gone deliberately back into the hands of those Indians while there was any other chance of life. Cooke also says that Glass then went to a trading post at the mouth of the Teton river.

(6) This event is confirmed by an entry in the *Missouri Intelligencer* of February 25, 1824.

(7) Cooke's account of this affair is very much colored, too much so to be true, and was probably the result of the natural growth which such stories undergo through many repetitions.

(8) Cooke says the younger of the two men was found at Henry's Fort; that he was petrified with fear when he saw Glass; but that Glass had compassion on him, and let him go on account of his

youth, his penitence, and, more likely, because he considered Fitzgerald, who was the older, the real culprit.

Cooke has no account of Glass' adventures beyond his arrival at
Henry's fort.

(9) "Although I had lost my rifle and all my plunder, I felt
quite rich when I found my knife and steel in my shot pouch. These
little fixins make a man feel right pert when he is three or four
hundred miles away from anybody or anywhere—all alone among
the painters [panthers] and the vile varmints." From the article in
Missouri Intelligencer.

(10) By Johnson Gardner, the well-known free trapper.

EDITOR'S NOTES

(A) Alter, in his *James Bridger*, page 21, says that none of the
early printed narratives used Bridger's name, and after quoting the
statement of La Barge from Chittenden, continues; "we are thus
accepting as an established fact the general belief that Bridger was
the junior trapper left on guard." He has no authority to either
confirm or contradict La Barge's statement.

Dale says, *Ashley-Smith Explorations*, page 87, "Tradition has it
that the younger of Glass's companions was James Bridger."

Alter quotes almost in full the various early versions of Glass'
escape.

(B) John G. Neihardt has told the story in verse, *The Song of
Hugh Glass.*

Chapter IX

THE TREACHERY OF MIKE FINK (1)

*Early life—A great shot—His friends Talbot and Carpenter—
Goes to St. Louis—Shoots off a negro's heel—Enters Ashley's
service—Quarrels with Carpenter—Slays Carpenter—Killed by
Talbot—Talbot drowned.*

Mike Fink, a character in early Western history, whose
well authenticated preformances were so remarkable as to
appear rather the creations of fancy than actual occurrences,
was a native of Pittsburg, Pennsylvania. He had little education and made ridicule of what he had. He used to spell his
name Mike Phink and he loved to affect the extremes of
barbarous jargon that characterized the language of the un-
lettered boatmen on the Western rivers. Mike early became
fascinated with the boatman's life, and the sound of the boat
horn was his most entrancing music. He learned to imitate its
notes, so that when he first took service in a keelboat he could
fill the office of trumpeter without any instrument. The river
life suited his tastes and he longed to visit its remotest ports—
even New Orleans, where, he had heard, the people spoke
French and wore their Sunday clothes all the week.

When the water was too low for navigation Mike spent
most of his time in Pittsburg and vicinity, killing squirrels and
shooting at a target for beef at the frequent Saturday shooting
matches and company musters of the militia. He soon became renowned as the best shot in the country, acquiring the
soubriquet of "Bangall," and on account of his extraordinary
skill he was excluded from participation in the matches. As a
price for this exclusion he was allowed the "fifth quarter"
of the beef, as it was then called—the hide and tallow. His
usual practice was to exchange his "quarter" at a dram shop
for whiskey, with which he treated everybody and particularly himself. He became fond of strong drink, but never was

intoxicated. He could drink a gallon in twenty-four hours and not show any effects of it.

His language was a perfect sample of the half-horse, half alligator dialect of the early race of boatmen. He was a good deal of a wit, a quality which won him the admiration, but at the same time excited the fears, of the whole boating fraternity; for he usually enforced his jokes with a sound drubbing if any one had the temerity to refuse to laugh at them. He used to say that he told his jokes to be laughed at, and that no one should make light of them. The consequence was that Mike always had about him a band of laughing sycophants who were as afraid of his frown as a vassal might be of the displeasure of his lord.

Mike used to proclaim himself—"I am a Salt River roarer, and I love the wimming, and as how I am chock full of fight." And indeed he had a *chère amie* in every port who would "fight their deaths" in his defense.

Among his confederates were two men conspicuous for their prowess and who were Mike's fast and confidential friends. Their names were Carpenter and Talbot. Each of the three was a match for the other in fighting and in marksmanship and were adepts in the virtues and mysteries of Mike's calling.

Mike's weight was about 180 pounds. He was five feet nine inches high; with broad, round face and pleasant features; brown skin, tanned by the sun and rain; blue but very expressive eyes, inclining to gray, broad white teeth; and square brawny form, well proportioned, with every muscle fully developed, indicating the greatest strength and activity. Except as to stature he was a perfect model for a Hercules.

As already stated, he was an expert marksman, and many of his shooting feats have been related by those who professed to have witnessed them. On one occasion while ascending the Mississippi River above the mouth of the Ohio, he saw a sow with eight or nine pigs on the river bank. He declared in boatman phrase that he "wanted pig," and took up his rifle to shoot one. He was requested not to do so, but nevertheless laid his rifle to his face, and as the boat glided up the river under easy sail, some forty or fifty yards from shore, he shot at one pig after another, cutting their tails off close to their bodies, but not doing them any other harm!

In 1821, while standing on the levee in St. Louis, he saw a negro on the river bank listlessly gazing at what was going on around him. He had a remarkably shaped foot peculiar to some African tribes. His heel protruded to the rear so far that his foot seemed to be as much in the rear as in front of the leg. This unshapely form offended Mike's eye and outraged his sense of symmetry. He determined to correct it. Lifting his rifle at thirty paces he actually shot the heel away, inflicting an ugly wound. The boy dropped to the ground, screaming "Murder!" Mike was indicted in the circuit court of the county, tried and found guilty (2). His plea in justification of the offense was that he wanted to fix the boy's foot so that he could wear a genteel boot. Mike's punishment, which is not stated, could not have been very severe, for he was at liberty in the spring of 1822.

Mike's particular friend, Carpenter, was also a great shot, and it was a common thing for him and Mike to fill a tin cup with whiskey and shoot it from each other's heads at a distance of seventy yards. The feat was always performed successfully, the cup being bored through without injury to the person supporting it. It was a favorite performance with these two men, who regarded it as fresh avowal of confidence in each other.

Mike had first visited St. Louis in 1814 or 1815 and was there frequently afterward. In 1822 he and his two friends, Talbot and Carpenter, enlisted in the company which General Ashley and Major Henry were organizing for their attempt to open up a trade with the mountain tribes. They enlisted in the threefold character of boatmen, trappers, and hunters. The company ascended as far as to the mouth of the Yellowstone, where a fort was constructed, from which the party was sent out in detachments to trap on the tributaries of the Missouri and the Yellowstone. Mike and his friends, with nine others, went to the Muscleshell River where they found a warm and commodious habitation for the winter.

During their sojourn here Mike and Carpenter fell into a deadly quarrel, which, however, was smoothed over for the time by the interposition of friends. The cause is not certainly known, but there seems to have been a woman in the case, a squaw for whose good graces they had become rival aspirants. On the arrival of spring the little party visited the fort, and here, over a draught of whiskey, they renewed their smothered quarrel. Again they made a treaty of peace, and in evidence of their sincerity Mike proposed that they repeat their familiar feat of shooting the whiskey cup from each other's head. This would not only be a test of reconciliation, but of mutual trust and confidence as well.

A preliminary question to be decided was which should have the first shot. To determine this Mike proposed to "sky a copper," or in modern phrase, to flip a copper. This was done and Mike won the first shot. Carpenter, who knew from long experience the uncompromising character of Mike's hatred, declared his belief in his companion's treacherous intent, and that he should surely be killed. But he scorned life too much to repudiate his contract, and accordingly he prepared to die. He bequeathed his rifle, bullet pouch, powder horn, belt, pistol and wages to Talbot, and then went out to the place where the trial was to occur. He filled his cup with whiskey and placed it on his head, while Mike was loading his rifle and picking his flint. Carpenter stood up at the proper place, erect and serene, without a change of countenance to indicate what was passing in his mind. Mike leveled his rifle at the distance of sixty yards. After drawing a bead he took down his rifle and smilingly said: "Hold your noddle steady, Carpenter, and don't spill the whiskey, as I shall want some presently." He again raised his rifle and in an instant Carpenter fell, expiring without a groan. The ball had penetrated his forehead in the center an inch and a half above the eyes. Mike coolly set the breach of his gun on the ground, and applying his mouth to the muzzle, blew the smoke out of the barrel, all the while keeping his eye upon the prostrate form of his oldtime friend. Finally he said: "Carpenter, you have spilled the whiskey!" He was told that he had killed Carpenter. "It is all a mistake," he said, "for I took as fine a bead on the black spot of the cup as I ever took on a squirrel's eye.

How did it happen?" He then cursed his rifle, the bullet, and finally himself.

In this remote region where the power of the law was not yet known, and among a party who had an exaggerated dread of Mike's prowess, the crime was permitted to pass off as an accident, and Mike was allowed to go at large. But Talbot, who was Carpenter's fast friend, was convinced of Mike's treacherous intent, and resolved upon revenge whenever an opportunity should offer. Some months afterward, Mike, in a fit of gasconading, declared that he had killed Carpenter and was glad of it. Talbot instantly drew his pistol, the same which Carpenter had bequeathed him, and shot Mike through the heart. Mike fell and expired without a word (A).

Talbot likewise was not called to account, for nobody had any authority to do so and few doubtless felt any inclination, as it was probably considered a just penalty for the killing of Carpenter. Moreover Talbot was a terrible enemy, ferocious and dangerous as a grizzly of the prairies. About three months later he was present in the Aricara battle under Colonel Leavenworth, where he displayed a coolness which would have done honor to a better man. He came out of the battle unharmed, but about ten days later while attempting to swim the Teton River he was drowned. Thus perished the "last of the boatmen" (3).

AUTHOR'S NOTES

(1) This story is given mainly verbatim from the *Missouri Intelligencer* of Sept. 4, 1829, quoted from *Flint's Western Review*, which in turn took it from an ephemeral publication called the *Western Souvenir*. The article was entitled "The Last of the Boatmen." Author not given.

(2) The writer of this article states that he himself had seen the record of the trial.

(3) Remarkable as this story is it has authentic confirmation. In General Clark's letter book on Indian Affairs, now in possession of the Kansas Historical Society at Topeka, there is a list of deaths among Ashley's and Smith, Jackson and Sublette's parties before 1830. The statement says that in 1822 Mike Fink shot Carpenter; that Fink was soon after shot by Talbot, who was later drowned in the Teton River. The year should be 1823.

The following notice appeared in the *St. Louis Republican* of

THOMAS FITZPATRICK

July 16, 1823: "By a letter received in town from one of General Ashley's expeditions we are informed that a man by the name of Mike Fink, well known in this quarter as a great marksman with the rifle, and is the same who some time since in this place shot off a negro's heel to enable him, as he said, to wear a genteel boot! was engaged in his favorite amusement of shooting a tin cup from the head of another man, when by aiming too low, or from some other cause, shot his companion in the forehead and killed him. Another man of the expedition (whose name we have not yet heard) remonstrated against Fink's conduct, to which he (Fink) replied that he would kill him likewise, upon which the other drew a pistol and shot Fink dead on the spot."

EDITOR'S NOTE

(A) Walter Blair and S. J. Meine have just published a life of Mike Fink.

Chapter X

THE ADVENTURES OF JOHN COLTER

Colter in Lewis and Clark expedition—Remains in the upper country—Enters Lisa's employ—Sets out to find the Crows—Crosses to Pierre's Hole—Fight with the Blackfeet—Colter starts for Fort Manuel alone—Crosses Yellowstone Park—"Colter's Hell"—Colter goes to Three Forks—Terrible adventure on Jefferson Fork—His miraculous escape—Results of Colter's adventures—His subsequent career.

John Colter was one of the private soldiers attached to the expedition of Lewis and Clark in the years 1804–06. When the returning explorers had arrived at their former winter quarters near the Mandan villages, some fifty-five miles above where Bismarck, North Dakota, now stands, Colter asked for his discharge in order that he might remain in the upper country and trap. He had met two hunters only the day before who were bound for the upper rivers and they offered him substantial inducements if he would accompany them. As his record on the expedition had been excellent, his commanding officers assented to the request, gave him his discharge, outfitted him in good shape, and he forthwith set out on his proposed expedition. This was August 15 or 16, 1806 (A).

Colter remained in the upper country all the following winter, but in what precise locality is not known. It is probable, from subsequent events, that it was in the valley of the Yellowstone. In the following spring he set out, apparently alone, to return to St. Louis, but on his way met the expedition of Manuel Lisa near the mouth of the Platte River. To this band of adventurers into an unknown country the service of a man like Colter, who had spent a winter there and had twice passed entirely through it, could not but be very important. He was persuaded (if persuasion was necessary) to join the expedition and accordingly turned back a second time from his journey towards home.

Nothing occurred on the voyage with which his name is connected until the arrival of the expedition at the mouth of the Bighorn. Lisa had expected to find the Blackfeet nation very hostile on account of the loss of one of their number at the hands of Captain Lewis the previous summer on his way back from the Pacific (1). It may have been a fear of this hostility that caused his unlucky decision to establish himself in the country of their enemies, the Crows. But it seemed that a detachment of Lisa's party met a band of Blackfeet, either before or soon after the arrival at the mouth of the Bighorn, from whom interesting and important information was obtained. Far from being hostile, these Indians evinced a pacific disposition and said that the provocation under which Captain Lewis acted was so obvious and flagrant that they had not cherished this act as a justification of hostility, and were ready to open relations of trade with the whites (B).

Lisa was greatly pleased at this prospect. He had already sent Colter to notify the surrounding bands of Indians of his arrival, and he probably directed him to proceed also to the Three Forks of the Missouri and confer with the Blackfoot nation. It was a perilous adventure and one requiring great courage and hardihood. "This man," says Brackenridge, "with a pack of thirty pounds weight, his gun and some ammunition, went upwards of five hundred miles to the Crow nation; gave them information, and proceeded from thence to several other tribes." It seems that when Lisa arrived in the country the Crows were in the upper end of the valley, probably on Wind River, and Colter had to travel a long distance to reach them. He then most likely secured the services of a party of the Crows to guide him by the best trail across the mountains, for he could hardly have followed so well by himself what is now, and doubtless was then, the best route through this exceptionally rugged country. All available evidence indicates that Colter traveled directly from Wind River to Pierre's Hole, crossing the Wind River Mountains by Union or Two-gwo-tee passes and the Teton range by the pass of the same name. The sublime and wonderful scenery and the remarkable topographical situation by which divergent streams flow from a common neighborhood to widely-separated river systems and the ease with which the mountains could be crossed (2), impressed Colter deeply. When he returned to St. Louis he drew the attention of Clark, Brackenridge and others to these remarkable features.

It is probable that it was in the valley of Pierre's Hole that "this party in whose company he happened to be," was attacked, as related by Brackenridge (C). This party, according to Biddle, was of the Crow nation (D) and the attacking party were Blackfeet (3). A fight ensued and Colter, by the necessity of the situation, was compelled to take part with the Crows. He distinguished himself greatly and received a severe wound in the leg. The Blackfeet were defeated, but not until they had seen the pale-face ally of their enemies to whom, no doubt, they attributed their discomfiture.

The Crows, having conducted their guest across the mountains, and probably not deeming it wise to linger until the vengeance of the Blackfeet should bring reinforcements upon them, left Colter at this point and returned to their country. This conclusion seems certain from Colter's own narrative to Brackenridge, who says that notwithstanding the wound in his leg, "he returned to the establishment entirely alone and without assistance, several hundred miles." Colter, upon his return to St. Louis, gave to General Clark a description of his route, which the latter placed upon the map accompanying the report of the Lewis and Clark expedition and legended it "Colter's Route in 1807." This map makes it clear that from Pierre's Hole Colter undertook to reach Lisa's Fort by the most direct route possible. Such was probably his plan. He knew that it would be folly for him now to proceed to the Three Forks, where he would become an instant victim of Blackfoot vengeance. The best thing to do was to make his way back to the fort and report to Lisa. To go by the way he had come would be to make a long detour and nearly double the distance over a direct line. Colter had a sufficient eye for topography to know that Lisa's Fort lay about northeast of his position. He accordingly launched into the dense pine forests that cover the country on the northern flank of the Teton Range and the southern portion of Yellowstone National Park. It may with difficulty be imagined what must have been his astonishment when, emerging from the forests upon the shore of that surpassingly beautiful mountain lake near the source of the Yellowstone River, he found its shore steaming with innumerable boiling springs and geysers. As a matter of fact Colter's route was carrying him directly across the present Yellowstone Park, from southwest to northeast. He saw the strange phenomena on the shore of Yellowstone Lake, and along the course of its outlet for a distance of some forty miles. There is no record that he ever mentioned having seen the Falls of the Yellowstone, but he could hardly have escaped them, considering the course of his journey as outlined on the map. He continued down the Yellowstone so long as it bore to the northeast on his general course, but left it by way of the valley of the East Fork where the main stream turns abruptly to the northwest. Thence he continued his course almost on the line of the present route to the northeast corner of the Park and eventually found his way back to Lisa's Fort (E).

This very remarkable achievement—remarkable in the courage and hardihood of this lone adventurer and remarkable in its unexpected results in geographical discovery—deserves to be classed among the most celebrated performances in the history of American exploration. Colter was the first explorer of the valley of the Bighorn River; the first to cross the passes at the head of Wind River and see the headwaters of the Colorado of the West; the first to see the Teton Mountains, Jackson Hole, Pierre's Hole, and the sources of the Snake River; and most important of all, the first to pass through the singular region which has since become known throughout the world as the Yellowstone Wonderland. He also saw the immense tar spring at the forks of the Stinkingwater [Shoshone] River, a spot which came to bear the name of "Colter's Hell."

Colter had now accomplished enough to entitle him to lasting distinction in the cause of geographical exploration; but honors of a more perilous character still awaited him. As soon as spring opened—for Colter could not have returned to Lisa's Fort before the arrival of winter—Lisa dispatched him again to visit the Blackfeet (F). Colter set out directly for the Three Forks of the Missouri where he seems to have employed his time trapping until the Indians put in appearance. He was accompanied on this expedition by a companion named Potts, very likely the same one who had been a fellow soldier in the Lewis and Clark expedition. Biddle relates that when these two men met the Blackfeet these Indians did not even yet evince hostile intentions, but that an altercation soon ensued, ending in a combat in which Potts was killed and Colter made his escape. This affair was probably the same as that related by John Bradbury in his *Travels in North America*, and better known through Irving's *Astoria*. Colter gave the account of his miraculous escape to the English naturalist immediately after his return to St. Louis in the spring of 1810. All other accounts are based upon Bradbury's. The simple and direct language in which the author has clothed his recital tells the story so well that even the skilful pen of Irving adopted it almost without change. The adventure is one of those remarkable experiences which have now and then occurred in our frontier history, almost beyond credibility, but nevertheless in their details clearly possible. The story is here repeated in the exact words of Bradbury (4):

"This man came to St. Louis in May, 1810, in a small canoe, from the headwaters of the Missouri, a distance of three thousand miles, which he traversed in thirty days. I saw him on his arrival, and received from him an account of his adventures after he had separated from Lewis and Clark's party; one of these, from its singularity, I shall relate. On the arrival of the party at the headwaters of the Missouri, Colter, observing an appearance of abundance of beaver there, got permission to remain and hunt for some time, which he did in company with a man by the name of Dixon, who had traversed the immense tract of country from St. Louis to the headwaters of the Missouri alone.

"Soon after he separated from Dixon, and *trapped* in company with a hunter named Potts; and aware of the hostility of the Blackfeet Indians, one of whom had been killed by Lewis, they set their traps at night, and took them up early in the morning, remaining concealed during the day. They were examining their traps early one morning, in a creek about six miles from that branch of the Missouri called Jefferson's

Fork, and were ascending in a canoe, when they suddenly heard a great noise, resembling the trampling of animals; but they could not ascertain the fact, as the high, perpendicular banks on each side of the river impeded their view. Colter immediately pronounced it to be occasioned by Indians, and advised an instant retreat; but was accused of cowardice by Potts, who insisted that the noise was caused by buffaloes, and they proceeded on. In a few minutes afterwards their doubts were removed by a party of Indians making their appearance on both sides of the creek, to the amount of five or six hundred, who beckoned them to come ashore. As retreat was now impossible, Colter turned the head of the canoe to the shore; and at the moment of its touching, an Indian seized the rifle belonging to Potts; but Colter, who is a remarkably strong man, immediately retook it, and handed it to Potts, who remained in the canoe, and on receiving it pushed off into the river. He had scarcely quitted the shore when an arrow was shot at him, and he cried out, *Colter, I am wounded.* Colter remonstrated with him on the folly of attempting to escape, and urged him to come ashore. Instead of complying, he instantly leveled his rifle at an Indian, and shot him dead on the spot. This conduct, situated as he was, may appear to have been an act of madness; but it was doubtless the effect of sudden and sound reasoning; for if taken alive, he must have expected to be tortured to death, according to their custom. He was instantly pierced with arrows so numerous that, to use the language of Colter, *he was made a riddle of.*

"They now seized Colter, stripped him entirely naked, and began to consult on the manner in which he should be put to death. They were first inclined to set him up as a mark to shoot at; but the chief interfered, and seizing him by the shoulder, asked him if he could run fast. Colter, who had been some time amongst the Kee-kat-sa, or Crow Indians, had in a considerable degree acquired the Blackfoot language, and was also well acquainted with Indian customs. He knew that he had now to run for his life, with the dreadful odds of five or six hundred against him, and those armed Indians; therefore he cunningly replied that he was a very bad runner, although he was considered by the hunters as remarkably swift. The chief now commanded the party to remain stationary, and led Colter out on the prairie three or four hundred yards, and released him, bidding him *to save himself if he could*. At that instant the horrid war whoop sounded in the ears of poor Colter, who, urged with the hope of preserving life, ran with a speed at which he was himself surprised. He proceeded towards the Jefferson Fork, having to traverse a plain six miles in breadth, abounding with prickly pear, on which he was every instant treading with his naked feet. He ran nearly halfway across the plain before he ventured to look over his shoulder, when he perceived that the Indians were very much scattered, and that he had gained ground to a considerable distance from the main body; but one Indian, who carried a spear, was much before all the rest, and not more than a hundred yards from him. A faint gleam of hope now cheered the heart of Colter; he derived confidence from the belief that escape was within the bounds of possibility; but that confidence was nearly fatal to him, for he exerted himself to such a degree that the blood gushed from his nostrils, and soon almost covered the forepart of his body.

"He had now arrived within a mile of the river, when he distinctly heard the appalling sound of footsteps behind him, and every instant expected to feel the spear of his pursuer. Again he turned his head, and saw the savage not twenty yards from him. Determined if possible to avoid the expected blow, he suddenly stopped, turned round, and spread out his arms. The Indian, surprised by the suddenness of the action, and perhaps of the bloody appearance of Colter, also attempted to stop; but exhausted with running, he fell whilst endeavoring to throw his spear, which stuck in the ground and broke in his hand. Colter instantly snatched up the pointed part, with which he pinned him to the earth, and then continued his flight. The foremost of the Indians, on arriving at the place, stopped till others came up to join them, when they set up a hideous yell. Every moment of this time was improved by Colter, who, although fainting and exhausted, succeeded in gaining the skirting of the cottonwood trees, on the borders of the fork, through which he ran and plunged into the river. Fortunately for him, a little below this place there was an island, against the upper point of which a raft of drift timber, had lodged. He dived under the raft, and after several efforts, got his head above the water amongst the trunks of trees, covered over with smaller wood to the depth of several feet. Scarcely had he secured himself when the Indians arrived on the river, screeching and yelling, as Colter expressed it, 'like so many devils.' They were frequently on the raft during the day, and were seen through the chinks by Colter, who was congratulating himself on his escape, until the idea arose that they might set the raft on fire (5).

"In horrible suspense he remained until night, when hearing no more of the Indians, he dived under the raft, and swam silently down the river to a considerable distance, when he landed and traveled all night. Although happy in having escaped from the Indians, his situation was still dreadful; he was completely naked, under a burning sun; the soles of his feet were entirely filled with the thorns of the prickly pear; he was hungry, and had no means of killing game, although he saw abundance around him, and was at least seven days' journey from Lisa's Fort, on the Bighorn branch of the Roche Jaune River. These were circumstances under which almost any man but an American hunter would have despaired. He arrived at the fort in seven days, having subsisted on a root much esteemed by the Indians of the Missouri, now known by naturalists as *psoralea esculenta*" (G).

From this time on deadly enmity toward the white race became the settled policy of the Blackfeet Indians. There is probably little doubt that it was the *apparent* favoritism of the white traders toward their enemies the Crows that turned the scale (6). For this appearance the action of Lisa in building his first post in Crow territory, and Colter's accidental presence in the ranks of the Crows when these Indians were attacked by the Blackfeet, are mainly responsible. Colter thus became in part the involuntary cause of that deadly feud which lasted beyond the lifetime of any of his contemporaries.

Colter remained on the upper rivers until after Lisa's return in the summer of 1809 with an extensive outfit of the newly formed St. Louis Missouri Fur Company. But he very wisely abandoned the country before the disastrous events of

1810 at the Three Forks of the Missouri. He set out for St. Louis about April 1st of that year and made the descent of the rivers in thirty days, a distance according to his own estimate, of some three thousand miles. Colter remained in St. Louis for a considerable time, and evidently talked a great deal about his adventures. He gave Clark important data for his forthcoming map of the Lewis and Clark expedition. He succeeded in making himself accounted a confirmed prevaricator, and a cloud of doubt and ridicule hung over his memory until far later years proved the truth of his statements.

Among those who esteemed Colter's accounts of sufficient importance to merit attention may be mentioned General William Clark, Henry M. Brackenridge, the author, and John Bradbury, the English naturalist. He was seen by Bradbury in the spring of 1810, immediately after his return to St. Louis. Bradbury also spent the forenoon of March 18, 1811, with Colter while en route up the Missouri with the Astoria expedition of that year. Colter had lately married and was living near the river above the point where the little creek La Charette empties into the main stream. He was full of admonitions in regard to the Blackfeet and urged the most careful measures to prevent trouble with them. He was himself very much disposed to accompany the expedition, but he was too recently married to be able to come to a decision not to remain.

This is the last positive record that we have of the discoverer of the Yellowstone Wonderland. In the *Louisiana Gazette*, St. Louis, December 11, 1813, there appeared a notice by the administrator of the estate of "John Coulter, deceased," calling for a settlement of all claims for or against the estate. The final settlement left a balance in favor of the estate of $229.41¾. The deceased may or may not have been the subject of this sketch; but if so, his terrible experiences among the Blackfeet might very easily account for his early demise. (H).

AUTHOR'S NOTES

(1) These Indians were Grosventres of the Prairie, but were always classed with the Blackfeet by the traders and trappers. See Part V, Chapter IX.

(2) "At the head of the Gallatin Fork and of the Grosse Corne

of the Yellowstone [the Bighorn river] from discoveries since the voyage of Lewis and Clark, it is found less difficult to cross than the Alleghany mountains. Colter, a celebrated hunter and woodsman, informed me that a loaded wagon would find no obstruction in passing." Brackenridge. The Gallatin river was mistaken for one of the upper branches of the Yellowstone, probably; but it is clear that Colter here refers to the Union or Two-gwo-tee pass at the head of Wind river.

(3) In all probability these Indians were Grosventres.

(4) See Bradbury's *Travels in North America*, Irving's *Astoria*, and the *Yellowstone National Park*, by the present author.

(5) For a parallel case to that of Colter see narrative of the escape of Oskononton by hiding under a raft in a river. Ross' *Fur Hunters of the Far West*, p. 189.

(6) "This adverse feeling arose from a jealousy prevalent among all savage (and some civilized) nations, of those who trade with their enemies. The Crows and Blackfeet are almost continually at war; the company detached a party to trade with the former; this gave offense to the Blackfeet, who had not the same opportunity of procuring arms, etc., the Hudson Bay factory being several days' journey from their hunting grounds, and with which they could not trade with equal advantage." *Louisiana Gazette*, July 26, 1810.

EDITOR'S NOTES

(A) Colter was born in Virginia and died at Charette, Missouri in 1813. See the editor's *John Colter, Discoverer of Yellowstone Park*. He joined the Lewis and Clark expedition at Maysville, Kentucky.

(B) Letter of Major Biddle to Colonel Atkinson, October 29, 1819, *American State Papers, Indian Affairs II*, page 201.

(C) James in his *Three Years Among the Indians and Mexicans*, definitely fixes the place of this battle. In 1810, while a member of Henry's party and at the place itself, Colter described the fight to him. James says the party were on their way from the Gallatin and that they reached the Three Forks the next day so the fight could not have been at Pierre's Hole. James, pages 52 and 53.

This means that the "Route in 1807" could not have been the same journey as the one on which the battle took place, for the "Route" is shown close to Yellowstone Lake and nowhere near the Three Forks. James says, page 57, Colter made many excursions from Lisa's Fort to the Three Forks.

(D) James says, page 52, Flatheads and Crows.

(E) A complete analysis of "Colter's Route in 1807" will be found in the editor's *John Colter, Discoverer of Yellowstone Park.*

Shortly after the publication of the editor's book, the late J. G. White of Cleveland, wrote the editor that in his opinion Colter went through South Pass on his memorable journey in 1807. He also considered that the "Colter's River" of the Lewis and Clark map of 1814, and there shown as an affluent of the "Rio del Norte" is really the Big Sandy, and that the "Rio del Norte" is the Green.

In this latter conclusion Mr. White simply follows Coues' error in his edition of Lewis and Clark, page 1153. They are clearly wrong, as an inspection of the Lewis and Clark map and a knowledge of the circumstances under which the nomenclature was used by Clark in making the map will demonstrate. The "Rio del Norte" is obviously the Rio Grande, as is shown by the fact that the elements in this part of Clark's map south of Colter's "Route" were taken by Clark from Pike's map published in his *Account* in 1810. Pike's map shows the supposed relation of the Arkansas and Platt rivers and on it is marked his stockade. Pike, in his map, calls the Rio Grande the Rio del Norte. That this is what he meant by the use of the name is shown by his locating Santa Fe on the banks of the stream. When Clark made his map, he did not carry it far enough south to show Santa Fe, but all the other features are exactly copied, including the location of Pike's stockade.

How Pike and Clark confused each other is set forth in the editor's *John Colter*, pages 53 *et seq.*, which also points out the gross exaggeration and false orientation of the "Route." There are obvious impossibilities shown on Clark's map. Lake Biddle (Jackson Lake) is shown draining into the Big Horn instead of correctly into the Snake.

Pike supposed that the sources of the Yellowstone and the Rio Grande were so close together that there was a point in between where a man could reach either within a day's journey. *Account* II page 8. He even thought he *saw* the "Pierre Juan" (Yellowstone). *Account* II, page 182. Of course, he was never within hundreds of miles. But all these errors were accepted by Clark and they duly appear on the Lewis and Clark map.

Therefore, when Clark showed Colter's River as an affluent of the Rio del Norte, he intended to show it as flowing into the Rio Grande. This eliminates Colter's River as flowing into the Green and of course, it cannot be the Big Sandy.

Ignoring the mistake in thinking that Colter's River emptied into the Rio Grande instead of the Snake, but taking into consideration only the closeness with which the "Route" skirts Lakes Eustis and Biddle, it seems highly improbable that Colter was ever far enough south to have reached South Pass, which is a considerable distance south of any point that he could have attained. Besides, the "Route" clearly shows that he was never south of the Big Horn, as by it he crossed several streams flowing only from the north into the Big Horn, so named on the map, and followed the Stinking Water River (Shoshone), also to the north of the Big Horn, down its course, or up, depending on which directions he made the circuit. Therefore, he could not possibly have reached any of the headwaters of the Sweetwater, all of which are, of course, well to the south of the Big Horn.

Dale, in his *Ashley-Smith Explorations*, page 29, asserts that "Colter's route in 1807 lies wholly west and north of Lake Eustis (Yellowstone)." This is in face of the clear showing on the Clark map of the complete encirclement of Lake Eustis, and the crossing of the head of "Colter's River" which is certainly a long distance south of the lake. Is it probable that Colter's River was so named because someone else went there?

(F) The expedition of the famous escape was not in the spring, for his companion Potts rented horses from Lisa for the trip as late as July. *Missouri Historical Society Collections* III, 256. It was evidently a free trapping venture.

(G) James gives a slightly different version.

(H) This was John Colter. He died of jaundice. His administrator sued James, who settled, on a note for $140.00. James' *Three Years*, page 93n.

PART *V. The Country and its Inhabitants*

Chapter I

THE ROCKY MOUNTAINS

View of the western country—The Continental Divide—The name "Rocky Mountains"—Physical aspect of the Rocky mountains—Attractions of mountain life—The Teton range—The Grand Teton—The Absaroka range—The Wind River mountains—The Bighorn mountains—The Black Hills—Other Wyoming ranges—Front and rampart ranges—Pike's Peak—Mount of the Holy Cross—The Spanish peaks—The Uintah mountains—The Wasatch range—Montana and Idaho ranges—The Blue mountains—The Sierra Nevadas—The Cascade range.

Were it possible for an observer to be poised far above the surface of the earth, near the locality where the Teton Mountains lift their majestic summits above the clouds, and were he endowed with a power of vision that could pierce to the uttermost verge of the horizon, he would see beneath and around him a panorama which it is here desired to fix clearly in the mind of the reader. It is a panorama of mountains and plains, of lakes and rivers, of forest-crowned hills and treeless deserts, that stretches away to the distant alluvial plains of the Mississippi on the east and to the broad expanse of the Pacific on the west.

The first and most obvious feature of the landscape, thus spread out like a map before the eye, is its vast aggregation of mountains. Except far to the eastward, peaks innumerable arise on every hand. Some extend in well-defined ranges like broken ridges on the surface of the earth; others stand alone like solitary protuberances from its crust. The variety of form and aspect is infinite. Here a pointed spire of primeval rock stands motionless among the shifting clouds; there a flat mesa or table, crowned with grassy sward, terminates in bold escarpments overlooking the valleys and plains below. Lofty fields of perennial snow, grey patches of rock where vegetation never thrives, broad acres of evergreen forest, wide-spreading slopes of native pasture—all combine to produce an effect which is different in every detail, yet displays as a whole a distinct uniformity of character.

Amid the seemingly purposeless and accidental distribution of these mountains, the eye may trace an irregular line across the country from north to south, along which the ground is higher than in the immediate vicinity on either side. It is the line which separates the waters that flow into the Atlantic from those which flow into the Pacific—the *height of land* between the two oceans, or, as it is commonly called, the Continental Divide. It is everywhere a line of deep sentimental interest, for it is not easy to realize that, from points so close together, streams should flow to destinations so widely separated. Little as the country may vary in its aspect on one side from that on the other, the imagination sees a difference, and the early traveler always considered himself "across the Rocky Mountains" when he had passed this dividing line. "Here, hail Oregon!" reads an old itinerary of the Oregon Trail when South Pass is reached. It mattered little that the greater part of his journey still lay before him, with mountains to cross more difficult than any yet encountered; to him it seemed that his labors were nearly over when he first saw the first tiny rivulet flowing to the very country whither he was bound.

The Divide is an extremely sinuous line, whose position may be best understood by consulting the map. Its general direction in passing from the Canadian to the Mexican border is a little east of south, crossing the northern boundary in the northwestern corner of Montana and the southern in the southwestern corner of New Mexico. Its total length is about 2,000 miles in passing through a little less than sixteen degrees of latitude. On the eastern slope the Mississippi system drains about 1,450 miles of this distance, and the Rio Grande the remainder, while on the western slope the Columbia drains about 730 miles and the Colorado system 1,270 miles.

It might quite naturally be supposed that the geological evolution of a continent would have left this height of land upon the summits of the more prominent ranges; and this is the case along a portion of the Bitter Root range between Montana and Idaho, the Wind River Mountains in Wyoming and several of the lofty ranges in the state of Colorado. Generally, however, it lies on lower ground. In the vicinity of Yellowstone Lake, for example, it is but a little higher than the lake surface, and in central Wyoming it extends for many miles over a desert plateau of comparatively low altitudes where the streams sink into the ground and never reach the true drainage of either ocean.

As the Divide is not generally on the crests of high mountains, passes over it are rarely difficult. The only characteristic passes are Union and Two-gwo-tee at the head of Wind River, a few over the range between Montana and Idaho, and several within the limits of the state of Colorado. In other places they are generally low and practicable, while in some sections, as in central Wyoming and northern New Mexico, the Divide can be crossed almost anywhere without discovering its actual location. The most celebrated crossing, the well-known South Pass, which holds so prominent a place in the early history of the West, scarcely deserves the name of a mountain pass. It is barely 7,500 feet high, and is situated in an open valley of gentle slopes in either direction, with little to mark it as a crossing of the main chain of the Rocky Mountains. But as a gateway between the Atlantic slope and the Pacific, it became the most noted pass in the mountains.

It is a noteworthy fact that a natural geographic line of so great interest as the Continental Divide should have been so little utilized in establishing the boundaries of modern political divisions. It forms a state boundary in only one place and that is for about one hundred miles between Montana and Idaho. During the period of the fur trade, however, it was the eastern boundary of the disputed territory of Oregon all the way from the Spanish to the Russian possessions.

It was the Continental Divide and the ranges in the immediate vicinity which were known to the traders and trappers as the *Rocky Mountains*. That name has now, however, no particular habitat and can scarcely be found upon any modern large scale map, where every separate range has its own local name. The term has come to mean, in the popular mind, the mountains between the Mississippi and the Pacific, just as "the Alleghenies" applies in a general way to the mountains between that stream and the Atlantic. The name itself is not a happy choice, for it might apply to any range of mountains in the world. It came into general use only in the present century. Early writers refer to these mountains as the Missouri, Mexican, Shining, Snowy, and Stony Mountains, until finally from the French *Montagnes Rocheuses* came the modern name. The general system was also at one time referred to by geographers as the great Chippewyan system, and it would have been well if this name had survived, as the name Appalachian has in the East.

The physical aspect of the Rocky Mountains is altogether characteristic. The traveler who passes hurriedly through them on the modern railroad is liable to contrast unfavorably their grey color, severe outlines and barren slopes with the verdure-clad hillsides of the Eastern states. Not so he, who, like the ancient trapper, frequents their unaccustomed haunts, comes in close contact with their wide and picturesque details, and observes their varying moods with the changes of each day and of the seasons of the year. This more intimate acquaintance discloses a wealth of beauty which the uniform green of the Eastern mountains does not possess, and it is said by reputable painters of natural scenery, that no mountains in the world, not even the Alps, afford scenes so satisfactory to the art as those of the Rocky Mountains.

The general appearance of the mountains is of a greyish color where vegetation is scarce. This results not only from the exposed areas of rock *in situ*, but from the disintegrated rock which covers the mountains in many places with a sterile soil. The reddish color of iron oxide is widely present, particularly in the smaller hills of the Bad Lands, while yellow and other colors are of frequent occurrence.

The greater number of the northern mountains have extensive grassy slopes, whose broad areas, inclined upward as on a mighty easel, and spread out in rolling stretches with gentle depressions between them, look like beautiful carpets of green or brown, according to the season, softened by the mellow haze of distance and burnished by the crimson rays of morning and evening sun. At the higher elevations, from five to ten thousand feet, forests of pine, fir and similar trees abound extensively and cover the mountains with a mantle of dark green or black. At frequent intervals throughout these forests are open spaces, filled with luxuriant grass, forming parks of faultless beauty amid the somber solitudes of the surrounding woods. Everywhere in these wild and sublime situations occur the always pleasing groves of the quaking aspen, a grateful relief either from the gloomy view of extensive forests or the uniform prospect of grass-covered slopes. Taken altogether, these varied arrangements of nature present an artistic appearance that reminds one of the cultivated sections in the mountain regions of Europe where man has contributed so much to enhance the beauty of nature.

The scenery of these mountains, moreover, is subject to continual and interesting change. Scarcely have the bleak storms of winter subsided, and while yet deep fields of snow lie upon the upper slopes, the soft blossoms of spring shoot eagerly from the scanty soil and oppose the gentle warmth of their blooms to the chill snow which is slowly receding before them. So profuse and beautiful are the flowers in these lofty regions that one would doubt if any other season could rival the springtime in beauty. But in truth the somber season of autumn is the most attractive of all. The early frosts cover the mountain sides with the most varied and gorgeous colors. The quaking aspen, which before was simply a mass of green upon the mountain side, now stands forth with tenfold greater distinctness in its rich autumnal foliage. The low growth of underbrush, which scarcely attracts the eye at other seasons, takes on a livelier hue, transforming the whole mountain sides into fields of pleasing colors. Even upon these inaccessible and apparently barren slopes, where the eye had not before detected any sign of vegetable life, may now be seen spots of crimson and gold, as if nature had scattered here and there rich bouquets of flowers and bunches of fruit.

It is not upon the surface of the earth alone that are to be seen the grandeur and beauty of these regions. Even the wild mountain storms which are frequent at certain seasons have an attraction peculiarly their own, and all the more remarkable by the very contrasts which they produce. If, in passing, they display on a terrible scale the power of the elements, on the other hand, they leave behind them, in the sun-gilded clouds among the mountain tops, the most peaceful and pleasing pictures which nature anywhere affords.

Again, in the long rainless season, the atmosphere, like the painter's brush, tints the hills, in ever-varying intensity, with the purple and blue of distance. For this is pre-eminently a land of cloudless skies. The risings and settings of the sun are on a scale of sublime magnificance, while the moon rides among the mountain peaks with a serene splendor unknown in less favored climes.

It was among scenes like these that the mountaineer of early days imbibed that strong love of wilderness life which made him restive ever after under the restraints of civilization. That he looked at nature with an artist's eye, that he was often conscious of his surroundings, that he ever paid much attention to these things, is scarcely probable. In his practical, hard-working life he doubtless often wished that there were no mountains, for they caused him many a wide detour and many a weary climb. So little use did he find for them that he gave very few of them names, and the mountain nomenclature of the West is mostly the outgrowth of a later period. Nevertheless he loved his rugged country and unconsciously yielded to those subtle influences which he made no attempt to analyse, but which bound him to wild nature with a force that he was unable to resist. The hardship of his life, the ever present perils which environed him, the ties of kindred and home, none of these could extinguish the passion for mountain life when once he had tasted its pleasures.

Having taken this general view of the Rocky Mountains as a whole, it will be of interest to notice more in detail some of the more important local ranges. Directly below our assumed point of observation lies the most noted historic summit of the West, the culminating peak of the Teton range. In early times this range was more commonly known as the Three Tetons (*Les Trois Tetons*), because from certain points, particularly from the west, three peaks stood out prominently above all the others. The range covers a comparatively small area, perhaps sixty miles long by ten to twenty broad, the notable part of it scarcely exceeding twenty miles in length. The Tetons are a prominent exception among the mountains of the surrounding country in that they rise in bold relief directly from the valleys around them. In general the mountains are so hemmed in by successive terraces of foothills that their true altitude can not be grasped by the eye; but the Grand Teton rises in sheer relief above the surface of Jackson Lake almost a mile and a half. The altitude of this peak is nearly thirteen thousand eight hundred feet, being the highest mountain of the central region north of Colorado, unless it be Fremont Peak in the Wind River Mountains, which is of almost exactly the same altitude (1).

It is not alone its great altitude that has made the Grand Teton so famous in frontier history. The topography of the surrounding country is such that its summit is visible at a great distance in almost every direction, while its appearance from wherever seen is striking and unmistakable. From Union Pass, for example, sixty miles east, it looks like a slender spire of pure outline piercing the sky, in appearance so remarkable that the beholder is forced to question whether it can really pertain to any mountain. It was the great prominence of this peak and its ease of identification from other mountains that made it so useful to the early travelers. Far and wide it was the beacon of the trapper. Familiar with its different aspects as seen from different directions, he could tell his position at once when his eye fell upon it.

Could this ancient monument disclose the record of what transpired within its horizon, it would make known some of the most interesting events in the annals of the fur trade. For this was the paradise of the trapper. In every direction meandered the streams along which he was wont to pursue his trade, and near by were the valleys where the rival companies gathered in annual conclave to fight the bloodless battles of their business. There is scarcely an acre of open country in sight of it that has not been the scene of forgotten struggles with the implacable Blackfeet, while far and near, in unknown graves, lie many obscure wanderers of whose lonely fate no record survives.

The pass by which the Teton range is crossed connects the valley of Jackson Hole on the east with Pierre's Hole on the west. It is not a very high pass, but a singular one in its extremely narrow and ridgelike character. The approach from either direction is excessively steep and the traveler scarcely reaches the top from one side before he begins the descent on the other. The pass was extensively used in early fur trade days, and it is still the only practicable connection between the two valleys.

As our observer, from his aerial vantage ground, looks to the eastward beyond the Continental Divide, range upon range of lofty mountains greets his eye almost to the limit of the horizon. In the near foreground is a rugged chain of mountains, known in modern geography by the name Absaroka (2), which fills almost the entire space between the Yellowstone and its principal tributary, the Bighorn River. It is one of the most compact mountain masses upon the continent, with fully a hundred peaks towering above the timber line, and it comes as near to being an impassable barrier as can be found in the Rocky Mountains.

To the southwest the Absarokas merge into the Wind River Mountains (3), one of the most famous ranges of the West. Viewed from whatever point, these mountains present a sublime and imposing spectacle. From the valley of Green River, that favorite summer meeting-ground of the trappers and traders, they appear like a solid rampart to the eastward, with Fremont Peak (13,790 feet) the commanding summit; while from across the valley of Wind River, on the other side of the range, they bound the southwestern horizon with a wavy line so lofty as scarcely to seem to rest upon the earth. Immense snowfields lie upon these dizzy heights throughout the summer, and feed the innumerable lakes and streams which unite to form the rivers on either side.

This mighty barrier lay directly in the route of travel between the valleys of the Yellowstone and Bighorn rivers on the northeast and those of Green River, Salt Lake and Snake River on the southwest and west. As a consequence, travelers had to bend out of their course and cross the mountains by the head of Wind River to the north, or in the other direction by South Pass at the head of the Sweetwater.

The Wind River Mountains are celebrated in fur trade history and native lore. The Indians clothed them with superstitious legends, as they always do any locality whose secret places they are unable to explore, while the scarcely less ignorant trapper felt a wholesome awe of their weird and gloomy retreats.

Beyond the valley of the Bighorn River, which lies at the eastern base of the Absarokas, rises the extensive range of the Bighorn Mountains (4). It is a typical example of detached mountain masses in the Far West. Extending north and south for one hundred and fifty miles between the Bighorn and Powder Rivers, it forms a compact barrier through which there are but few practicable passes. The range abounds in fine scenery and is the home of a great number of lakes of Alpine beauty. Several of the peaks attain great altitude, the highest, Cloud Peak, being 13,300 feet high. This was likewise a range with which the trapper always had to reckon, for it lay directly in his route from the trapping grounds of the Bighorn to those of Powder River.

Far to the eastward of the Bighorn Mountains, across a dreary waste of reddish hills and broken, uninviting country, the observer may descry the dark and shaggy eminences of the Black Hills, the extreme eastern outlier of the Rocky Mountains. The dense forests of pine and stunted, wind-torn cedars gave to these hills, when seen from a distance, the dark appearance from which is derived their name. Like most of the other early names of the Northwest, this one was used by the French. Long before any American had visited these parts, *Les Cotes Noires* were well known to the Creole trader and voyageur. The name is now restricted to the mass of mountains enclosed by the two forks of the Cheyenne River, in the modern states of Wyoming and South Dakota, but it had a far broader application in the early times.

The Black Hills, though not to be compared as mountains with those farther west, were nevertheless a notable and important range. Harney Peak, the commanding summit, is

7,368 feet high. The scenery of the hills is, in many places, grand and sublime, and certain localities, like that of Sylvan Lake and the Spearfish cañon, bear high comparison with the finest scenery on the continent. The abundance and variety of floral growth add an element of beauty which is one of the chief attractions.

These mountains were famous in Indian lore, and many were the legends concerning their mysterious labyrinths, and the dangers and terrors concealed within them. No other mountains in the entire West surpassed them in this regard. At the same time they were a great resource to the surrounding tribes, who made annual excursions thither in quest of wood for the various uses of their manner of life.

To the trapper, the Black Hills were the best known, as they were the nearest, mountains that he was wont to frequent. They were rich in the commercial products which were the objects of his pursuit, and his operations embraced the entire region.

Extending southwesterly from the Black Hills of Dakota, southerly from the Bighorn range, and southeasterly from the Wind River Mountains, are many detached spurs and isolated peaks which merge together in the region along the Upper North Platte and the Laramie Rivers, and extend thence southerly to the high mountains of Colorado. These ranges are now known under a variety of local names, but in the fur trade period they were collectively a part of the Black Hills. Probably the most noted summit in those scattered groups is Laramie Peak, nearly fifty miles west of old Fort Laramie, and one of the best known landmarks of this region.

The territory embraced within the modern political divisions of Colorado and Northern New Mexico is a typical mountain region. It is here that the Rocky Mountains appear in all their grandeur—massive, lofty and sublime. The principal peaks are nearly all over 14,000 feet high. In marked contrast with other portions of the West, where the approach to the main ranges is through a long succession of foothills, extending perhaps hundreds of miles, the mountains of central Colorado rise at once in full magnitude directly from the prairies. This is notably true of the Front and Rampart ranges, which face the plains to the north and south of Denver. As seen from far out on the prairies they appear like a mighty wall of corrugated outline, projected against the western sky, while from the mountains themselves the far-stretching savannas resemble the unbroken vista of the ocean.

Two prominent peaks stand out from these ranges distinctively visible for a hundred miles to the eastward. They are Long's Peak in the Front range, and Pike's Peak at the extremity of the Rampart range. The former peak was named in 1820 for Major Stephen H. Long, whose exploring party discovered it. It is 14,271 feet high. Pike's Peak is now the best known summit of the Rocky Mountains, and holds a prominence with the traveling public which the Grand Teton formerly held with the trappers and traders. Pike's Peak, though previously known to the Spaniards, was first seen by Americans, so far as we positively know, in 1806, when it was visited, though not ascended, by Lieutenant Z. M. Pike, of the United States Army, whose name, after many vicissitudes and changes, it now bears. The Grand Teton was not discovered until a year later, when it was probably seen by John Colter. Pike's Peak is 14,147 feet high, or 347 feet higher than the Teton summit. Like the latter, it rises in sheer relief a mile and a half above the valley below. The summits of these two mountains are strikingly different, one being of rounded outline, and comparatively easy of access; the other a rocky pinnacle, which it is almost impossible to climb.

In southern Colorado the Sangre de Cristo and Culebra ranges are similarly situated to the Front and Rampart ranges farther north, although they do not rise so directly from the eastern plains. At the southern extremity of the Sangre de Cristo range is Blanca Peak (14,464 feet), dominating the valley of the Upper Rio Grande, and the highest mountain in Colorado. A little to the eastward of the Culebra range rise the Spanish Peaks (12,720 feet), two prominent outlying summits which were noted landmarks during the periods of the Santa Fe trade and subsequent exploration.

Back of the easternmost line of the Colorado Mountains a continuous succession of ranges extends to the western boundry of the state, so diversified in detail that it would be impossible in the space here available to describe them. In the central portion of the state they are of lofty and massive proportions, extending in every possible direction, and controlling the topography of the country. Farther west their appearance changes materially, assuming more the character of bad lands, though on a stupenduous scale, and they are known, from their peculiar forms, as mesas, book cliffs, buttes, and the like (5).

The mountain passes of Colorado are the most noted in the Rocky Mountains, now that South Pass has lost its former prominence. The great development of this region, owing to the discovery of valuable mineral deposits, has given to the question of getting over the high ranges, an importance which it did not possess during the fur trade era. Many new passes, never crossed by the trapper, have been found by the engineer, and these, as well as the old ones, are among the chief modern attractions in this home of mountain scenery.

The mountainous sections of Colorado were not frequented by the trapper to the same extent as were the regions farther north. Possibly the very difficulty of traversing the country made it less desirable to operate in. It was, of course, well known, and its streams were worked for beaver, but it did not compare in this respect with the region about the sources of the Missouri, Columbia, and Green Rivers.

Passing from the broken and rugged terrain of Colorado into the northeastern corner of Utah, a remarkably compact and imposing chain of mountains is encountered, to which the name of Uintah has been given. It extends almost due east and west for about a hundred miles, and forms such a solid mass that very few practical crossings have been discovered in modern times. The culminating summit of the range is Gilbert Peak, 13,687 feet high. These mountains lie directly athwart the course of Green River, which is forced to make a detour of about sixty miles to the eastward in order to get by them. The country round about was famous trapping territory, as may be inferred from the fact that nearly all of its many streams bear names that were given by the trapper.

Extending north and south through the state of Utah, and for a long distance forming the divide between the valleys of Green River and Great Salt Lake, is a prominent chain of mountains known by the name of Wasatch. Nearly east of the southern extremity of Great Salt Lake it forms a junction with the Uintah Mountains. A little farther north it is broken by a deep rift, through which a railroad now finds its way. Still farther north it rises again in a bold mass of mountains which occupies the interior of the horseshoe formed by the course of Bear River.

The entire region to the northward between the valleys of Green River on the east and Bear and Snake Rivers on the west is filled with mountain ranges, known under different names, but forming part of a general system which extends from the Wasatch and Uintah Mountains on the south to the Teton and Wind River ranges on the north. These mountains abound in fine streams, which made them a favorite resort of the trapper. The great highway across them in the early days was that now followed by the Oregon Short Line Railroad.

Extending from the region of the Yellowstone National Park along what is now the boundary line between Montana and Idaho is a long and almost continuous range of mountains which makes a broad sweep from the west to the north, and finally leaves the territory of the United States in northwestern Washington. The southern portion of this range, to about latitude forty-six degrees, is still known on some maps by the name of Rocky Mountains. North of this point it bears the name Bitter Root as far as it forms the state boundary. It then takes the name Coeur d' Alêne, and extends in a northwest direction across the narrow strip of Northern Idaho and the northeast corner of Washington into the British possessions. The southern portion of this range, as above described, lies on the Continental Divide, but this line leaves it just north of latitude forty-six, swings eastward to the near vicinity of Helena, Montana, and then extends north to the boundary.

The whole of Western Montana is very mountainous, and the name of the state was well chosen. The mountains extend far eastward to the center of the state in smaller detached ranges, such as the Judith, Belt, Little Rocky, and Bear Paw Mountains. In that section immediately north of the National Park, they assume a massive and lofty character, which denotes their close connection with the Absaroka range already described.

The entire country among these mountains was a fruitful one to the trapper, and was frequented as much as any in the West. The ranges had numerous and easy passes, and were not, except in the few places already noted, formidable obstacles to travel. Several of the most important Indian tribes made their home in the country round about. The region was therefore one of great activity in the days of the fur trade, although it was mainly exploited by British companies in that portion which lay on the Pacific slope.

West of the Bitter Root Mountains in central Idaho the the country is excessively broken by ranges of mountains that separate the eastern tributaries of Snake River. The Salmon River and Clearwater Mountains are the most important. They extend across the state westwardly to and beyond Snake River, which has cut its way through them in one of the most most imposing cañons in the world. To the west of Snake River these mountains continue into Oregon, where the range extends first southwest and then west well toward the center of the state. They are here known as the Blue Mountains, and are particularly noted in fur trade history as the difficult barrier that lay between the Columbia River and the upper course of the Snake. The topography of the country was such that all travel between these rivers, the Snake and the Columbia, was compelled to traverse this range. The same necessity exists today and the railroad now follows essentially what was once the Oregon Trail.

Southwardly from the Salmon River and Blue Mountains, through southern Idaho and Oregon, Western Utah and Eastern Nevada, even to the borders of California and Arizona, was a region which, though not mountainous in the sense of those just described, contained many broken and detached ranges, isolated peaks and buttes, and singular irregularities of ground which fall under none of the usual designations.

These eminences are not generally of great altitude, but owing to the surrounding topography are often visible at immense distances and therefore serve as important landmarks. The Three Buttes of the Snake River plain are conspicuous examples.

There remains to be considered that extensive mountain system which lies parallel to the Pacific Coast and forms the final barrier between the Mississippi Valley and those of California and Oregon. In its southern portion it is known as the Sierra Nevada, and farther north as the Cascade range.

The Sierra Nevada is probably the most extensive and massive array of mountains in the United States, if not in North America. Its lofty peaks, its successive ranges, which give great depth to the system, its never-melting snow fields and its deep and gloomy cañons have made it a most formidable barrier to travel, which even at this day is crossed in but few places. The principal mass of these mountains extends upwards of two hundred miles parallel to the San Joaquin Valley of California. In this portion of its course are found its loftiest peaks, reaching to an altitude of nearly 15,000 feet. In the western foothills is the marvelous cañon of Yosemite, and nearby a grove of those gigantic redwood trees which are one of the wonders of nature.

The Sierra Nevadas break down somewhat in northern California, and merge for a short distance with the Coast range, which lies close to the ocean. Klamath and Pitt Rivers here find their way through the range from the eastern side to the Pacific. North of Klamath the name Cascade begins, and continues to the British boundary. The principal gap through the Cascades is where the Columbia River makes its way to the ocean, although there are other practicable openings both north and south.

The Sierra Nevada and the Cascade ranges abound in noble peaks, including some of the loftiest in the country. Owing to their proximity to the coast, and the low altitude of the valleys to the westward, their elevation is more apparent than in other sections of the mountains. The three most notable peaks are situated respectively at the southern, central, and northern portions of the range. Mt. Whitney, in

Southern California, is the highest peak in the United States, with an elevation of 14,898 feet. In the space between the Sierra Nevada and Cascade ranges is Mt. Shasta, 14,350 feet, one of the best known mountains in the West. Mt. Ranier, north of the Columbia River in Washington, has an altitude of 14,444 feet, and is plainly visible from sea level on Puget Sound. It is one of the few mountains in the world which stands out in full relief, and it affords perhaps the most perfect example of a single mountain peak to be met with in nature.

The mountain ranges last considered were not of great importance in the American fur trade, because in only three or four instances did the operations of the American companies reach so far. The streams of the Cascade range, however, were thoroughly exploited by the Hudson Bay Company, and were as rich a field as the West afforded. The expeditions of the Astorians and of Nathaniel J. Wyeth to the Columbia, and of J. S. Smith and I. [J.] R. Walker to California, were the only instances in which Americans ever seriously attempted to develop the fur trade of these mountains.

AUTHOR'S NOTES

(1) The Grand Teton is one of the most difficult mountains to climb of which there is any knowledge. To the present time (1901) it has been ascended by white men only twice; by Messrs. N. P. Langford and James Stevenson in 1872, and by Messrs. William Owen, Frank S. Spalding, John Shive, and Frank Peterson in 1898.

(2) This name as here applied is of recent date and is intended to commemorate the tribe of Indians (Absaroka, or Crows) who dwelt in the valley of the Bighorn river to the eastward of these mountains.

(3) This name more probably arose from the prevalence of southwest winds on the mountains than from any characteristic of the valley itself, as the name might imply. Union Pass, near the head of Wind river, is one of the windiest places in the world, and the trees and other vegetation are so bent over by the constant blast that in many instances they stand more nearly horizontal than vertical.

(4) This name is of course derived from the animal of the same name, *Ovis Montana*, which formerly abounded in this region, and is still occasionally seen there.

(5) Among the loftier peaks of central Colorado may be mentioned the Mount of the Holy Cross, a name which dates from the

fur trade period. Its modern application, however, is not the same as it was then. It now belongs to a mountain some fifteen miles northwest of Leadville, Colorado—a noble peak 14,176 feet high—on the face of which there is a cross formed by the perpetual snows which gather in longitudinal and transverse chasms on the mountain side.

As noted by Farnham, 1839, the name applied to a conical hill about eight hundred feet above the general level. The cross was formed by "two transverse seams of what appeared to be crystallized quartz." The upper end of the cross was "about 100 feet below the summit." "The upright was about 60 feet in length; the cross seam about 20 feet, thrown across the upright near its top." "The trappers have reverently named this peak the Mountain of the Holy Cross."

Singularly enough this mountain is not far distant from the modern Holy Cross Mountain. As near as can be determined from the imperfect description it was just north of the pass over the Continental Divide near Breckenridge, Colorado.

Chapter II

VALLEYS AND PLAINS

The typical mountain valley—Valleys along the Three Forks—
The Gallatin Valley—Valley of the Three Forks—Great Bend
of the Yellowstone—Gardner's Hole—Jackson Hole—Jackson's
Little Hole—Pierre's Hole—Upper Green River valley—
Brown's Hole—Odgen's Hole—Cache Valley—The Grande
Ronde—Old and New Parks and Bayou Salade—San Luis
Valley—The Plains—Change in the country westward from the
Missouri—The Bad Lands—The "Great American Desert"—
Prairie roads—Storms of the prairies—Prairie fires—The
mirage—The plains not a trapping country.

The "holes" of the mountains, as they were called by the
trappers, were of paramount importance in the business of the
fur trade, as indeed they have been in all enterprises which
man has carried on among the mountainous regions of the
earth. Nothing in nature is more beautiful than a typical
valley in the Rocky Mountains. Around it tower the eternal
hills, like faithful sentinels, to guard and protect it. Perennial
streams of crystal water, fresh from the pure snows on the
mountain sides, flow down from every direction into the
plains below. Converging lines of foliage mark the courses of
these streams as they mingle one with another, until all are
united in a broad ribbon of verdure, which meanders across
the valley and finally leaves it through some opening in the
surrounding hills. Scattered here and there are groves of the
quaking aspen, but generally the lowlands are covered with
nutritious grasses, which enjoy here a more healthy and luxuriant growth than in the arid tracts below the mountains.
The flowers of spring likewise bloom in greater profusion and
with more exquisite colors than where nature has deprived
them of moisture which they require.

These mountain valleys must be distinguished on the one

hand from extensive basins, like that of the Bighorn River,
which comprise a great variety of topography, and on the
other, from those contracted openings through the mountains
which fall more properly under the designation of cañons.
The open valleys here considered were in the nature of parks,
grateful oases in the waste of rugged country, where the wild
game loved to gather and the mountaineer found rest from his
prodigious labors. In these charming retreats he was wont to
pitch his camp, where there were water and grass for his stock,
wood for his fire, shelter from the tempest, and convenience
to the objects of his pursuit. What he did not find here,
unfortunately, was protection from savage foes, who, like
their pale face brethren, loved the valleys and made them
their home.

There were hundreds of these valleys in the Rocky Mountains, but it will here be possible to refer only to a few of the
more important. Each of the three forks of the Missouri had
its parks or basins. The beautiful valley of upper Red Rock
Creek, the source of Jefferson Fork, known in recent years as
Centennial Valley, was a much frequented spot in early times.
Near the sources of the Madison there were also numerous
parks, which are still without distinctive names; but which
were familiar resorts to the hunters and trappers. All of these
valleys were connected by easy passes over the Continental
Divide with the equally important basin of Henry Lake, one
of the ultimate sources of the Columbia.

Along the lower course of the Gallatin and its principal
tributary, the East fork, is one of the most extensive and
beautiful mountain valleys in the West. It is the vacant bed
of an ancient lake, surrounded by a cordon of mountains which
are flecked here and there with patches of snow and are
clothed in the varying hues of the atmosphere, dependent
upon their distance from the beholder. The valley is upwards
of thirty miles long, with a remarkably even topography and
a beautiful supply of water from the Gallatin and its various
tributaries. It was the scene of great activity during the entire
period of the fur trade and yielded untold wealth to the coffers
of the traders.

The immediate valley where the Three Forks unite to

form the Missouri is of very limited area, but was of great importance in the early days. A glance at the map will show its stragetic and commercial relation to the surrounding country. A short distance to the eastward lay the valley of the Yellowstone, while to the south, by easy passes over the Divide, access was had to the Snake River Valley and the region beyond. North and west lay an extensive country prolific in the fruits of the chase. The Three Forks themselves and their numerous tributaries were the best trapping ground on the continent. All of these considerations appealed strongly to the early traders, and very soon after the return of Lewis and Clark, in 1806, attempts were made to found a trading post there. These efforts, though more than once repeated, always failed on account of the hostility of the Blackfeet Indians; and a sort of fatality has hung over the spot even to the present day. In recent years, the government went to the upper end of the East Gallatin valley to found a military post, where has also arisen the principal town in this part of the country. The ground around the Three Forks has been staked out into streets and blocks of a city yet to be, but not a house stands upon the spot. It is a singular fact, and is accounted for by some, on the ground that the valley was the immemorial fighting ground of hostile tribes, while the soil was sterile on account of the alkali washed down from the higher sections. Be this as it may, it seems as if nature had ordained that this meeting place of the sources of the world's longest river should remain unchanged by the hand of man.

The Great Bend of the Yellowstone, where Livingston, Montana, now stands, was a picturesque spot hemmed in by lofty hills and a convenient point to the trappers, who often passed their winters there. In ascending the Yellowstone from the Great Bend to its source, a series of cañons is passed between which the valley spreads out into open parks, where the bottom lands and hillsides are carpeted, like the green hills of France, with meadows so uniform and lawn-like as scarcely to seem the product of unaided nature.

In an open valley of most attractive surroundings on one of the upper tributaries of the Yellowstone, a free trapper, Johnson Gardner, plied his trade as far back as 1830, and gave

the river and valley his name. "Gardner's Hole" was the uncouth name of this beautiful spot which every tourist now
sees as he enters the Yellowstone National Park.

South of this government reservation lies one of the most
celebrated of all the mountain valleys, still known by the
name first given it, Jackson Hole (1). The name embraces the
whole valley along the eastern base of the Tetons from the
north shore of Jackson Lake to the mouth of the Little Grosventre River, a distance of upward of forty miles.

A most striking feature of this wonderful valley is its
extremely flat topography, surrounded as it is by some of the
most rugged mountains on the continent. It beauty is greatly
enhanced by the presence of several lakes which lie immediately at the base of the Teton range, and in whose placid
surfaces these mountains stand reflected as from the most
perfect mirror. The landscape thus formed has been the despair
of painters of natural scenery since the valley became frequented by students of nature. Neither pen nor pencil, nor
the modern perfection of the photographic art can reproduce
its marvelous beauty.

Whatever the trapper may have thought of the scenic
attraction of this valley, he certainly loved the spot, and it
was always one of the favorite haunts. It was a most convenient base of operations. From north to south through it
flowed the Snake River, with its sources mainly in the Yellowstone Park farther to the north. Three large tributaries joined
the main stream in this vicinity and all were full of beaver
when the trapper first visited them. Jackson Hole was thus
a point from which small trapping parties could explore the
many branches of these larger streams and to which they
could return with the fruits of their labors. It was probably
also safer from Indian incursions than were other valleys less
difficult of access. There was no easy way to get into it, and
from most directions it was then, and is still, exceedingly
difficult to enter at all.

Another valley which bore the name of Jackson was Jackson's Little Hole. It was situated at the source of Hoback
River just across the Divide from Green River, and was the

first camping place after leaving Green River for Jackson or Pierre's Hole.

From Jackson Hole a trail led across Teton Pass to the scarcely less celebrated locality of Pierre's Hole (2). The Teton or Pierre River drains the western slope of the Teton Mountains. It rises in Teton Pass, and flows slightly west of north for about thirty miles, when it turns due west and flows into Henry Fork of Snake River. It was that portion of the valley that lay along the northerly course of the stream to which the name Pierre's Hole applied. The open valley is about twenty-five miles long, and five to fifteen broad. On the right hand, looking down stream, rises the mighty wall of the Teton range, while on the left is the much less lofty range of the Snake River Mountains. Through the center of the valley wound the inevitable line of trees which showed where the waters from the mountains were flowing, and many a tributary could be discovered coming in from the highlands on either side. The valley is a most attractive one, and is now being rapidly filled up with industrious settlers.

Pierre's Hole was a particularly favorite resort of the trader. Several of the annual rendezvous were held here, and there are still in existence papers of the Rocky Mountain Fur Company which bear the date, "Pierre's Hole, under the Three Teton Mountains." The events of the year 1832, which are narrated in detail elsewhere, would alone make the valley famous.

About seventy miles southeast of Jackson's Hole was an amphitheatre-shaped basin situated where Green River emerges from the Wind River Mountains in a westerly direction and turns due south on its long journey to the Gulf of California. The valley was not so closely hemmed in by mountains as were those just described, but it was even more important to the fur trade. It was a favorite rendezvous for many years, and witnessed some of the most notable gatherings of Indians and traders that ever took place in the mountains.

Two hundred miles by the river channel below the locality just described, Green River flows for sixty miles in a direction nearly due east along the northern base of the Uintah range. Some twenty-five miles of this distance is through an open valley from five to six miles wide, hemmed in by the mountains in the most effectual manner. The river enters and leaves it through dismal, deep, and impassable cañons, and take it all in all, it is little else than a solitary mountain prison, surrounded with the grandest scenes of nature, but cut off entirely from the outside world. This was the famous Brown's Hole (3) of the trappers known in modern geography by the more pleasing name of Brown Park. In the later years of the fur trade the valley was much frequented by the trappers, who even maintained at one time an inferior trading post there.

Near the northeastern shore of the Great Salt Lake there was a deep recess in the range of lofty mountains to the east, known in early times as Ogden's Hole, where now the city of Ogden, Utah, stands. It was a sheltered cove of striking form and beauty, and no doubt was frequented by the retainers of that noted trader whose name it now bears (4).

The most important valley near Great Salt Lake, however, was that traversed by Bear River in Northern Utah and Southern Idaho. It was an extensive valley, bounded on the east by a noble range of mountains, and on the west by smaller hills, where all conditions were to be found that made a desirable stamping ground for the trapper. Today it is the home of a busy population, with ten or more thriving villages all in sight at once. It is still known by its original name of Cache Valley, which arose from some unrecorded circumstance possibly from the cache of beaver furs belonging to Peter Skene Ogden which shadowy tradition says was "lifted" by General Ashley, to the latter's great financial advancement (5).

A little valley which deserves a passing notice lies in the eastern flank of the Blue Mountains in Oregon, directly on the line of the old Oregon Trail. It was named by the French, from its form, Grande Ronde, and was a well-known camping and resting place on the Trail.

The principal open valleys in the Colorado mountains are those now known as the North, Middle and South Parks, but which the trappers knew as the New and Old Parks and the Bayou Salade (6). In them the North Platte, Grand and South Platte Rivers respectively find their sources. They are typical mountain valleys, although considerably larger than those just described. They were great resorts for the trappers, and the Bayou Salade in particular was a favorite retreat for both the white man and the Indian.

On the upper course of the Rio Grande there were two notable valleys, known by the names of Taos and San Luis. Taos was the northernmost of the Spanish settlements in New Mexico and was a famous place in the annals of the fur trade. The San Luis Valley, as an opening among rugged mountains, is one of the most striking in the entire West. Surrounded by lofty peaks, among which is the dominating summit of Sierra Blanca in the Sangre de Cristo range, it is itself as smooth and even as the flattest prairie—so uniform in surface that the railroads which radiate from Alamosa in the center of the valley extend in almost straight lines for a distance of from twenty-five to fifty miles. The trappers who plied their calling in these valleys and the country to the westward were mostly connected with the Santa Fe Trade and brought their furs either to Santa Fe or Taos for sale or shipment to the United States.

Such are a few typical mountain valleys among the hundreds that were known to the trapper. His claim upon them has long been transferred to a more civilized posterity, who have utilized the stream where he once trapped for beaver to extract from the soil a less precarious livelihood than they ever yielded to him. Their beauty and grandeur remain and their utility has been increased, but the romance of their early occupation by white men has permanently passed away.

What was included in the term "plains," as used in frontier history, it would be difficult to say. "Across the plains" generally meant from the Missouri River to one's destination, whether across the prairies of Kansas, the staked plains of Texas, the sand hills of Nebraska, the Bad Lands of Dakota, the sage brush tracts scattered everywhere throughout the West, the lava wastes of Idaho, or the alkali deserts of Utah, Nevada, and California. The term "prairies," in popular use, referred more specifically to the region between the Missouri River and the foothills of the mountains, those broad and treeless areas, often rolling and diversified, yet as often flat as the level sea, lying in part within the region of rains and luxuriant vegetation, and in part in the arid zone beyond.

To convey an idea of the external aspect of the country which the trader and trapper passed over and lived in while absent from the frontiers, it will be expedient to follow them in a journey from the Missouri to the heart of the mountains and note these features which especially appealed to them in the line of their particular business.

For one hundred and fifty miles out from Independence, or say to the 98th meridian, the traveler was in a country agriculturally rich. Here nature reveled in exuberant growth, for there was a bountiful soil, abundant rain, and dew in the morning, as in the most favored localities in the East. All descriptions of the prairies in the early days abound in enthusiastic praise of this delightful region, and nearly all foresaw in it the home of populous communities yet to be. With little qualification this was true of the country north and south, within these limits of longitude, to the boundaries of the United States. Although it lay mostly out of the timber belt, the soil was exceedingly fertile, and whatever man might intelligently cultivate was bound to flourish there.

But as the traveler held on his way another one hundred and fifty miles, or say to the 101th meridian, a notable change came over the face of the country. The rolling hills sank into the even plains, as uniform and monotonous as the naked ocean. Look in whatever direction he might, no undulation of the ground restricted the limit of vision, and it needed only a passing sail to make the illusion complete. He observed that the soil was less deep and rich, the rains evidently much less frequent, the water very scarce except in the larger streams, the trees along the river less abundant, and vegetation generally less luxuriant, if not actually dwarfed and scanty. Before the western limit of this belt was reached there began to appear infallible signs which denoted proximity to the desert. Among them were the sage brush, the cactus, and the prairie dog, those singular products of the vegetable and animal worlds which seem to flourish only where nature is parched and dry. The soil also began to show a white efflorescence denoting the presence of the dreaded alkali, which from here on would render many of the streams and pools unfit for drink and would fill the air along the road with suffocating dust.

The third belt of the three degrees of longitude, extending to the 104th meridian, carried the traveler into the worst features of the plains country. He found himself in the hilly region which betokened proximity to the mountains, whose glistening crests he could already discern in the distance. Rock began to appear in the bluffs along the streams. In some localities, as in the valley of the North Platte, the elements have carved these rocks into remarkable shapes to which the early traveler gave such names as Court House, Chimney, and the like. Generally, however, the exposed rock has been mellowed down by the action of time into gentler slopes where vegetation finds a precarious foothold.

A curious and remarkable region in this zone is that comprising the sand hills of Nebraska. These rounded hills, composed of sand with a thin covering of turf, are often of considerable height, and are so like one another that it is impossible to distinguish between them. Landmarks are wanting, and once off the trail one is almost certain to get confused as to his bearings. Not even the dense and trackless forest is so easy a place to get lost in. These hills, though useless for agriculture, afforded fair grazing for the buffalo.

Farther north in Dakota between the Black Hills and the Missouri is a tract of country where nature seems to have outdone herself to render her aspect hideous and forbidding. The whole country is cut up by gullies, or *coulées*, while the ancient surface of the ground is indicated here and there by harder material, which has resisted the action of time and stands aloft above the general level. The elements have carved these hills into the most varied and fantastic shapes, sometimes like the domes and towers of a city, and again unlike anything which art or nature has elsewhere produced. In some of the hills or bluffs there is a distinct stratification, the appearance of which was confused by the paths of the mountain sheep in former times, as it is by domestic sheep now. The soil has an oily, slippery consistency when wet which makes it impossible at such times to clamber up the steep slopes.

On these barren, ashy hills no vegetation thrives, or in such lonesome, sickly forms as are found only where life pines and languishes from the poverty of nature. Little animal life is seen except the snake and the lizard, unless indeed from some lofty pinnacle the stately bighorn surveys in solitary independence the scene of desolation around him.

These are the Bad Lands, the *Mauvaises Terres* of the French, and present the hopeless side of the Western country, a true picture of the Great American Desert. In one form or another the Bad Lands are found over a vast extent of country. The whole region between the Black Hills and the Bighorn Mountains, extending north to the Missouri, contains tracts of this character. The valley of the Bighorn is full of bad lands. South of the Sweetwater River in Wyoming are extensive areas which differ essentially from the Dakota bad lands, but surpass them, if possible, in general worthlessness. Here may be seen those soda lakes where the alkali of the plains exhibits itself in a concentrated form, which has annihilated every form of life within it. In this strange and uninviting region are extensive fossil remains, which indicate that in past geological time, conditions more favorable to life prevailed here. The Pacific side of the mountains even outdoes the Atlantic slope in its desert appearance. The valley of Green River from its source to its mouth abounds in bad lands of one form or another. In Colorado and Utah the broken character of the country is on a stupenduous scale, cut up with impassable cañons and walled in in every direction by lofty and almost vertical cliffs. The vast lava plains of Snake River with their suffocating dust, the barren deserts of Utah and Nevada with their salt fields and waterless stream beds, and the lifeless wastes of southern California are a part of this scene of widespread desolation. To the south the picture is equally uninviting. It would be difficult to say what proportion of the immense region of New Mexico and Arizona is of this worthless character, but it is large enough. To the east of the mountains the Cimarron Desert, so often fatal to human life from its lack of water, is a fair example of the evil conditions which geologic evolution has imposed upon this country.

As already observed, these desolate tracts present the

hopeless side of the Western country and constitute in the aggregate the Great American Desert. The early geographers were not wrong in placing such a desert on their maps, much as they have been ridiculed for doing so. The error lay rather in its location and in their failure to note the many important exceptions. While it was then true, and will so remain until geologic and climatic changes shall have worked a revolution in this country, that west of the 103rd meridian and east of the Sierra Nevadas there is not a point from which one can not find within a radius of a hundred miles true desert conditions; still the country was not all of this character. There were the thousand valleys through which coursed perennial streams destined to make them rich with cultivated fields, and there were the mountains with their hidden treasures of wealth; while even the desert tracts yielded a scanty pasturage which in the aggregate sustained countless multitudes of grazing animals. These were very important exceptions to the rule of the desert, and their existence has confounded nearly all the early predictions concerning the future of this country.

Having considered the general character of the country which the traveler had to pass through in crossing the "plains," it remains to notice some of their more striking peculiarities which had a practical bearing upon these overland journeys and upon the business for which they were undertaken. Except in the spring of the year the roads over the prairies were excellent, the fords practicable, and traveling a comparatively easy matter. Not so in the season of rains, when the roads were converted into quagmires, the streams were unfordable, and camping wretchedly uncomfortable. In general the outgoing expeditions of spring encountered great difficulties from high water both on the prairies and in the mountains; but on their return in the autumn these obstacles had mostly disappeared. The drawbacks of spring travel were in some degree compensated by the balmy and invigorating air of that season, while the better conditions that prevailed later in the season lost some of their advantage from the parched and dusty state of the country, which was hard both upon man and beast.

The storms of the prairies, whether in summer or winter,

were always characterized by great severity. The cyclonic character of the summer storms has become well known since the country has settled up. They were the same in the early days, and many are the records of demolished camps, stampeded herds, drenched and damaged cargoes, when these terrific tempests have descended upon the solitary caravans of the plains. In winter the prairie blizzard was then, and is now, death to the wayfarer who is caught in it away from shelter. Consequently travelers rarely ventured across the plains in winter, and death has overtaken more than one rash adventurer who has wandered too far from a safe retreat.

A common peril on the prairies after the spring rains had ceased and the grass had become dry was the prairie fire. How these could have been so frequent (7) as they seem to have been is a mystery. When the conditions were ripe for one of those fires—that is, when the growth of grass had been abundant, but had become dry, and when a brisk, dry wind was blowing, the phenomenon was one of marvelous beauty, if viewed from a point of safety, but of peril and terror when the beholder stood in its way. The speed of the fire over the prairies depended of course largely upon the wind and was therefore a very variable quantity; but that at times it exceeded that of the fleetest horse there is abundant evidence. Likewise the intensity of the fire varied greatly. When driven by a strong wind over areas of tall dry grass it was a veritable traveling furnace, and no matter how great its speed nor how quickly past, it was death to whatever it touched. In other instances, with a mild wind and short grass, the line of flame could anywhere be crossed with impunity. The spectacle of a strong prairie fire at night was one of the most magnificent that nature affords. The long sweeping line of fire stretching from one part of the horizon to the other, the lambent flames soaring high into the air, the flitting forms of animals driven suddenly from cover, and the reflection of the brilliant light in the clouds, composed a scene of truly terrible sublimity.

The usual method of avoiding the danger of these fires was to start one in the immediate vicinity of the person or company in peril. This fire, at first small and harmless, would soon burn over an area large enough to form a safe asylum, and when the sweeping cohorts of flame came bearing down upon the apparently doomed company, the mighty line would part as if by pre-arrangement and pass harmlessly by on either side.

Among the most singular, and at times the most distressing, phenomena of the plains were the mirages. Although these were seen in nearly all parts of the West, it was in the southern plains that they were most prominent. To see them to the best advantage requires favorable conditions both physical and mental. Not alone must the plain, the atmosphere, and the sun be right, but the effect will be greatly heightened if the mental state of the beholder has been suitably prepared for the phenomenon. To this end, suppose him to be journeying over one of those barren, even tracts which so extensively abound to the south of the Arkansas, and particularly in the Cimarron Desert. The sun is almost unendurable in its intensity; the ground is parched and dry; the grass withered and sparse; no tree or shrub relieves the landscape; no sign of water is visible anywhere; while the oppressive heat and the cravings of thirst tax his endurance to the utmost. In the midst of his suffering comes a promise of relief. Several miles ahead of him in a gentle depression he distinctly sees a body of water; it may be a river, more probably a lake. Its surface gleams in the sun and here and there it is roughened by passing breezes. The shore line is distinct and is bordered with objects that look like trees. The sight inspires new life; the spirits rise; and the pace of the traveler is quickened with fresh energy. It is wasted effort on the part of more experienced companions to urge caution in trusting so implicitly to appearances. Confidently he pushes forward with his eyes fixed on the refreshing sight before him. But as he nears it a change comes over the scene. The surface of the lake begins to show gaps and breaks that he had never noticed on any other lake. These gaps increase as he approaches; the water surface diminishes; it begins to have a trembling, shimmering appearance; it finally vanishes from sight; and when the traveler reaches the spot he is still surrounded by the same cheerless landscape over which he has already traveled so far. With what tenfold power does his thirst now come back, enhanced by the bitter disappointment! The lesson of the mirages or "false ponds" was hard to learn and it required many a chastening such as has been described to place one fully on his guard against it.

The cause of the phenomenon of the mirage is not perfectly understood, and has received a variety of explanations, some maintaining that it is due to refraction alone, others to reflection. Strange as it may seem, these false appearances, if we may trust the many accounts of observers, are sometimes erect, at other times inverted. The necessary conditions of an effective mirage are a broad plain with an extensive horizon free from conspicuous undulations; a dry, hard ground which will reflect readily the rays of the sun; warm, dry and clear weather, so that the eye can scan the ground for several miles. Wislizenus holds that the true mirage always shows objects double, the lower erect by refraction through the stratum of air next to the ground, and the upper inverted by reflection against the surface of a different stratum some distance above. Whatever may be the true explanation, the delusion is a perfect one, and its tantalizing effect upon the thirsty wayfarer was often more distressing than the thirst itself.

The plains were not, strictly speaking, trapping territory, for the beaver and other fur-bearing animals dwelt mainly within the mountain regions. But they were the home of the buffalo, and the buffalo was the life of the fur trade. The countless herds of these useful animals which overran the territory of the Far West, supplying the necessities of life to its nomadic population, were a product of the plains country, and but for this limitless expanse of grazing territory, their existence in such enormous multitudes would have been impossible.

AUTHOR'S NOTES

(1) Named for David Jackson, of the firm of Smith, Jackson and Sublette, who did business in this region from 1826 to 1830. (Ferris.)

(2) "It receives its name from an Iroquois chieftain, who first discovered it, and was killed in 1827 on the source of the Jefferson river." (Ferris.)

(3) This name is understood to have been given for the trader who first did business in the valley.

(4) Peter Skene Ogden, a leading spirit of the Hudson Bay Company in the decade between 1820 and 1830.

(5) See Part II, Chapter XVI.

A. W. Ferris, in *Life in the Rocky Mountains*, says that the valley was named from circumstances that there an employe of Smith, Jackson and Sublette, while engaged with others in building a cache in the side of the bank, was killed by the bank caving in. "His companions," says Ferris, "believed him to have been instantly killed, *knew* him to be well buried, and therefore left him." It is quite possible that the writer was somewhat mixed as to the locality of this accident. An exactly similar mishap occurred in the Wind River valley in 1830.

(6) Where the names New and Old, as applied to the North and Middle Parks, came from, I do not know. Sage says that the modern North Park was not at first as much frequented by hunters as was the Middle Park, and as a result game increased in it at the expense of its southern neighbor. When the hunters began to be drawn to it extensively they called it the New Park in distinction from that which they had been longer acquainted. New or North Park was also called the Bull Pen by the trappers.

The word bayou in the early French usage in this country meant a slack water slough connected with some larger stream. "In township 12 South Range 76 West, on the south Fork of South Platte river in South Park, Colo., are two saline lakes and a salt creek. It was anciently a great resort for buffalo and was given the name Bayou Salade by the trappers." (Berthoud.)

(7) "The prairies are on fire in every direction" is a frequent entry in the old Fort Pierre journals.

Chapter III

RIVERS AND LAKES: THE MISSOURI SYSTEM AND THE PLAINS RIVERS

Importance of streams to the trapper—The three great river systems—Their historical associations—Their relation to the fur trade—The Missouri River—Its length—Its name—Mouth of the Marias—Mouth of the Yellowstone—The Yellowstone and its tributaries—Locality of the Mandans—Locality of Fort Pierre—The Platte River—Mouth of the Kansas—Mouth of the Missouri—Physical characteristics of the Missouri—The Plains rivers—The Arkansas—The Cimarron River—The Canadian River—The Red River—The Rio Grande.

Although the mountain systems of any country are the primary factors in determining its topography, they are from a practical point of view, of less importance in human affairs than are the streams of which they are generally the source. Particularly true was this of the business of the fur trade. Except in the case of certain desert tracts, the mountains were the principal barriers to travel which the trapper had to cross in his ubiquitous wanderings. The valleys of the streams, on the other hand, were the universal routes of travel and the places of abode during his sojourn in the wilderness. Every thing that he required was to be found there. Along their banks were groves of cottonwood which furnished wood for fuel, temporary huts, trading posts and boats, and ample shelter both from the heat of summer and the cold of winter. He also found there the various animals of which he had need, and particularly the beaver, whose capture was the main object of his labors. In the larger valleys dwelt the Indian tribes with whom he traded so extensively. The great rivers furthermore afforded him the cheapest means of transporting his furs to market. Everything contributed to give the water courses of the country an importance which no other physical feature possessed. This may account for the prominence given to the delineation of the streams upon the early maps, as may be seen by comparing them with modern railroad maps; and also for the fact that nearly all the streams, quite unlike the mountains, bore well-known names given by the trappers, most of which they retain to the present day.

The water courses of the West which were of importance to the trapper belonged nearly all to the three great systems— the Missouri, on the Atlantic slope, and the Colorado and Columbia on the Pacific. There were besides a few streams in the southwest, such as the Arkansas and the Rio Grande, and also many on the Pacific coast; and there were the lakes and rivers of the Great Basin which do not flow into the ocean. It is a noteworthy fact that within a distance of fifty miles from the Grand Teton, where our imaginary observer is stationed, lie the sources of the three river systems just referred to. To the northeast the Continental Divide sweeps into a full quarter circle from a little west of north to a little south of east, and just beyond it are the sources of the Three Forks of the Missouri, the Yellowstone, and the Wind and Bighorn rivers. About a hundred miles southeast, one of the tributaries of the Platte, a water of the Missouri finds its source. Within the arc of the circle just described lie the sources of Snake River, the southern branch of the Columbia, while southeast in the direction of Fremont Peak, are the headwaters of Green River, the principal source of the Colorado, the area drained by these three systems within the United States, nearly all of which were operated in by the fur companies, are approximately as follows:

The Missouri system above Independence....................	490,000	square miles
The Colorado system...............	248,000	,, ,,
The Columbia system within the United States...................	220,000	,, ,,
The Arkansas and Canadian above their junction...................	146,000	,, ,,
The Rio Grande above El Paso.......	42,000	,, ,,
The Great Basin...................	215,000	,, ,,

The Missouri River, being much longer than the Colorado and the Columbia, has a gentler slope and a slower current. As is well known, it is navigable nearly to its source. The rivers across the Divide, on the other hand, have a rapid fall, broken by frequent cascades, and flow for long distances through cañons of immense depth. They are not navigable with safety except in their lower courses.

An interesting historical coincidence connected with these river systems relates to the territorial expansion of the United States. Upper Louisiana comprised the valley of the Missouri and its tributaries. A large part of the cession from Mexico lay in the valley of the Colorado. Oregon comprised the watershed of the Columbia with limited territory besides. It is a pleasing reflection that these extensive regions, embracing conditions so various, and even civilization so unlike, have fallen, in the process of time, under one government; and that, as these rivers find their sources among the perennial snows, so the communities that dwell in their valleys look to a common fountain head for the blessings of national life.

In the business of the fur trade the fields of operation of the several companies conformed in a broad sense to the natural divisions of the country based upon these drainage systems. The Missouri Fur Company and its successor, the American Fur Company, confined their business mainly to the watershed of the Missouri. The Rocky Mountain Fur Company had its center of operations in the valley of Green River, but its parties frequented also the headwaters of the Missouri and Columbia and the valley of Great Salt Lake. The British Fur Companies west of the mountains occupied the watershed of the Columbia. The Santa Fe traders operated in the Arkansas and Rio Grande valleys.

To the individual trapper the innumerable ramifications of these streams were a familiar field of labor. It was his duty to seek them out and explore them for beaver. In carrying out this duty during two score years it may be doubted if there was a rivulet in all the mountains, capable of sustaining a beaver family, that he did not visit. He was acquainted with all the sources of all the rivers in the trans-Mississippi region, and many a stream which is unknown and unvisited today was familiar to him.

THE MISSOURI SYSTEM

Both in its physical characteristics and in its eventful history, the Missouri River must be ranked as one of the most remarkable streams upon the globe. Its source is farther from the sea than that of any other, the distance from the head of Red Rock Creek, the upper source of Jefferson Fork, to the Gulf of Mexico being 4,221 miles. Of this distance 398 miles is above the mouth of the Jefferson, 2,547 miles is in the Missouri proper from Three Forks to the mouth, and 1,276 miles is in the Mississippi. The total length of the Mississippi River is 2,553 miles, half of which is on each side of the mouth of the Missouri. It thus appears that the Missouri River is longer than the entire Mississippi and more than twice as long as that part of the latter stream above the junction of the two. This fact has led to the frequent observation that the name which applies to the lower course of the Mississippi ought to have followed the Missouri (1).

From the Three Forks the Missouri flows almost due north to the junction of a large stream from the west, the Marias River. In this distance it passes through the celebrated "Gates of the Mountains," a stupendous cañon of vertical walls about eighty miles below the Forks. One hundred and fifty miles farther down it flows over a succession of cataracts known as the Great Falls of the Missouri, which extends for a distance of eight miles and includes four distinct cataracts and many rapids, the total fall in the whole distance being over 500 feet. The Lower or Great Fall is truly the Niagara of the West, and ranks among the world's greatest cataracts; but owing to its remote situation it will probably never receive the homage from the lovers of nature that it deserves. On the other hand, if developments now in progress continue, the mighty power of these falls will yet be harnessed effectually into the service of man (A).

About thirty-seven miles below the Great Falls, or two hundred and twenty-four miles below the Three Forks, is the head of navigation on the Missouri, distant 2,285 miles from the sea. Its elevation above sea level is 2,565 feet, nearly half a mile. From this point the river descends like an interminable winding staircase to the level of the sea, and with so gentle a slope that great boats can ascend it the entire distance.

The locality at the mouth of the Marias River was a place of much importance in the fur trade. At this point the Missouri abandons its northerly course and turns completely to the eastward. This was the center of the Blackfoot territory and here was established the first successful trading post among those Indians, from which, after many changes, sprang the celebrated Fort Benton, perhaps the best known post upon the river.

From the mouth of the Marias the general course of the river is eastward for several hundred miles, flowing within a hundred miles of the British boundary all the way. On the north it receives the waters of Milk River and on the south those of the Muscleshell, the only two considerable tributaries above the Yellowstone and these important in length rather than volume of flow.

At the distance of 786 miles below the Three Forks is the mouth of the Yellowstone River, the largest tributary of the Missouri. The confluence of these two streams was one of the most important situations in the West, not only during the fur trade era, but through the entire period of frontier history. Commanding as it did the commerce of both streams at a time when all trade of that region followed the river valleys, it possessed an importance which in modern times it has completely lost. Here stood the greatest of the American Fur Company's posts, Fort Union, where transpired many stormy events during the more than thirty years of its existence. It was in the country of the Assiniboine Indians, but many other tribes also made it their principal center of trade.

The Yellowstone River is one of the most noted rivers on the continent. It is not only a great river, in itself worthy of high comparison, but it comes from a region which in recent times has acquired celebrity throughout the world as that singular place where nature seems to be still engaged in finishing the work of manufacturing a planet. The river comes mainly in its upper course from the Yellowstone National Park. It flows through the beautiful Yellowstone Lake, over a distance of fifty miles a combination of grandeur and beauty unparalleled upon any other river in the world (B).

From its source it flows north a hundred and fifty miles to the Great Bend of the Yellowstone, where it turns abruptly to the east. It then flows nearly due east for about a hundred miles, when it turns gradually to the north and finally flows northeast to its junction with the Missouri. It receives no tributaries worthy of mention from the north, but many important ones from the other side. Of these the principal one is the Bighorn River, which, in its upper course, bears the name of Wind River.

The valley of this stream throughout its entire length was a popular one with the fur companies. It was the home of the Crow tribe of Indians, a splendid fur-bearing country, and was always much frequented by trappers. It drained the Absaroka Mountains on the west through the Grey Bull and Stinking-water rivers, and the Bighorn Mountains on the east; while its upper course gathered up the waters from the northern slopes of the Wind River Mountains. The region at the mouth of the Bighorn was long the site of a trading post, which was moved here and there at different times to satisfy the whims of the Indians.

Below the mouth of the Bighorn, the Rosebud and Tongue rivers bring down the waters from the northern slopes of the Bighorn Mountains, and still farther down, the important stream of Powder River somes in with the drainage of nearly the whole eastern slope of that range. The valley of the upper course of Powder River was a favorite wintering ground for the trappers on account of the abundance of game and pasturage to be found there.

From the mouth of the Yellowstone the Missouri flows at first in a general eastern course, but trends gradually in a southerly direction until it arrives at the site of the old Mandan villages, where it turns completely to the south. In this distance of 255 miles the only tributary of any note is the Little Missouri, a long but unimportant stream from the south which rises west of the Black Hills in Wyoming.

The locality of the old Mandan villages has been known to white men for one hundred and sixty years, and has ever since been an important situation. Hither came De la Verendrye in the years about 1740 on his uncertain course toward the Western Ocean. The location is near the British line and was easily reached from the Red River settlements—a fact which gave it great importance in those times when British influence was a formidable menace upon our border. It was at this point that Lewis and Clark passed the winter of 1804 and 1805. Trading posts were established here at an early date and continued until they were superseded by the military posts and Indian agencies of later times.

From the site of the Mandan villages the Missouri pursues a southerly course, with a slight trend to the east, to the site of old Fort Pierre and the modern city of Pierre, the capital of South Dakota. In this distance of nearly three hundred and fifty miles no tributaries of moment come in from the east. On the west there are several streams of great length but little volume, of which the principal ones are the Heart, Cannon Ball, Grand, Moreau, and Cheyenne rivers, the last being the largest and most important. The two forks of the Cheyenne, which unite in the main river just east of the Black Hills, completely encircle that mass of mountains. Their junction was an important trading center for the Indian bands in that vicinity.

With the possible exception of the site of Fort Union the position of Fort Pierre was the most important upon the upper river. It was the heart of the Sioux country and controlled the trade of the numerous bands of Indians belonging to that tribe. It was at an angle in the course of the stream where its direction changed from south to southeast and was nearer than any other point on the river to old Fort Laramie on the Platte. It therefore commanded all of the trade of the Black Hills and much of that from the Upper Platte valley.

The course of the Missouri below Fort Pierre is southeast to the mouth of the Niobrara, thence due east nearly to the mouth of the Big Sioux River, and thence slightly east of south to the mouth of the Platte. Of the tributary waters received in this distance, the Teton, White, and Niobrara on the west are the most important. The Teton came in near the site of Fort Pierre and trading posts belonging to one company or another stood near its mouth during the entire period of she fur trade. The river was familiarly known down to 1830 at the Little Missouri. After that period it was long known as the Teton; but now the name Bad River seems to have become a fixture.

Wind River flowed through the desolate Bad Lands of South Dakota and its valley was the route of travel between Pierre and Laramie.

The Niobrara rises far west at the southern base of the Black Hills and enters the Missouri at the northeast corner of the modern state of Nebraska. It is, in its lower course, a strong swift stream, and was always known, until recent years, by its French name, *L' Eau qui Court*, or simply as the *Qui Court* (3). This stream, like those just mentioned, had trading posts upon its borders.

On the east shore the most considerable tributaries are the James (4) or Dakota River, the Vermilion, and the Big Sioux. The James is a very lengthy stream which flows from north to south across both Dakotas, but carries a comparatively small volume of water. In its valley an extensive trade was carried on in fur trading times.

At the mouth of the Vermilion stood a considerable trading post and on the Big Sioux there was another though less important one.

The neighborhood of the mouth of the Platte River early acquired and has always held great prominence as a commercial center. Many trading establishments and two or three military posts have been built here and now two flourishing cities with numerous smaller towns have taken their place. The situations of these several establishments were a little above the mouth of the Platte, but it was undoubtedly the junction of that stream with the Missouri which controlled their location. The local trade here was principally with the Omahas, Iowas, Otoes, and Pawnees, in addition to which there was an extensive outfitting trade for expeditions to Oregon and the Far West.

The mouth of the Platte River was, in these early days, the division point between the upper and lower Missouri. So important a landmark was it then considered that the voyageurs came to treat it as the equator of the Missouri, and it was a regular thing to subject the uninitiated to the rude jokes which are familiar to the navigator upon the high seas as an incident of crossing the line.

Of all the tributaries of the Missouri the Platte (5) is the most remarkable and interesting, and is surpassed in size, though not in length, by the Yellowstone alone. The extreme length of the Platte is about a thousand miles. Its two branches, the North and South, rise respectively in North and South Parks of the state of Colorado. The North Fork flows nearly north into Central Wyoming, where it turns to the east by a gradual curve, passing through a sublime and beautiful cañon of red sandstone, when, gently turning to the right, it takes a southeasterly course into the state of Nebraska. The South Fork descends abruptly from the mountains in an easterly direction and then flows north for a considerable distance along their eastern base, past the site of the city of Denver, after which it turns to the northeast and joins the larger fork at the site of the modern town of North Platte in Nebraska. Thence the united streams pursue an easterly course to the Missouri River.

The principal tributaries of the North Fork are the Sweetwater and the Laramie rivers (6). The Sweetwater joins the main river where the latter makes its great bend to the east. It is a very notable stream in that its course was followed by the Old Oregon Trail from Independence Rock near its mouth to South Pass at its source. The Laramie was an important stream in the fur trade era, for near its mouth were the trading establishments of Fort John and Fort Platte, which were later succeeded by Fort Laramie, the most famous military post on the frontier.

The South Fork of the Platte received many tributaries from the mountains, among them the Big Thompson, the St. Vrain, and the Cache à la Poudre. The locality of the mouths of these streams was likewise important in fur trade history, there having been no fewer than three trading posts established there.

The Platte proper is one of the most extraordinary of rivers. Its fall is very rapid, and its bed being composed of fine sand, one would expect that the rapid current would erode a deep channel through it. No such result, however. The broad bed of the river stands almost on a level with the surrounding country, while the water flows back and forth in such sinuous and irregular courses as to increase in a marked degree the length of the channel. The sand washed up in one place is dropped in another and the bed is built up as fast as it is cut down. Thus it results that so unresisting a material as fine sand withstands the action of the current better than a harder material, for it is certain that if this river with its heavy fall were flowing over solid rock it would have carved out a deep and cañon-like bed.

To see the Platte in all its glory one must see it during the spring floods. Then it spreads over its entire bed, upwards of a mile wide, and rivals the Mississippi itself in pretentiousness of appearance. But one has only to look a little closely to see through the thin veneer of this imposing appearance, and to discover, instead of a deep and powerful volume of water, sand bars innumerable, which show their glossy backs above the water and disclose the deceptive character of the stream. Irving very aptly characterized the Platte as "the most magnificent and the most useless of rivers," and a modern satirist has described it as a river "a thousand miles long and six inches deep."

The navigation of such a stream was of course largely out of the question. Bullboats, or flatboats made of buffalo hide, have descended from above Fort Laramie, but where one such attempt has succeeded, probably ten have failed. From the mouth of the Loup Fork of the Platte near where the Pawnee villages were located boats did frequently descend the short distance to the Missouri to trade with those Indians.

Despite its uselessness as a stream the Platte has won a permanent place in the history of the West. If boats could not navigate its channel, the "prairie schooner" could sail along its valley, where lay the most practicable route across the plains. It led the overland traveler by gradual and imperceptible ascents from near the level of the ocean to the very summit of the Continental Divide. Along it lay the old Oregon Trail, most famous of the overland highways, and along the main river in modern times was built the first transcontinental railroad (7).

From the mouth of the Platte River the Missouri continues its course slightly east of south to the mouth of the Kansas River, the site of the modern Kansas City. This is the seventh important locality on the course of the stream at which it is worth while to pause. The river here turns abruptly to the east, and holds its course for nearly four hundred miles to its junction with the Mississippi. At this important bend travelers to Santa Fe or the mountains left the river. It was the eastern terminus of the Oregon and Santa Fe Trails and became the principal outfitting point for the entire West. Near by stood the military post of Fort Leavenworth, while the small towns of Independence and Westport became the progenitors of the modern Kansas City.

The Kansas, or Kaw, River, which joins the Missouri from the west at Kansas City, is a large and important tributary. It rises in eastern Colorado and flows eastward through the entire state of Kansas. Its two tributaries are the Republican and Smoky Hill rivers, of which the first flows for a considerable distance through Southern Nebraska. In the valley of the Kansas River dwelt a tribe of Indians of the same name, for whose accommodation a trading post was long maintained about ten miles above the mouth.

Between Kansas City and the mouth of the Missouri there are several tributaries, but only one of any importance in the present connection. This is the Osage River, which comes in from the southwest a little below the present site of Jefferson City, Missouri, and along the valley of which dwelt the powerful tribe of the Osage Indians. Lieutenant Pike ascended this stream on his famous Southwestern expedition in 1806.

The eighth and last important locality on the course of the Missouri is that near the mouth of that stream. Here was the city of St. Louis, the principal fur trading mart in the United States and the base of operations for the entire Western country. Its history and its relation to the fur trade have been fully noted in another place.

The physical characteristics of the Missouri River over the navigable portion of its length are the same as those of the

Lower Mississippi. For nearly the whole distance below Fort Benton it flows through a valley built up from alluvial deposits, with nothing like a hard or rocky bed to hold it in place. The fall is rapid, the current swift, and the soft banks are therefore always undergoing erosion. The shoreline here recedes and there advances as the earth which falls into the stream in one place is dropped in extensive bars in another. At certain seasons this action is rapid and destructive and hundreds of acres in a single locality are frequently washed away in the course of a few days.

The river naturally develops a succession of bends which are often very pronounced. In many instances the opposite portions of these bends approach very close to each other, so that while the river distance around may be several miles, the distance across may be only a few hundred feet. In time this narrow neck is cut through, a large body of land is transferred to the other shore, and the old bend becomes another of those crescent shaped lakes which abound throughout the valley. Thus the channel of the river is ever migrating from one side of the valley to the other, changing its length, readjusting its slopes, destroying extensive and fertile bottoms, building up new land, and giving rise to never-ending disputes in the ownership and jurisdiction of property. In recent years the government has undertaken to harness this refractory stream, for now that farms and cities line its course, these destructive raids are becoming an evil that must be attended to. The problem, however, is one not easy to solve and it will be generations yet before the river is imprisoned within fixed limits.

A river whose bed is composed of sand or alluvium can not have a clear current. That of the Missouri always has a muddy appearance and in seasons of high water the amount of sediment which it carries is very great. The current has no uniform or regular flow, but is everywhere whirling and boiling in ceaseless internal commotion. The bottom has no stability. It is a mass of moving sand drifts which are building here and washing away there and shifting their position continually. The navigator can never tell where the channel will be twenty-four hours ahead. The constant cutting of banks fills the bed of the river with fallen trees which are drawn along by the powerful current until they become anchored in the bottom, forming the most dangerous obstacles to navigation. These obstacles are called snags and sawyers, or sometimes "breaks," from the appearance which they produce where they lie a little beneath the surface. They come almost entirely from cottonwood trees.

The newly formed lands along the river bottoms are generally covered with willows which often attain considerable size. Their growth is of astonishing rapidity, and scarcely is a new sand bar formed and uncovered by the water, when the thick tender crop is seen shooting vigorously upward. As these willows are extensively used in regulating works on the river, it seems as if nature, in giving this stream its wild and unruly character, has provided the means ready at hand by which it may be placed under control.

Of all the Western rivers the Missouri was by far the most important to the trader. It would be impossible to estimate the great amount of business that has been transacted upon it, or the strange and unusual adventures it has witnessed. Its navigation is a science by itself. As a business it has now wholly passed away, but its record will survive as one of the most important chapters in the history of the West.

PLAINS RIVERS

Under this title will be briefly described two characteristic streams of the arid region of the Southwest: the Arkansas and its tributaries and the Rio Grande. The Red River lies between them, but it plays very little part in the operations of the fur trade.

The most striking characteristics of the plains streams are their great length and comparatively small drainage area. The Canadian branch of the Arkansas, for example, through the five hundred miles of its course has a watershed which averages scarcely fifty miles wide. The same is true of the North Canadian and the Cimarron. Even in a humid climate these streams would be small in comparison to their length. In a region where rain rarely falls, most of them are totally dry for considerable distances and long periods. The water which flows from the mountains is not sufficient to overcome the seepage and evaporation on the plains in the dry season and even the main Arkansas is a very small stream in its course through Western Kansas and Eastern Colorado.

The Arkansas is the best type of the plains streams as well as the most important in this section of the country. It was often spoken of in early times as the "River of the Plains."

Only that portion which lies above the mouth of the Canadian is of interest in connection with the fur trade. Below this point the river enters the humid belt and takes its character almost entirely from the local drainage. In fact if the upper two-thirds of its course were wiped out of existence, the difference could scarcely be noted at the mouth of the stream.

The sources of the Arkansas are in the Rocky Mountains to the westward of Pike's Peak. This part of its course is full of magnificent scenery, most of which is now accessible by means of the Colorado railroads.

The Arkansas River bore the unique distinction among Western streams of being an international boundary. Prior to the war with Mexico it was the frontier between the United States and that country from the 100th meridian to its source. This fact gave it an artificial importance which it in no way possessed as a natural water course.

For about one hundred miles west from the Great Bend of the Arkansas, the main line of the old Santa Fe Trail followed the north bank of the river, while a branch of the Trail followed it to the foot of the mountains. The upper course of the Arkansas was a great resort for traders and trappers and here arose the well-known Bent's Fort which held commercial sway for many years over the surrounding country.

The Cimarron River is important as being on the line of the Santa Fe Trail, which followed its course for nearly ninety miles. It was generally dry, but there were two or three permanent springs which came to be well known, and marked the stages of the journey as effectively as do the oases of an eastern desert. The country bordering the valley was of a desert character and was infested with bands of hostile Indians. It was the scene of much suffering and frequent loss of life during the Santa Fe trade.

The Canadian rises in the mountains northeast of Santa Fe and is here a strong, full stream, but it quickly loses this character when it gets well away from the hills. In its upper course it flows for a long distance through a reddish soil which imparts its color to the water. This circumstance coupled with the general trend of the valley and its correspondence with what was known of the Red River of the Natchitoches, led to a mistaken identity of the two streams. Down to the year 1820 the Canadian was always supposed to be the upper course of Red River. Under this assumption Major Long in that year descended the former stream on his intended exploration of the sources of the latter. It was not until he had reached the lower valley of the Canadian that he discovered the error under which geographers, travelers, and the local Spanish authorities had hitherto labored—an error which had become the more firmly fixed in geography from having the sanction of that eminent authority on New Spain, the Baron von Humboldt.

The Red River lies south of the Canadian and empties into the Mississippi in latitude 31°, being the most southern of the great western tributaries of that stream. Its sources do not extend beyond the boundaries of Texas. The name Red, or its Spanish equivalent, was applied in these early days to a great number of streams, and it was only by adding some qualifying descriptive that the particular river meant could be understood. Thus the Red River here considered was then known as the Red River of the Natchitoches. As geographical nomenclature has become more established other names have been given to most of these streams, and the name Red River, as applied in this section of the country, is now restricted to the great southern tributary of the Mississippi.

The Rio Grande was a typical plains river—a bold, dashing stream where it descended from the mountains, but utterly insignificant in its lower course except in seasons of flood. In ordinary times it could not so much as float a canoe, for in parts of its course it flowed almost entirely underground, and today it is incapable of furnishing the water required for the irrigation of the neighboring country.

The valley of the Rio Grande above Santa Fe is one of great beauty, particularly in those localities where it expands into open prairies like the San Luis Valley. In its upper course it was a great resort for the trapper and it was from this section that the ancient overland trail started for southern California.

The chief importance of the Rio Grande Valley lay in its connection with the Santa Fe trade, which was so long maintained between the frontier settlements of the United States and Mexico. It was here that were located the historic villages of Santa Fe and Taos—one the capital and chief town of northern Mexico, and the other its northernmost settlement.

AUTHOR'S NOTES

(1) From this very general view there is excellent reason to dissent. It is not clearly a logical rule that the name of a stream should follow the longest tributary. The size and importance of a river may be more rationally gauged by the volume of flow than by the length of channel. From this point of view the Ohio has the strongest claim to the name and the Missouri the weakest, for the latter stream discharges less water than either of the others. But there are other reasons why neither the length of the stream nor the volume of flow should in this case control, and why the name as it actually applies is exactly right. The Mississippi river flows nearly south through its entire course; it is obviously the trunk stream and all others merely laterals. It divides the country into two great sections, the east and west. On one side the streams come mainly from the Alleghenies, on the other side from the Rockies. The Mississippi is the great central water course which gathers up the drainage from both sides and conveys it to the sea. Political divisions are based upon it. For almost its entire length it is a boundary between states. The phrases "trans-Mississippi" and "beyond the Mississippi," so well established in our national literature, would have no meaning if either of the great tributaries carried the name. In fact the naming of this stream is one of those striking instances where the common sense of the multitude is better than the wisdom of the wise, for no doubt if the matter had been left to some learned geographer or society of savants the name would have been placed on the Missouri river to the perpetual inconvenience of future generations.

The first known reference to this stream was by Marquette, who saw it in 1673. Upon a crude sketch which he made of the country through which he passed, the Missouri river appears under the name of Pekittanoui. In the region whence it was supposed to flow, were noted the names of several tribes of Indians and among them the Oumessourit tribe which lived nearest the mouth, though some distance from it. From this tribe, at an early date, the river came to be known. The name passed through nearly every combination of its letters which the eccentricity of orthographers could devise, but had settled down to its present form before the close of the eighteenth century. The word seems indubitably to have meant, as applied to the Indian tribe, *Living at the Mouth of the Waters*. Their own name for their tribe was Ne-o-ta-cha (Say) and had the same signification. The most probable theory is that the word Missouri or *Oumessourit* was the equivalent or translation of this name by some other tribe or nation, probably the Illinois, from whom it passed to the French. There seems to be no foundation for the popular notion that the name is simply characteristic, and means, *Muddy Water*.

(2) By recent enactment the Legislature of Wyoming has changed the name of this river to Shoshone.

(3) The translation of this name, Running Water, is still retained on the upper course of the Niobrara, but curiously enough, where the river is a sluggish stream and has none of the characteristics that gave rise to the name.

(4) James river, or "The Jim" as it was more commonly called, or again, the Dakota, was always known to the traders as the *Rivière à Jacques*, often written *Au Jacques*, and even *O Jacques*. The name was given for one of the earliest traders who frequented the valley.

(5) The name Platte is characteristic and arises from the extremely shallow character of the stream. It use dates from 1739. In that year two brothers, Mallet, with six companions undertook to reach Santa Fe from a point on the Missouri somewhere near the present site of Sioux City. They left the river on the 29th of May and arrived at the Platte June 2. ("*Le 2 Juin ils tombèrent sur une rivière qu'ils nommèrent la Riviere Plate.*" De Margry.) The party ascended the main stream and the South Fork to the mountains and reached Santa Fe on the 22nd of July.

(6) For origin of these two names, see Part II, Chapter XXVI.

(7) However useless the river Platte may seem to have been in its earlier history, it has been utilized to a remarkable degree in later times for irrigation, and it is not improbable that in the course of time its entire flow will be drawn out upon the neighboring lands.

EDITOR'S NOTES

(A) There is now at the falls a thriving city of 28,000. The power has been harnessed, and the electric power developed smelts ores and operates railroad trains which make the falls easily accessible.

(B) The month before Clark went in canoes down the Yellowstone in July, 1806, the Canadian Laroque had explored its lower course. *Journal de Laroque* (L. J. Burpee, Ed.) In *Publications des Archives Canadiennes*, No. 3, 1911, page 3.

Chapter IV

RIVERS AND LAKES: THE COLORADO AND COLUMBIA SYSTEMS AND THE GREAT BASIN

The Colorado of the West—Its cañons—Its name—Green River —Its tributaries—Grand River—The Lower Colorado—Snake River—Its source—Physical characteristics—Lower course— Tributaries—The Upper Columbia—Historical importance of the Columbia—The name "Oregon"—The Great Basin—Great Salt Lake—Its Tributaries—Its history—Sevier Lake—Humboldt River and Lake—Other features of the Great Basin— Political boundaries.

THE COLORADO SYSTEM

The Colorado with its tributaries forms one of the most remarkable river systems on the globe—remarkable in its magnificent mountain sources, in its cañons of unsurpassed and unapproachable grandeur, and in the strange and forbidding country through which it flows, carrying the chill waters of a northern clime to the burning shores of a tropical sea. It is preëminently a system of cañon rivers. No other known stream can approach it in this regard. From the point where Green River enters the Flaming Gorge at the southern boundary of Wyoming to the lower end of the Grand Cañon of the Colorado, a distance of upwards of a thousand miles, ninety per cent at least of the channel length lies in the bottom of cañons whose walls vary in height from a few hundred to several thousand feet. In some places the walls recede in successive terraces, in others they are nearly vertical, while the swift river follows its devious course at almost unfathomable distance below, hidden from view, and practically shut out from the light of day. All the tributaries of this stream likewise flow through cañons, whose majesty and beauty are excelled only by those of the main stream itself (1).

Of the tributaries of the Colorado, the Green River, which is really the main stream, is the largest. Coming down to the west from the Wind River Mountains, where it is fed by lakes of Alpine magnitude and splendor, it turns nearly due south and holds this direction until it crosses the southern boundary of Wyoming. The upper course of Green River was a great place of rendezvous for the traders and trappers. Here Bonneville built his "Fort Nonsense" and here the Rocky Mountain and American Fur Companies assembled annually for many years to transact the business of the mountains. All of the tributary streams, and there were hundreds of them, abounded in beaver, the valleys were frequented by buffalo, and all the conditions were present to make it a veritable paradise for the fur trader.

In its course through western Wyoming, Green River receives many important tributaries, nearly all of which still retain the names given them by the parties of General Ashley between 1824 and 1830. On the east the two largest are the New Fork and the Big Sandy, both of which rise in the Wind River Mountains. New Fork drains a large section of the mountains and is a fine, bold stream. The origin of its name is uncertain. The Big Sandy, so called from the character of the country in its lower course, was on the line of the Oregon Trail for part of its length, and one of its branches flowed out of South Pass.

On the west there are twelve considerable tributaries from the state of Wyoming. Horse Creek, near the upper end of the valley, where so many annual rendezvous were held, received its name from the circumstance that Thomas Fitzpatrick was robbed of his horses there by the Crow Indians in 1824. La Barge Creek was named for the father of Captain Joseph La Barge, the well-known Missouri River pilot and boat owner. Fontenelle Creek was named for Lucien Fontenelle, who was later a leader of the mountain expeditions of the American Fur Company. Black Fork, a large mountain stream, and its tributary, Ham's Fork, were well known to the trappers. Both names date from Ashley's time, but it is uncertain for whom they were given. Henry Fork is believed to be named for Andrew Henry, whose name the north fork of Snake River also bears.

Soon after Green River crosses the southern boundary of Wyoming it turns abruptly to the east and flows in that direction for about sixty miles into the northwest corner of Colorado. Along the lower portion of this course was situated the valley of Brown's Hole. After leaving this beautiful valley the river turns abruptly to the southwest, rounding the Uintah range, and then pursues its course for several hundred miles, trending more and more to the south, until it is joined by the Grand River, the two together forming the Colorado (A).

The course of Green River over this distance is through a succession of cañons, and only in a few places does it come out into open country where an easy approach may be had to its banks. The most important of these openings is where the Denver and Rio Grande railroad now crosses, and where the old Spanish trail from Abiquiu, New Mexico, to Los Angeles, California, crossed in the early part of the century.

The largest tributaries from the east along this stretch of the river are the Yampah or Bear and the White River which drain a large section of northwestern Colorado. The headwaters of these streams were good trapping territory and on an upper tributary of the Yampah the trader Henry Fraeb once had a post.

On the west the Uintah River is considerably the largest tributary between Henry Fork and the mouth of the Grand. It drains the southern slopes of the Uintah Mountains and was a splendid trapping country. For many years the trader Robidoux maintained a post on its banks. Price River valley has been utilized in modern times to carry the railroad up the slopes of the Wasatch range. San Rafael River, which also rises in the Wasatch Mountains, is the last considerable tributary of Green River.

Grand River, the great eastern tributary of the Colorado of the West, lies almost entirely in the state of Colorado, and drains fully one-quarter of the mountain area of the state. The main stream rises in Middle Park, Colorado, between the sources of the North and South Platte. It flows through a series of magnificent canons, and several open valleys, which were once barren, but are now converted by modern enterprise into prosperous fruit farms. The principal tributary of Grand

River is the Gunnison, which comes in from the south and joins the main stream a few miles east of the Colorado-Utah line (2). It is a large and important stream, and its valley abounds in sublime and beautiful scenery.

The watershed of the Grand River was all good trapping territory, although not so much frequented by the traders as were the streams farther north. Only one post seems to have existed in the entire valley and that was Robidoux's post on the Gunnison, at the mouth of the Uncompahgre, its principal southern tributary.

The Colorado River proper below the confluence of the Green and Grand has but little connection with the history of the fur trade. The physical character of the country precluded access to the river for the greater part of its length until it emerged from the Grand Cañon near the mouth of the Virgin River. By that time it was in a latitude where the trapping business was no longer profitable. Most of its tributaries, likewise along this stretch of the river, were shut in between the walls of deep cañons and, like the main stream, were inaccessible. However interesting and attractive this region may now be to lovers of natural scenery, it was not so to the people of the fur trade, and was but little frequented by them.

The only tributary of the Colorado from the west that will here be referred to is the Virgin River, which drains a large section of Southern Utah and enters the main stream near the point where it turns to the south after its westwardly course through the Grand Cañon. In 1826 Jedediah S. Smith named it Adams River for the President. Its present name would seem to be of Spanish origin, although there is a suggestion of a possible origin in the fact that the name of one of Smith's men, who passed along the stream and was later killed in California, was Thomas Virgin.

Of the eastern tributaries the Rio San Juan, the Little Colorado, and the Gila are most important. The latter stream, which enters the Colorado at the southern boundary of the United States, has an extensive watershed including all of Southern Arizona and Southwestern New Mexico. It was too far south to be of any importance in the fur trade.

THE COLUMBIA SYSTEM

The sources of the Snake, the south fork of the Columbia, are inextricably interlaced with those of the Missouri, Yellowstone, and Green rivers. The principal branch comes from the Yellowstone Park, where it drains Shoshone, Lewis and Heart lakes, which lie just across the Divide from Yellowstone Lake. Flowing south from the Park, it skirts the eastern base of the Teton range, passing through Jackson Lake and Jackson Hole, and finally, after rounding the southern extremity of the range in a deep and rugged cañon, it turns off to the northwest. In its course of fifty miles along the base of the Tetons it receives great accessions from the east, the principal tributaries being Buffalo Fork, Grosventre and Hoback rivers. Just at the point where it crosses the state line between Wyoming and Utah it receives two more large tributaries from the south, the Salt and John Day rivers (3).

The Snake follows its course to the northwest for upward of a hundred miles, when it is joined by a tributary of almost equal magnitude from the north. This is Henry Fork of Snake River, which rises in Henry Lake, just across the Divide from Red Rock Lake, the source of Jefferson Fork of the Missouri. Before it reaches the main Snake it is augmented by an important tributary from the southeast, the Teton or Pierre River, which drains the valley of Pierre's Hole, at the western base of the Teton range.

From the junction of the two branches of the Snake, the main stream flows at first directly south. It has now acquired those peculiar qualities which give it a distinct character among the streams of the West. Starting from the same elevation as does the Missouri, and reaching the sea in half the distance, it is much more rapid and torrential than the eastern stream. It flows with a strong current almost from the start, and its dark gloomy waters, moving here in silent but dreadful power, there in loud and violent impetuosity, breathe danger and treachery at every foot. Many indeed have been the lives lost in its uncertain crossings. For a great distance in Southern Idaho it flows through ancient lava fields in a narrow gorge of varying depth, and over a constant succession of rapids and cascades. In many places not even the usual trees line the water's edge, and a traveler two hundred yards away would never suspect the presence of a great river, for the narrow cleft in the even plain is quite indiscernible unless from some neighboring elevation. Through portions of this gorge the river has wrought a most weird and fantastic channel, with winding and broken shoreline and rocky islets, all black and dismal like the aspect of the surrounding country. Once in a while it comes forth from its lava prison, and, as if for joy at its temporary release, disports itself over miles of country, in many separate channels, lined with dense groves of willow and cottonwood. Its harsher characteristics become accentuated as the river approaches the Blue Mountains. It is all the way an unnavigable stream, and only at rare intervals has it been possible to establish safe ferries.

From the junction with Henry Fork to the mouth of the Salmon River, the course of the Snake is approximately that of a great semi-circle, extending southwest, west, and around to the north. It flows over three immense cataracts, the American, Shoshone, and Salmon Falls, and receives many large tributaries on either hand. Of these the more important only will be noted. The Portneuf River, so named for a Canadian trapper murdered on its banks by the Indians, comes in from the southeast about fifteen miles above the American Falls. It was an important stream in early years, for it led almost directly from the great bend of the Bear River, whence the Oregon Trail passed over to the valley of the Snake. The modern railroad also follows the valley of the Portneuf. The mouth of this stream was the locality of the well-known Fort Hall, the most important trading post, and later the chief military post, of the Snake River valley.

The other tributaries on the left bank of the Snake are the Raft River, Goose Creek, Salmon Falls River, and Owyhee River, which all flow nearly north. The Owyhee is a large stream, and rises as far south as Northern Nevada. The Malheur, Powder, and Grand Ronde rivers collect the drainage from the eastern slopes of the Blue Mountains. Nearly all of these streams were familiar to travelers along the old Oregon Trail.

On the right bank of the Snake only one important tributary, the Malade, is received until the river enters upon its long northerly course where it now forms the boundary between Idaho and Oregon. Exactly at the point where this natural boundary begins, and opposite the mouth of the Owyhee, the Boise River joins the Snake. This was an important stream. Its course was nearly due west, and the Oregon Trail followed it all the way from the modern site of Boise City to its mouth. A few miles below the confluence of the Snake and the Boise stood a Hudson Bay Company post, and at this point the Oregon Trail crossed the Snake on its way over the Blue Mountains to the Columbia.

Below the Boise the principal eastern tributaries of the Snake are the Payette, Weiser, Salmon, and Clearwater rivers. The courses of the Payette and Weiser are peculiar, being nearly south, parallel to the course of the Snake, but flowing in the opposite direction. The eastern limit of their watersheds is not far distant from the parent stream.

Salmon River is a large and important stream. Its main source is in Central Idaho, whence it flows north to the site of the modern Salmon City. Here it is joined by a large tributary from the southeast, the Lemhi River, which carries the western waters from the ranges along the Continental Divide between Idaho and Montana. Below the confluence of these two streams the main river takes a westerly course and flows nearly across the state to within a few miles of the Snake River. Here it turns abruptly to the north, and parallels the Snake very closely for about forty miles before it enters the main stream. The Salmon River had a notable history in the fur trade and pioneer period. Its valley was a rich trapping territory, and was the home of the Nez Perce tribe of Indians.

Clearwater River, also a large stream, and the last important tributary of the Snake, joins the latter stream where it turns from its northerly course westward toward the Columbia. Like the Salmon River, the Clearwater finds its source in the mountains along the eastern boundary of Idaho, and flows entirely across the state. It rivaled its sister to the south in its wealth of beaver fur, and its valley was likewise occupied by the Nez Perce Indians.

The course of the Snake through the range which connects

the Blue Mountains with those east of the river is in a cañon which ranks among the most wonderful in the world. It attains its greatest magnitude near the mouth of the Salmon River, where both streams are in the bottoms of gorges of black volcanic rock, perhaps three thousand feet deep, through which they flow with torrential velocity, their white, foamy surface forming a marked contrast with the gloomy majesty of the walls which enclose them.

Below the mouth of the Clearwater the Snake is navigable to its outlet. It flows in a considerable curve to the north, through the region known as the Great Plain of the Columbia, and enters the latter stream three hundred and thirty-six miles from the sea.

The Upper Columbia drains the territory comprised in part of Washington, Idaho, Montana and British Columbia. It enters United States territory already a great river, swollen by the thousand streams which the lofty mountains of these northern regions afford. Its course and those of its tributaries are exceedingly irregular and broken, difficult to follow on the map, and forming a striking contrast to the more regular course of the rivers east of the Divide. The region of its sources abounds in noble lakes, and the scenery is on a scale of grandeur scarcely equalled in any of the mountains to the south. It was a splendid region for the trapper, and every one of its streams yielded an annual tribute to the coffers of the Hudson Bay Company, or its predecessor in those parts, the Northwest Company. From the utmost source of the Columbia, the fur company's trail lay across the Divide to the sources of the Saskatchewan, whence it led east to the Red River Valley, Lake Superior, and to Montreal.

Where the Columbia crosses the international boundary, it receives Clark's Fork from the east with the waters of Northern Idaho and Northwestern Montana. The valley of this stream is also a region of notable lakes, of which the principal are the Pend d'Oreille, Flathead, and Missoula, and it gives rise to hundreds of the finest streams in the mountains. It was the home of those staunch friends of the whites, the Flathead Indians, and was a favorite haunt of the hunter and trapper.

The distance on the Columbia from the mouth of Clark's Fork to the mouth of the Snake is four hundred and sixteen miles. The only notable tributary on the left or south bank is the Spokane River, an important stream on whose banks stood a trading post, Spokane House, some ten miles below the modern site of Spokane City.

The course of the Columbia, in the state of Washington, is first south one hundred and twelve miles to the mouth of the Spokane, thence slightly north of west for about one hundred miles, to where the tributary Okanagan comes in from the north. This was the site of an important trading post which accommodated the Indians dwelling in the country to the north.

From the Okanagan to the mouth of the Snake the general course of the Columbia is a little east of south. The only considerable tributary received in this distance is the Yakima, which comes in from the west with the drainage of a large extent of the Cascade range in Central Washington.

From the mouth of the Snake the Columbia continues southeast for a short distance, when it turns abruptly to the right and holds a course nearly due west for about one hundred miles. At this important bend two small but notable tributaries flow in from the northern slopes of the Blue Mountains. These streams, the Walla Walla and the Umatilla, are important ones in the fur trade and missionary history of Oregon. It was in this vicinity that the Oregon Trail, after crossing the Blue Mountains, came to the Columbia River.

Three great tributaries join the Columbia between the Snake River and the sea, and all come in from the south. They are the John Day (4) and the Des Chutes rivers, which bring in the contributary waters of the Blue and Cascade ranges in Central Oregon; and the Willamette, a large stream which is fed by both the Coast and Cascade ranges, and drains the extensive and beautiful valley between. The latter stream enters the Columbia near the site of the modern city of Portland, and opposite old Fort Vancouver, the most important locality on the Pacific slope during the fur trade era. Here the British companies had their Pacific coast establishment, and from this point they ruled as lords of the country for fully two score years.

As if deflected from its course by the impact of the Willamette, the Columbia, at its junction with this stream, turns sharply to the north and continues in this direction for about forty miles, when it swings in an easy curve to the left and holds a course due west to the ocean. For many miles above the mouth of the river it expands into a broad estuary, where ocean vessels ride in safety, and it finally enters the Pacific over what was in early times one of the most dangerous bars known to navigation.

Like all the rest of the Western country, the valley of the Columbia west of the Cascade range presented every gradation of quality from rich and fertile bottom lands to the most barren and worthless desert. Large sections of the Great Plain of the Columbia, as the region between that river and the Snake, and above their junction, is called, are fertile lands and will yield to reclamation. But in the days of the fur trade this country had no value except for grazing the few horses which were required in a business where boats were the usual means of transportation. The true trapping country was farther up, among the thousand tributaries and mountain lakes that were spread over an area four times as large as New England. All of this region ranked with that above the headwaters of the Missouri in its abundance of beaver.

The Columbia was not a navigable stream in the same sense that the Missouri was, but was subject to far greater extremes. The character of the Missouri was practically uniform from its mouth to the head of navigation, and a boat which could navigate it at its outlet could navigate it all the way. Not so with the Columbia, which, in one part of its course or another, could accommodate every known kind or size of craft, but in which the navigation was nowhere continuous for large steamboats for more than about two hundred miles. For one hundred miles above the mouth ocean vessels can pass with ease and safety. For fifty miles farther up, or to the Cascades, river boats can navigate at all seasons of the year. Here navigation was formerly completely interrupted, and the traders had to make portages, whose natural difficulty was greatly enhanced by the presence of thieving and treacherous bands of Indians. In modern times a canal eliminates this obstacle altogether. Nearly fifty miles farther up is another rapid, where the river is compressed into a narrow channel with such a turbulent current that the passage of boats in either direction is out of the question. Above The Dalles, as this place is called, the most serious obstruction is Priest rapids, but by the aid of the cordelle, portages could be avoided, and navigation was practically continuous in small craft to Boat Encampment, near the source of the river, where the British trail started for the East. It was also possible to ascend the Snake River in boats to about thirty miles above the mouth of the Clearwater.

In spite of its many rapids and the difficult portages at The Dalles and Cascades, boats were the universal means of transportation during the fur trade era from the mouth to the source of the Columbia. The lighter craft ascended the tributaries for long distances, and if the total navigable length of all these streams, as actually used by the traders, could be determined, it would be found to amount to more than two thousand miles.

The valley of the Columbia has but an incidental interest in the history of the United States fur trade. Only one important enterprise was ever undertaken there by an American company, and that was Mr. Astor's project in 1811-13. Nathaniel J. Wyeth undertook to found a business there twenty years later, but wholly without success. Jedediah S. Smith, Joshua Pilcher, and Captain Bonneville succeeded in obtaining a glimpse of the resources of the valley, but scarcely so much as carried away a beaver skin. The British companies held absolute commercial sway over that region, and its fur trade history therefore relates mainly to the history of those companies.

No river upon the continent, and few upon the globe, have held a larger place in history, considering the time that it has been known, than this "River of the West." Whether viewed by the business man or poet, its effect upon the imagination of the pioneer was the same. One saw in its valley a land full of the possibilities of material greatness; the other a land full of the grandeur and beauty of nature and hallowed by the traditions and activities of man. Both alike, as they looked out upon the wide-spread rolling ocean beyond the headlands that guarded its entrance, felt that there were no limits to the greatness of the coming time,

"When through this gate the treasures of the North
 Flow outward to the sea" (5).

The very name of the river—the original name, Oregon— was enshrined in poesy while yet the existence of the stream was an unsolved mystery. The adventures of the fur trader, the trials of the missionaries, the perils of the navigator, the sufferings of the resolute emigrant, and the political contro- versy of a quarter of a century, are all inseparably interwoven with its history (6).

THE GREAT BASIN

To the westward of the valley of the Colorado lies an immense territory with no rivers that flow into the sea. Its area is over 200,000 square miles, comprising portions of California, Oregon, and Utah, and nearly all of Nevada. It is known in the geography of the United States as the Great Basin. Its most salient hydrographic feature is the Great Salt Lake, with an area of 1,700 to 2,100 square miles, according to the height of its fluctuating surface. It is a body of water without outlet and of excessively saline quality. The lake is now scarcely a tenth of its former size, for the Quaternary Lake Bonneville, as traced out by geologists, had an area of nearly 20,000 square miles, was a freshwater lake, and drained north into Snake River, making the Great Basin, geologically at least, a portion of the Columbia Valley.

The tributaries of Great Salt Lake all come from the east- ern shore, the country to the west being a barren, waterless waste known as the Great Salt Lake desert. The mountains to the east of the lake yield many perennial streams, such as the Bear, Ogden, and Weber rivers. Of these Bear River is the most important and is quite a large stream. Its course is peculiar. Rising on the other side of the Wasatch range, almost due east of the Great Salt Lake, it flows north through Wyoming and Utah into the state of Idaho, where it turns completely about and flows south into the lake. Bear River was an important stream in the early days, for along a portion of its valley lay the famous Oregon Trail, and this importance it retains to the present day as the route of the Oregon Short Line Railroad.

Bear Lake occupied the center of a large, marshy tract which drained into Bear River a short distance west of the Wyoming boundary. It was first known to the trappers as Black Bear Lake, and later as Bear Lake. To Ashley's men in 1826 it was known as Little Lake, in distinction from the Great Lake farther west. At that time Bear River was spoken of by Ashley as "a water of the Pacific Ocean."

Next to Bear River, Weber River is the largest tributary of Great Salt Lake. It rises directly west of the sources of Bear River and flows northwest into the lake. Weber Cañon, and the picturesque gorge along one of its branches, known as Echo Canon, form an opening through the Wasatch range which was utilized by the first transcontinental railroad.

Near its mouth Weber River is joined by a tributary from the east known as Ogden River, a beautiful stream which drains that remarkable nook in the mountains, elsewhere referred to as the "Ogden Hole" of the trappers, and now occupied in its lower portion by the city of Ogden, Utah.

The third stream of importance emptying into Great Salt Lake joins that body of water near its southeastern extremity and is known, since the Mormons settled in its valley, as Jordan River. It flows due north from another considerable lake now called Utah Lake, a body of fresh water fed by the drainage of the western slopes of the Wasatch range through nearly a degree of latitude. Provo River, Spanish Fork, and Salt Creek are the principal tributaries of Utah Lake.

The early history of Great Salt Lake is intimately bound up with the history of the fur trade. There is no certain evidence that any white man ever saw the lake until the hunter and trapper came. Father Escalante, in 1776, came as far north as Utah Lake, but did not see the Great Salt Lake. On a map of North America "engraved for Guthrie's New System of Geography" in 1811, and "drawn from the best authorities," and a very good map of the known portions of the continent, there is represented a considerable lake very nearly in the same latitude and longitude as Great Salt Lake. It shows the lake without an outlet and thus avoids the error involved in the Rio Buenaventura myth, which represents the lake as flowing through a river of that name into the Pacific— an error which Captain Bonneville is generally given the credit of correcting. On this map there is no name to the lake, but instead the following legend: "Lake, etc., laid down according to Mr. Lawrence, who is said to have traveled through this country to California in 1790 and 1791." Nothing farther in this connection has come to light, but it leaves unsettled a very interesting question as to who actually first saw this lake.

The first party of white men to have passed anywhere near the lake were the Astorians in 1811-12. The detached party left by Hunt at Fort Henry went south at least as far as to Bear River. When Stuart and Crooks returned in the summer of 1812 they met this party and were guided by Miller, one of their number, to this stream and ascended its course for a considerable distance. Although very near to the lake, there is no positive evidence that Miller's trapping party actually saw it.

It is highly probable, although here again the direct evidence is lacking, that the Northwest and Hudson Bay people saw this lake prior to 1824. Donald McKenzie worked all through the country around the headwaters of the Snake before 1820, and Ross quotes a letter written by him from "Black Bear's Lake" in 1819. It seems scarcely possible that so large a trapping party could have passed so much time in this vicinity without discovering the Great Salt Lake.

So far as indubitable proof goes, the discovery of the lake is connected with the expeditions of General William H. Ashley which penetrated these regions in 1823-26. A party of Ashley's men were encamped for the winter of 1824-25 in Cache Valley and were trapping on Bear River and its tributaries. Here a controversy arose as to the course of Bear River after it left the valley. A wager was laid and James Bridger was selected to follow the river and determine the bet. This he did, and soon arrived at its outlet in Great Salt Lake. Tasting the water he discovered it to be salt, and on reporting to his companions, all assumed that it was an arm of the Pacific

Ocean. But in the spring of 1825 four men in skin boats explored its shore line, and found that it had no outlet (7).

The discovery of Great Salt Lake can therefore hardly be considered a settled question in history (B). It is possible that before 1824 the Spaniards may have seen it, or that white men from the eastward may have penetrated so far, or that it may have been discovered by Andrew Henry's men or by the Astorians. It is probable that it was known to the trappers of the Northwest and Hudson Bay Companies. But none of these things are as yet certainties. The situation may be concisely stated by saying, that while Bridger is the first white man whom we positively know to have seen Great Salt Lake, we do not positively know that he was the first to see it.

The essential facts in regard to Great Salt Lake, such as its location, approximate size, lack of outlet, and quality of water, were thus definitely known as early as the spring of 1825. In fact, the geographical nomenclature of the valley dates in no small degree from the Ashley expeditions, although to some extent from the Hudson Bay Company explorers. Ogden River is named of course for Peter Skene Ogden, who came into the valley at least as early as 1825. The tributaries of Bear River, such as Tulloch's and Smith's forks, are probably named for Samuel Tulloch and Jedediah S. Smith. The name Weber River dates from his time, but the identity of the individual for whom it was given is lost (C). Utah Lake was then known by its present name and Sevier Lake was called Ashley Lake. A tributary of Utah Lake is now called Provo River, and near its mouth is the modern Provo City, Utah. It was so named for Etienne Provost [Provot], who was with these expeditions and one of the most noted mountaineers of that time (8).

To the south of the present valley of Great Salt Lake lie Sevier Lake and its long tributary, Sevier River. This valley occupies a large part of Southwestern Utah and geologically is a part of old Lake Bonneville. The Sevier River rises near the southern end of the Wasatch range, flows north along the western base of these mountains for a hundred and fifty miles, and then turns southwest for about seventy-five miles into Sevier Lake. The similarity between its course and that of

Bear River, the principal tributary of Great Salt Lake, is striking. Sevier Lake has no outlet and the characteristics of the Great Lake at the north are accentuated here. The water is shallow, and even before the advent of civilization a large part of the area probably became bare and covered with salt every summer from evaporation. In later times irrigation has so far absorbed the waters of the Sevier River that the lake has become practically dry.

Westward of the valley of the Great Salt Lake along the eastern base of the Sierra Nevada Mountains lies another extensive section of the Great Basin. Here are many lakes, all without outlet to the ocean. Among them the more important are the Humboldt Lakes, the Carson Lakes, Walker and Pyramid Lakes, and Lake Tahoe. There are also many others extending along the base of the mountains as far north as to the present state of Oregon.

The most considerable river of this section is the Humboldt, which flows into the Humboldt Lakes, or as they are often called, the Sinks of the Humboldt. It takes its rise about one hundred miles west of Great Salt Lake and flows in a direction generally south of west for some three hundred miles. About midway of its course it receives a tributary from the south of considerable length but insignificant proportions. The Humboldt was long known as Ogden River, from the Peter Skene Ogden already mentioned. Ogden married an Indian woman from one of the tribes of the valley, calling her name Mary, and from this circumstance the river was also at one time known as Mary River (9). In Leonard's account of the Walker expedition in 1833, the stream is invariably called Barren River and the Lakes into which it flows Battle Lakes. The name Humboldt was bestowed by Fremont, and is an instance of the violence so often done by explorers to existing geographical nomenclature without justifiable cause. The river should have retained its original name, Ogden.

At the southern extremity of the Great Basin, lying mostly within the state of California, is a desolate waste which is in the most emphatic sense a desert. It is of very low altitude, some portions even lying below the level of the sea. The water which would naturally collect there is carried off by the excessive evaporation of that region. In this section are Lake Owen, Death Valley, and the Sinks of the Mohave.

Only that portion of the Great Basin which lay along the western slope of the Wasatch range was much frequented by the American trapper. The Hudson Bay Company monopolized the fur business in the region to the northwest, while little was ever done by the traders in that to the southwest (10).

AUTHOR'S NOTES

(1) The earliest use of the name Colorado, as applied to this river, has not come to the author's notice. It is of course very ancient as American history goes, and only an intimate acquaintance with early Spanish manuscripts of the northern provinces of New Spain could settle the question. For a time the name applied to the whole river, but now only to that portion below the junction of the Green and Grand. That part of the stream now called the Green river was very commonly known down to 1840, as the *Seeds-kee-dee*, or Prairie Hen river. It generally so appears in the literature and correspondence of the times. The name Green river began to come into general use about 1833, although it dates back as far as 1824. Its origin is uncertain. Bancroft says it was given for one of Ashley's men, but it certainly was in use before Ashley was in the country, for William Becknell has left a narrative of a trip he made from Santa Fe to Green river in 1824, and the name was evidently a fixture at that time among the Spanish. Fremont says that it was the "Rio Verde of the Spaniards" and adds that "the refreshing appearance of the broad river, with its timbered shores and green wooded islands, in contrast to its dry sandy plains, probably obtained for it the name of Green river." This does not seem unreasonable, although some who are well acquainted with the characteristics of the river are more inclined to attribute the name to the appearance of the water, which is a very pronounced green, than to the foliage of the valley, which is in no marked degree different from that along other streams in this locality.

At the time Ashley and his men entered the valley of Green river in 1824 it was supposed to flow into the Gulf of Mexico. Various hints in the correspondence of the times show this to be the case, and it is averred even that General Ashley thought so when he started to descend the river in a canoe in 1825. It is certain, however, that the Astorians understood the identity of the stream in 1811-12 for they called it the "Colorado or Spanish" river. (See *Missouri Gazette*, May 15, 1813.)

(2) As late as the era of the Pacific railroad surveys, the name Grand river was used to describe the southern branch, now called the Gunnison. After Captain Gunnison's exploration of the valley of the latter stream and his tragic death in 1853 his name was given to the tributary, while the name Grand became permanently fixed on the main stream. The latter was, prior to this time, called Blue River, but this name is now applied to the stream which drains the valley comprised in the modern Summit County of Colorado.

(3) It is unfortunate that modern geography has made a mistake in perpetuating the name of this stream. It should be John Gray. There was a John Gray in the Hudson Bay Company service under Alexander Ross, and a person by the same name, but whether the same individual or not is uncertain, in the American Fur Company's service between 1830 and 1835. Both John Grays (if different individuals) were distinguished hunters, and from one of them came the name Gray's Hole as applied to a valley on the stream which is now called John Day. The hunter who bore the latter name was never near this stream.

(4) This stream is named for the John Day who figures in the overland Astorian expedition of 1811-12.

(5) *Sunset at the Mouth of the Columbia.* (Mrs. Victor.)

(6) The origin of the name "Oregon" has puzzled geographers and historians as almost no other name has. It is so beautiful and sonorous and has become so deeply fixed in the popular mind that the desire to know whence it came is an unusually strong one. It was first used by Jonathan Carver in 1778, but without the slightest clue to his authority save that he received it from the Indians (E). But none of the tribes with which he had intercourse had any such word. There is much reason to think that it came from the Spanish. Early writers refer to it as the "Oregon of the Spaniards." One of the first, if not the first, attempts at explanation, appeared in the *Missouri Republican* of St. Louis in 1825 in which "A Subscriber" explained the origin of the name as a Spanish word "*oregano,*" a plant of the wild marjoram species, which was said to flourish on the banks of the river. In a subsequent issue, a person who signed himself "Patrick" took the "Subscriber" to task for being "after robbing the whole country of the best part of its name" which, he averred, was in full, Teague O'Regan, a family name in the island of Erin. Captain Bonneville thought that the *oregano* was the wild sage which grew so abundantly in portions of the valley. Other writers have sought to associate the name with the storms of the coast by deriving it from the French word *Ouragan,* hurricane.

Still another explanation is that it is from the Spanish *orejon*, lop-eared, or hanging ears, descriptive of a species of rabbit, and also of an Indian tribe found in these parts.

None of these explanations, unless probably the first, merits serious consideration, and so the name is still wrapped in impenetrable mystery. If it was really the creation of historian or geographer who coined it from "airy nothing" and gave it a "local habitation and a name" on this most interesting river, then all praise to the genius who created it. That it was an acceptable name time has amply proven, and the circumstances of its history have endeared it to the popular mind. Bryant built it skilfully into his "Thanatopsis" where he says:

"Lose thyself in the continuous woods
Where rolls the Oregon and hears no sound
Save his own dashing."

The picture was a pleasing one, "Oregon" a pleasing word, the poem a great one, and all combined to fix the name in the hearts of the people. Hall J. Kelley was, we believe, the first one to transfer it to the country drained by the river, which he did in his impassioned writings on the subject beginning about 1815. Then followed the long and bitter controversy over the "Oregon Question," at one time not very far from war, until the name became one of the most familiar in our geography. (For a careful inquiry into the origin of this name, see footnote p. 17, vol. 34, Bancroft's *History Western States*. It is by Mrs. Frances Fuller Victor, probably the ablest living authority on the history of Oregon.)

The nomenclature of the streams of the Columbia Valley, with the exception of the main river and a few of its larger tributaries, is mostly the work of the Northwest and Hudson Bay companies. Nearly all the names date before 1820.

(7) See Warren's Memoir of Exploring Expeditions West of the Mississippi River.

(8) See further, Chapter XVI, Part II.

(9) Beckwourth connects the origin of this name with the Lewis and Clark expedition, but his theory is more absurdly impossible than are most of even *his* stories.

(10) This may be as suitable place as any to note the political boundaries of the trans-Mississippi country during the period of the fur trade. The Spanish and later the Mexican line commenced at the mouth of the Sabine river and coincided with the east and northern boundary of Texas as far as to the 100th Meridian, which it followed to its intersection with the Arkansas. Ascending this

stream to its source in the mountains it thence followed the 106th Meridian to its intersection with the 42nd parallel of latitude. This parallel formed the northern boundary of the Spanish possessions westward to the Pacific ocean. The British American line was the same as at present as far west as to the crest of the Rocky mountains. The disputed territory of Oregon was bounded on the north by the Russian possessions at latitude 54 degrees 40 minutes, on the east by the Continental Divide, on the south by the 42nd parallel, and on the west by the Pacific Ocean.

EDITOR'S NOTES

(A) The Grand is now called the Colorado.

(B) Nor has time brought forth any conclusive evidence. In fact, claims have been brought forth for several more discoveries. It seems a congressional committee reported in 1826, Nineteenth Congress, first session, H. R. 213, that one Samuel Adams Ruddock went to Oregon in 1821 from Santa Fe by way of the Chamas, Colorado, "Lake Timpenagos" (Great Salt Lake) Multnomah and Columbia. This discovery is more than doubtful since the report makes Great Salt Lake a headwater of the Multnomah.

Through the courtesy of W. A. Struble, the editor has been furnished with a copy of a clipping, probably from the Jackson, Iowa *Sentinel* about 1906. This is a sketch of the life of John H. Weber, from information furnished by his son to the newspaper. According to the sketch, John H. Weber went to the mountains in 1822 and remained five years. During this time he and Henry each commanded a detachment of trappers and he himself discovered Great Salt Lake, Weber River and Weber Cañon. No date is given, and the account has many obvious inaccuracies. He is represented as being a fellow proprietor with Ashley and Henry, and in general, his importance is obviously greatly magnified. While credence cannot be given to these claims of discovery, Weber was apparently a member of one of Ashley's detachments and probably this is the source of the name of the river and cañon.

Claims have also been put forth for Peter Skene Ogden, but the interpretation of Ogden's *Journals* leads to the conclusion that he did not reach Great Salt Lake until after Bridger's visit. T. C. Elliott in the Oregon Historical *Quarterly*, Volume XI, page 358, considers that Ogden possibly reached Salt Lake in 1825, but as Dale points out, page 46, this is highly improbable as later entries by Ogden show him traveling in the immediate neighborhood and describing what he saw as being new to him. Ogden was certainly at Great

Salt Lake in 1828. *Journals* for December, 1828, Oregon Historical *Quarterly*, XI, 388.

It is also possible that Miller, Hoback, Robinson and Rezner of the Astorians, or some of them, reached the lake as Chittenden points out in Part II, Chapter 11, but it is not probable in view of the fact that there is no contemporary or nearly contemporary statement that they were there.

The claims of Etienne Provot, one of Ashley's free trappers, seem to have more substance. He was in the neighborhood and on Weber River not far from Ogden's Hole not later than the winter of 1824-1825 and very possibly preceded Bridger. See Dale, *Ashley-Smith Explorations*, page 103 *et seq*.

Robert Campbell many years afterwards, in a letter to the compiler of the Railroad Exploration Reports in the fifties, states positively "James Bridger was the first discoverer of Great Salt Lake," and says that Bridger's description of the discovery is corroborated by Tullock. However, as Dale points out, *Ashley-Smith Explorations*, page 104, Provot had a breach with Ashley in 1826 and Campbell, as one of the succeeders to Ashley's business, might have had a motive to overlook Provot's claims.

(C) Probably named for John H. Weber. See Note B.

(D) Ashley knew the Green was the Colorado. See editor's note I, Part II, Chapter 16.

(E) An earlier use in the form "Ouragon" was in a petition to King George made in 1765 by Major Robert Rogers regarding a proposed search for the northwest Passage. It appeared in print in London the following year. See T. C. Elliott in Oregon Historical Society *Quarterly*, XXI, 341; XXII, 91; XXIII, 42.

Chapter V

FLORA

Vegetable productions of importance to the trapper—The cotton-wood—The quaking aspen—The conifera—The cedar—The willow—Council Grove—The Big Timbers—The Cross Timbers—Sage brush—Greasewood—Cactus—The grasses—Wild fruits—Edible roots—The maize—Plants used for tobacco.

The preceding pages have been devoted to a description of the topography and physical aspects of the country in which the American fur trade was carried on. It is now in order to consider, not in exhaustive technical detail, but from the practical standpoint of the hunter and trapper, the varieties of life which flourished there. The vegetable productions which had any appreciable influence upon their manner of life were very few. The woods, grasses, fruits, edible roots, the troublesome sagebrush, greasewood, and cactus, the maize, and a few domestic plants introduced by the trader, comprise the number.

The most important tree in the business of the fur trade, and in many parts of the West practically the only tree, was the cottonwood. There were several species of the genus *Populus*, but the most important was the *Populus deltoides occidentalis* (A), the broad-leaved cottonwood of the lower rivers found only along the water courses, where it grew into every variety of form and size, from diminutive, misshapen shrubs to stately trees of more than five feet diameter and upward of seventy feet high. In the higher altitudes it had a narrower leaf and was called *Populus angustifolia*.

A grove of large cottonwoods with stately trunks and widespreading tops, is not surpassed in beauty by any other variety of forest. In a region like the Western country, totally devoid of trees except high among the mountains or in the valleys of streams, the sight of these long lines of foliage was always welcome to the hunter for the comfort it promised, as it is now to the lover of nature because of the beauty which it displays.

The cottonwood was used in these early days for a variety of purposes. In the first place it was a grateful shelter both in winter and summer. It supplied the hunter with fuel for his warmth and cooking, logs for temporary huts, and food for his horse. This last use will seem surprising to many, yet it was a universal one upon the plains, when grazing was impracticable, as it often was in winter. The bark was one of the most nutritous foods. The horses liked it and throve upon it as well as upon oats. It is recorded that Kenneth McKenzie at Fort Union kept some of the horses of superior quality for the chase exclusively, and for their better training fed them only upon cottonwood bark (1). Although elk and deer obtained the bark by browsing from the younger shrubs, horses, if in considerable numbers, were fed on the bark obtained from larger trees. In such cases it was customary to cut down the trees and shave the bark from them with ordinary draw knives. The shavings were then cut up into short pieces and fed to the animals. Great care was taken not to feed the bark in a frozen condition lest the sharp edges, keen as steel with frost, lacerate the horses' mouths and stomachs. Animals were occasionally lost from neglect of this precaution.

The cottonwood was extensively used in the manufacture of boats, particularly the "dugouts" or log canoes which were so much used on the Missouri and its tributaries. It likewise supplied palisades for the forts, logs for the houses, fuel for the steamboats, and every other want for which wood was required. It was usually manufactured with the axe alone, but at the larger posts there was a more complete equipment. Timber and boards were sawed by erecting a stage on which the logs were rolled, high enough so that a man could stand erect underneath. Two men then sawed the log, one standing above, the other underneath, and together operating the saw. The use of cottonwood as timber was more from necessity than on account of its quality, which was really very inferior. As a general thing it was the only timber available, the low dwarf cedar being unfit for lumber, and the pine and fir of the mountains being too far away.

Another species of the genus populus was the *Populus tremuloides*, the quaking asp, or the *tremble* of the French. It was sometimes found in the valleys, as along the *Rivière aux Trembles*, or Poplar River, in Montana, but more generally on the mountain sides, where it grew in small, compact copses which greatly enhanced the beauty of the scenery. The superstitious voyageurs thought that this was the wood of which the Cross was made and that ever since the crucifixion its leaves have exhibited that constant tremulous appearance which has given rise to the name. The wood of the quaking asp was preferred by the trappers as a fuel for cooking, because it had little odor and did not taint the meat (B).

The mountains were extensively covered above an altitude of 7,000 feet, with forests of pine, spruce, balsam, and fir. The more important species were *Pinus flexilis*, or Rocky Mountain white pine (C); the *Pinus Murrayana*, or lodge pole pine, and sometimes called black pine from its appearance in forest masses; *Picea Engelmanni*, a spruce flourishing near the timber line; *Abies Subalpina* balsam, found near the snow fields and a very beautiful tree (D); and the *Pseudotsuga Douglasii*, the Douglas spruce, largest of the conifera, sometimes attaining a diameter of five feet. It was only where these forests descended into the lower valleys that they were of much use to the trapper. The pine made a good fuel and its boughs were often used for bedding. The forests also afforded shelter from storms. But as a general thing the part which they played in the hunter's life was that of an obstacle to travel. They were often very dense, difficult to pass through, with little or no game in them, and in the springtime powerful retainers of the winter snows. They delayed to a great extent the passage of the mountains in spring, and by holding the snows till the period of hot weather, increased the mountain freshets in June and contributed to render the streams more impassable.

The cedars were very numerous and grew in the widest variety of situations. The *Juniperus communis Alpina* (E) which flourished extensively on the hillsides, and the *Juniperus Virginiana* (F), commonly called the red cedar, were the principal varieties. The cedars of the mountains and foot hills grew in the most distorted and twisted shapes as if from the long actions of storms and winds. Sometimes their tops spread out into wide canopies, affording ideal spots on which to camp. For lumber, fuel, etc., they were not so useful owing to the difficulty of cutting and splitting. These trees are to be seen in any part of the West, and frequently in those barren and forbidding situations where it would seem that no life could flourish.

On some of the islands of the Missouri the red cedar flourished in great abundance and was there a most useful tree. It furnished timber for the trading posts and fuel for the steamboats. The various Cedar islands along the river, particularly those in the Sioux country, were named from the presence of this tree.

Along nearly all of the streams there were growths of willows of greater or lesser density—*Salix rostrata* is the most common of the several varieties. These often amounted to extensive thickets, almost impenetrable, making the approach to streams a matter of the greatest difficulty, while they crowded so close upon the borders that it was impossible to follow the bank. The trapper had therefore to wade the stream or betake himself to the open bottoms. These thickets were a most serious obstacle in trapping operations, but at the same time they were a source of food for the beaver and the wild game and a splendid concealment from savage foes.

Although the plains of the West and most of the foothills and bad lands were barren of trees, there were here and there extensive forest lands which came to have considerable celebrity in the life of the plains. The country around the Black Hills was an example. While much of this section was mountainous and the forests there strictly mountain forests, still the trees extended down to the very plains and far out from the base of the mountains.

On the headwaters of the Neosho was the celebrated forest of Council Grove which contained several varieties of timber. It was of great importance to the Santa Fe caravans.

The Big Timbers of the Arkansas were a large body of cottonwood on the north side of the Arkansas River, extending for several miles along the river at some distance below the site of Bent's Fort. In a country almost devoid of trees, even along watercourses, this extensive forest was of more than unusual importance and was a great resort for both Indians and traders.

The forest section known as the Cross Timbers lay rather outside the territory embraced in this work, being mainly in Texas and Indian Territory, and it extended from the Brazos River northwesterly to the Canadian River. South of the Canadian a branch of the Cross Timbers extends westwardly and then northerly across the North Fork of the Canadian, where it finally disappears. This hilly, wooded section is the line between the lower well-watered prairies and the high, arid plains. It is covered with a thick growth and a wide variety of trees mostly of dwarfish, stunted size. The underwood is so overgrown with vines and shrubbery as to be in places almost impassable.

What the prairie-dog was among the animals of the plain, the sage brush and greasewood were to the plants—products so generally useless that it has ever been a mystery what their purpose in the economy of nature may have been. It is an observation often made that a discovery of some beneficial use for the sage would render available vast regions of the country which must otherwise apparently forever remain in a state of non-productiveness.

There are more than twenty species of the genus *Artemisia*. The most common, and the one to which the sage brush strictly applies, is the *Artesmisia tridentata*. The term sage refers more properly to the other varieties, although, in popular use, fine distinctions were not drawn, and the names sage and sage brush were indefinitely applied to everything of the *artemisia* characteristic. It is worthy of note that lands where the true sage brush flourishes are reasonably free from alkali and are generally fertile. The several varieties vary greatly in size, the *tridentata* occasionally attaining a height of from fifteen to twenty feet, and forming dense miniature forests. These large growths constitute as formidable an obstacle to travel as does a thicket of willows. The larger shrubs make a quick, hot fire, but a very transient one, and so are not esteemed a good fuel in comparison with wood. They are said to have been extensively and even exclusively used, however, by some of the tribes of the Columbia where wood is unknown.

One useful purpose which the sage brush serves, when its growth is very dense, is as a shelter from the storms of winter. Both in the earlier times when wild game grazed on the plains, and now when their place is taken by domestic herds, this otherwise useless plant has been the means of saving the lives of thousands of animals every winter.

This plant has the widest area of growth of any of the plants of the plains. From the 100th meridian westward to the Pacific it is almost never out of sight and its appearance becomes so familiar as scarcely to attract attention.

The greasewood (*Sarcobatus Vermiculatus*) resembles somewhat in external appearance the sage brush and like it flourishes only in the arid regions. Its distinguishing peculiarity, apart from its well-marked appearance, is the fact that it flourishes in an alkaline soil. The ash of the burned plant has been found to contain twenty-two per cent of potash and twenty four per cent of soda. Its presence is a sure indication of black alkali, and it is now recognized among farmers that where greasewood flourishes it is useless to attempt cultivation. The plant itself, like the larger sage brush, grows from four to eight feet high, and contrary to what might be expected, affords browsing to cattle and sheep.

The cactus in its various forms is an exceedingly troublesome plant, where its growth is abundant, for its sharp thorns pierce the shoes or moccasins of pedestrians, and injure the feet of horses and mules. The prickly pear (*Cactus Opuntia*) (G), is the most common of the plants. When in full bloom it is very attractive and it is said to have been much used for food. Another variety of cactus is the little spherical form (*Mamalaria Missouriensis*) that grows in great numbers on the prairies, and though its armature of thorns is less powerful than that of the prickly pear, it is still a very troublesome plant. Farther south on the plains of Arizona the giant cactus (*Cereus giganteus*) thrives with its weird and strange forms towering like ruined columns in every direction.

Among the most important vegetable productions of the plains, so far as the business of the fur trade was concerned, were the grasses, for upon them depended not only the sustenance of nearly all the native herbivorous animals, but also that of the beasts of burden which acompanied the expeditions. As a general thing the grasses were of excellent quality, and no country in the world can excel the Western plains as a grazing country. The growth on the lower prairies, where rain is more abundant, is more luxuriant than upon the high plains, and of course more plentiful on the stream bottoms than upon the table lands or hills. One most valuable quality of these prairies grasses is that they retain their nutritive power apparently quite as well after the season of growth is over as before, so that wherever the snow in winter does not cover the ground too deeply the grazing herds find sustenance as easily as in the summer time.

The three grasses that were the chief reliance of herbivorous animals were the gramma grass (*Boutelona aligostacha*) (H), the buffalo grass (*Bouchloe dactyloides*), and the bunch grass (*poa tenuifolia*). The gramma grass had a wide distribution throughout the West, and was often called buffalo grass. It sometimes grew to a height of ten inches on the ranges. It is one of the native grasses which has been improved successfully under irrigation.

Buffalo grass likewise had a wide distribution, but unlike the gramma grass it is dying out before the advance of cultivated grasses.

Of all the grasses, however, the bunch grass was the most widespread and important. It is a rich nutritious food for stock and equally good in winter as in summer. In fact, the term "bunch grass" in the Western country has become synonymous with excellence of quality in any line.

All over the West were to be found wild fruits which were an occasional resource for food when other means failed. Plums, bull berries, haws, cherries, service berries, and native varieties of the common fruits—raspberries, blackberries, strawberries and huckleberries, were met with. These fruits were gathered extensively by the Indians, who had effective methods of preserving them. To the hunter and trapper they were an entirely secondary means of subsistence.

There were numerous edible roots throughout the Western countries which were a substantial resource among the Indians, though rarely used, except under the compulsion of want, by the whites. The more important were the camas root (*Camassia esculenta*), the Indian turnip or *pomme blanche* of the French (*Psoralea esculenta*), the bitter root, and the wild onion, of which there were several varieties. The Indian women had an interesting method of gathering and preparing the common roots. After a sufficient quantity had been collected, holes were dug in the ground and lined with stones upon which a fire was built of sufficient strength to heat them thoroughly. The ashes were then carefully removed, and the stones were covered with fresh, leafy twigs, upon which the roots were placed until the hole was filled. The top was then covered over first with a layer of leaves and then with a layer of earth upon which a fire was maintained until the roots were thoroughly cooked. As thus prepared they formed an excellent food.

The *Psoralea esculenta* was used in a dry and pounded state by the Indians. It was a nutritious food and extensively used.

The gathering of these roots at certain seasons and curing them for future supply was a regular business with most of the tribes who dwelt in the Great Basin. To such an extent did they depend upon this kind of food that they became known by the opprobrious epithet of "Rootdiggers" or simply "Diggers."

The maize or Indian corn was the most important plant regularly cultivated by the Indians, and among the tribes in permanent villages it was a common food. The planting was usually done in May. The ground was prepared with a utensil made of the shoulder blade of a buffalo, prior to the advent of the traders, but after that with the common hoe. The seeds were planted in rows and the corn was hoed two or three times during the season, pains being taken to bank the earth against the hills for the better retention of the moisture. The harvest generally took place in October. The cornfields were unfenced and were frequent objects of raids by hostile tribes.

The traders made extensive use of the maize and all the larger posts had mills to grind it.

When the traders began to get a permanent hold on the country, they introduced along the Missouri some of the more common and hardy vegetables such as pumpkins, beans, etc., while every important post had its regular garden in which a variety of products was raised for the use of the inmates.

With a people who set so high a value as did the Indians upon the pipe as an indispensable feature of their ceremonial intercourse with the whites and with each other, the material used in the pipe had an importance by no means to be despised. The Indians cultivated a native tobacco in the early days (*Nicotiana quadrivalvis*), but when they came to use the white man's tobacco they always mixed with it a substance called kinikinik which consisted of the leaves or inner bark of certain shrubs. Among those more commonly used were the leaves of the smooth sumac (*Rhus Glabra*) (I); the inner bark of the red-osier dogwood or so-called red willow (*Cornus stolonifera*) and the leaves and bark of the bear berry (*Arctostaphylos uva ursi.*)

Such is a catalogue of the principal uses which the hunter derived from the plant life of the West. The cottonwood for forts, houses, boats, forage and fuel; cedars for building, willows for browsing, grasses for grazing, roots and wild fruits for food, the cactus and sage as obstacles, and the mountain forests for the general uses of lumber, when convenient of access—these were about the extent of his direct dependence upon or relation to the flora of the country.

AUTHOR'S NOTES

(1) "About four o'clock the horses were brought in much fatigued; on giving them meal bran moistened with water they would not eat it, but preferred the bark of the cottonwood."—Journal of Lewis and Clark.

EDITOR'S NOTES

(A) The correct botanical name of the common Cottonwood of the Rocky Mountains is *Populus occidentalis*. It is closely related to the *Populus deltoides* of the Mississippi valley but is not the same.

(B) The bark of *Populus tremuloides* and other species of Populus constitute the most important food of the beaver.

(C) *Pinus flexilis* is more often called "Limber Pine" although "Rocky Mountain White Pine" is in frequent usage.

In some places the White-bark Pine (*Pinus albicaulis*) is more common than the *Pinus flexilis*. It is a timber-line tree and therefore grows at higher altitudes. Probably at the time the *American Fur Trade* was written, botanists did not distinguish between these two species.

(D) The present name of the Balsam of the Rockies is *Abies lasiocarpa* instead of *Abies subalpina*.

(E) The present name of the *Juniperus communis alpina* is *Juniperus communis siberica*.

(F) The correct name of the Rocky Mountain Red Cedar is *Juniperus scopulorum* instead of *Juniperus virginiana* which is an eastern tree.

(G) *Cactus Opuntia* is not the correct botanical name. The correct genus name is *Opuntia*. There are several species of *Opuntia* in the Rocky Mountains. One of the commonest is *Opuntia polyacantha*.

(H) The genus name of the Gramma Grass is correctly spelled *Bouteloua*.

(I) The smooth Sumac of the Rocky Mountains is *Rhus cismontana*. *Rhus glabra* is an eastern species.

The notes on this chapter on the flora have been furnished to the editor by Dr. W. B. McDougall of Los Angeles, California.

Chapter VI

FAUNA: THE BUFFALO, BEAVER, AND BEAR

Great importance of the buffalo—Description—Flesh of the buffalo—Appearance and habits—Methods of capture—Buffalo butchering—Territorial range of the buffalo—Rapid disappearance—Commercial importance of the buffalo—The importance of the beaver in the fur trade—Description of the beaver—Method of capture—The beaver skin—Commercial importance—The grizzly bear—The most dangerous American quadruped—Method of attack—Notable encounters with grizzly bears—The black bear.

Under the above title will be considered the three representatives of animal life on the plains and in the mountains with which the trader and trapper, as well as the Indian, were most familiar and which entered most largely into the daily life of the natives and the business of the fur trade.

More than the horse to the Arab, the camel to the pilgrim in the desert, the reindeer to the Laplander, the seal to the Esquimau, or the elephant to the Hindoo, was the BUFFALO to the trans-Mississippi Indian. History affords no other example where a single product of nature, whether animal or vegetable, has filled so large a place in the life of a people. The self-sustenance of the tribes of the plains would have been impossible without it, and when the buffalo disappeared these tribes fell back upon the government in hopeless dependence for the very necessities of existence.

This remarkable animal (*Bos Americanus*) furnished nearly everything that the Indians wanted, and in the life of the trapper as well it was the principal resource. Almost every part of its huge body was utilized, and a volume would be required to catalogue its manifold applications. The hide was dressed in a variety of ways, each special treatment having its particular use. The lodge of the Indian, his bed and covering

when asleep, his clothes, his weapons of war, his shield in
battle, kettles for his food, boats for crossing the river,
material for his saddle and halter, strings for his whip and
bow, hair for ornamenting his dress—all these and many other
articles were made from the robe that grew around this most
useful animal. His bones, likewise, from the short, curved,
strong horns to the hoofs that supported him, were manufactured into an endless variety of articles that entered into every
part of the domestic life of the Indian.

The flesh of the buffalo was the most wholesome, palatable, and universally used of that of any wild animal. The
extent of its use, that is, the degree to which the entire animal
was thus utilized, depended upon its abundance. When there
were multitudes at hand the epicurean palate rejected all but
the choicest morsels, but in time of scarcity every part of the
flesh did duty as food. The greatest luxury was the tongue and
this was often the only part taken. The hump ribs and the
tenderloin came next in favor, while smaller parts, such as the
marrow bones, liver and gall, and parts of the intestines, were
often devoured with avidity while the process of butchering
was still going on. The fleece fat upon the animal's back was
generally thick and rich and was an important article in the
process of cooking.

All authorities unite in praising the excellence of buffalo
meat, and the true plainsman would never admit that the
domestic beef could approach it. It always agreed with the
digestion and it seemed impossible to overeat of it. Combined
with the healthfulness of the open-air life on the prairies or in
the mountains, it formed a perfect food whose virtues became
widely known; and many an invalid has recovered his health
on the plains with no shelter but the sky and no food but the
meat of the buffalo.

It was not always, however, that the hunter or traveler
had the buffalo with him, and it became necessary to provide
in times of plenty against the times of deficiency. This was
ordinarily done by the process of jerking or drying the meat.
The flesh was cut up in thin strips and hung up in the open air
to dry, after which it could be kept indefinitely without
deterioration. The Indians had another process of curing

buffalo meat, equal, if not superior, to the most approved canning processes, and wholly free from the use of chemicals or embalming preparation which too often cast suspicion upon the preserved meats of the present day. This was the much used pemmican. It was prepared by cutting the flesh into thin slices, thoroughly drying it, preferably in smoke, until it was hard and crisp; then pulverizing it by pounding upon a stone, and finally mixing it with an equal weight of buffalo tallow or marrow fat. Sometimes it was seasoned with powdered wild cherry, stone and all. The whole mixture, before hardening, was introduced into skin bags, shaken down compactly, and then sealed tight. In this way it would last indefinitely and was always ready for use without cooking. It formed a very palatable as well as nutritious food.

These manifold and important uses did not exhaust the purposes which this most valuable animal subserved. In those regions where wood was scarce, and that was nearly everywhere except upon the larger streams and in the mountains, the dried ordure of the buffalo supplied an excellent and ready fuel. Finally, to push the range of utility to the extreme limit, there are instances on record where the lonely hunter, caught unexpectedly by a prairie blizzard, has slain and disemboweled a buffalo, and, crawling inside the huge body, has found a safe refuge from the tempest.

For so useful an animal, and one of such mild and inoffensive habits, the buffalo was terrible in appearance, misshapen, unwieldy, and ponderous. Its massive, shaggy front, its matted mane almost concealing the small, bright eyes, and its short, curved, powerful horns, altogether gave it an aspect of ferocity which was quite out of keeping with the actual instincts of the animal.

The color of the buffalo was dun or dark brown inclining to black and was remarkably uniform throughout the species. Variations from the common color were so rare that the Indians attributed such as were met with to supernatural causes. Thus the white buffalo was an object of worship among most of the plains tribes, and a white buffalo skin was considered great medicine, the possession of which was a mark of distinction.

In its habits the buffalo was a thoroughly gregarious animal, being rarely seen alone, unless, from injury or age, it was
unable to keep up with its companions. Not only was the
buffalo generally seen in herds, but the smaller herds were
usually parts of larger ones. Great multitudes of these animals
migrated from one section to another, and when they were
passing any place their numbers were often beyond the power
of the mind to estimate.

It will readily be seen that the business of capturing
animals so useful and necessary was an important one. The
buffalo hunt was the highest sport which could engage the
skill of the hunter. The animal was not keen except in its
sense of smell, which was very acute and warned him with
certainty of danger from the windward. In his flight he displayed a sort of stupid persistence, rushing madly along, often
into the very teeth of destruction, and he was not alarmed at
the crash of a rifle so long as he saw neither smoke nor hunter.

The methods of capture were various. With the Indians
wholesale destruction was commonly resorted to by alluring
vast herds at full gallop to the brink of a precipice or into the
mouth of an artificial enclosure. The force of the mass behind
crowded those in advance ahead until they fell upon each
other at the foot of the cliffs or in the enclosures, and were
thus slaughtered by the hundreds. A great deal of skill, and
favoring conditions of wind, as well as the most adroit management on the part of the Indian, who, clad like a buffalo,
acted as a decoy to the herd, were essential to the complete
success of the maneuver. These hunts were matters of great
ceremony among the Indians. Days and weeks were devoted to
preparation, with the most rigid laws against individual
hunting or frightening of the herds, and with due observance
of the established religious rites of the tribes.

The true sportsman-like attack was by direct onslaught on
horseback, or, as it was sometimes called from the manner of
approach, the "surround." It was managed with the same
ceremonious preliminaries that were observed in all great
buffalo hunts by the Indians. The attack was made by riding
in careful order, under strict discipline, directly upon the herd
until the latter had fully scented the danger, when the hunters

broke into a wild gallop, each free to go where he chose, and fell pell-mell upon the herd, chasing and slaying, amid the thunder of hoofs, the bellowing of the frightened beasts, and the clouds of dust raised in the mad rush of so many animals. So completely panic-stricken would these mighty herds become, and so little sensible of where to flee, that most of them fell victims of their pursuers, and the ground where the attack took place would be strewn with hundreds of dead bodies. Now and then a luckless hunter would be unhorsed, or even slain in the confusion of the chase, when some infuriated monster turned too quickly upon him.

The scene of these hunts, after they were over, was one field of carnage, or gigantic slaughter house, in which the women were everywhere busy, securing the trophies of the day. Theirs truly was the laborious part, and days were required to gather the hides and meat and the other fruits of a few hours' hunt.

The practical American hunter, when not bent on sport for sport's sake, but after meat for *its* sake, adopted a much simpler, more direct, and quite as efficacious means of securing his game. This was the method of "still hunting," which consisted, as the name suggests, in stealing unobserved upon the intended victim. Generally a small band was preferable. It was not a difficult thing to crawl from the leeward to within sure rifle shot without being discovered. Then choosing the best concealment the ground afforded, the hunter would commence the work of destruction by firing at the fairest mark. The animals, seeing nothing, and hearing only the report, would not generally flee, but stand still in apparent wonderment. Presently the wounded animal falls, and the companions, smelling its blood, gather round it and try to make it rise, and even lick its wounds; or they would go on grazing, apparently thinking that their companion has lain down to rest. Meanwhile the hunter's rifle is busy, shot upon shot is heard, and victim after victim falls, until, either because there are no more to kill, or because he is surfeited with slaughter, he rises and surveys his conquest (1).

The buffalo was a difficult animal to kill. A ball upon its shaggy head or neck fell off as from a panoply of steel. Wounds in the nether portion of the body were rarely fatal. It was only in the region of the heart that the blow was sure, and the Indians and white hunters sought out this region in all their attacks. The animal was not ordinarily pugnacious or dangerous, and only when smarting with its wounds would it turn upon its enemy. But its rage at such times made it a formidable adversary, and lucky was the hunter who could keep out of its way.

In the spring of the year when the ice moved on the Missouri river, great numbers of these animals were drowned in attempting to cross after the ice had become broken up. In some years their bodies floated down the stream in such numbers as to render the air almost unendurable to boat crews on their way up the river. It was a very singular thing that the Indians liked this kind of buffalo meat better than any other, and no matter how advanced in decomposition it might be, they would tow it ashore and use it in preference to fresh meat.

The butchering of the slain buffalo, as practiced by the American hunter, was an art *sui generis*. It proceeded in exactly the opposite way from that employed in dressing domestic cattle. Instead of turning the body upon its back, it was placed in a reversed position, and held there by spreading out its legs to serve as props. The skin was then parted along the spine and cleaved down the sides. The rest of the process depended for thoroughness upon the wants of the party. If meat was plentiful only the choicest parts were taken. The tongue, hump ribs, and fleece fat were always included, as well as the marrow bones, and generally the gall and liver. As piece after piece was severed from the trunk, it was deposited in a pile on the clean grass, and after the butchering was over it was packed on the horses or mules and borne to camp.

The hungry hunters did not by any means always await the slow process of cooking, although this was rushed to the utmost. Some would take the choicest parts and eat them *au naturel*, while others would pare from the roast rarely done slices and keep it turning and cooking anew. Voracious appetites were one of the features of life upon the plains, and the richest repast which the wealth and luxury of cities could afford was nothing to the crude meals of buffalo meat around the unsheltered camp fires on the broad prairies.

It is difficult to appreciate, at this distant day, how dependent upon the existence of one species another can be, as illustrated in the relation of the buffalo to the Indian, and it will not excite surprise to know that the one entered largely into the religious life of the other. Many customs and ceremonies had reference to it, and with the dying warriors were always buried the implements of the chase for use in the Spirit Land. It is also easy to understand with what prophetic vision the Indian saw the downfall of his race linked with the extermination of the buffalo, and could measure his own decline by the rate at which these animals were disappearing before the advance of civilization.

It remains to touch upon the territorial range and inconceivable numbers of the buffalo in the days of its unlimited growth. The researches of naturalists have shown pretty clearly that it roamed over all the country between the Alleghenies and the Rocky mountains. There is no satisfactory evidence that it ranged extensively on the coast, or beyond or within the mountains on either side. Its later appearance as far west as the Salt Lake Valley was probably due to pressure from the east. North and south it roamed from near the Gulf to as far as 60° north latitude. At the time of which this history treats, the buffalo had entirely disappeared from east of the Mississippi, and in 1807 had already receded as far as the 97th meridian. It was a common saying during the era of the fur trade that the buffalo was retreating before the white man at the rate of ten miles a year, and this is perhaps not an exaggerated measure of his certain and continuous disappearance.

The multitude of these animals, even in later years, was from all obtainable evidence, literally innumerable. There have been many attempts to estimate his probable number, from the size of particular herds, from the quantities of bones collected since his extermination and from other data; but while the attempt can, of course, never succeed with the least degree of precision, the proof is incontrovertible that they numbered millions and millions. It is a well-vouched fact that railroad trains have been stopped to let the herds pass over the track, while the delay of steamboats on the Missouri from a similar cause was by no means a rare occurrence. The innumerable trails worn by these animals may still be seen in many places, silent but impressive proofs of the vastness of the multitudes that used them.

Marvelous, however, as were the numbers of the buffalo, their complete disappearance from the face of the earth is more marvelous still. Ages of geological history were required to bring about the decline and disappearance of species that once flourished here, but the avarice of the hunter and trapper and the wanton cruelty of the sportsman have sufficed to exterminate the buffalo in the space of a single generation (2) (A).

The chief articles of commerce obtained from the buffalo were his skin, tongue, and tallow. In the matter of bulk, if not in number, the buffalo robes exceeded all other furs combined. They were mostly shipped from the immediate valley of the Missouri, because their weight and bulk made transportation by caravan difficult. The American Fur Company sent down to St. Louis, in 1840, 67,000 robes. In 1848 there were received at St. Louis 110,000 robes and other skins, mostly buffalo. These robes were scattered all over the United States and Europe and were everywhere used for lap robes and overcoats. A few of these old garments may still be seen in the West.

The quantity of tongues annually sent down to St. Louis was immense and in the single year of 1848 reached the number of 25,000. Tallow was likewise extensively shipped. A novel method of transporting it occasionally resorted to was to fill log canoes or dugouts with it, close them over tightly with skins and let them float down the river.

The great importance of the BEAVER in the life of the hunter and trapper arose almost entirely from the commercial value of its fur, which is one of the finest that nature produces. At this early period in particular it was in great demand. An average price was four dollars per pound, and as the little animal carried from one to two pounds on its body the premium for its destruction was from four to ten dollars, according to its size and the prevailing price of furs. As the streams of the West—of the whole country for that matter—originally swarmed with these animals in numbers that rivalled the illimitable buffalo herds of the plains, it will be readily understood what a mine of wealth here lay open to the industry of the trader and trapper.

Every stream of the West was as rich as if sands of gold covered its bottoms—a richness, moreover, which, if gathered with judgment and not to the degree of extermination, would renew itself by natural increase.

The American beaver (*Castor Canadensis*) is a small animal of very striking appearance and of amphibious habits. It is never found except near water courses and only near those which are lined with shrubbery. As with the whole animal kingdom, its peculiar methods of life have the single aim of securing it food, shelter, and protection. The beaver and his family live in lodges which are built near the shore, with the living room above water, but with a sub-aqueous passage whose outer opening is in the stream. In small streams, where the water is too shallow to conceal this passageway, or protect it from ice in the winter, the beaver builds dams to increase its depth. This part of his domestic economy makes the beaver a unique creature in the animal creation. It is the wonder of engineers how he can accomplish what he does. It is true that the dams are never high, only two or three feet, and much oftener less; but even for that height it is astonishing how such structures can withstand the pressure against them; for they are nothing but masses of sticks piled together in all directions and plastered up with mud. They are very effective, however, and nature soon strengthens them by causing shrubbery to grow upon them until finally they are so firmly interwoven with roots that they resist the stoutest floods. Moreover, the beaver believes in maintaining what he has built and so goes over his work with regular annual repairs. These are made both upon the dam and the lodge late in the season when the beaver is ready to house himself for the winter.

The cutting of trees by the beaver has a threefold purpose —the construction of the dam, the building of the house, and the supply of food. The beaver's diet is vegetable, and mainly the bark of trees, soft shrubs and the like. A large supply of sticks sufficient for the winter's need is gathered every fall. As the bark is gnawed from these during the winter they are carried out of the lodge and thrown either on the dam for use in reenforcing it or into the stream below, where they are washed away.

The beaver is often given more credit for sagacity in felling trees than he deserves. One has but to examine his work to see that he has comparatively little idea of the art as a successful woodsman practices it. He gnaws around the entire circumference and with a tree standing vertical his work would not have perceptible influence upon the direction of falling. But as it is usually the case that trees on the bank of a stream lean towards it, such trees when cut off, fall into the stream. The beaver shows no sagacity in this, unless in selecting those trees that have a decided inclination from the vertical and in the direction in which he wishes them to fall.

With that wonderful adaptation which nature shows in all her works, the anatomical makeup of the beaver is admirably suited to his mode of life. For cutting wood he has four powerful incisor teeth, two in each jaw, deeply planted, and curved in form, the upper ones being something more than a semicircle, and the lower ones something less. Powerful jaw muscles enable him to do his work, while extraordinary salivary glands provide the means of digesting his peculiarly dry and hard food. The tail of the beaver, like a powerful sculling oar, makes him a successful and expert navigator, while it enables him, with the further aid of his peculiarly shaped hind legs, to sit bolt upright when engaged in the work of cutting down trees.

As beaver fur was the great staple of the fur trade, and widely sought everywhere, trappers became very expert in their knowledge of the habits of the little animal and the best methods of taking him. They could readily tell, from the appearance of a lodge, the probable number of inmates and where they could most successfully entrap them. The universal mode of taking the beaver was with the steel trap, in the use of which long experience had taught the hunters great skill. The trap is a strong one of about five pounds weight, and was valued in the fur trade period at twelve to sixteen dollars. The chain attached to the trap is about five feet long, with a swivel near the end to keep it from kinking. The trapper, in setting the trap, wades into the stream, so that his tracks may not be apparent; plants his trap in three or four inches of water a little away from the bank, and fastens the chain to a strong stick, which he drives into the bed of the stream at the full chain length from the trap. Immediately over the trap a little twig is set so that one end shall be about four inches above the surface of the water. On this is put a peculiar bait, supplied by the animal itself, castor, castorum, or musk, the odor of which has a great attraction for the beaver. To reach the bait he raises his mouth toward it and in this act brings his feet directly under it. He thus treads upon the trap, springs it and is caught. In his fright he seeks concealment by his usual method of diving in deep water, but finds himself held by the chain which he cannot gnaw in two, and after an ineffectual struggle, he sinks to the bottom and is drowned. Not infrequently he wrests the chain from the stake, drags the trap to deeper water before he succumbs, or, taking it to the shore, becomes entangled in the undergrowth. In such cases he may cause the trapper much laborious and uncomfortable search, particularly if he has to wade deep streams in cold weather.

Generally the beaver was skinned near the place of its capture, and only the skin, the tail, and the castorum glands were taken to camp. Here other persons than the trappers attended to the work of cleaning, dressing, curing, and properly marking the skins. On the average it took about eighty skins to make a pack of one hundred pounds, the value of which was from three to five hundred dollars in the mountains. The packs were prepared with the utmost care, the choicest furs being placed in the inside. The great value of such property caused it to be guarded with much solicitude, for a single Indian could carry away, unaided, the rich produce of a year's hard labor.

The flesh of the beaver, except the tail, was not used for food, unless in scarcity of other supply. The tail was considered one of the richest delicacies whicht he mountains afforded, taking rank with the most favored parts of the buffalo.

The beaver also supplied another article of commerce, a

secretion from two small glands in its body. This was always known in the commerce of the mountains as castorum. In the arts it is more commonly called castor. In the mountains its value was about three dollars a pound. The castorum was used as the beaver's bait, and thus the little animal itself supplied the means of alluring its race to destruction.

The extensive use of beaver fur in the early years of the century caused an immense exportation from America to Europe, reaching as high as 200,000 skins annually. This great draught on the supply led to the rapid extermination of the beaver. It so happened, however, that at the time when this process had begun to show its effects, an unfavorable change came over the beaver market of Europe which helped to counteract it. Silk largely supplanted the use of this fur in the manufacture of hats, while other kinds of fur took its place in other uses. The price fell so that the trapping was no longer profitable, and nature, responding to the relief thus produced, began to recuperate her resources. In later years, although the price of beaver did not fully recover its old figure, its exportation began to increase, until it finally very nearly recovered its former magnitude.

The king of American wild beasts was the GRIZZLY BEAR (*Ursus horribilis*), the only animal which the hunter looked upon as really dangerous. It is distinguished from any other species of bear by several marked characteristics, such as facial profile, shape of anterior claws, color of hair, and lack of ability to climb trees. The color varies greatly, and the name grizzly is not an inapt description of it, although the preponderance of white was such, in the average specimen, that the name "white bear" was more commonly used by the hunter. In size the grizzly bear averaged about six feet in length from nose to tip of tail, but they were often found to measure nine, and instances are mentioned of the enormous length of fourteen feet. A weight of five hundred pounds was common. The grizzly was an exceedingly powerful animal, and extremely tenacious of life. He was not naturally pugnacious; very rarely attacked a man without provocation, and even when wounded frequently attempted to escape. But at such times it was the general experience that he was disposed to fight, and if thoroughly roused his strength and rage were terrible. It was often noted as a remarkable fact that when struck by a bullet he started instantly in the direction from which it came without waiting to see his enemy. However this may be, when once launched on his work of revenge, nothing could withstand him. His attack was from a standing position, first by means of a blow from his fore foot, which was then followed by gnashing and tearing with mouth and claws.

It was always of the first importance for the hunter to aim well in attacking these dangerous brutes. A shot between the eyes or behind the ear was most effectual, for bears have been known to survive several minutes and run a long distance after being shot through the heart. The great danger to the hunter was that of being caught with an empty gun after having inflicted a wound not mortal. It required coolness and composure rarely exemplified to stand and face calmly an enraged grizzly, even with a gun loaded. "Never be alarmed at a bear's rush" says a hunter of experience. "Never fire in a hurry. The bear will always stop, rise on his hind legs, and prepare to strike a sidelong blow with his fore feet. At this moment, when his head is extended, and in a position in which the ball will not glance, aim between the eyes and fire, and the bear will fall dead." Very good advice, but it would have been much more to the point to have given a recipe for cool nerves and the power to await calmly the approach of the ferocious monster, deliberately calculating the precise spot and moment for the fatal blow. The same authority adds that "two hunters of experience, armed with breech loaders, never hesitate to attack a bear. While he prepares to strike one, they will both get a good shot, one in front and the other behind the ears."

We find that all unlucky encounters with grizzly bears have resulted from this one cause: that the bear has been wounded, but not fatally, and has turned upon his assailant before the latter could reload his rifle or escape; or has so terrified the other hunters that they have either forgotten to shoot, or have lost the power of effective aim. The history of the fur trade is full of incidents of this nature. The majority were harmless and even ludicrous, but many resulted in injuries of a serious nature, while there were not a few instances of actual death.

One of the most noted encounters with a grizzly bear in the whole history of the west was that of Hugh Glass in 1823. This remarkable episode is made the subject of a separate chapter in another section of this work. The fury of the bear in this attack upon Glass was terrible, and left the victim in a state in which all hope of recovery was despaired of.

Another instance, and this time a fatal one, occurred near a camp of hunters on Purgatory River, in the present state of Colorado, November 13, 1831. It was perhaps the only instance on record where a grizzly bear has been known to climb a tree after its victim, but it appears that the tree was very much inclined, so that the bear had no difficulty in walking up it (3).

Another fatal encounter brings up a well-known name in the fur trade history of the West—that of the Sublettes. Andrew, one of the four Sublette brothers, of St. Louis, went to California after the discovery of gold there, and settled near Los Angeles. Grizzly bears of more than ordinarily ferocious type abounded there. The Indians rarely molested them, nor the Spaniards either, except when compelled to from their frequency around the ranches. But Sublette was not of this disposition. A famous bear hunter, passionately fond of the sport, he lost no time in testing the reputed qualities of the California type. In one of his encounters, accompanied by a powerful dog, himself a good bear fighter, he wounded one bear, when its mate suddenly pounced upon him from the bushes. With unloaded gun, he was compelled to battle with the aid of his dog and knife alone. He slew both bears, but himself received wounds from which he never recovered. A pathetic feature of this incident was the faithfulness of the dog, not only on the field of battle, but by the sick bed, and afterward by his master's grave, where he lingered inconsolable, refusing food and drink, until death came to his relief.

It would be easy to multiply these incidents, for they were

of frequent occurrence, and are well attested by reputable witnesses. They all justify the propriety of the zoological name—*Ursus horribilis*.

The fur of the grizzly bear did not have a high value, although it was generally saved, as opportunity afforded, and sent to market.

The BLACK BEAR (*Ursus Americanus*) was everywhere met with in the mountainous regions. It was an inoffensive animal and rarely dangerous, even when wounded. Its fur was valuable, and formed a regular part of the trade.

AUTHOR'S NOTES

(1) An instance of this, in which the hunter was the well-known adopted Crow chief, Edward Rose, is related in the Journal of the Atkinson Expedition of 1825, where an account is given of the killing of six buffalo. "Rose, an interpreter, one of the party, covered himself with bushes, and crawled into the gang of these bulls, and shot down the six on the ground before the others ran off."

(2) Some of the causes which contributed to the rapid disappearance of the buffalo are noted by Dr. F. V. Hayden who visited the Upper Missouri county several times between 1850 and 1860: "As near as I could ascertain, about 250,000 individuals are destroyed every year, about 100,000 being killed for robes. At the present time, the number of males to the females seems to be in the ratio of ten to one, and this fact is readily accounted for from the fact that the males are seldom killed when the cows can be obtained. Skins of females only are used for robes, and are preferred for food. Besides the robes which are traded to the whites by the Indians, each man, woman, and child requires from one to three robes a year for clothing.

A large quantity are employed in the manufacture of lodges, and an immense number of animals, which it would be difficult to estimate, are annually destroyed by wolves and by accidents." *Trans. Am. Phil. Soc.* vol. XII., New Series, 151.

(3) This incident is related in the Journal of Jacob Fowler, edited by Dr. Elliott Coues, F. P. Harper, New York, 1898, p. 41.

EDITOR'S NOTE

(A) In 1889 Hornaday estimated the number of wild and unprotected buffalo in the United States at 85, and in the rest of North America at 550. To these he added 256 in captivity, and 200 under protection in Yellowstone Park, a grand total of 1091. Since his tabulation, poachers at one time brought the number in Yellowstone Park down to 30.

So near was the buffalo to joining the Great Auk. Rigid protection has now brought back the numbers to tens of thousands, and there seems to be no longer any danger of extermination. In fact, in the year 1926 the Canadian government found it necessary to kill not less than 1,800 in the National Park at Alberta, because the increase had outgrown the available food supply. In 1933, there were similarly killed 2,000 head in the Wainwright herd.

The American Bison Society reports that a survey made in the early part of 1934 showed 4,404 buffalo in the United States and 17,043 in Canada.

Chapter VII

FAUNA: OTHER SPECIES OF INTEREST IN THE FUR TRADE

*The fur-bearing animals—The elk—The deer—The antelope—
The mountain sheep—The wolf—The panther—The prairie dog
—The horse—the dog—The term " game"—Birds of little im-
portance in the fur trade—Fishes—The salmon—Its great
importance—Description—Method of capture—The rattlesnake
—The mosquito—Ants and grasshoppers—The honey bee.*

Besides the beaver, there were many other animals which
had no particular value except for their fine furs. Among these
may be mentioned the large red, common red, and silver FOXES
(*Vulpes macruris, fulvis* and *argentalis*); the OTTER (*Lutra
Canadensis*); the MINK (*Putorius vision*); the RACCOON (*Procyon
hernandezi*); several varieties of SQUIRREL (*sciurus*); POLE CAT
(*Mephitis mephitica*); and the MUSKRAT (*Ondetra zibethicus*). All
of these animals were regularly hunted, and their furs were
annually shipped in considerable quantities to St. Louis. None
of them present any particular features of interest.

The ELK (*Cervus Canadensis*, or American Elk), was always
an important animal to the hunter and trapper, although for
flesh mainly. Next to the Buffalo it was probably the most
generally eaten. Its wide distribution, large size, and comparative ease of capture made it a great resource when buffalo
could not be had. Its meat was excellent, and a good elk steak
ranked well with domestic beef. The hide of the elk was but
little used, except for certain special purposes, being inferior
for general use to that of other wild animals. Its horns, likewise, were not used except in ornamentation. Fences were
made of them, doorways were ornamented with them, and in
a variety of ways the stately antlers of this noble animal did
service in adorning the abodes of men (1).

There were various species of the DEER, the most prominent
of which were the blacktail, or mule deer (*Cariacus Virgini-*

anus). Of these the first was considered the most important as game, and ranked with the elk in this regard. The deer was an excellent object for the sportsman's rifle, and good meat for his camp. The skin also was an important article of commerce; and shaved deer skins in particular formed no inconsiderable part of the cargoes which the American Fur Company brought annually from the Indian country.

The ANTELOPE (*Antilocapra Americana*) was one of the most interesting animals of the plains, although of little practical importance except for food, and then only when other game was scarce. Its flesh was considered very good, and it is said that its hide was used for saddles. Its great attraction for the hunter lay in its remarkably agile and watchful habits, which made its capture difficult, and an excellent test of sportsman-like skill.

The antelope has been called the gazelle of the prairies, and was the swiftest animal of the plains. It was quick of sight, acute of ear and smell, and ever alert for danger. Its flight was rarely direct, but broken and irregular, now this way and now that, pausing every little while to look at its pursuer, until finally it would disappear.

It was generally seen on the prairies in groups, rarely, however, within gunshot, or in depressions, where it could be approached under cover. It is said of the antelope that its curiosity afforded the surest way to capture it, and no less an authority than Audubon confirms this statement from his own experience. The usual method was to take a piece of red or scarlet cloth and tie it to a stick or ramrod. Then the hunter would lie down upon the prairie and alternately raise and lower the cloth. The curiosity of the antelope would be aroused, and he would circle round and round the spot, gradually coming nearer and nearer, his head erect, his movement full of suspicion, yet unable to overcome his curiosity at the strange object before him, until he would finally approach within the range of the hunter's rifle.

The MOUNTAIN SHEEP (*Ahsata*, or Bighorn), the *grosse corne* of the French (*Ovis Montana*), was to the Bad Lands what the Antelope was to the prairie: one of the most difficult animals to capture. Wonderfully agile, it possesses a skill in climbing rugged places and in getting about among crags and precipices that has ever been the wonder of those familiar with its performances. Its home was in the mountainous country, and as its color was not easily distinguishable from its environment, it was more generally observed when in its favorite position on the crests of cliffs, where its form stood out in clear relief against the sky. Among these inaccessible fastnesses the bighorn reared its young, and here was its sure refuge from its enemies. It derived a large part of its subsistence from the scanty herbage of these places, although it descended to the valleys for the more abundant grass to be found there.

The most striking feature in the appearance of the animal is its enormous head, neck, and horns. In a specimen mentioned by Irving, the horns were three feet eight inches long, and five inches through at the base. It is hard to conceive what use nature can have designed for such a ponderous impediment. It was a common belief among the hunters that the animal made use of its horns in leaping from cliff to cliff. Where the distance was too great to alight in safety upon its feet, it was said to fall upon its enormous horns, which, with its powerful neck, easily withstood the shock. There is no evidence that this theory was correct, although it is interesting enough to make one wish that it were. The broken horns of the male, often observed, are not, according to Audubon, due to this cause, as many hunters suppose, but to battles which the animals indulge in with each other.

The flesh of the bighorn was of excellent quality, and was rated among some Indian tribes as superior to buffalo meat. The great difficulty of procuring it, however, made it something of a rarity. No important commercial use was made of the skin or other parts of the animal; but its head and horns have always had a high value for ornamentation.

The WOLF was the most ignoble of the inhabitants of the plains. It personified cowardice, beggary, craftiness, deceit, mercilessness, and all the group of evil qualities that are comprised in the term *wolfishness*. It was the shark of the plains, and it followed the caravans for whatever it might find along the route, such as the refuse of camps, or the remains of buffalo and other game slain by the hunters. It delighted to disinter the bodies of persons who died on the way, and only the most thorough protection could save the graves of the dead from this desecration. It was essentially a cowardly animal, and attacked only the feeble and young, unless with overpowering numbers. Bands of wolves would indeed slay huge buffalo by their incessant annoyances; some say by constantly biting at the buffalo's tongue until it was destroyed, when death would result from starvation; others by biting the tendons of the legs until the animal was disabled, when it could be safely dispatched. Its methods were always stealthy and its attacks indirect. In the night it filled the air with its unearthly and hideous howlings, and gave an impression of power out of all proportion to what it really possessed. Such was the wolf, an animal of little matter to man, yet one that he had to take account of because of its troublesome habits. We shall notice but two of its varieties.

The American GREY WOLF (*Canis Lupus Occidentalis*) was the largest of the wolves and the most troublesome. Its length was about three feet and its color a dingy grey, though subject to much variation. The animal was rarely, if ever, known to attack man, even when impelled by extreme hunger. On the prairies it was generally found in the vicinity of buffalo herds, where it attacked the feeble and brokendown animals or the young calves. It is often said that wolves killed buffaloes and even the fleet antelope by chasing them in a circle, being frequently relieved by fresh runners, until the victim fell from exhaustion. Examples have been known where wolves have killed tethered animals during the night, and have also dragged articles almost from under the heads of the sleeping owners. They were always a source of extreme annoyance.

A much smaller species of wolf, but an exceedingly common one, was the COYOTE (*Canis Latrans*). It was a cowardly animal, rarely venturing, even in numbers, to attack large game, but its depredation in a smaller way, and its irrepressible night howlings, made it one of the greatest nuisances of the plains.

These are the two varieties of wolf which mainly concerned the trapper. They were never used for food except in case of necessity. The skin of the grey wolf, though gathered to some extent, was not of great value in the market, and formed an insignificant part of the fur trade.

The AMERICAN PANTHER (*Felis concolor*), the "painter" of the trappers, is of very little importance in fur trade history. Its flesh, however, was accounted the choicest which the wilderness afforded, not excepting even the tail of the beaver or the most delicate morsels from the buffalo. "Painter meat" was the synonym of anything which was particularly excellent.

The WILD CAT (*Lynx rufus*), and the COLUMBIA LYNX (*Lynx Canadensis*), were met with in different parts of the west, but received only scant attention from the hunters.

The PRAIRIE DOG (*Cynomys Ludovicianus*) is one of the most numerous and interesting, yet utterly useless, animals of the prairies, and is referred to here, not because the hunter derived any benefit from it, either for food or fur, but because it always excited the curiosity of travelers in that country. There is no quadruped of the plains that receives more attention in the narratives of the time than does the prairie dog.

As seen in different localities it varies greatly in size, in some places being fully fifteen inches in length, and in others scarcely five. Whether these differences are specific or not is not clear. The little animal resembles slightly in form and habits the woodchuck or ground hog of the East. It is much smaller, however, lighter in color, and more gregarious in its habits. It burrows in the ground as the woodchuck does, but always in villages or colonies, and such a thing as the solitary dwelling of a prairie dog is scarcely to be seen. Its "towns" or "villages" usually contain a great number of habitations, and the passerby will see the white mounds, where the earth has been thrown out of the holes, scattered thickly in every direction. Upon these he will find the little inmates gathered singly or in groups, some sitting erect on their haunches, others with their heads aimed toward the holes ready to dart in on the instant, and others still capering from one mound to another. They set up a shrill but diminutive yelp, which, in a large town, makes a continual clatter. Upon the too near approach of the visitor they utter a succession of yelps, shake their short tails with incredible rapidity, and dart into their holes. So remarkably quick are they in concealing themselves that it is only with great difficulty that they can be taken. It requires a good shot to hit one, and then the chances are that even if the shot is mortal the animal will escape beyond reach before it dies. Attempts to drown the dogs out of their holes, and likewise to dig them out, have almost invariably proved unsuccessful.

The prairie dog dwells always upon the arid prairie, and feeds exclusively upon the short prairie grass. It would seem that it lives without water. The towns make dangerous ground for horseback riding, on account of the frequent holes, in which the horses are liable to stumble.

A remarkable peculiarity of these villages is that they are likewise inhabited by the rattlesnake and a species of owl. Stansbury says that in passing through one of these towns several of the dogs were shot by members of the party, but when it was attempted to reach into the holes and pull them out, they were invariably met with the ominous rattle of the dreaded reptile. Whether the rattlesnake and the owl are enemies or friends of the prairie dog, naturalists have left undetermined, but it would hardly seem as if such close companionship could be compatible with very bitter enmity.

The HORSE (*Equus Caballus*), in its wild or domesticated state, was everywhere met with throughout the West during the period of the fur trade. It was, however, a comparatively recent arrival there, for it was not native to America, but was a descendant from the horse introduced by the Spaniards into Mexico. It multiplied with great rapidity, and in its wild state overspread the southern plains, where it was captured by the Indians and scattered over every part of the West. The wild horse or mustang of the southern plains was very common in the early times of the Santa Fe Trail. He is described as a very beautiful animal when wild, although presenting nothing of extraordinary attraction when reduced to a domesticated condition. The mustangs generally moved in droves of considerable size, and occasionally caused the trader no little trouble by dashing in among his stock. The latter were much more inclined to adopt the habits of the mustang than the former the restraints of domestic bondage.

The mustang was an animal of considerable commercial

importance, and thousands of them were caught for the market. They were generally taken with the lasso, and were easily tamed. A method of capture sometimes resorted to was that of "creasing," which consisted in shooting a rifle ball through the top of the neck so as to cut a nerve at that point. The animal was rendered momentarily insensible and before he recovered was securely fastened. The method required such fine marksmanship as to be rarely resorted to, on account of the large proportion of animals killed. Pike relates that the Mexicans sometimes caught them by means of an artificial enclosure similar to the buffalo pen of the northern Indians.

There was a tradition in the early days of a mustang of marvelous beauty, a stallion, perfect in form and milkwhite in color save for a pair of black ears. It was as fleet as it was beautiful, and no horseman was ever able to take it. It was reported to have been seen in nearly every part of the West, but its existence was doubtless one of those myths which always abound in a country not yet reduced to a matter-of-fact civilization.

The horse of the Indian was an animal of greatest usefulness to the tribes, as indeed it has been to the human race in all ages. The Indian pony was an inferior animal to the breeds which have been developed in civilized communities, but it was nevertheless strong and enduring, and seemed to fit in perfectly with the Indian's mode of life. So important were these animals that their capture or theft was considered the greatest object of Indian wars and forays, and innumerable were the hostile encounters of which they have been the cause.

The importance of the horse in the business of the fur trade can scarcely be overestimated. Except in the immediate vicinity of the Missouri river it was the universal reliance for transportation. It was the hunter's inseparable companion, and its loss was about the greatest calamity he could suffer. Many a promising venture has ended in disaster because of the loss of horses. The guarding of these animals against the cunning wiles of the Indians was an object of never-ending solicitude, and many were the lives lost in repelling attempts to steal them.

Scarcely less in importance to the Indian than the horse was the DOG, a long, slender, wolfish animal, whose general appearance clearly denoted its consanguinity with the cowardly denizens of the plains. The Indian dog was an inseparable feature of Indian life. They were present in large numbers in every village, and white visitors found them an intolerable nuisance. Before the advent of horses among the Indians, dogs were used as beasts of burden, and continued to be so used in later times in the winter season, when they were the only animal that could successfully stand the long sled journeys over the snow. The flesh of the dog was the greatest delicacy the Indian could offer his guest, and all narratives of Western adventure abound in references to this hospitality so repugnant to the white man, but which he perforce must accept in order to avoid giving offence to his host.

This may be a proper place to consider the meaning of the term "game" as used by the hunters. It referred to those animals whose flesh was good for food, and which were regularly sought by the hunter for that purpose, and included not only several of the quadrupeds already noticed, but certain of the birds and fishes presently to be referred to. The presence of game in the different sections of the country was one of the most uncertain things that hunters or trappers had to consider, and its varying quantity at different times was a phenomenon which it is difficult to explain. At one time it was found in plenty; at another, in the same locality, it was impossible to find enough to save one from starvation. All books of early Western travel complain of the scarcity of game, some in this place, some in that. The truth seems to be that a migratory habit was characteristic of all game, and it did not remain in any fixed locality. Doubtless careful observation and study might have discovered the law of these movements, so that it could have been predicted where the game was most liable to be found at certain seasons. But this was never done, and the hunter was therefore always vibrating between plenty and want—this week luxuriating in the wealth of buffalo meat, and the next reduced to the very brink of starvation. A precarious sort of life was that which relied for subsistence solely upon the capture of game.

The winged portion of the animal creation in the Far West filled a very small place in the life of the hunter and trapper.

In a land of large game, the hunting of birds had little attraction, for ordinarily meat could be much more easily procured from other sources. On the lower Missouri and in the southwest the wild turkey abounded, and was extensively used for food. Everywhere upon the water courses wild geese and the several varieties of ducks were met with and were often captured by the hunters when nothing better was at hand. The same was true of the numerous varieties of ground birds, such as the prairie chicken, sage hens, grouse, pheasants, and the like. For the capture of winged game, whether birds of the bush or water fowl, the hunters attached to the large parties regularly carried fowling pieces.

As to the other birds, they have no practical connection with the business of the fur trade. The swan, eagle, crane, hawk, raven, magpie, and buzzard abounded, some very generally, others in certain localities, but the hunter had little use for them, unless he sought to imitate the Indian by ornamenting his person with their plumes and feathers.

Fishes, likewise, with few exceptions, were of small importance in fur trade history. The numerous species that inhabited the Missouri were used to a considerable extent at the trading posts. The mountain trout, where they could be found, were also used in times of necessity. For the most part, however, the catching of fish was pretty tame sport, and never a substantial resource for food.

The principal exception to this general rule was the SALMON (*Oncorhynchus chavicha*), whose home was on the Columbia and its tributaries. This wonderful fish was to the tribes of the lower Columbia what the buffalo was to those on the plains, so far at least as it was possible for one to supply the place of the other. The salmon, of which there were several varieties on the Columbia, was a large fish, weighing from fifteen to twenty-five pounds, with frequent specimens of a much larger size. The shape of the fish and the color of the flesh are well known. Its muscular power was very great, and was called into constant play in its attempts to ascend the rapids of the rivers. The chief characteristic of the salmon that has a practical interest in this connection is its ascent of the river in the spawning season, for it is this that gives the fisherman a chance to exercise his trade to great advantage. The salmon begin to ascend the river in the month of April, and so vast are its numbers that one reputable author, who wrote from personal observation, declared that it would be as easy to count the pebbles on the beach as the fish in the water. The Columbia and its tributaries are obstructed with frequent cataracts and cascades. Here the salmon find great difficulty in ascending and here they display the great muscular strength which they possess. The delay in climbing these rapids causes them to accumulate in great numbers immediately below, and at these places the fisherman gather to take them. Some of the cascades, like the Salmon Falls on the Snake River, have been famous fishing points from the earliest times. In their long journey up these difficult rivers, the labor of ascent wastes their flesh, and their bodies become scarred from contact with the rocks, until by the time they reach the upper rivers they are reduced to mere skeletons, covered over with the mutilations they have undergone.

The salmon, having reached the remotest headwaters of the tributaries, brings forth its young, and never again, it is said, descends to the sea. But the young descend in the fall, and after a period of four years, according to some authorities, themselves ascend the river to the place of their birth, which in turn becomes the place where they die. It is indeed an interesting order of life, that of the salmon of the Columbia River, and it has always had a great attraction for observers of nature.

To the tribes of the lower Columbia, the salmon was the principal source of subsistence. Even to the Nez Perces and the Shoshones, in the valleys of the Snake and Salmon rivers, it was a great reliance, although those tribes depended also upon other game. The Indians took the salmon with a kind of seine or basket, and also with the spear, and during the fishing season they gathered in great numbers at the fishing points, camping along the banks, and covering the rocks around with their spears and nets. Not only did the Indians live on these fish during the fishing season, but they collected a store sufficient for the rest of the year. They had a very effectual method of preparing it, similar to that of preparing pemmican, another evidence that neither canned beef nor canned salmon is a strictly modern invention.

The salmon has become a great article of commerce, and fortunately it cannot be exterminated as the buffalo has been, although it is said to have been greatly reduced in numbers.

Among reptiles we shall notice only the RATTLESNAKE (*Crotalus confluentus*) as the single species that played any part of note in the life of the hunter and trapper. The fatal character of the bite of the rattlesnake caused it to be regarded with a degree of dread quite out of proportion to the real danger. Deaths from its bites were of the greatest rarity, particularly among men. Mules and horses more frequently suffered. But there were enough of these incidents to inspire a respectful dread of the loathsome animal, and it was really more of a terror than the grizzly itself. Mountaineers who never quailed before a "white bear" were completely unnerved by the sound of the stealthy rattle, and nothing in all their experience was so abhorrent as the suspicion that this subtle creature was creeping into bed, even if with no other purpose than to avail itself of the warmth of the hunter's body. In many localities these snakes swarmed in prodigious numbers. Generally they dwelt in crevices in the rocks, and it was not uncommon to find them by the hundreds basking in the sun. On the prairies they were mostly found at the prairie dog villages, not from any probable affinity for that animal, but because its burrows afforded a convenient lodging.

The size of the rattlesnake varied from two to six feet in length. Its distinguishing features were its brownish spotted color, its teeth, which consisted of two fangs in the upper jaw, through which was emitted the fatal poison; its rattles, which were at the end of its tail, and which gave an infallible warning of its presence never to be mistaken by one who had heard it; and the peculiar spiral coil into which it threw itself whenever it attempted to strike or bite.

The rattlesnake was not an aggressive reptile, and there is no evidence that it ever attacked without provocation, although the provocation might be wholly unintentional on the part of the offender. Accidents from these snakes most often occurred from coming upon them unawares, stepping upon them, or otherwise interfering with their liberty.

The skin of the rattlesnake and its teeth and rattles were often used for ornamentation, while its flesh was occasionally used for food, when necessity compelled a resort to it. By some it was considered a delicacy, and it was a common saying that, but for the repulsiveness of the reptile itself, its flesh would rank with that of other animals.

Besides the rattlesnakes, the lizards, horned frogs, and similar reptiles are mentioned by the writers in the early times, but they played no important part in the life of the trapper.

Among insects, by far the most important, because of its intolerable annoyances, was the MOSQUITO (*Culex mosquito*). Scarcely any other member of the animal kingdom received more attention than this from the early traveler. It abounded everywhere except upon the naked prairie, and was particularly numerous in those places which were most frequented by man, the river valleys and the forests which lined the streams. So fierce and incessant were their attacks that at times they completely absorbed the energies of the individuals, and have been known to cause the death of horses.

Strange as it may seem, their strength and voracity increase with the latitude, and they are more terrible the farther north they are met. It is as if all their energies were concentrated into the shorter season, and that their power increased inversely with the length of time in which it was exercised. With these explanations the reader of the literature of this period will be less inclined to belittle the virility of the mountaineer and explorer for giving so much space to the consideration of so diminutive a creature. He will see how far-reaching may be its influence when it destroys the aim of the rifle, interferes with the explorer when making important observations, causes the pilot to let slip his wheel in dangerous places, to say nothing of destroying sleep and so inflaming the skin as to unfit one for work. Of all the pests of the prairies the mosquito was incomparably the worst. With it must also be classed the various kinds of flies that annoyed the horses at certain seasons.

In the Great Basin the more degraded nations used ANTS for

food. They were collected in large quantities, washed free from the dirt in which their mounds were built, and then crushed into a kind of pastry, which was much relished by the Indians. It is also recorded that these insects were frequently eaten alive by the handful as scooped up from the anthills.

Father De Smet gives an interesting account of the use which these same Indians make of GRASSHOPPERS and of their method of catching them. They begin by digging a hole ten or twelve feet in diameter and four or five feet deep. They then take long branches of sage brush and surround a field of three or four acres, more or less, according to the number of persons engaged in the work. They stand about twenty feet apart and commence by thrashing the ground to frighten up the grasshoppers, thus continually driving them towards the pit, until all fall into it. It often happens that a few acres will yield enough of these insects to fill the hole prepared for them. "They [the Indians] have their tastes like other people" observes Father De Smet. "Some eat the grasshoppers in soup; others mash them and make a kind of pie of them, which they harden or bake in the sun or dry by a fire; others still take pointed sticks, on which they string the larger grasshoppers, and as fast as they are sufficiently roasted the poor Indians regale themselves until the repast is entirely consumed."

Another interesting insect that played no inconsiderable rôle in the pioneer period of the country along the lower half of the Missouri River, was the common HONEY BEE. Like the white man, the bee was an intruder into these remote solitudes, where he preceded the settler by only a few years. The Indians were accustomed to say that they could tell that the white man's advance was near wherever the honey bee came. The abundance of these insects was astonishing, if we may accept the many corroborated accounts of the explorers. Their hive was almost always in hollow trees, occasionally, however, in hollows of rocky bluffs. So plentiful were the "bee trees" in early times that search for them in certain localities was as much a part of the hunter's labor as was the search for game. Honey was a common article of food on the frontier and considerable quantities were at one time shipped to St. Louis.

AUTHOR'S NOTE

(1) In the thirties there was a notable monument of elk horns on the prairie near the Missouri river above the mouth of the Yellowstone. It had been gradually built up by the Indians, who, whenever they passed, placed each a brace of antlers upon it, until, at the time of Maximilian's visit in 1833, it was about eighteen feet high and fifteen feet through at the base, forming a most unusual and striking object.

Chapter VIII

NATIVE TRIBES: GENERAL OBSERVATIONS

The predatory tribes—Their shelter, dress, etc.—Subsistence—
Methods of life—Good fur gatherers—Their rovings—Perma-
nent village tribes—Huts and villages—Convenience of villages
for purposes of trade—Habitat of the stationary tribes—Routine
life of the tribes—War; its terrible meaning to the Indian—At-
traction of Indian life—Its unfortunate extinction—The Algon-
quian family—The Siouan family—The Shoshonean family—
Other families—Importance of ethnic relations in the life of
the tribes.

The trans-Mississippi Indian differed in no essential particular from his Eastern brother. Such differences as there were
were those of environment, and these had not continued long
enough to develop permanent characteristics. The denizen of
the treeless prairies must needs have led a somewhat different
life from him of the Eastern forest, but not so different that
either would have found it difficult to adapt himself to the
situation of the other. It thus happened that the frontiersman
of Kentucky or Illinois, who had been reared in the midst of
savage neighbors, found his experience perfectly adapted to
the changed conditions of the Western plains in his onward
march beyond the confines of civilization. The Indian there was
like the Indian with whom he was already familiar, and his fertil-
ity of resource quickly made him master of the new situation.

Before taking up a consideration of the separate tribes with
which the trader had to do, it will be well to note those general characteristics which were common to most of them. The
greater part of the Western tribes were wandering or predatory, while a few along the Missouri valley and in the southwest dwelt in permanent villages. Even the predatory tribes
had their particular habitat or country, to which the always
returned from their excursions, but they were essentially a

nomadic people, moving from place to place, and making long journeys for the purposes of the chase or of war.

The shelter of the predatory tribes consisted of the immemorial conical tent or tepee, which was made of poles and skins. The poles rested on the ground on the circumference of a circle, and were bound together in a sheaf near the top, leaving a small section of the upper nappe projecting into the air. Upon this framework was stretched a covering made of buffalo skins. A hole was left at the top for the egress of smoke from the fire, which was built in the center of the lodge. A small, low door was provided by drawing up from the ground the flap of one of the skins. This simply-constructed shelter was exceedingly comfortable as tents go, and was set up, taken down, packed and moved with remarkable facility.

The Indian's clothing, before the white man came, was made almost exclusively of skins, and was ornamented with feathers, the teeth of animals, and numberless other gew-gaws, which were obtained from a variety of sources. His feet were shod in leather moccasins, and heavy robes gave him the extra protection which the colder seasons required. In the summer he wore very little clothing, and his children practically none. He painted his body in the most grotesque and repulsive manner, and among some tribes, even resorted to mutilation or deformation. After the trader came, the cloth blanket largely replaced the skin robe as an article of apparel.

An Indian chief, decked out in all the finery which savage ingenuity could devise, was, according to all accounts, an imposing personage. His wild and motley apparel struck the imagination of the hunters, and they always sought to imitate it in their own dress. It is related that the free hunter was never more satisfied than when he had made this imitation so perfect that he was taken for an Indian.

The wandering tribes, and even those who dwelt in permanent villages, were mostly expert horsemen. The horse was exceedingly important to their manner of living; and the business of securing horses, which was mostly by theft from their neighbors, was the highest calling, with the exception of war, of which, indeed, it was generally the principal motive.

In moving from place to place, the impedimenta of the

tribes were loaded by the squaws upon the characteristic travois—two long poles crossing over the horse's back and trailing on the ground behind him, with crosspieces fastened to them for supporting the load—and the camps were struck and pitched with marvelous facility and dispatch.

Their subsistence was mainly the fruit of the chase, for their migratory habits were not suited to agricultural pursuits. They were generally excellent hunters, and depended largely upon the buffalo for support. Their primitive weapons were the bow and arrow, but these were, to a great extent, replaced in later years by the more effective weapons introduced by the traders.

These Indians were good fur gatherers, and were always sought by the trader. Generally one or more posts were established in the heart of their country, while itinerant traders were sent to accompany the various bands in their wanderings and trade for their furs as soon as they were taken.

As a general thing the wandering tribes were among the most stalwart and robust of their race, fond of the attractions of dress, haughty and vainglorious on occasion, much given to pomp and bluster, yet withal stubborn fighters, and, as their subsequent history has proven, foemen worthy of the white man's steel. The extent of their rovings was very great, particularly those of the Crows and Blackfeet, who were met in almost every section of the West from the Spanish provinces to the British possessions. At no other time were they so lawless and dangerous as in their raids into distant sections, especially if the purpose of their forays had not been successful.

Numbers of the western tribes along the Missouri River had permanent villages where they spent most of their time and to which they returned from their excursions. The essential peculiarities which this difference in mode of life developed related mainly to shelter and food. These Indians had fixed huts of large size and stable construction. They were situated close together, without any very regular order, except that they were often set in a circular row with a considerable space in the center. The huts themselves were usually circular in shape with conical or slightly vaulted roofs. The outer walls were supported by a row of posts, and in the center were four

longer posts with suitable cross timbers at the top to receive
the upper ends of rafters of which the lower ends rested upon
cross timbers supported by the outer posts. A brush wattling
was spread over the rafters and sides of the hut, which were
then covered with straw and thickly plastered with mud. The
huts so made were very strong, as may be judged from the fact
that the Indians frequently congregated upon them in considerable numbers.

The fire was built in the center of the lodge and a hole was
left in the top for the egress of the smoke. The beds were
arranged around the walls and were often covered with a can-
opy of skins. A whole family usually occupied a lodge, in
which was also reserved a space for the horses when there was
danger of capture. The articles belonging to the family were
variously bestowed, and a single door, closed by a skin cur-
tain, gave access alike to man and beast. Among some of the
tribes the form of the huts was polygonal, the octagon being
the usual figure, while by one tribe at least, a rectangular
form was used.

In regard to subsistence, permanent residence in fixed
localities made possible the development of a crude agriculture, and around these villages there were fields of corn, and
the more common vegetables introduced by the white man.
Although these tribes frequently made long excursions from
home, their roamings were rarely so distant or diversified as
those of other tribes. The Pawnees were possibly an exception to this rule, while the Aricaras were also fond of a
predatory life.

The permanent village accommodated itself to the business
of the fur trade much better than did the wandering village.
It was a simple matter to maintain establishments where the
places of abode were fixed, and posts were accordingly found
at one time or another at or near all of these villages. These
tribes, moreover, were more uniformly friendly to the whites
than were those restless spirits whose very wanderings developed in them the character of freebooters and pirates. To
this rule the Pawnees and Aricaras were the only exceptions.

The country of the stationary tribes in the immediate
valley of the Missouri was simply that where their villages

were located, and whenever they went beyond this they did so at the sufferance, or in defiance, of their neighbors. This was particularly true of the Minnetarees, the Mandans, and the Aricaras. The Pawnees and the Osages, on the other hand, were recognized as controlling a wide area of territory.

The routine life of the tribes, as it existed during the trapping era, was simple in its general scheme, but in detail full of incident and adventure. When in camp in the case of the predatory tribes, or when residing in fixed villages, the life was a quiet one, filled up largely with the work of women, the sports of the children, and the gossip and interchange of views of the men. When the season came for laying up a supply of food, as when the buffalo drew near, great preparations were made both for the sport of hunting and for the care of the meat. These were seasons of activity and excitement as well as of hard work, and the subsequent comfort of the village depended on how well the work was done. Moreover the gathering of robes was the Indian's great source of revenue, and he had a care to lay in a goodly store for trade whenever he should go to the company's posts, or their traders should come to reside with him.

The tribes often had, however, more serious work on hand than that of providing subsistence and securing robes and furs. Their enemies might be on the warpath, and their very existence might depend upon the most active and energetic measures of defense. It is difficult to realize what a mighty question this was to the Indian. War among civilized countries is terrible, but with them prisoners are not killed, private property is supposed to be respected, noncombatants are left uninjured, and only such destruction of life and property is permitted as is necessary for the direct crippling of the enemy's military power. Not so in the wars of the Indian. His theory of war was extermination. Not only did he kill all he could in battle, but he slew prisoners, destroyed the enemy's property, whether of a military character or not, carried of or killed his women and children. War, therefore, had a terrible meaning to the Indian, and the attack of an enemy was like a destroying whirlwind, spreading ruin and devastation in its path.

But the Indian did not always await the onslaught of his enemy. The village was frequently called upon to depart on some perilous enterprise of war to avenge the death of some of their number or to secure such spoils as they might find. Then, too, they made frequent excursions on peaceful errands, as when they visited friendly tribes, or sought some locality where buffalo were plenty, or went to a timbered section to find poles for their lodges. There were, in short, in the Indian's mode of life, demands of business quite as imperious to him as were those of civilized life to his pale-face brother.

That the white man found much to his taste in the wild, free life of the Indian is amply proven by the willingness with which so many abandoned the blessings of civilization for the hardships of the wilderness. There was in the Indian character and manner of life much to admire. In spite of the absence of the ideals of civilized life, in spite of revolting uncleanliness, loose and dissolute habits, and an utter absence of mercy toward an enemy—in spite of the fact that the Indian was a true savage, he was nevertheless not disliked by those who knew him most nearly. Since he was first known he has been admired for his rude eloquence, his deeply religious nature, his fine sense of right and justice, his steadfastness to his friends, his wild and manly sports, his love of the chase, and his bravery in war. It will ever be a source of poignant regret among the millions of those who helped despoil him of his country, and who look with pity upon a fate which they were powerless to avert, that there could not have been reserved in all this vast continent a true home for the Indian—a place where he could have led the life he used to lead when he chased the deer and buffalo, trapped the cunning beaver, and made war upon his enemies. Such was the life for which alone he was fitted, and we have yet to see any departure from it that has not resulted disastrously to his race.

The tribes with which this work has mainly to do belonged, with few exceptions, to three great linguistic stocks—the Algonquian, the Siouan, and the Shoshonean.

The Algonquian family was distinguished for noble tribes, stalwart warriors, and a high type of aboriginal development. It occupied some of the fairest portions of North America, both East and West. Its western territory extended from the Great Lakes to the Rocky Mountains and lay mainly in what is now British territory. Those tribes which resided wholly or in part within the territorial limits of the United States were the Arapahoes, the Cheyennes, the Blackfeet, and the Gros-ventres of the Prairie.

The most important of all the linguistic stocks to the purposes of this investigation was the Siouan. It occupied nearly the whole of the immediate valley of the Missouri, with a wide extent of territory on either side. It was a well-developed race both intellectually and physically and in its individuals the Indian was seen in its purest type. Among the well-known tribes of this family which figured prominently in the American fur trade were the Crows, the Assiniboines, the Minnetarees, the Mandans, the Sioux, the Poncas, the Omahas, the Iowas, the Otoes, the Kansas, the Osages, and the extinct tribe from which the great river takes its name, the Missouris.

The Shoshonean family dwelt in the Great Basin and in the valleys of the Snake River and the Colorado of the West, with one wandering tribe in the plains. While it included some of the most virile tribes, it included also some of the most degraded and pitiable upon the continent. Those with which we shall here come in contact were the Shoshones or Snakes, the Utahs, the Pai-Utes, or Diggers, the Bannocks, and the Sheepeaters—all mountain tribes—and the Comanches who roamed over the prairies on the south side of the Arkansas.

Besides these three important families there were the Caddoan, represented by the Pawnees and the Aricaras; the Kiowan by the Kiowas; the Athapascan, by the Apaches and the Navajos; three different stocks, represented by the Pueblos; the Shahaptian, whose principal tribe was the Nez Perces; and the Salishan, which included the Flatheads. There were also many other stocks in the country along the Pacific coast, but they were outside of the theater of the American fur trade.

A knowledge of the ethnic relations of the various tribes is of practical value in explaining certain peculiarities of Indian history, even in those early days when the commercial mind of the traveler never dwelt upon such matters. The various alliances among the tribes usually followed those relationships. How it was that the Aricaras and the Cheyennes were preëminently the horse-dealing tribes among the northern Indians may be understood when it is known that their kindred, the Pawnees and the Arapahoes, with whom they were on terms of friendly intercourse, dwelt in or roamed over the country where the mustang flourished. The ubiquitous wanderings of that terrible tribe, the Grosventres of the Prairie, throughout the country to the south of their own, are explained when it is remembered that these Indians were closely related to the Arapahoes, and were wont to make frequent excursions to the country of that tribe. Other equally important deductions will reward the labor of the student who takes pains to bear these relationships in mind (1).

AUTHOR'S NOTE

(1) Before taking up the following brief account of the various tribes of the West, it will be well to remind the reader of what was said in the preface of this work: That the purpose of these descriptions is not to present an exhaustive treatment of the subjects considered, but solely to show their relation to the business of the fur trade. Into the boundless fields of the ethnography and archaeology of the aborigines west of the Mississippi it is not intended to enter at all. The purpose here in view will have been attained if the reader is given a clear idea of that portion of the political history of the tribes which relates to their intercourse with the fur trader. It was in this intercourse that the Indian Question had its origin, and here began, for better or worse, that process which must eventually result in reducing the Indian to a civilized order of life.

Chapter IX

NATIVE TRIBES OF THE MISSOURI BASIN

The Blackfeet—Their territory—Origin of name—Division of the tribe—The Grosventres of the Prairie—Habitat of the various Blackfoot bands—Importance of the Blackfeet to the traders —Characteristics of the tribe—The Crows—The Crow country— Characteristics of the tribe—Relation to the traders—Their horse-stealing propensities—The Assiniboines—The Minnetarees—The Mandans—The Aricaras—Their history—Their treachery—Their staples of trade—The Sioux nations—History —Characteristics—The Yanktonais—The Tetons—Importance of the Sioux tribes to the trader—Their attitude toward the traders—The Cheyennes—Tribal history—Characteristics— Great horse dealers—The Pawnees—Tribal history—Relation of Pawnee Loups to Aricaras—Characteristics of the Pawnees— Under Spanish influence—Relations with the traders—Lower Missouri tribes—The Poncas—The Omahas—The Kansas— The Osages—The Iowas—The Otoes—The Missouris.

THE BLACKFEET (*Algonquian*)

Coming now to a more detailed enumeration of the various tribes, the first to arrest our attention is that of the terrible Blackfeet, the scourge of the upper Missouri country during the whole of the period considered in this work. The territory of the Blackfeet was the watershed of the Missouri above the mouth of, and including, the Milk River, although it may be a doubtful question if the territory above the Three Forks ought not rather to be considered as common or fighting ground of the various tribes. The heart of the Blackfoot country may be taken as in the immediate valley of the Missouri near the mouth of the Marias, where the river makes its great bend from north to east.

There were included under the general term Blackfeet four distinct bands; the Blackfeet proper (*Siksikau*), the Piegan (*Pikuni*), the Bloods (*Kainah*), and the Grosventres of the Prairies or the Falls Indians (*Atsina*), numbering all told about 14,000 souls. Early writers mention also the Surcies and the Little Robes, but these two bands were not prominent in the tribal history of the nation. By the fur traders these Indians were all included under the general term Blackfeet (1), for they dwelt in the same country, spoke similar dialects, and much resembled each other in personal appearance. But to those well acquainted with them there was always a well-recognized distinction. With two of the bands in particular the trader became intimately acquainted, although for exactly opposite reasons. The Piegans were peaceably disposed to the whites as a general thing, and the first successful trading post established in Blackfoot territory was built at the mouth of the Marias River, the usual habitat of this band, and was honored with their name. It was with the Piegans that the principal trade in this part of the country was conducted (2).

The Grosventres of the Prairie, on the other hand, were the most relentlessly hostile tribe ever encountered by the whites in any part of the West, if not in any part of America, and the trapper always understood that to meet with one of these Indians meant instant and deadly hostility. The greater part of the many conflicts between the whites and the Blackfeet were with this tribe. Such was the case in the famous battle of Pierre's Hole in 1832. The origin of this hostility is traced in another chapter of this work (3), but its long continuance is still without adequate explanation.

The tribal affinity of the Grosventres was with the Arapahoes, and the two tribes always maintained a feeling of friendship for each other. They once lived together with another kindred tribe, the Cheyennes, near the headwaters of the Mississippi and the Great Lakes. For some cause they migrated westward, the Cheyennes first branching off to the south, and later the Arapahoes to the southwest, while the Grosventres kept on to the west until they reached the foothills of the mountains. The close relationship between the Grosventres and the Arapahoes was a matter of great conse-

quence in fur trading times. It was the custom of the Grosventres to visit their friends every two or three years. They
went sometimes by way of the Crow country and the Black
Hills, but generally by the headwaters of the Snake and Green
rivers and the mountains of northern Colorado, in order to avoid
the Crows, who were the most powerful and uncompromising
of their enemies. As nearly all the intermediate tribes through
whose country they passed were hostile to them, their excursions were always occasions for bloody conflicts. It was inevitable that the trappers who overspread this entire country
should have frequent encounters with them, although it has
puzzled many writers to understand why this band should
have been met with in such widely separated localities. It was
on one of their return trips from the Arapahoes that they fought
the trappers in Pierre's Hole, as elsewhere narrated (4). The
name Grosventre, as applied to the large eastern tributary of
Snake River in Jackson Hole, and also to a neighboring range
of mountains, was given from the circumstance that the Grosventres passed along this stream on their way to the Arapahoes about the year 1830.

The Grosventres were also commonly called Falls Indians
in this early day, from the fact, it is said, that they lived near
the Falls of the Saskatchewan. In common usage they were
called Blackfeet by the traders and trappers, and very few
understood their true tribal relations. Their own language
was difficult to acquire, and as they understood the Blackfoot
language they always used it in their intercourse with the
whites. This tended further to confuse the distinctions between the two tribes, and accounts for the fact that so many
of the hostile acts of the Grosventres were charged up to the
account of the Blackfeet. Thus it has always been commonly
understood that it was a Blackfoot Indian that Captain Lewis
killed on his return from the Pacific in the summer of 1806,
but it was, as a matter of fact, a Grosventre.

Next to the Grosventres, the Blood Indians were the most
troublesome to the traders. They were bitterly hostile, but
their wanderings did not so often bring them into contact
with the whites. The Siksikau, or Blackfeet proper, were also
very hostile.

As the several bands roamed over pretty much the same territory, it is difficult to say just what the usual habitat of each was; but, broadly speaking, the Siksikau dwelt northeast in the valley of Milk River; the Bloods near the sources of the Marias and Milk; the Piegans west of the Missouri along the lower course of the Marias; and the Grosventres along the south shore of the Missouri from the Great Falls to the Judith Basin, although some authorities place them north on the south fork of the Saskatchewan.

All of the Blackfoot bands belonged to the predatory class of Indians and their wanderings were very extensive. As they were hostile to nearly all the surrounding tribes, and as they were constantly invading their neighbor's territory, they lived in a perpetual state of warfare. Another source of trouble with their neighbors was the fact that Judith Basin was one of the most popular buffalo regions in the entire West, and the tribes from beyond the mountains, such as the Snakes, Nez Perces, and Flatheads, annually repaired thither for their supply of meat. Such visits were more than likely to result in hostile encounters.

For two reasons the Blackfeet Indians were of great importance in the fur trade: their country was the richest beaver country of the West and the Indians themselves were the most hostile. Abundant riches and deadly peril were therefore the conflicting influences which actuated the bold invader of this coveted region. Every portion of it is marked by struggles, now mostly forgotten, between the whites and natives, and history will never know how many of the early trappers fell before the savage hatred of this terrible tribe.

The Blackfeet were splendid examples of their race, well formed physically, fond of athletic sports, excellent horsemen, great hunters, proud of the gaudy ornaments of dress, inordinately fond of liquor and gambling, addicted to the usual native vices of filth, beggary, and small thieving—in short they were true savages so far as the term can be properly applied to the aboriginal American. Their reputation for courage—even of the native quality—has been disputed, but their almost continuous record of war shows that they were not afraid of battle.

It seems most unfortunate that a better understanding could not have been brought about at an early date between the Blackfeet and the whites. The common verdict of those who became acquainted with these Indians on a peaceable footing is that they were a very tractable and intelligent tribe to get along with, and later experience confirms this view. But in some way the key to the situation could not be found until a score of years had left its record of bloodshed upon the history of this region.

THE CROWS (*Siouan*)

These Indians, with the Minnetarees, belonged to the Hidatsa substock of the Siouan family. The native name of this tribe is Absaroka, which is said to signify a species of hawk. The French translated it *Corbeau* and called the tribe *les Corbeaux*. The translation of this name into English gives the designation by which these Indians have been universally known, since the white man found them. Although modern writers divide the tribe into different bands, particularly the Crows proper and the mountain Crows, these distinctions never obtained among the trappers. The tribe was not numerous and probably did not number over 10,000 souls in its best days. Their country, always so known, the true Absaroka, or home of the Crows, was the valley and watershed of the Bighorn River. It extended, to be sure, considerably to the eastward, and may be said to have included the valleys of the Rosebud, Tongue, and Powder rivers, and also a strip of territory on the north bank of the Yellowstone. But still, when mention was made of the "Crow country," the valley of the Bighorn was always meant, the heart of Absaroka being in the lower portion of the valley near the mouth of the Little Bighorn.

The Crows were considered to be the best formed physically of any of the Western Indians. Tall, graceful, pleasant in physiognomy, they were exceptionally fine looking. In dress and ornamentation likewise they excelled most other tribes. They made a particular point of developing long hair, which they regarded as a great ornament. But however much they might excel other tribes in physical development, they were in no degree behind them in the vices and defects of Indian character.

The Crows were the equestrian tribe of the Missouri valley. In proportion to their numbers they possessed more and better horses than any other. They were the most expert of horse stealers and the most skilful robbers among the Missouri tribes. For this reason, rather than on account of any hostile intent, they caused a great deal of trouble to the traders in every part of the West. They always professed friendship for the whites and usually were peaceably disposed toward them. There is in fact almost no record of their having killed white men or having made war against them; but very many instances of their having committed robberies upon them.

The principal enemies of the Crows were the Sioux and Blackfeet. With the latter tribe they were never at peace in the early days, and the history of their relations to each other is one of unremitting hostility. The allies of the Crows were the Minnetarees and the Mandans.

A peculiarity of the Crow nation was their fondness for having white men among them. In the cases of Edward Rose and James P. Beckwourth the tribe adopted them, made them chiefs, and no doubt profited greatly from their leadership. There is no other tribe whose history is so full of romantic adventure, and the country of no other so abounded in the wildness and weirdness as well as the beauty of nature.

The Crows were exclusively a wandering tribe, never having lived in fixed villages. They were encountered by trappers in almost every part of the trans-Mississippi region. They were great buffalo hunters and the fur companies regarded them as the best robe producers of any of the Indian tribes. They were, however, very exacting, and gave the traders no little trouble to satisfy their whims in the matter of trading posts. The American Fur Company in the course of twenty years built four posts for their accommodation, and the Missouri Fur Company two; but the Indians were never satisfied and wanted the location changed continually. The method of trading which proved most satisfactory was to send traders with small outfits of merchandise to reside in villages, moving from place to place as the Indians moved, and by their presence encouraging them to make robes.

THE ASSINIBOINES (*Siouan*)

These Indians were true representatives of the Siouan stock and even called themselves by the native family name, Dakota, or Nakota, as they more commonly pronounced it. During the best days of the fur trade they numbered some 28,000 souls. Their territory bordered on the Missouri river from the mouth of Milk River to below the mouth of the Yellowstone and thence extended north to the Saskatchewan and east to the Assiniboine River. It lay mostly outside what is now the territory of the United States. The tribe comprised no fewer than eight distinct bands, some of which are often mentioned in the fur trade correspondence.

The Assiniboines resembled closely the other Sioux tribes —tall, rather slender, with broad faces and high cheek bones. Their clothes were the usual leathern make of the plains Indians, and a characteristic feature was the headdress adorned with two horns. The ornamentation was in other particulars similar to that of other Indians. Although armed to some extent in these times with guns, they all had bows and arrows.

They were a wandering tribe of Indians, living in movable tents, and their chief resource for subsistence was the buffalo. They were very expert in driving the buffalo into the parks or pens which have already been referred to. There was a noted enclosure of this sort within ten miles of Fort Union and around it were the bones of thousands of buffalo slain there.

The Assiniboines were an equestrian tribe, though not so well supplied with horses in these early times as were some of their neighbors. Like all other tribes they considered horse stealing a legitimate business.

They were generally friendly to the whites, though not to be trusted, and they did not scruple to rob when they could do so with impunity. They were also good robe-makers and were an important tribe to the traders. Fort Union, which was in their territory, was their great trading point.

As this tribe, like the Blackfeet, resided in both American

and British territory, there was sharp competition for their custom on both sides of the line; and much of the complaint of the American traders about the use of liquor by the British related to its use among these Indians.

THE MINNETAREES (*Siouan*)

These Indians were commonly known as the Grosventres of the Missouri, the last three words being added to distinguish the name from that of the Grosventres of the Prairie (*Algonquian*). There was nothing in the physical characteristics of either of the tribes to justify the name. Minnetaree is the name by which the Mandans called these Indians. It was always spelled as here given in the early years, but the modern official orthography is Minitari. The true tribal name was Hidatsa, but it was formerly rarely heard in popular use.

Under the name Hidatsa the Minnetarees and the Crows were once united in a single sub-stock of the great Siouan family. They migrated from the southeast at some not very remote period, and, for causes not clearly understood, separated, the Minnetarees stopping near the Mandans on the Missouri, and the Crows moving farther to the westward. It is probable that the origin of their distinctive tribal names arose in some way from this separation.

After this event the Minnetarees gradually abandoned the wandering life and settled down in permanent villages like the Mandans, from whom, through long association, they adopted many customs. Their huts were of the same general pattern as those of their new neighbors, and like the latter they had separate villages for summer and winter use. Their home was on the right bank of the Missouri near the mouth of Knife River. At the time of the visit of Lewis and Clark their number was estimated at 2,500 souls.

Early writers describe the Minnetarees as the tallest and best formed of the Missouri Indians, excepting only their kindred, the Crows. They delighted in elegance of costume and made use of all the ornamentation characteristic of Indian ingenuity in these matters.

They were generally friendly to the traders, although there are records of some outrages committed by them. There are two or three posts in their neighborhood at one time and another, but they were later all merged in the large post of Fort Clark, which accommodated both their own trade and that of the Mandans.

The Minnetarees found their natural allies in the Crows and Mandans, and although liable to frequent misunderstandings with other tribes, their record is not that of a warlike nation.

THE MANDANS (*Siouan*)

Of no other tribe of the Missouri valley are there extant so many complete and circumstantial accounts by early writers as of the Mandans. This arose from the fact that the situation where the tribe has dwelt since it became known to white men was one of great strategic and commercial importance. Its relation to the surrounding country has been explained in another place. It was for many years the farthest point to which the operations of the traders were carried up the Missouri and the tribe thus became familiarly known to the fur companies both north and south of the national boundary. Travelers likewise in these remote regions rarely got beyond the Mandans prior to 1830 and naturally devoted a great deal of attention to the tribe where they turned back on their expeditions. Thus from one cause or another these Indians received a large share of attention from the early explorers of the Missouri valley.

The tribal history of the Mandans is exceedingly obscure; but one fact stands out with only too great certainty, and that is their terrible misfortunes as a result of their contact with the white race. Our first knowledge of them locates them on the Missouri River considerably below their later location, where they dwelt in nine villages, two on the west shore and seven on the east. They must have numbered at the time at least 6,000 souls. The hostility of the Assiniboines and Sioux through many years gradually depleted their numbers, while the smallpox on different occasions made such terrible havoc among them as to threaten their extermination. The different bands consolidated with one another as the tribe diminished, until at the time of the visit of Lewis and Clark there were only two villages numbering between 1,500 and 2,000 occupants. It was in this situation that they were found by the traders who came first from the British companies and later up the Missouri from St. Louis. In 1837 the tribe experienced its last visitation of the smallpox, which carried off all but about thirty of its people. This terrible calamity, which resulted in the almost complete extermination of an interesting and important Indian tribe, is described in another part of this work.

The Mandans were a prominent example of stationary tribes living in permanent villages. They had separate villages for summer and winter use, the latter being located in the forest where it was better protected from the fierce blizzards of the northern prairies. The winter village was occupied about four months of the year.

These Indians were an agricultural tribe, if that term can be appropriately applied to the crude method by which the natives cultivated the soil. The principal product was the maize, but they also raised certain vegetables introduced by the whites.

Their main reliance for subsistence was, of course, the buffalo. Their country was in the very heart of the buffalo range and at certain seasons these animals roamed in countless thousands over the surrounding hills. At such times they were taken in great numbers without difficulty. At other times it was necessary to make long excursions to find them.

Physically the Mandans were rather above the average Indian in stature, though scarcely the equals in this respect of the Minnetarees and Crows. They were robust and broad-shouldered. Their countenances were not so striking in the aquiline nose and high cheek bone as the other Siouan tribes The eyes were dark brown, the mouth and jaw broad, the hair long and black and cultivated to great length. A greyish mixture was very common in the hair of many and was a characteristic feature. The teeth were very fine and remarkably permanent, even in old age. The complexion was of a brown, copperish tinge, although it many individuals it approached white very nearly. The women were short, robust, and not handsome even for Indian women. The men were notoriously vain in matters of dress, and exercised great ingenuity in ornamentation.

The Mandans were a peaceably disposed tribe and were always on terms of friendship with the whites. The Sioux and Assiniboines were their enemies and the Crows and Minnetarees their allies. The traders always maintained one or more posts in their neighborhood. The chief staples of trade were the robes and tongues of the buffalo, but they also collected a large amount of beaver fur.

THE ARICARAS (*Caddoan*)

Next to the Blackfeet the Aricaras were more dreaded by the whites than any other northern tribe. Though not so continuously hostile as the Blackfeet they were more treacherous, and the outrages and loss of life suffered at their hands form a mournful chapter in the history of the Missouri valley.

The Aricaras, commonly called Rees by the traders, were one of the principal divisions of the Caddoan family whose pristine habitat seems to have been in the vicinity of the Red River of the Natchitoches. In their migration north the Pawnees and the Aricaras parted company, the former settling down on the waters of the Kansas and Platte rivers, and the latter going north to the heart of the Sioux country on the Missouri. The tribe was once much more numerous than when it became known to the traders, and the remains of its ancient villages can be traced all the way from the Niobrara to the Cannon Ball River along the shores of the Missouri. The Aricaras claimed no particular country except that which they actually occupied. At the time of the voyage of Lewis and Clark they probably numbered 3,600 souls.

Prior to 1830 they lived in clay huts similar to those of the Mandans and Pawnees, but in this and other matters they resembled more closely the former tribe, although kindred to the latter. In physical appearance they were tall and well formed, and their women were considered the handsomest on the Missouri. In their manner of life they did not differ essentially from the tribes among whom they dwelt and with nearly all of whom they were on terms of hostility, if not of actual war.

The principal characteristic of the Aricara Indians, so far as it relates to the fur trade, was their treacherous and warlike attitude toward the whites. What can have been the cause of their bad faith and their many atrocities has always been a mystery. They were friends today and enemies tomorrow. One party of trappers they would treat with hospitality; the next they would seek to destroy. After Colonel Leavenworth's campaign, which was supposed to have subdued them, they became more troublesome than ever before. They abandoned their old villages and moved up to the neighborhood of the Mandans. They soon returned, however, and some years later migrated, it is said, to the North Platte. It was their depredations and murders committed upon trading parties in that region that induced N. J. Wyeth and others in 1833 to return from Green River to the States by way of the Bighorn, Yellowstone and Missouri rather than risk the journey across the plains; and also led to the military expedition to the upper Platte under Colonel Dodge in 1835.

The Aricaras were, in spite of their character of duplicity, useful Indians to the traders, who always had a post among them when they resided on the Missouri. They were good robe-makers and beaver hunters, but their chief staple of trade was horses; and it was from them that the traders obtained a goodly part of their supply. The overland Astorian party in 1811 outfitted with horses at their villages and General Ashley did the same thing in 1823 just before his disastrous experience at their hands.

THE SIOUX NATIONS (*Siouan*)

In popular usage the term Sioux was restricted to the tribes of the Siouan stock who dwelt in the "Land of the Dakotas" and who were called by the name Dakota. The term Sioux was of Algonquian origin, "expressing enmity or contempt," and through the medium of the Canadian French descended upon the Dakota tribes in its present corrupted form.

The Sioux undoubtedly came from the eastward and reached their historic habitat in comparatively late prehistoric times. When they became known to the traders in the latter part of the 18th century their country embraced what is now the state of South Dakota with contiguous territory all around its borders. The population of those tribes who dwelt in the valley of the Missouri cannot have exceeded at that time 15,000 souls.

In physical appearance the Sioux were true Indians, the characteristics of the race being especially marked in them. Although not so fine looking and well formed as the Minnetarees and Crows, they were nevertheless of stalwart physique and great physical power. They were mostly of medium stature, slender yet muscular, with oval features, prominent cheek bones and slightly aquiline nose. They wore long hair braided to the full length, although in some of the bands the custom prevailed of shaving off the hair except a tuft on the top of the head.

The Sioux were typical plains Indians and presented in the highest degree the characteristics which aboriginal life on the prairies developed. They were exclusively a nomadic people and their wanderings extended far beyond their proper country; but they were not equals in this respect of the Crows and Blackfeet. They were among the most warlike and aggressive of the Western tribes and were everywhere held in terror by their enemies. All of their neighbors, such as the Omahas, the Aricaras, the Cheyennes, the Mandans, and the Minnetarees, suffered calamities at their hands from which they never recovered.

There were three important divisions of the Sioux tribes with which the Missouri traders had to do—the Yanktons, the Yanktonais, and the Tetons.

The Yanktons lived in the southern portion of the Sioux territory along the Missouri River in the valleys of the James, the Vermilion, and the Big Sioux, and even as far east as the headwaters of the Des Moines. They numbered about 1,000 people. They were the least troublesome of all the Sioux tribes and gave the traders comparatively little annoyance. Posts were maintained at different times for their convenience at the mouth of each of the tributaries of the Missouri mentioned above.

The Yanktonais, or Yanktons of the Plains, occupied the upper valleys of the James and Big Sioux rivers, and even that of the Red River of the North on the east and a long stretch of the Missouri valley on the west. They numbered about 2,500 souls. They were on the whole the most dreaded by the traders of any of the Sioux tribes. They were treacherous, stealthy, vindictive, and caused a great deal of trouble. It was a frequent pastime with them to fire from some secure hiding place upon boats passing along the river. Small parties were never safe in their country, while the loss of life and property at their hands during the period of the fur trade was such as to cause never-ending solicitude on the part of those who did business with them.

The modern classification gives two divisions of the Yank-tonais, the Upper and Lower; but one never finds this distinction in the literature of the fur trade era. There was a Sioux band, then well known, but now not recognized, the ·Teton Saone, or simply the Saone, which may have been a part of the Yanktonais tribe. They resided on both sides of the Missouri in the section where Bismarck and Mandan now stand. It was presumably among these Indians that the "Sawon" post, so often mentioned in the journals and correspondence of the American Fur Company, was maintained.

The Tetons were a very important tribe of the Sioux and numbered about 5,000 souls. They dwelt mostly west of the Missouri and overspread the country as far west as to the Black Hills and the North Platte, while they ranged north and south from the Pawnee country to the Mandans. Like the Yanktonais they were exceedingly troublesome in the early years of the fur trade and greatly annoyed boat parties ascending the river. So far did they interfere with navigation that they came to be known as the pirates of the Missouri. The Tetons, however, dropped their hostile attitude much sooner than did the Yanktonais, and in later years gave the traders little or no trouble.

The Tetons embraced several distinct bands, with each of which trading posts or houses were maintained. These bands were the Boise Brulés, who lived on both sides of the Missouri near the mouths of the White and Teton rivers; the Sans Arcs; the Blackfeet (*Sihasapa*); the Minneconjous; the Two Kettles; the Ogallalas, who dwelt at the headwaters of the White and

Niobrara rivers at the southeastern base of the Black Hills; and the Hunkpapas.

For several reasons the Sioux tribes were the most important of any with which the fur traders had to do. They were the most numerous. Their country was one continuous range for the buffalo who were wont to frequent every part of it. As a result the traffic in buffalo robes was exceedingly heavy, and the quantities of these peltries that were shipped from the Sioux country were very great. The Sioux were also good beaver hunters, and contributed great quantities of these finer kinds of fur. The various trading companies had posts all over their country from James River to the Black Hills, and the total number of these establishments, large and small, that were built during the fur trade era, would probably exceed one hundred. Fort Pierre, located nearly in the center of the Sioux country, was the greatest of these posts, and a very important establishment in its day.

But if the custom of the Sioux was a matter of great importance to the traders, the open hostility of some of the bands and the doubtful friendship of others were not less so. The location of the Sioux tribes on both sides of the Missouri placed the navigation and trade of the upper rivers very largely at their mercy. In the earlier expeditions the American traders met with much opposition from these Indians. They were at the time largely under British influence, and during the War of 1812 came very near taking sides against the United States. Then they were enemies of most of the tribes above them, and did not like to have the whites go up there to trade. Moreover, they acted to some extent as middlemen between the whites and those tribes, compelling the traffic to pass through their hands to their great advantage. They did not like to see this business interfered with. All these considerations, and the natural jealousy with which they saw the advent of the white men, made them regard the approach of the American traders with an unfriendly eye. More than once they turned back the early expeditions. But as time wore on and the traders became firmly established among them, this hostile feeling passed largely away. There is no doubt that if, at this time, a wise and judicious policy had been pursued towards these Indians, they might have been led to their new destiny without serious difficulty or misunderstanding. The Sioux were blessed beyond most tribes with sound practical sense. They knew that their former method of life could not endure and all that they asked was that, in the inevitable process of change, the government should keep its faith with them. When they saw the agents of the government year after year and decade after decade violating its promises, the smoldering fires of bitterness were fanned again into flame, until they burst into that terrible conflagration that raged so furiously in the decade around 1876 (5).

THE CHEYENNES (*Algonquian*)

These Indians seem formerly to have been associated with the Arapahoes and the Atsina (Grosventres of the Prairie), and to have dwelt in what is now the state of Minnesota. Their western migration was probably under pressure from the Sioux, and their southern deflection from their western course was probably due to pressure from the Assiniboines, with whom they were never after at peace. Broken and dispirited with their accumulated misfortunes, they finally found an abiding place at the eastern base of the Black Hills among the upper tributaries of the stream that bears their name. Owing to some internal dissensions, a small number of the tribe seceded prior to 1820 and joined the Arapahoes. Later the rest of the tribe followed suit, until by 1840, all seem to have gone to the country of their kindred.

The Cheyennes are said to have formerly dwelt in permanent villages, but their lot of misfortune had driven them to a wandering life like that of their new neighbors. In spite of their disastrous experiences, they were a virile race, superb horsemen, tenacious of their ancient rights, and able to acquit themselves with credit when occasion required. They were much at war with the surrounding tribes, and the name of Cheyennes everywhere inspired, if not terror, at least respect. With the whites they were generally, though not always, on friendly terms.

The traders found these Indians profitable fur gatherers, but the principal traffic with them was in horses. These they obtained in their frequent excursions to the southern plains, and made a regular business of selling them to the whites and to other Indians. It was in their village that the Astorians completed their outfit of horses in 1811. For the trade of these Indians the American Fur Company regularly maintained one or more trading posts in their country.

THE PAWNEES (*Caddoan*)

The Pawnees, during the period of the fur trade, lived within the present limits of the state of Nebraska, and during the greater part of the time upon the Loup Fork of the Platte. They consisted of four distinct villages, the Grand Pawnees, the Republican Pawnees, The Tapage or Noisy Pawnees, and the Skidi or Pawnee Loups, nearly always called in early literature the Panimahas. In these later years of the eighteenth century, the Republican Pawnees moved south to the northern branch of the Kansas, which has since been known by their name. They rejoined the other villages on the Loup Fork probably about 1815.

The Pawnee Loups seem to have been later arrivals in the trans-Missouri country than were the other tribes. They claimed to be a distinct people, but their language proves an affinity. It was with this branch of the Pawnees that the Aricaras were associated, and the two formerly dwelt east of the Mississippi. After their migration across the Missouri, the Loups were conquered by the other Pawnee tribes, while the Aricaras went farther north. The Loups joined their conquerors and remained thereafter associated with them.

The Tapage Pawnees were the least important of the four bands, and are not mentioned at all by several of the early explorers. Thus Pike, in 1806, mentions only the three larger bands, and likewise Long, who passed through their villages fourteen years later. At that time the Pawnees were living 60 miles above the mouth of the Loup. The Grand Pawnees were farthest down stream, and numbered about 3,500 people. Three miles above them were the Republican Pawnees, with a population of about 1,000. The Pawnee Loups lived four miles farther up, and numbered about 2,000 souls.

The Pawnees belonged to the permanent village tribes, and were consequently agriculturalists as well as hunters.

Their lodges were very large, some 60 feet in diameter, circular in form, with conical roofs of flat slope. To judge from pictures of them they were not unlike, in general appearance, when seen from a distance, the thickly-clustered oil tanks in a modern petroleum district.

The agricultural productions of the Pawnees were maize, pumpkins, and squashes. The maize they raised quite extensively, but left it largely to take care of itself. When the spring planting was done, they set out on hunting or foraging expeditions, and did not return until near the time for harvest. In the winter they cached the harvested corn and went off again to hunt for meat and robes.

The Pawnees were physically a well-formed and vigorous people, tall, slender and muscular, exhibiting the peculiar physiognomy of the Indian race. Their great athletic accomplishment was horsemanship, in which they ranked with the Crows on the north and the Comanches on the south. For a tribe who resided in permanent villages, they led a remarkably predatory life, and rivaled in this respect their tent-dwelling neighbors. Their excursions were generally south and southwest, and they were scarcely ever encountered in the country to the north and west.

These Indians were at one time and another at war with nearly all the surrounding tribes, and do not seem to have had any steadfast allies. A late high authority upon their history states that they were uniformly friendly to the whites. But this was not the case during the period of the fur trade, at which time they rivaled the Comanches as terrors of the southern plains. Gregg says of them that they were "among the most formidable enemies of the Santa Fe traders," and the name Pawnee was held in the same degree of dread by the traders of the south as were the Blackfeet by the traders of the north. Whatever may have been their disposition in later times, they harbored no feeling of love for the whites at this early day. They held a relation to the Spanish government for several years analogous to that held by the Sioux to the British. The Spanish regarded them somewhat in the nature of allies, or at least as very friendly disposed toward them, and this fact of itself made them hostile to Americans. Lieutenant

Pike noted this hostility when he visited the Pawnees in 1806, and it did not die out for many years after (6).

The trade of the Pawnees was principally in robes, the gathering of which was a great business with them. The traders never built a post in their country, but conducted the business from their establishment near the Council Bluffs. Men were sent with outfits of merchandise to reside with the Indians while at their villages and to follow them on their expeditions. The produce of the trade was shipped down the Loup Fork and the Platte in bull boats, where it was incorporated in the larger cargoes coming down the Missouri.

THE PONCAS (*Siouan*)

Four of the lower Missouri tribes, *viz.*: the Poncas, the Omahas, the Kansas, and the Osages, were once a single tribe dwelling in the Ohio valley near the Wabash River. With them was also another band called the Kwapa. When the tribe migrated westward, the Kwapa separated from the others at the Mississippi, and the main body began the ascent to the Missouri valley. The Osages separated from the larger group at the Osage River, settling in the valley of that stream, and the Kansas followed suit when they reached the valley of the river which bears their name. The Omahas and the Poncas gradually made their way farther up the river, and finally themselves parted company, the Omahas settling on the west bank of the Missouri at a considerable distance above the Platte, while the Poncas located near the mouth of the Niobrara.

Such, in simple outline, are supposed to have been the movements which carried a great tribe from the forest country east of the Mississippi to the treeless plains of the central West. The movement doubtless consumed a long period of time, and was marked by wars and other important events, which are now lost to history. The four sub-tribes had long been settled in their new homes when the white man found them, and remained there during the whole period of the fur trade.

In physical characteristics and in tribal customs the Poncas resembled their kindred, the Omahas. They had been oppressed through many years by the Sioux, and reduced by the small-pox, until, when the traders came, they numbered but little more than 200 souls. They were always on friendly terms with the whites, and a regular trading post was maintained in their territory.

THE OMAHAS (*Siouan*)

Although this seems to be the correct form of the name, it was more usually spelled Maha in the first half of the 19th century. The Omahas were once a powerful tribe, but the oppressions of the Sioux and a terrible epidemic of the small-pox in the latter years of the 18th century had reduced their numbers to about 400. Their habitat was on the west bank of the Missouri, about one hundred miles above the modern city which bears their name. Naturally a warlike tribe, their spirit had been broken by their great misfortunes, and they seem not to have gone to war to any great extent after the traders settled among them. On account of this quiet life they do not figure prominently in annals of Western adventure. They did, however, produce some of the most noted chiefs of any of the Indian tribes, and among them the great chief Black Bird, who died of the smallpox a few years before the arrival of Lewis and Clark.

The Omahas were a popular tribe with the traders, and seem to have been industrious fur gatherers. They dwelt in permanent villages, but were absent on their hunting excursions several months of the year. All of the leading fur companies maintained trading posts near the old Council Bluffs for the convenience of these Indians and other tribes in the vicinity.

THE KANSAS (*Siouan*)

This tribe dwelt in the valley of the river which bears their name, and their village was located a few miles above its mouth. They had a population of about 1,500. They lived in mud huts not unlike those of the Mandans, and followed a life similar to that of the tribes around them. They were generally at peace with their neighbors, who were indeed of their own stock. With the whites they were also usually at peace, although they committed many outrages upon small parties.

They cultivated maize and followed the chase, but became indolent and lazy as their dependence upon the government increased. A permanent trading post was maintained among them.

THE OSAGES (*Siouan*)

This great nation was the first in the Missouri valley to have a regular trade with the whites. Many years before the Louisiana Purchase, trading posts had been built in their country. At the time of the general migration westward from east of the Mississippi, the Osages settled in the country along the Osage River and between that stream and the Missouri. Subsequently they divided into smaller bands. The first separation, which Pike places early in the 18th century, was into two tribes, the Great and Little Osages, but later the Little Osages, finding themselves too weak for self-protection, located near the large village. A third division, which Pike calls the Arkansas Schism, was brought about by the white traders. For many years prior to 1800 Mr. Pierre Chouteau had monopolized the trade of these Indians, but at about the above date, or perhaps a little earlier, Mr. Manuel Lisa obtained from the Spanish authorities an exclusive grant of their trade. Incensed at this action, Mr. Chouteau, who had the monopoly of trade on the Arkansas, intrigued with the Indians and succeeded in drawing so large a part of the tribe to his post that he practically nullified the value of Lisa's monopoly, and led to a permanent division of the tribe.

The Osages, like the Omahas, Otoes, and Kansas, lived in permanent villages, but their huts were rectangular in plan, in which respect their architecture differed materially from that of the other tribes. The huts were supported by vertical posts, the center row under the ridgepole being twenty feet high and the outside rows about five feet. Poles and rafters gave support to the roofing of brush, bark, and dirt. These huts were sometimes sixty feet long. Fires were kindled on the ground under the ridgepole and the smoke escaped through openings in the roof.

In language, customs, and dress the Osages were like their kindred tribes. They were of especial importance to the trader by reason of their large property in horses, which they obtained through annual excursions to the southwestern plains. They were good judges of these animals, and the traders relied on them largely in organizing their expeditions, for these were made up on the very borders of the Osage country.

The Osages were on the whole friendly to the whites, but their marauding parties did great mischief to small bands of trappers or hunters. There was much complaint of them by the Santa Fe traders, and many unprovoked outrages were committed by them. Permanent posts were always maintained in their country.

THE IOWAS (*Siouan*)

There were three other tribes who dwelt in the lower Missouri Valley, and were familiarly known to the traders. They were the Iowas, the Otoes, and the Missouris, who all sprang from a common stock which was closely related to the Winnebago division of the Siouan family. What their course of migration was is unknown, but they had crossed the Mississippi before they first fell under the observation of white men.

The pristine home of these Indians was practically what is now the state which bears their name. They were found within the historic period in almost every part of that region. Once a powerful tribe, they, like their neighbors, had been ruined by the smallpox and the Sioux, and they were a small tribe of only 800 people when the American traders opened relations with them. They traded principally at Robidoux post at Black Snake Hills, where St. Joseph, Mo., now stands, and also to some extent at the Council Bluffs.

THE OTOES (*Siouan*)

From at least as far back as the middle of the 18th century the Otoes dwelt on the banks of the Platte about forty miles above its mouth. They lived in dirt villages like the other tribes of the lower Missouri. They present no characteristics notably different from the surrounding tribes, and the history during the fur trade period was uneventful. Their trade all went to the establishments at Council Bluffs.

Iatan was the name of a noted chief of the Otoes who held

sway over the tribe from about 1825 to 1840, when the fur trade was in its most flourishing condition. He earned his name from a hard-fought battle between his tribe and the Comanches or Iatans, in which the latter were utterly routed. His native name was a long word which signified "Prairie Wolf." Iatan was a popular chief, even with other tribes, and was frequently called into the councils of the Pawnees.

THE MISSOURIS (*Siouan*)

This tribe, though of little importance in the fur trade, is an interesting one historically. From it is derived the name of the great river on whose shores they dwelt (7), and where they were actors in events of deep significance in the history of the trans-Mississippi territory. Within the knowledge of white men the tribe resided near the mouth of the river, but they were driven off by the Illinois and were found early in the 18th century farther up the Missouri on its left or north bank not far below the mouth of Grand River. It was here that the tragedy occurred in 1720 in which a Spanish expedition against the Missouris was destroyed by these Indians. Near by, on an island, the French erected their first post in the Missouri Valley (8). Sometime after this event they suffered a misfortune from which they never recovered, and which marks the termination of their separate tribal existence. They were attacked by the Sac and Fox Indians, and were almost annihilated. The remnants of the tribe dispersed among the Osages, the Kansas, and the Otoes, where they were found by the traders.

AUTHOR'S NOTES

(1) The origin of the name "Blackfeet" is said by tradition to arise from the fact that in some other tribal disputes of this nation the Siksikau separated from the rest of the tribe, then on the Saskatchewan river or even farther north, and resolved to take up their new abode in the south. It was in the fall of the year when they reached the valley of the Missouri, and prairie fires had swept the country in every direction. After traversing this burnt district until their moccasins were black with the ashes, they were met by a band of Crows, who, from their appearance, called them Blackfeet.

The tradition may not be entitled to any greater weight than the following which accounts for the bitter hostility of these Indians to the whites. When they first saw the effects of firearms they were so much impressed that they wanted to know where they could procure some powder. They were told that it was a kind of grain, which, if sowed in the spring, would, like any other grain, multiply in the harvest. They procured a large quantity at great cost and made the experiment. Nothing could ever induce them afterwards to treat the white man as a friend.

(2) Kenneth McKenzie, in his account of the establishment of Fort Piegan says: "The Piegan band of Blackfeet is warmly attached to our interests. They are the beaver hunters of their nation. The other bands trade robes and provisions principally."

(3) Part IV, Chapter X.

(4) See Part IV, Chapter II.

(5) The Sauteurs of Spirit Lake frequented the Missouri river valley a great deal in the latter years of the trade. They were exceedingly troublesome in 1843.

(6) As late as 1811 an officer belonging to the government trading factory at Fort Osage made a visit to the Kansas and Pawnees. He left Fort Osage May 11; reached the Kansas May 19, at a point about one hundred miles above the mouth of the Kansas river; found several American flags in the village; left village May 22 and reached Republican Pawnees one hundred and twenty miles farther; continued journey and crossed Platte about 28th; came to Pawnee villages on Loup Fork, one hundred miles above mouth; found Pawnees in close relation with Santa Fe; one Spanish flag found; also a letter from Governor of Santa Fe thanking Pawnees for their loyalty. It is evident that at this date the Republican Pawnees were still on the Republican Fork of Kansas river.

(7) See Chapter III, this Part.

(8) See Appendix F.

Chapter X

NATIVE TRIBES: OF THE SOUTHWEST AND THE TRA-MONTANE COUNTRY

The Paducas—Trading custom of the Paducas—The Arapahoes
—Tribal history—Characteristics—Relation with the traders
—The Kiowas—The Comanches—Habitat—Characteristics—
An equestrian tribe—New Mexican tribes—The Pueblos—
Meaning of term as applied to the Indians—Characteristics—
The Navajos—The Apaches—The Shoshones or Snakes—
Their country—Characteristics—The Bannocks—The Pai-utes
—The Utahs—Their Country—Characteristics—The Sheep-
eaters—The Mokis and Mojaves—The Nez Perces—Other
names for the tribe—Confusion as to the name Flathead—
Country of the Nez Perces—Characteristics of the tribe—Rela-
tion to the missionaries and the traders—The Flatheads—
Other tribes of the Columbia Basin—Peculiarities of the
coast tribes.

THE PADUCAS

In the earlier notices of the country, near the base of the Rocky Mountains at the headwaters of the Platte and Arkansas Rivers, before exploration had penetrated so far, the name Paduca was applied to the native inhabitants that were supposed to be located in that section. The first extensive report upon these Indians appears to have been by Bourgemont, in 1724, but the precise application of the name has never been determined. As the country came to be known, the tribes who dwelt there were found to have other designations, and the name Paduca consequently fell into disuse. In one form or another the name is found in the vocabularies of the several Siouan tribes, and by them was applied to the Comanches. This, however, was not the understanding of the earlier authorities, who knew of the existence of the Comanches, or Iatans, as they were called, but who still referred to the Paducas as a distinct people. Even Pike, who was one of the first to identify the Paducas with the Comanches, directly contradicts himself in his tabulated statement of the Indian tribes of the West, in which he mentions the Paducas as being at war with each other. Furthermore, the habitat of the Comanches in historic time has been south of the Arkansas, while that of the Paducas was always located on the headwaters of the Platte, and one of the principal branches of that stream bears the name Paduca on some of the older maps. It is therefore clear that, whatever may have been the Sioux name of the Comanches, the name Paduca was not considered by the earlier writers as belonging to that tribe. On the whole the explanation given by Dr. James, in his narrative of Long's Expedition of 1820, and which is followed by Gallatin in his *Synopsis of the Indian Tribes of North America* (1836), appears the most reasonable of any—that the name Paduca was formerly applied collectively to the tribes living at the headwaters of the Platte, who have since become known under the separate names of Arapahoes, Kiowas, etc.

The Paducas, or more properly the Arapahoes, who were the principal tribe of the Paduca country, formerly held a sort of fair on a tributary of the South Platte near the site of the modern city of Denver, Colo. The stream was at one time known, from this circumstance, as Grand Encampment creek. At this rendezvous the Arapahoes acted as middlemen in the exchange of articles obtained from Spaniards on the south with those obtained through their kindred, the Grosventres and the Cheyennes, from the British on the north. It is conjectured by some authorities that the name Arapahoe signifies "he who buys or trades," and has reference to this early custom. However this may be, the fact itself is an interesting one in connection with our present studies, disclosing as it does the advancing shadow of the trader long before his actual appearance upon the scene.

THE ARAPAHOES (*Algonquian*)

In the western migration of the Arapahoes and Grosventres, as already noted, the Arapahoes went to the headquarters of the Missouri, and then, turning south, made their way to the eastern base of the Rocky Mountains, in what is now the state of Colorado. These Indians are described in the modern scientific classification as the Southern Arapahoes, the Northern Arapahoes having remained on the headwaters of the Yellowstone. Be this as it may, no such distinction was known to the traders and trappers, and no Indians of this name are ever spoken of as dwelling in the northern mountains. When the Arapahoes are mentioned the tribe in the valley of the South Platte is always meant.

In physical characteristics the Arapahoes resembled their neighbors very closely. In stature they were rather inferior to the Missouri Indians, but much like them in physiognomy and dress. A distinctive feature of their tribal custom was the tattooed breast. They gave great attention to the hair, which they permitted to grow to great length, sometimes even increasing its length by the use of false hair. Their clothing was like that of the tribes farther north, but contained in addition blankets and other articles obtained from the Spaniards.

The Arapahoes were exclusively a wandering tribe, living in skin tents, and during the period of the fur trade numbered about 2,500 souls. With most of their neighbors, except the Utahs and Pawnees, they were at peace. In the earlier years of the trade they were very hostile to Americans, but in 1832 Captain Gant, of the firm of Gant and Blackwell, established a trading post in their country on the Arkansas River and succeeded in gaining their confidence. At that time they were uniformly friendly to the whites. While not aggressively warlike, they were good fighters, and were held in high respect by their enemies. They were a brave, candid and honest people, and were much less given to beggary and thieving than were most other Indians. They have proven among the most peaceable of tribes, and the most willing to be led in the new pathway of civilization.

The Arapahoes were an important tribe to the traders, and their country was always one of active operations. Not only were they good fur producers, but they were accomplished traders themselves, from their long experience already alluded to, in this sort of business. Many posts were established in their country upon the headwaters of both the Arkansas and the South Platte.

The Kiowas

So far as known this tribe is of an independent linguistic stock and its history is very obscure. Modern research claims to have traced its course of migration from the headwaters of the Missouri southeastward through the country of the Crows, who became their allies, and that of the Sioux and Cheyennes, who became their enemies. What their first alliances were when they reached the Paduca country is uncertain. They are known to have been in close association with the Arapahoes, and as late as 1820 Long found them so associated as if in permanent union. But it is equally certain that their later and stronger alliance was with the Comanches. Their habitat, therefore, was that of their associates, and comprised the entire Arapahoe and Comanche country. If it were possible to designate any one situation as more resorted to by them than another, it was the valley of the Arkansas on the south side near the Purgatory River.

The Kiowas were not a tribe well known to the traders, and almost no mention is made of them in the annals of the times. A late authority says that they were "the most predatory and blood-thirsty" of the prairie tribes, and that "they have probably killed more white men in proportion to their number than any of the others." This statement is not at all borne out by the records of the fur trade, in which encounters with the Kiowas are rarely mentioned. It is possible that these Indians have been given credit by later historians for many outrages committed by the Comanches. The long and close association of the two tribes would make an error of this kind possible. On the other hand, the same cause may have led the traders to suppose that they were being annoyed by the Comanches when in reality it was the Kiowas. In either case it is a fact that the literature of the fur trade has very little to say of the Kiowas but a great deal of the Comanches.

There was a early trading post of the American Fur Company named Fort Kiowa. Strange to say, it was located on the Missouri River near the mouth of White River, far away from the actual home of the Kiowas.

The Comanches (*Shoshonean*)

These Indians were the only tribe of the great Shoshonean family who dwelt exclusively upon the plains. They were formerly federated with the eastern Shoshones, who still reside in Wyoming, but from some cause, supposed to be the pressure of their enemies, the Sioux, the two bands separated, the Comanches moving southwest into the plains while their associates turned back into the mountains. Their habitat was south of the Arkansas, in portions of what are now Oklahoma, Texas, and New Mexico.

The Comanches were, in the fullest sense, a wandering people, and it is doubtful if any other American tribe led an existence of such continuous movement from place to place. They, of course, had no permanent villages, but lived in skin tents, and their entire domestic economy was ordered with reference to the supreme condition of mobility. It is even impossible to fix upon any locality in their country which they frequented more than another. They moved north and south, according to the season, but for the rest they went wherever fortune promised to be most propitious.

The worldly wealth of the Comanches and the prime object of their solicitude was the horse. They were the most expert horsemen among the American Indians, not even excepting the Pawnees and Crows. They were trained to ride from infancy, and their remarkable skill in handling their animals has been the wonder of all who have witnessed it. They marked their animals with a slit in the ear, and they could not be induced for love nor money to part with their favorite steeds.

In personal characteristics they were not particularly different from the Arapahoes. They wore less clothing than the northern tribes, for their climate did not require so much, but they were quite as proud and fastidious about what they did wear. It is noted of these Indians, as a remarkable exception, that they did not care for liquor.

The Comanches were a very dangerous tribe, and were enemies to nearly all their neighbors, whether white or red. They were the terror of the southern plains, and their name carried a shudder wherever it was heard, from the Brazos to the Rio Grande del Norte. They were of very little use to the traders, for they were not good fur gatherers, but they always had to be reckoned with on account of their abandoned and lawless character. Some of the most lamentable tragedies of the Santa Fe Trail are chargeable to them.

THE PUEBLOS

The Indians who dwelt in the northern provinces of Mexico, which are now comprised within the territories of New Mexico and Arizona, played little part in the history of the fur trade, and only a brief reference will be made to them here. They were too far south for a profitable fur-bearing country, and it was only occasionally that the regular fur traders came in contact with them. The Santa Fe trader had limited dealings with them, and they were, of course, encountered along the trails between the Rio Grande valley and California.

The Pueblos dwelt mainly in the valley of the Rio Grande del Norte. The name Pueblo has no ethnic significance in this connection; that is, it is not in any sense a tribal or family name, but refers to those tribes of Indians in New Mexico who built and occupied the characteristic villages called pueblos. They comprised at least three distinct linguistic stocks, of which the Keresan and Tanoan were the more important. They were distinguished from surrounding tribes by their peaceful and unwarlike nature, the fixity of their abode, their quiet pursuit of peaceful vocations, and their marked advance in the cruder arts of civilized life.

The Pueblos of New Mexico were an industrious, prosperous and numerous people when the Spaniards entered their country, but the effects of the political and religious system which was imposed upon them were sufficient, in the course of two centuries, to reduce them to scarcely a tenth of their former number. In the course of long intercourse with their conquerors, they adopted many of the Spanish customs, while the latter borrowed extensively from the Pueblos, so that, with continuous intermarriage, the result was an amalgam in which the predominent element was a matter of doubt.

These Indians exercised no particular influence upon the American fur trade; but owing to the similarity of their food, dress, and other articles of daily life to those of the Mexicans, the Santa Fe trade did undoubtedly receive material assistance from them. They were always on friendly terms with the Americans.

The Navajos (*Athapascan*)

These Indians are said to have numbered, during the era of the fur trade, about ten thousand people, and their country lay west of Santa Fe between the Little Colorado and San Juan Rivers as far as to the Colorado of the West. They dwelt in rude huts, somewhat resembling those of northern permanent villages. The characteristic production of their tribal life, which has given them a wide notoriety, was the Navajo blanket, an article of such close texture that it is nearly as impervious to water as a rubber blanket. The value of a genuine Navajo blanket, like a genuine Oriental rug, is very great. Many of these blankets found their way East through the medium of the Santa Fe traders.

The Navajos were never subjugated by the Spaniards, with whom they remained in a state of almost perpetual hostility. Neither did the Catholic missionaries make any permanent impression upon them. A peace arrangement was generally made between them and the New Mexican government every spring, on terms dictated by the Indians. It was a wily move on their part to secure sufficient tranquillity to plant their crops and conduct their trade. At the close of the season their predatory habits were generally resumed. They seem to have directed their hostile efforts only against the Mexicans. There is no evidence that they were unfriendly to the Americans, and the fur traders operated freely in their country.

The Apaches (*Athapascan*)

The various tribes that fall under the above designation occupied the vast territory now comprised in the southern half of the territories of New Mexico and Arizona. The Apaches were a wandering tribe without fixed habitations, using skin tents when they used any. Taken all in all, they have probably been the most troublesome Indians within the territorial limits of the United States. They are the only Indians who, in their habitual state, lived neither upon agriculture nor upon the chase, but by robbery from surrounding peoples. In their whole career of more than two centuries, the Spanish and Republican governments never subjugated nor converted them and, in fact, seemed to have existed only by their sufferance. They were too shrewd to wish to drive the Spaniards out entirely, for it was from them that their chief tribute came. They were wont to conclude a temporary peace with one province while waging war on another, and the booty obtained from the latter they would trade in the former. In this way they laid a tribute upon the provinces, which constituted in large part their subsistence. While the raids of the Apaches did not reach the extent of actual extermination of the white population, and probably were not intended to, they had, in later years, caused the abandonment of most of the ranches which were located away from the villages, and the country wore a depolulated appearance in consequence. It is said that the Mexican population was gradually diminishing from this cause in the years immediately preceding the American conquest.

The Apaches for many years were rather friendly than otherwise to the American traders, and the Mexican authorities concluded from this that there was some mutual understanding or alliance; but there never was. In 1838 the treacherous conduct of a party of Americans in killing a large number of Apaches whom they had accosted as friends put an end to the amicable relations between the two peoples. Among the problems which the conquest of New Mexico brought to the United States, the most difficult one was the Apache problem, and this it took nearly two score years to settle.

The Shoshones or Snakes (*Shoshonean*)

These Indians were the type of the Shoshonean family, and the name Snake (1) was of such general use as almost to obscure the family name. The tribe dwelt in the upper portions of the valleys of Green and Snake Rivers and the northern portion of Bear River Valley. What their population was at the time when the traders first came to their country is very uncertain, for it is not known just what bands of Indians different writers intended to include in their estimates.

In physical characteristics the Shoshones were inferior to the tribes heretofore described, The precarious livelihood which they were able to extract from the poverty of the country could not sustain a stalwart physique, and they did not present that appearance of hardy manhood that was generally observed among the Indians farther east. They were, however, excellent horsemen and good warriors, and their martial prowess, if not to be compared with that of the Blackfeet and Crows, was held in wholesome respect by the neighboring tribes.

They were exclusively a wandering tribe. The necessities of subsistence, which was mainly derived from the buffalo and the salmon, compelled long excursions, either to the lower rivers, where fish were taken, or to the plains of the Missouri, in quest of buffalo. From the nature of their means of subsistence, these Indians partook of the traits and customs of both the fishing and hunting Indians.

While the Shoshones were a brave, active and shrewd people, they were, on the other hand, suspicious, treacherous and jealous. They were not openly hostile, but were such inveterate beggars and thieves that they were considered an intolerable nuisance. With the whites they were always at peace after their first few years of acquaintance. They were good fur gatherers, though not so useful in this respect as the Missouri Indians. There were only two trading posts in their territory, Fort Boisé, in the western portion, and Fort Hall, in the central. The establishment of both these posts, however, arose from peculiar conditions of competition among the traders, and not from any real necessity to accommodate the trade of the Indians. The usual method of exploiting the resources of the Snake country was by means of white trapping parties, who also traded such furs as the Indians might have to sell.

The Shoshones were on friendly terms with the Nez Perces and Flatheads at the north, but were generally at war with the Crows, Blackfeet, and Utahs on the eastern border of their country. Necessity compelled them to go annually into the country of the Blackfeet to hunt buffalo, but on such occasions they went in sufficient force to bid defiance to their enemies. Frequently these expeditions were made in alliance with the Nez Perces or Flatheads.

THE BANNOCKS (*Shoshonean*)

The Bannocks were the most warlike of the Shoshone tribes except the Comanches, and in this respect compared favorably with the plains tribes across the mountains. But while they were better specimens of Indian manhood than were certain other tribes of this stock, they were of a more troublesome character than the Snakes, and had the reputation of being a sort of lawless banditti, frequently infesting the routes of travel and causing trouble to the emigrants. The trappers had many hostile encounters with them, and kept a careful watch upon them whenever in their vicinity. One of the earliest notices of them is the pursuit of one of their bands in 1824 by a party under James Bridger, then a young man, for the purpose of retaking some horses which they had stolen. The country of the Bannocks was the territory between the Great Salt Lake and Snake River, and it lay athwart both the Oregon and California Trails.

PAI-UTES OR ROOT DIGGERS (*Shoshonean*)

These were the most degraded and pitiable of all the Indian tribes of the West. They dwelt in that desolate waste to the west and south of Great Salt Lake, where nature has dealt with a more niggardly hand than in any other part of the country. The barrenness of the country was reflected in the character of the inhabitants. They were inferior in stature, almost devoid of clothing, and nearly always in a condition bordering on starvation. Their degradation is attested by the fact that they subsisted to a considerable extent upon ants, other insects and vermin, and also upon roots, from which fact they were called by the opprobrious epithet of Root Diggers, or simply Diggers. In the winter they sought shelter among the sage brush and lived upon grass seed, or anything that the scanty gratuity of nature afforded them. They had no horses, and were armed only with the bow and arrow. They were "destitute of all the necessaries that make life even desirable." As a rule they were friendly to the whites, more perhaps through fear than otherwise. They were harmless through incapacity to do harm. They were, however, disposed to theft, and at times made their annoyances from this cause almost insufferable. This was the excuse offered for the frightful massacre of these Indians by the Walker party in 1833, of which an account is given elsewhere.

The name Root Diggers has by some writers been restricted to the tribe of Pai-Utes; but it was used with reference to several tribes. It was an epithet derived from a manner of life, and the trappers applied it to any of those degraded peoples who dug roots for a subsistence, or depended upon other equally precarious means.

The Utahs (*Shoshones*)

The Utahs dwelt north of the Navajo country in the valleys of Green and Grand Rivers. The crest of the Wasatch range on the west and the Uintah Mountains on the north denoted the limits of their country in those directions. They are said to have numbered about 2,500 souls.

They were a predatory tribe, never having lived in fixed villages. In physical development they ranked with the Bannocks and Shoshones, and were rated as the best horsemen living west of the mountains. They bore an excellent character among the hunters, as being less addicted to thieving, dishonesty, gambling, and other native vices, than were most of the other tribes. They were a thrifty race as Indians go, well clothed, and were industrious in gathering furs. While not belligerent in character, they were a brave and warlike people when occasion made war necessary. Their excursions for buffalo brought them into frequent contact with the Cheyennes, Arapahoes, and other eastern tribes, with whom they had many deadly encounters.

Their country was rich in beaver, and was well known to the traders, who built no fewer than four trading posts within it. These were Robidoux's two posts on the Uintah and Gunnison Rivers, Fort Davy Crockett in Brown's Hole, and Fraeb's post on the Yampah. Trails led from their country to Santa Fe, and they were well known to the New Mexicans, whose language, it is said, they understood.

THE TUKUARIKA OR SHEEPEATERS (*Shoshonean*)

This small and insignificant tribe was distinguished as being the only tribe of Indians ever known to have regularly dwelt within any part of that singular region which is now the Yellowstone National Park.

THE MOKIS AND THE MOJAVES

In the far south dwelt two tribes, the Mokis (*Shoshonean*), in the valley of the Colorado Chiquito, and the Mojaves (*Yuman*) on the lower course of the Colorado of the West, who are occasionally mentioned in fur trade literature. It was the latter tribe who massacred the party of Jedediah S. Smith in August 1827, while crossing the river on a raft en route to California.

THE NEZ PERCES (*Shahaptian*)

These Indians were frequently called by the name Chopunnish, and by their own name, Sahaptin. The name Flathead was also applied to them in ignorance of actual tribal distinctions on the coast, and much confusion has arisen thereby. For example, the famous Flathead deputation to St. Louis in 1832 for the purpose of seeking religious instruction was undoubtedly composed of Nez Perce Indians. There is, in fact, a great deal of the nomenclature of the western tribes which is still without adequate explanation, for the customs which would seem to have given rise to certain names had almost entirely passed away even in the days of the fur trade. Thus one of the most intelligent and observing of the traders (2), who spent five years in the Far West from 1830 to 1835, and passed one winter among the Flatheads, refers to these incongruities as follows: "Several tribes of mountain Indians, it will be observed, have names that would be supposed descriptive of some national peculiarity. Among these are the Blackfeet, Flatheads, Pend d' Oreilles, Nez Perces, Grosventres, etc. And yet it is a fact that of these the first have the whitest

feet; and there is not among the next a deformed head; . . .
there is not among the Nez Perces an individual having any
part of the nose perforated; nor do any of the Pend d' Oreilles
wear ornaments in their ears; and finally, the Grosventres are
as slim as any other Indians, and corpulency among them as
rare." Whether the Nez Perces ever did wear nose pendants
does not seem to be a matter of definite record, and it may well
be doubted. It was a name given by the French, and probably
with no more reason than were the names *Grosventre* or
Pied-noir. But it is a fact that the Nez Perces did follow to
some extent the custom of flattening their heads, although it
died out after the advent of the white man. Mrs. Whitman
(1836) records her impressions upon finding children undergoing this process of deformation, and there is a positive
record by an eye-witness that the deputation of Indians who
went to St. Louis in 1832 had flattened foreheads (3). It was,
in fact, the Nez Perces rather than the tribe which bears the
name Flatheads, that practiced this deformation, and it was
one of the few mountain tribes that did so, although the custom prevailed extensively among the natives of the coast.
The early nomenclature, which still obtains, was therefore
given in ignorance of actual conditions, and is largely mis-
leading. That this same confusion of names existed before the
advent of the white man is evident from the following observation from Lewis and Clark: "The custom, indeed, of
flattening the head by artificial pressure during infancy prevails among all the nations that we have seen west of the
Rocky Mountains. To the east of that barrier the fashion is
so perfectly unknown that there the western Indians, with
the exception of the Snake nations, are designated by the
common name Flatheads." It is singular that this name should
finally have settled on the tribe where the practice prevailed
the least (4).

The country of the Nez Perces was the lower watershed of
the Snake River, including particularly the valleys of the
Clearwater and Salmon Rivers on the east, and the Grande
Ronde River on the west. The tribe was the most important
of the Shahaptian stock, and played a notable part in the fur
trade and missionary history of the Columbia Valley. Physi-

cally they were a well-developed race, and compared favorably with the tribes east of the mountains. They were an equestrian tribe, and were well supplied with horses. Their subsistence was both the salmon and buffalo. They made annual excursions to Judith Basin to lay in their supply of meat, and the trail habitually followed in these journeys is still well known to the white inhabitants of that country.

All later accounts agree that the Nez Perces were a highly honorable tribe in their dealings with the whites and with other Indians, although a different impression was made upon the Astorians. They were a brave and powerful tribe, and their relations with all their neighbors, except the Blackfeet, were friendly. They were always staunch friends of the whites, and it can never cease to be a matter of keen regret that their tribal history could not have been brought to an end without the mournful tragedy of the war of 1877.

One of the most noteworthy characteristics of this tribe and of the Flatheads also was their deeply religious nature. They eagerly sought instruction in the Christian religion, adopted its rites and ceremonies with zeal, and became the most fruitful field for missionary effort of any of the Western tribes.

Although the Nez Perce country belonged commercially to the Hudson Bay Company, the American traders operated in it extensively. It was rich in beaver fur, and this, with the abundance of horses to be had from these Indians, made them an important tribe to the trade. Fort Nez Perce or Walla Walla, a Hudson Bay Company post, was located on Snake River a little above the mouth of the Walla Walla.

THE FLATHEADS OR SALISH (*Salishan*)

The Flatheads here referred to dwelt in the extreme western part of Montana between the Continental Divide on the east and the Bitter Root range on the west. Their country was drained by Clark's Fork of the Columbia, and its center was near the large and beautiful Flathead Lake.

The characteristics of the Nez Perce Indians were accentuated in the Flatheads. They were extremely receptive of religious influences; always friendly to the whites, and to most of the neighboring tribes; brave and vigorous in battle, and intensely warlike when war was unavoidable. Nearly all of their hostile encounters were with the Blackfeet, but these were many. If we may accept the evidence of Father De Smet, whose affection for these Indians made him rather partial towards them, they were more than a match in battle with their enemies.

The Flathead country was very rich in beaver, and was a great resort for trappers. The Hudson Bay Company maintained a regular post there.

Other Tribes of the Columbia Valley

The valley of the Columbia lying outside the pale of the American fur trade, except in the country of the Shoshones, Nez Perces, and Flatheads, no detailed notice will be given of the tribes dwelling there. The number of these tribes was very great. In the upper Columbia valley were the Pend d' Oreilles, Coeur d' Alênes, Spokanes, Cayuses, Walla Wallas, and Umatillas, who resembled in characteristics and customs the Flatheads and the Nez Perces. The Indians along the lower Columbia were a very different sort of people, owing to their different environment and means of subsistence. The Indians of the plains and the central mountain regions were horsemen, accustomed to the most hardy exercise in the pursuit of game and war and they were generally muscular and well formed. The coast Indians, on the other hand, subsisted principally upon fish, passed their time largely on or around the water, paddling in their canoes, or engaged in the unathletic work of still fishing. They were less strong physically than the plains Indians, of inferior build, and in no sense comparable to them as specimens of physical manhood. They became, indeed, very expert in the arts that pertain to canoe navigation and fishing, but they were physically ill-formed, with "broad, flat feet, thick ankles and crooked legs."

The tribes near the mouth of the Columbia were generally friendly to the whites, and were of great importance in the early fur trade of this section. They were much addicted to small thieving and were inveterate gamblers, though not so fond of liquor as most other tribes. They were excellent traffickers, having quickly learned the white man's value of their wares and were as shrewd as any one in driving a bargain.

Near the Cascades and Dalles of the Columbia dwelt some of the most troublesome tribes to be found in the entire West. They were sagacious and shrewd, but entirely without conscience, and were the boldest and most successful thieves and robbers among the aboriginal tribes. This locality had long been a trading emporium between the Indians of the upper and lower Columbia, and the Indians there seem to have acted as middlemen in the traffic. During the career of the Pacific Fur Company on the Columbia these Indians were a constant peril to expeditions passing up and down the river.

AUTHOR'S NOTES

(1) Alexander Ross is authority for the statement that this name arose from the characteristic of these Indians in quickly concealing themselves when once discovered They seemed to glide away in the grass, sage brush and rocks and disappear with all the subtlety of a serpent.

Father De Smet gives the following: "They are called Snakes because in their poverty they are reduced like reptiles to the condition of digging in the ground and seeking nourishment from roots."

(2) W. A. Ferris, *Life in the Rocky Mountains*.

(3) See Appendix D.

(4) A striking illustration of this confusion of names is found in a little incident which occurred in St. Louis when one of a deputation of Indians from these distant tribes died there and was buried in the Catholic burying ground. The record of burial refers to this Indian as a "Nez Perce of the Choponeek tribe, a nation called by the name Flathead."

APPENDICES

A

COPY OF LETTER FROM PIERRE MENARD TO PIERRE CHOUTEAU

An account of the first attack by the Blackfeet upon the Missouri Fur Company at the Three Forks of the Missouri in the summer of 1810.

Below are given, in the original and corrected French and in English translation, copies of a letter found among the Chouteau papers. It is probably the only document in existence that was written upon the identical spot where the old fort of the St. Louis Missouri Fur Company stood at the Three Forks of the Missouri. It narrates an important event in the series of disasters which overtook the company in that quarter, and is a genuine messenger from that forlorn band under Henry who later, when driven from this position, crossed the Divide and built the first trading establishment upon Columbia waters. The original of this letter, in four pages, written upon a sheet of fine light blue paper, full letter size, and still in excellent preservation, is in the possession of Mr. Pierre Chouteau of St. Louis. The names in brackets marked are as printed in the *Louisiana Gazette* of July 26, 1810, from an interview with Menard.

trois fourches du Missourie 21 Avrill
1810

Monsieur   ⎱
Pierre Chouteau eqr ⎰
                    Monsieur et beau frere

Je matandais Pourvoire vous Ecrire Plus Favorable que Je ne suis Ameme de le faire a present Les prospect de vent nos yeux il lia dix Jours etait Beaucoup Plus flateurs quil le sont aujourhuit un party de nos Chasseurs on Etez de fait Par les pied noirs le 12 du present il lia heus Deux homme De tuez tous leurs castors pilliez et Beaucoup de pieges De perdues et lamoniton de plusieur de nos Chasseurs et 7 de nos Chevaaux Nous avont Etez aleure poursuite maist malheureusement nous navont pas pux les rejoindre Nous avon ramasse 44 piege et 3 chevau que nous avont Ramene icy et nous Esperont trouvez Encore quelque piege Set malheureuse afaire a toute afet Decouragez Nos Chasseurs Il ne veulle plus aller a la chasse icy il en partira se pendent de mains 30 qui son tous de gens a gage les 14 Lous et 16 Fransais il vont allondroit ou les autres on Etez De fait Je ne leur donne que 3 pieges Chaque ne croient point prudent Dans risque daventage et surtous lorsque il ne doive point Se Se pare et La moitier devent tonjours Etres au campement. Le parti qui a etez de faite Consistait Au onze personne et les trois quare Etait a lez tendre Leurs piege Lorsque les Sauvages on fonce au campement Le deux person tuez Son James Chique (Cheeks) et un nomez haire (Ayres) Angage de Mes Crou (Crooks) et McLanell (McLellan) que Mess Silvestre (Chouteau) & Auguste (Chouteau) avait equipe Pour chasse de Moitiez il manque autres ses deux Le Jeune Hulle (Hull) qui etait du meme camp et flyharte (Freehearty) et son homme qui Etait campez Environ 2 mill Plus haut Nous avont trouvez 4 des piege de se derniers et La place ou les Sauvages les on poursuive mait nous navont point trouvez la place ou il on Etez tuez Dans le Campement ou les deux premier on Etez tuez Nous avon trouvez un Pied noire qui avait aussi Etez tuez et en suivant leure trase Nous avon vus quil En avait une autre de Blesse dangereusement tous les Deux Sil le blese meure on recu Leure more de la main de Chique (Cheeks) car il ni a que Lui qui sai defendue Set malheureuse affaire nous Cause une perte considerable maist Je ne croi pas pour Sela de vaire perdre Courage Les ressource de Se payis Son imance en Castors il est vrait que nous ne feront rein Se printemp mait Je me flate que nous feront Lautone prochaine Jes pert que Dici a mon De pare Jevairais les Ser pent et les taite plate Mon Intention est de les faire Reste icy Si Je puis et de les Encourage a la Guere Contre Les pied noirs Jusqua Se que nous puission Enprend pri Son nice et en renvoiez un poure faire des proposion de pais Seque Je croi Srat ayse En leur Lesent des traiteurs au bat de la

Chute (word torn out) Si nous navont point La paix avec Ses
ma- (rest of word gone) ou quil ne Soi point detruit nous ne
devont point pense a havoire detablisement icy assure Madame
Chouteau de mon estime la plus Sain Saire ainsi que vos
Chers enfants at Croiez Moix pour La vie votre Devouez
                                        (Pierre Menard
Nous nous atendont tous les jours Devoire)
les pied noire icy et nous Le desiront)

                        Trois Fourches du Missouri, 21 Avril, 1810.
Monsieur   ⎫
Pierre Chouteau eqr ⎬
                  ⎭
                    Monsieur et beau-frere

Je m'attendais pouvoir vous écrire plus favorablement que
je ne suis à même de le faire à present. Les prospects
devant nos yeux il y a dix jours etaient beaucoup plus
flatteurs qu'ils ne sont ajourd'hui. Une partie de nos
chasseurs a été défaite par les Pieds-noirs le 12 du présent.
Il y a eu deux hommes de tués, tous leurs castors pillés, et
beaucoup de pièges de perdus, et l'amonition de plusieurs de
nos chasseurs, et 7 de nos chevaux. Nous avons été à leur
poursuite, mais malheureusement nous n'avons pas pu les
rejoindre. Nous avons ramassé 44 pièges et 3 chevaux que
nous avons ramenés ici, et nous esperons trouver encore
quelques pièges. Cette malheureuse affaire a tout à fait de-
couragé nos chasseurs. Ils ne veulent plus aller à la chasse
ici. Ils en partiront cependant demain 30, qui sont tous de
gens à gage, les 14 loués et 16 Français. Ils vont à l'endroit où
les autres ont été défaits. Je ne leur donne que 3 pièges chacun,
ne croyant point prudent d'en risquer d'avantage, et surtout
lorsqu' ils ne doivent point se séparer, et las moitié doivent
toujours être au campement. La partie qui a été défaite consistait en onze personnes, et les trois quarts étaient allés tendre
leurs pièges lorsque les sauvages enfonçaient le campement.
Les deux personnes tués sont James Chique [Cheeks] et un
homme Haire (Ayres). engagés de Messrs Crou [Crooks] et
McLanell [McLellan] que Messrs Silvestre [Chouteau] &
Auguste [Chouteau] avaient équipés pour chasser de moitié.
Il manque, outre ces deux, le jeune Hulle [Hull] qui était du

même camp, et flyharte [Freehearty] et son homme qui étaient campés environ 2 milles plus haut. Nous avons trouvé 4 des pièges de ces derniers et la place où les sauvages le ont poursuivis, mais nous n'avons point trouvé le place où ils ont été tués. Dans le campement où les deux premiers ont été tués nous avons trouvés un Pied-Noir qui avait aussi été tué, et en suivant leur trace, nous avons vu qu'il y en avait un autre de blessé dangereusement. Tous les deux, si le blessé meurt, ont reçu leur mort de la main de Chique [Cheeks], car il n'y a que lui qui s'est défendu. Cette malheureuse affaire nous cause une perte considérable, mais je ne crois pas pour cela devoir perdre courage. Les ressources de ce pays sont immenses en castor. Il est vrai que nous ne ferons rien ce printemps, mais je me flatte que nous ferons (quelque chose) l'automne prôchaine. J'espère que, d'ici à mon depart, je verrai les Serpents et les Tête-plates. Mon intention est de les faire rester ici, si je puis, et de les encourager à la guerre contre les Pieds-noirs, jusqu'a ce que nous puissions en prendre prisonniers, et en renvoyer un poure faire des propositions de paix, ce que je crois sera aisé en leur laissant des traiteurs au bas de la chute [du Missouri.] Si nous n'avons point la paix avec ces ma[udits (?)], ou qu'ils ne soient point détruits, nous ne devons point penser à avoir d'etablissement ici. Assurez Madame Chouteau de mon estime le plus sincère ainsi que vos chers enfants, et croyez-moi pour la vie votre devoué.

Pierre Menard,

Nous nous attendons tous les jours de voir ⎱
les Pieds-noirs ici, et nous le désirons. ⎰

(Address on back of letter)
Monsieur Pierre Chouteau
St. Louis

Faveur de Mr. ⎱
Wm. Bryante ⎰

(Brief put on after
receipt of letter).

Lettre de Monsr.

P. Menard du
21 Avril 1810.

THREE FORKS OF THE MISSOURI,
April 21, 1810.

Mr. Pierre Chouteau, Esq.,

DEAR SIR and BROTHER-IN-LAW:—I had hoped to be able to write you more favorably than I am now able to do. The outlook before us was much more flattering ten days ago than it is today. A party of our hunters was defeated by the Blackfeet on the 12th inst. There were two men killed, all their beaver stolen, many of their traps lost, and the ammunition of several of them, and also seven of our horses. We set out in pursuit of the Indians but unfortunately could not overtake them. We have recovered forty-four traps and three horses, which we brought back here, and we hope to find a few more traps.

This unfortunate affair has quite discouraged our hunters, who are unwilling to hunt any more here. There will start out tomorrow, however, a party of thirty who are all gens a gage, fourteen loues and sixteen French. They go to the place where the others were defeated. I shall give them only three traps each, not deeming it prudent to risk more, especially since they are not to separate, and half are to remain in camp.

The party which was defeated consisted of eleven persons, and eight or nine of them were absent tending their traps when the savages pounced upon the camp. The two persons killed are James Cheeks, and one Ayres, an engage of Messrs. Crooks and McLellan whom Messrs. Silvester and Auguste (Chouteau) had equipped to hunt on shares. Besides these two, there are missing young Hull who was of the same camp, and Freehearty and his man who were camped about two miles farther up. We have found four traps belonging to these men and the place where they were pursued by the savages, but we have not yet found the place where they were killed.

In the camp where the first two men were killed we found a Blackfoot who had also been killed, and upon following their trail we saw that another had been dangerously wounded. Both of them, if the wounded man dies, came to their death at the hand of Cheeks, for he alone defended himself.

This unhappy miscarriage causes us a considerable loss, but I do not propose on that account to lose heart. The resources of this country in beaver fur are immense. It is true that we shall accomplish nothing this spring, but I trust that we shall next Autumn. I hope between now and then to see the Snake and Flathead Indians. My plan is to induce them to stay here, if possible, and make war upon the Blackfeet so that we may take some prisoners and send back one with propositions of peace—which I think can easily be secured by leaving traders among them below the Falls of the Missouri. Unless we can have peace with these (ma—?) or unless they can be destroyed, it is idle to think of maintaining an establishment at this point.

Assure Madame Chouteau of my most sincere esteem as well as your dear children, and believe me always your devoted   PIERRE MENARD.

We are daily expecting to see the Blackfeet here and are desirous of meeting them.

B

LETTER FROM MANUEL LISA TO GENERAL CLARK

On the conduct of Lisa's office as Indian agent.

St. Louis, July 1st, 1817.

To His Excellency, Governor Clark:

Sir:—I have the honor to remit to you the commission of sub-agent, which you were pleased to bestow upon me, in the summer of 1814, for the Indian nations who inhabit the Missouri River above the mouth of the Kansas, and to pray you to accept my resignation of that appointment.

The circumstances under which I do this, demand of me some exposition of the actual state of these Indians, and of my own conduct during the time of my sub-agency.

Whether I deserve well or ill of the government, depends upon the solution of these questions:

1. Are the Indians of the Missouri more or less friendly to the United States than at the time of my appointment?

2. Are they altered, better or worse, in their own condition at this time?

1. I received this appointment when war was raging be-

tween the United States and Great Britain, and when the activity of British emissaries had armed against the Republic all the tribes of the Upper Mississippi and of the northern lakes. Had the Missouri Indians been overlooked by British agents?

No. Your excellency will remember that more than a year before the war broke out, I gave you intelligence that the wampum was carrying by British influence along the banks of the Missouri, and that all the nations of this great river were excited to join the universal confederacy then setting on foot, of which the Prophet was the instrument, and British traders the soul. The Indians of the Missouri are to those of the Upper Mississippi as four is to one. Their weight would be great, if thrown in the scale against us. They did not arm against the Republic; on the contrary, they armed against Great Britain and struck the Iowas, the allies of that power.

When peace was proclaimed more than forty chiefs had intelligence with me; and together, we were to carry an expedition of several thousand warriors against the tribes of the Upper Mississippi, and silence them at once. These things are known to your excellency.

To the end of the war, therefore, the Indians of the Missouri continued friends of the United States. How are they today when I come to lay down my appointment? Still friends, hunting in peace upon their own ground, and we trading with them in security, while the Indians of the Upper Mississippi, silenced but not satisfied, give signs of enmity, and require the presence of a military force. And thus the first question resolves itself to my advantage.

2. Before I ascended the Missouri as sub-agent, your excellency remembers what was accustomed to take place. The Indians of that river killed, robbed and pillaged the traders; these practices are no more. Not to mention the others, my own establishments furnish the example of destruction then, of safety now. I have one at the Mahas more than six hundred miles up the Missouri, another at the Sioux, six hundred miles further still. I have from one to two hundred men in my employment, large quantities of horses, and horned cattle, of hogs, of domestic fowls; not one is touched by an Indian;

for I count as nothing some solitary thefts at the instigation of white men, my enemies; nor as an act of hostility the death of Pedro Antonio, one of my people, shot this spring, as a man is sometimes shot among us, without being stripped or mutilated. And thus the morals of these Indians are altered for the better, and the second question equally results to my advantage.

But I have had some success as a trader; and this gives rise to many reports.

"Manuel must cheat the government, and Manuel must cheat the Indians, otherwise Manuel could not bring down every summer so many boats loaded with rich furs."

Good. My accounts with the government will show whether I receive anything out of which to cheat it. A poor five hundred dollars, as sub-agent salary, does not buy the tobacco which I annually give to those who call me father.

Cheat the Indians! The respect and friendship which they have for me, the security of my possessions in the heart of their country, respond to this charge, and declare with voices louder than the tongues of men that it cannot be true.

"But Manuel gets so much rich fur!"

Well, I will explain how I get it. First, I put into my operations great activity; I go a great distance, while some are considering whether they will start today or tomorrow. I impose upon myself great privations; ten months in a year I am buried in the forest, at a vast distance from my own house. I appear as the benefactor, and not as the pillager, of the Indians. I carried among them the seed of the large pompion, from which I have seen in their possession the fruit weighing 160 pounds. Also the large bean, the potato, the turnip; and these vegetables now make a comfortable part of their subsistence, and this year I have promised to carry the plough. Besides, my blacksmiths work incessantly for them, charging nothing. I lend them traps, only demanding preference in their trade. My establishments are the refuge of the weak and of the old men no longer able to follow their lodges; and by these means I have acquired the confidence and friendship of these nations, and the consequent choice of their trade.

These things I have done, and I propose to do more. The

Aricaras, the Mandans, the Gros-Ventres, and the Assiniboines, find themselves near the establishment of Lord Selkirk
upon the Red River. They can communicate with it in two
or three days. The evils of such communication will strike
the minds of all persons, and it is for those who can handle
the pen to dilate upon them. For me I go to form another
establishment to counteract the one in question, and shall
labor to draw upon us the esteem of these nations, and to
prevent their commerce from passing into the hands of
foreigners.

I regret to have troubled your excellency with this exposition. It is right for you to hear what is said of a public
agent, and also to weigh it, and to consider the source from
which it comes. In ceasing to be in the employment of the
United States, I shall not be less devoted to its interests. I
have suffered enough in person and property, under a different
government, to know how to appreciate the one under which
I now live.

I have the honor to be, with the greatest respect, your
excellency's obedient servant.

MANUEL LISA.

C

NOTES ON THE ASTORIAN ENTERPRISE

Numbers of the Astorians—Arrivals and departures from
Astoria—Deaths among the Astorians—Biographical notes—
Loss of the *Tonquin*.

THE NUMBER OF THE ASTORIANS

The Astorians, properly so-called, included those persons
in the service of the Pacific Fur Company who went to the
Columbia by the *Tonquin*, the *Beaver*, or by Hunt's overland
expedition. There were a few scattering arrivals besides these.
The *Tonquin* arrived within the mouth of the Columbia
March 25th, 1811, and the *Beaver* May 9th, 1812. One de-
tachment of Hunt's party arrived January 18, 1812; another
February 15, 1812; a third (Crooks and Day) May 10, 1812;

and a fourth January 6th, 1813. The principal departures were by the *Tonquin* June 1, 1811; by Stuart's overland expedition June 29; 1812; by the *Pedler*, April 3, 1814; and by the North-west brigade April 4, 1814.

ARRIVALS

By the *Tonquin*: There sailed from New York by the *Tonquin* 22 crew and 33 passengers. There were taken on 24 Sandwich Islanders, making the total of 79. There were left at the Islands 2 (crew) leaving 77 who arrived at the mouth of the Columbia. There were lost in crossing the bar 8 (4 passengers, 3 crew and 1 Sandwich Islander), leaving 69 who entered the Columbia. There sailed on the *Tonquin* 27 (16 crew, 3 Astorians and 8 Islanders). There remained at Astoria 42 (27 whites and 15 Islanders). One of the crew had left the ship and remained at Astoria.

The Overland Expedition—West: The total number of persons who left the Aricara villages July 18, 1811, with Mr. Hunt, was 64, as we learn definitely for the first time on the journey at the Caldron Linn, November 8, 1811. The number is arrived at as follows:

September	2 Left among the Crows Edward Rose	1
October	1 Trapping party detached at Snake river	4
October	10 Trapping party detached at Fort Henry	5
October	28 Antoine Clappine drowned at Caldron Linn . .	1
October	30 Reed and 3 men set out down river from Caldron Linn, 2 returning	2
October	31 McLellan's party sets out from Caldron Linn . .	4
October	31 McKenzie's party sets out from Caldron Linn . .	5
November	9 Hunt's party sets out from Caldron Linn	23
November	9 Crooks' party sets out from Caldron Linn . . .	19
		64

This number includes 1 woman and 2 children. The number given by Crooks is 60, but he doubtless omitted Rose and the woman and children.

Jan. 18, 1812, arrived at Astoria, parties of Reed, McLellan and McKenzie	11
Feb. 15, 1812, arrived at Astoria, Hunt's party	34

May 10, 1812, arrived at Astoria, Crooks and Day   2
Jan. 6, 1813, arrived at Astoria, Carson, Delauney, St. Michael,
    Dubreuil, LaChapelle, Landry, and Turcot   7
Still detached, including Rose (for Cass and Detaye, see next line)   5
Perished—Clappine, Detaye, Cass, Carriere, Provost   5
                                                                 ——
                                                                64

The total number who reached Astoria was 54.

On the *Beaver*: Irving says that the *Beaver* sailed with 1 partner, 5 clerks, 15 American laborers and 6 voyageurs, and took on 12 Islanders. One of the company's men died en route which would leave in all 38. Franchere places the number who arrived at Astoria at 33, and Cox, who was one of the passengers, at 36.

Fugitive Arrivals: There were 7 arrivals from various sources, but none of them of importance.

The total number of persons who entered the company's service on the Columbia, including the Islanders and fugitive arrivals, was therefore 144. This is a maximum number, the minimum given by any authority being 135.

Perished

The following is the number of Astorians who are known to have lost their lives during the continuance of the enterprise:

On the Columbia Bar   4
In the *Tonquin* Massacre   3
On the *Beaver*   1
Of the Overland Party   5
With Reed on Snake river   01
Lost at Astoria from various causes (Ross)   4
                                                               ——

    Total   27

Ship crews lost:

On Columbia Bar (including 1 islander).   4
Tonquin Massacre (including 8 islanders)   24
On the *Beaver*   2
Shipwreck of the *Lark*   8
                                                                ——

    Total   38

    Grand Total   65

Biographical Notes

Cox, Ross, was one of the clerks of the Pacific Fur Company; came to Astoria in the *Beaver* and entered the Northwest service in 1813. He was commonly known by the soubriquet of "Little Irishman." He remained on the Columbia six years, ascending the river nine times and descending it eight. His chief importance in Astorian history arises from the fact that he published an account of the enterprise which, although the least trustworthy of the original authorities, is still an important work. Its title is Adventures on the Columbia River, London, 1831.

Day, John, a hunter in the overland party under Hunt. According to Irving he was a Virginia backwoodsman, but had for several years been on the Missouri in the service of Crooks and others. He was about forty years old in 1811, six feet two inches high, in form erect, with a step elastic, and "a handsome, open, manly countenance." He was a true representative of the American hunter. He joined Hunt's party and went with the overland expedition to Astoria. He was somewhat broken in health at this time and fell behind with Crooks on Snake River when Hunt went on with the main party in the winter of 1811-12. He and Crooks were robbed of everything and stripped naked in the following spring on the Columbia. A large southern tributary of the Columbia that enters the river at this point is still called John Day's River.

Not liking the prospect at Astoria, Day resolved to return with the overland party under Robert Stuart; but before he reached the Walla Walla he became violently insane and was taken back to Astoria. Irving says that he died within a year, but this must have been a mistake for he was certainly alive in the spring of 1814 (A). As a matter of fact Day seems to have remained in the service of the Northwest Company for upwards of seven years and to have died in the upper Snake River country in 1819. Ross speaks in his Fur Hunters of a "defile where the veteran John Day died in 1819," and elsewhere refers to "Day's Valley." It was somewhere near Godin River. Ferris repeatedly refers to this valley as "Day's Defile."

Dorion, Pierre, a half-breed, and son of the Dorion who accompanied Lewis and Clark on a portion of their expedition across the continent. He was hired by Hunt as an interpreter and joined the overland expedition with his Indian wife and two children. He figures frequently in Irving's account of the expedition and generally in an interesting way. His death at the hands of the Indians near Boise River, Idaho, has already been related.

Dorion's wife was a woman of remarkable fortitude and perseverance, as will be seen from her experiences as related in the text. She and her children were still living in Oregon in 1850. One of the boys, Baptiste Dorion, was guide to the naturalist, Townsend, on a trip along the Columbia in 1834.

Franchere, Gabriel, one of the clerks who sailed in the *Tonquin*. His service on the Columbia was entirely at Astoria, and he was an eye witness of all the events which transpired there from March 25, 1811, when the *Tonquin* entered the Columbia, until April 4, 1814, when he left Fort George for home. Whatever is known of Franchere is to his credit. He was a man of ability and strictly honorable in all his relations. It is greatly to his honor that he had no hand in the negotiations connected with the transfer of Astoria and emphatically disapproved of McDougal's conduct.

Franchere did an inestimable service to the cause of Western history in leaving an admirable account of events at Astoria. It is written in a clear, simple and direct style, and is our best authority, except Irving's work, upon Mr. Astor's great enterprise. Franchere's Narrative was written in French and published in Montreal, 1819. An edition in English was published in 1854.

Franchere, after his return to Montreal, continued his connection with the fur business. He was engaged to the Northwest Company for several years, and in 1833 was employing men in Montreal for the American Fur Company.

Hunt, Wilson Price, chief partner in the Pacific Fur Company, except Mr. Astor, and leader of the overland Astorian expedition. Born at Asbury, New Jersey, date uncertain. Went to St. Louis in 1804 and was in business with John Hankinson in that city until Mr. Astor began to negotiate with him concerning his proposed enterprise on the Pacific. After the affairs of the Pacific Fur Company were wound up Hunt returned to business in St. Louis. In 1822 he was appointed postmaster of St. Louis by President Monroe. He was one of St. Louis' prominent business men and was highly respected by those who knew him. The events of his life which are most important in the present connection have already been related.

Miller, Joseph, "a gentleman well educated and well informed, and of a respectable family in Baltimore. He had been an officer in the army of the United States, but had resigned in disgust at being refused a furlough, and had taken to trapping beaver and trading with the Indians." (Irving.) Miller was with Crooks and McLellan in 1809 and joined the Pacific Fur Company with these gentlemen. The same imperious temper which drove him out of the army caused him to quit the new company when Hunt's expedition was about half way across the continent. After spending the fall and winter trapping and roving over the country until from one cause or another he was reduced almost to starvation, he was picked up by Robert Stuart in 1812 and acted as guide to Stuart's party from Snake to Bear river. For this very excellent service he was taken to task by the rest of the party, who thought that he was leading them too far to the south. They accordingly abandoned his guidance and made their senseless detour to the north. Miller's course was exactly right and to him belongs the credit of opening that part of the Oregon Trail which lay between Snake and Bear rivers.

It is quite possible that Miller may have seen Salt Lake in the winter of 1811-12.

Miller returned to St. Louis with Stuart's party and nothing further is known of him.

Reed, John, a clerk in the Pacific Fur Company, an Irishman by birth, and one of the unluckiest of the Astorians. His unfortunate affair with the tin box on the Columbia, and his untimely death on the Boise have already been related. Nothing is known of him except his connection with Astoria.

Ross, Alexander, a clerk of the Pacific Fur Company, who sailed with the *Tonquin*. After the downfall of Astoria he entered the Northwest service and remained there for many years. Much of his work was in the country around the headwaters of the Snake River. The greatest service which Ross performed was the publication of his two works, Adventures on the Oregon or Columbia River and Fur Hunters of the Far West. Both of these works are valuable contributions to the history of the fur trade.

Stuart, Robert, of Scotch extraction and a nephew of David Stuart. Both were partners in the Pacific Fur Company and both sailed in the *Tonquin*. Young Robert Stuart appears to have been a man of great ability and spirit. It was he who forced Captain Thorn, at the pistol's mouth, to turn about the ship at the Falkland Islands. He was selected to take charge of the returning overland expedition, although he had not crossed the country before and although there were in the party both Crooks and McLellan, who had crossed. After the affairs of the Pacific Fur Company were closed up, Crooks and Stuart entered Mr. Astor's service on the Great Lakes. When Crooks rose to the general agency of the company, Stuart was placed in charge of the Northern Department with headquarters at Michilimackinac. Many of his letters may still be seen in the old Astor letter books.

Loss of the Tonquin

The following account of the loss of the *Tonquin* appeared in the *Missouri Gazette* of May 15, 1813, being the first published account of that disaster. It has never before been reproduced:

"Loss of the Ship *Tonquin* near the Mouth of the Columbia.

"A large ship (The *Beaver*) had arrived from New York after a passage of near seven months, with merchandise and provisions for the company. It was here we learnt with sorrow that the story of the *Tonquin* having been cut off was but too true. The circumstances have been related in different ways by the natives in the environs of the establishment, but that which, from their own knowledge, carries with it the greatest appearance of truth is as follows: That vessel, after landing the cargo intended for Astoria, departed on a trading voyage to the coast north of Columbia River with a company of (including officers) 23 men, and had proceeded about 400 miles along the seaboard when they stopped on Vancouver's Island at a place called Woody Point, inhabited by a powerful nation called Wake-a-ninishes. These people came on board to barter their furs for merchandise, and conducted themselves in the most decorous and friendly manner during the first day, but the same evening information was brought on board by an Indian, whom the officers had as interpreter, that the tribe where they then lay were ill-disposed and intended attacking the ship next day. Captain Jonathan Thorn affected to disbelieve this piece of news, and even when the savages came next morning in great numbers, it was only at the pressing remonstrance of Mr. McKay that he ordered seven men aloft to loosen the sails. In the meantime about 50 Indians were permitted to come on board, who traded a number of sea otters for blankets and knives; the former they threw into their canoe as soon as received, but secreted the knives. Every one when armed moved from the quarter deck to different parts of the vessel, so that by the time they were ready, in such a manner were they distributed that at least three savages were opposite every man of the ship, and at a signal given they rushed on their prey, and notwithstanding the brave resistance of every individual of the whites they were all butchered in a few minutes. The men above, in attempting to descend, lost two of their number, besides one mortally wounded, who, notwithstanding his weakened condition, made good his retreat with the four others to the cabin, where, finding a quantity of loaded arms, they fired on their savage assailers through the skylights and companion-way, which had the effect of clearing the ship in a short time, and long before night these five intrepid sons of America were again in full possession of her. Whether from want of abilities or strength, supposing themselves unable to take the vessel back to Columbia, it cannot be ascertained. This fact only is known, that between the time the Indians were driven from the ship and the following morning, the four who were unhurt left her in the long boat in hopes of regaining the river, wishing to take along with them the wounded person, who refused their offer saying that he must die before long and was as well in the vessel as elsewhere.

"Soon after sunrise she was surrounded by an immense number of Indians in canoes (who had) come for the express purpose of unloading her, but who, from the warm reception they met with the day before, did not seem to vie with each other in boarding.

"The wounded man showing himself over the railing, made signs that he was alone and wanted their assistance, on which some embarked, who, finding what he said was true, spoke to their people who were not any longer slow in getting on board; so that in a few seconds the deck was considerably thronged, and they proceeded to undo the hatches without further ceremony.

"No sooner were they completely engaged in thus finishing this most diabolical of actions, than the only survivor of the crew descended into the cabin and set fire to the magazine containing nearly nine thousand pounds of gunpowder, which in an instant blew the vessel and every one on board to atoms.

"The nation acknowledge their having lost nearly one hundred warriors, besides a vast number wounded, by the explosion, who were in canoes round the ship. It is impossible to tell who the person was that so completely avenged himself, but there cannot exist a single doubt that the act will teach these villains better manners and will eventually be of immense benefit to the coasting trade. The four men who set off in the long boat were two or three days after driven ashore in a gale and massacred by the natives."

EDITOR'S NOTE

(A) For a discussion of this see Coues, *Henry-Thompson Journals*, page 856.

D

THE "FLATHEAD DEPUTATION" OF 1832

[Letter from G. P. Disoway to the *Christian Advocate* and *Journal* and *Zion's Herald*, Friday, March 1, 1833.]

THE FLATHEAD INDIANS

The plans to civilize the savage tribes of our country are among the most remarkable signs of the times. To meliorate the condition of the Indians, and to preserve them from gradual decline and extinction, the government of the United States have proposed and already commenced removing them to the region westward of the Misissippi. Here it is intended to establish them in a permanent residence. Some powerful nations of these aborigines, having accepted the proposal, have already emigrated to their new lands, and others are now preparing to follow them. Among those who still remain are the Wyandots, a tribe long distinguished as standing at the head of the great Indian Family.

The earliest travelers in Canada first discovered this tribe while ascending the St. Lawrence, at Montreal. They were subsequently driven by the Iroquois, in one of those fierce internal wars that characterize the Indians of North America, to the northern shores of Lake Huron. From this resting place also their relentless enemy literally hunted them until the remnant of this once powerful and proud tribe found a safe abode among the Sioux, who resided west of Lake Superior. When the power of the Iroquois was weakened by the French the Wyandots returned from the Sioux country, and settled near Michilimackinac. They finally took up their abode on the plains of Sandusky, in Ohio, where they continue to this day.

The Wyandots, amounting to five hundred, are the only Indians in Ohio who have determined to remain upon their lands. The Senecas, Shawnees, and Ottawas have all sold their Ohio possessions, and have either removed or are on their way to the west of the Mississippi. A small band of about seventy Wyandots from the Big Spring have disposed of their reservation of 16,000 acres, but have not accepted the offered lands of the government in exchange. They will retire into Michigan, or Canada, after leaving some of their number at the main reservation of Upper Sandusky.

The wonderful effects of the Gospel among the Wyandots are well known. Providence has blessed in a most remarkable manner the labors of our missionaries for their conversion. Knowledge, civilization, and social comforts have followed the introduction of Christianity into their regions. To all of the Indians residing within the jurisdiction of the states or territories the United States propose to purchase their present possessions and improvements, and in return to pay them acre for acre with lands west of the Mississippi River. Among the inducements to make this exchange are the following: perpetuity in their new abodes, as the faith of the government is pledged never to sanction another removal; the organization of a territorial government for their use like those in Florida, Arkansas, and Michigan, and the privilege to send delegates to Congress, as is now enjoyed by the other territories. Could the remaining tribes of the original possessors of this country place implicit reliance upon these assurances and prospects, this scheme to meliorate their condition, and to bring them within the pale of civilized life, might safely be pronounced great, humane, and rational.

The Wyandots, after urgent and often repeated solicitations of the government for their removal, wisely resolved to send agents to explore the region offered them in exchange, before they made any decision upon the proposal. In November last the party started on the exploring expedition, and visited their proposed residence. This was a tract of country containing about 200,000 acres, and situated between the western part of Missouri and the Missouri River. The location was found to be one altogether unsuitable to the views, the necessities, and the support of the nation. They consequently declined the exchange.

Since their return, one of the exploring party, Mr. William Walker, an interpreter, and himself a member of the nation, has sent me a communication. As it contains some valuable facts of a region from which we seldom hear, the letter is now offered for publication:

Upper Sandusky, Jan. 19, 1833.

Dear Friend:—Your last letter, dated Nov. 12, came duly to hand. The business part is answered in another communication which is inclosed.

I deeply regret that I have had no opportunity of answering your very friendly letter in a manner that would be satisfactory to myself; neither can I now, owing to a want of time and a retired place, where I can write undisturbed.

You, no doubt, can fancy me seated in my small dwelling, at the dining table, attempting to write, while my youngest (sweet little urchin!) is pulling my pocket-handkerchief out of my pocket, and Henry Clay, my only son, is teasing me to pronounce a word he has found in his little spelling book. This done, a loud rap is heard at my door, and two or three of my Wyandot friends make their appearance and are on some business. I drop my pen, dispatch the business, and resume it.

The country we explored is truly a land of savages. It is wild and romantic; it is a champaign, but beautifully undulated country. You can travel in some parts for whole days and not find timber enough to afford a riding switch, especially after you get off the Missouri and her principal tributary streams. The soil is generally a dark loam, but not of a durable kind for agriculture. As a country for agricultural pursuits, it is far inferior to what it has been represented to be. It is deplorably defective in timber. There are millions of acres on which you cannot procure timber enough to make a chicken coop. Those parts that are timbered are on some of the principal streams emptying into the great Missouri, and are very broken, rough, and cut up with deep ravines; and the timber, what there is of it, is of an inferior quality, generally a small growth of white, black, and bur oaks; hickory, ash, buckeye, mulberry, linwood, coffee bean, a low scrubby kind of birch, red and slippy elm, and a few scattering walnut trees. It is remarkable, in all our travels west of the Mississippi river, we never found even one solitary poplar, beech, pine, or sassafras tree, though we were informed that higher up the Missouri river, above Council Bluffs, pine trees abound to a great extent, especially the nearer you approach the Rocky mountains. The immense country embraced between the western line of the State of Missouri, and the Territory of Arkansas, and the eastern base of the Rocky mountains on the west, and Texas and Santa Fe on the south, is inhabited by the Osage, Sioux (pronounced Sooz), Pawnees, Comanches, Panchas, Arrapohoes, Assinaboins, Riccarees, Yanktons, Omahaws, Blackfeet, Ottoes, Crow Indians, Sacs, Foxes, and Iowas: all a wild, fierce, and war-like people. West of the mountains reside the Flatheads, and many other tribes, whose names I do not now recollect.

I will here relate an anecdote, if I may so call it. Immediately after we landed in St. Louis, on our way to the West, I proceeded to Gen. Clark's, superintendent of Indian affairs, to present our letters of introduction from the Secretary of War, and to receive the same from him to the different Indian agents in the upper country. While in his office and transacting business with him, he informed me that three chiefs from the Flathead nation were in his house, and were quite sick, and that one (the fourth) had died a few days ago.

They were from the west of the Rocky mountains. Curiosity prompted me to step into the adjoining room to see them, having never seen any, but often heard of them. I was struck with their appearance. They differ in appearance from any tribe of Indians I have ever seen: small in size, delicately formed, small limbs, and the most exact symmetry throughout, except the head. I had always supposed from their being called "Flatheads," that the head was actually flat on top; but this is not the case. The head is flattened thus:

From the point of the nose to the apex of the head, there is a perfect straight line, the protuberance of the forehead is flattened or leveled. You may form some idea of the shape of their heads from the rough sketch I have made with the pen, though I confess I have drawn most too long a proboscis for a Flat-head. This is produced by a pressure upon the cranium while in infancy. The distance they had traveled on foot was nearly three thousand miles to see General Clark, their great father, as they called him, he being the first American officer they ever became acquainted with, and having much confidence in him, they had come to consult him as they said, upon very important matters. Gen. C. related to me the object of their mission, and, my dear friend, it is impossible for me to describe to you my feelings while listening to his narrative. I will here relate it as briefly as I well can. It appeared that some white man had penetrated into their country, and happened to be a spectator at one of their religious ceremonies, which they scrupulously perform at stated periods. He informed them that their mode of worshipping the Supreme Being was radically wrong, and instead of being acceptable and pleasing, it was displeasing to him; he also informed them that the white people away toward the rising of the sun had been put in possession of the true mode of worshipping the Great Spirit. They had a book containing directions how to conduct themselves in order to enjoy his favor and hold converse with him; and with this guide, no one need go astray; but every one that would follow the directions laid down there could enjoy, in this life, his favor, and after death would be received into the country where the Great Spirit resides, and live for ever with him.

Upon receiving this information, they called a national council to take this subject into consideration. Some said, if this be true, it is certainly high time we were put in possession of this mode, and if our mode of worshipping be wrong and displeasing to the Great Spirit, it is time we had laid it aside. We must know something about this; it is a matter that cannot be put off; the sooner we know it the better. They accordingly deputed four of the chiefs to proceed to St. Louis to see their great father, General Clark, to inquire of him, having no doubt but he would tell them the whole truth about it.

They arrived at St. Louis, and presented themselves to Gen. C. The latter was somewhat puzzled being sensible of the responsibility that rested on him; he, however, proceeded by informing them that what they had been told by the white man in their own country was true. Then went into a succinct history of man, from his creation down to the advent of the Saviour; explained to them all the moral precepts contained in the Bible, expounded to them the decalogue; informed them of the advent of the Saviour, his life, precepts, his death, resurrection, ascension, and the relation he now stands to man as a mediator—that he will judge the world, etc.

Poor fellows, they were not all permitted to return home to their people with the intelligence. Two died in St. Louis, and the remaining two, though somewhat indisposed, set out for their native land. Whether they reached home or not is not known. The change of climate and diet operated very severely upon their health. Their diet when at home is chiefly vegetables and fish.

If they died on their way home, peace be to their manes! They died inquirers after the truth. I was informed that the Flatheads, as a nation, have the fewest vices of any tribe of Indians on the continent of America.

I had just concluded I would lay this rough and uncouth scroll aside and revise it before I would send it, but if I lay it aside you will never receive it; so I will send it to you just as it is, "with all its imperfections," hoping that you may be able to decipher it. You are at liberty to make what use you please of it.

Yours in haste,

Wm. Walker.

G. P. Disoway, Esq.

The most singular custom of flattening the head prevails among all the Indian nations west of the Rocky mountains. It is most common along the lower parts of the Columbia river, but diminishes in traveling eastward, until it is to be scarcely seen in the remote tribes near the mountains. Here the folly is confined to a few females only. The practice must have commenced at a very early period, as Columbus noticed it among the first objects that struck his attention. An essential point of beauty with those savages is a flat head. Immediately after the birth of the child the mother, anxious to procure the recommendation of a broad forehead for her infant, places it in the compressing machine. This is a cradle formed like a trough, with one end where the head reposes more elevated than the other. A padding is then placed upon the forehead, which presses against the head by cords passing through holes on each side of the cradle. The child is kept in this manner upward of a year, and the operation is so gradual as to be attended with scarcely any pain. During this period of compression the infant presents a frightful appearance, its little keen black eyes being forced out to an unnatural degree by the pressure of bandages. When released from this process the head is flattened, and seldom exceeds more than one or two inches in thickness. Nature with all its efforts can never afterward restore the proper shape. The heads of grown persons often form a straight line from the nose to the top of the forehead. From the outlines of the face in Mr. Walker's communication I have endeavored to sketch a Flathead for the purpose of illustrating more clearly this most strange custom. The dotted lines will show the usual rotundity of a human head, and the cut how widely a Flathead differs from the rest of the great family of man. So great is this difference as to compel anatomists themselves to confess that an examination of such skulls and ocular demonstrations only could have convinced them of the possibility of moulding the head into this form. The "human face divine" is thus sacrificed to fantastic ideas of savage beauty. They allege also, as an apology for this custom, that their slaves have round heads, and that the children of a brave and free race ought not to suffer such a degradation.

This deformity, however, of the Flathead Indians is redeemed by other numerous good qualities. Travelers relate that they have fewer vices than any of the tribes in those regions. They are honest, brave, and peaceable. The women become exemplary wives and mothers, and a husband with an unfaithful companion is a circumstance almost unknown among them. They believe in the existence of a good and evil Spirit, with rewards and punishments of a future state. Their religion promises to the virtuous after death a climate where perpetual summer will shine over plains filled with their much beloved buffalo, and upon streams abounding in the most delicious fish. Here they will spend their time in hunting and fishing, happy and undisturbed from every enemy; while the bad Indian will be consigned to a place of eternal snows, with fires in his sight that he cannot enjoy, and buffalo and deer that cannot be caught to satisfy his hunger.

A curious tradition prevails among them concerning beavers.

These animals, so celebrated for their sagacity, they believe are a fallen race of Indians, who have been condemned on account of their wickedness by the great Spirit, to their present form of the brute creation. At some future period they also declare that these fallen creatures will be restored to their former state.

How deeply touching is the circumstance of the four natives traveling on foot 3,000 miles through thick forests and extensive prairies, sincere searchers after truth! The story has scarcely a parallel in history. What a touching theme does it form for the imagination and pen of a Montgomery, a Mrs. Hemans, or our own fair Sigourney! With what intense concern will men of God whose souls are fired with holy zeal for the salvation of their fellow beings, read their history! There are immense plains, mountains, and forests in regions whence they came, the abodes of numerous savage tribes. But no apostle of Christ has yet had the courage to penetrate into their moral darkness. Adventurous and daring fur traders only have visited these regions, unknown to the rest of the world, except from their own accounts of them. If the Father of spirits, as revealed by Jesus Christ, is not known in these interior wilds of America, they nevertheless often resound the praises of the unknown, invisible Great Spirit, as he is denominated by the savages. They are not ignorant of the immortality of their souls, and speak of some future delicious island or country where departed spirits rest. May we not indulge the hope that the day is not far distant when the missionaries will penetrate into these wilds where the Sabbath bell has never yet tolled since the world began! There is not, perhaps, west of the Rocky mountains, any portion of the Indians that presents at this moment a spectacle so full of interest to the contemplative mind as the Flathead tribe. Not a thought of converting or civilizing them ever enters the mind of the sordid, demoralizing hunters and fur traders. These simple children of nature even shrink from the loose morality and inhumanities often introduced among them by the white man. Let the Church awake from her slumbers and go forth in her strength to the salvation of these wandering sons of our native forests. We are citizens of this vast universe, and our life embraces not merely a moment, but eternity itself. Thus exalted, what can be more worthy of our high destination than to befriend our species and those efforts that are making to release immortal spirits from the chains of error and superstition, and to bring them to the knowledge of the true God. G.P.D.

New York, Feb. 18, 1833.

The following letters were published in the *Christian Advocate* of May 10, 1833.)

THE FLATHEAD INDIANS

The following correspondence and communication will be read with great interest. Is it not the voice of Heaven to us? The field opens gloriously. Read Mr. M'Allister's letter below. The men are ready; let the Missionary Society have the means. Let the whole Church become a missionary band; not for this object particularly, but for every subject. These documents necessarily shorten our notice of the missionary anniversary of our Church, held on the evening of the 23rd of April, but we shall continue it in our next.

ST. LOUIS, Mo., April 16. (1833.)

Dear Brethren:—The communication respecting the Flat Head Indians, which appeared a few weeks since in your paper, and the call of Dr. Fisk, have excited considerable attention. I have just received a letter from Brother Brunson, propounding several questions, which he wished me to have answered here, so that the desired information might be rendered available to the Christian public. I called immediately upon General Clark, who received me kindly. He informed me he was just answering, or had just answered, some communications upon the subject. I was struck with the propriety of an immediate communication from this place; I therefore send you this, sincerely wishing it may be useful.

General Clark informed me that the publication which had appeared in the *Advocate* was correct. Of the return of the two Indians nothing is known. He informed me the cause of their visit was the following: Two of their number had received an education at some Jesuitical school in Montreal, Canada, had returned to the tribe, and endeavored, as far as possible, to instruct their brethren how the whites approached the Great Spirit. The consequence was a spirit of inquiry was aroused, a deputation appointed, and a tedious journey of three thousand miles performed, to learn for themselves of Jesus and him crucified. Will not these Indians rise up in the day of judgment to the condemnation of hundreds and thousands who live and die unforgiven in Christian lands?

I had the good fortune to become acquainted with Mr. Campbell, who was one of the first traders among those Indians. He left on yesterday for the Rocky Mountains and the country beyond. A few hours before his departure he favored me with the enclosed letter, which I wish you to publish with these remarks. Mr. Campbell is a very intelligent and gentlemanly man, and you may rely upon his information.

Yours as ever,

E. W. Sehon.

Rev. Mr. Sehon:

Dear Sir:—In compliance with your request I shall give you a few very brief answers to the questions you have put respecting the Flat Head Indians.

1. Prospects of a mission? I cannot pretend to say what prospects there would be in a religious point of view. The Flat Head Indians are proverbial for their mild disposition and friendship to the whites and I have little hesitation in saying a missionary would be treated by them with kindness.

2. Distance from St. Louis to Council Bluffs? The distance is about five hundred miles.

3. Whether suitable interpreters can be obtained for the Flat Head Indians? There would be some difficulty to have religious matters explained, because the best interpreters are half-Indians, that you could not explain to their minds the matter you would require to have told to the Indians.

4. The number of the Indians? There are about forty lodges of these Indians, averaging, say seven Indians to a lodge.

5. Do steamers go as far as the Council Bluffs? With the exception of the American Fur Company's steamboats, which ascend as high as the Yellow Stone, none go as far as the Bluffs.

6. Do fur traders go to the Flat Head country, and at what seasons of the year, and will they allow the missionaries to go in their company? There is every season one or more companies leaving St. Louis in the month of March, and I doubt not but they would willingly allow a missionary to accompany them; but the privations that a gentleman of that profession would have to encounter would be very great, as the shortest route that he would have by land would not be less than one thousand miles, and when he reached his destination he would have to travel with the Indians, as they have no permanent villages, nor have the traders any houses, but, like the Indian, move their leather lodges from place to place throughout the season.

Very respectfully, your obedient servant,

Robert Campbell.

St. Louis, April 13, 1833.

St. Louis, April 17, 1833.

Messrs. Editors:—The visit of the Flat Head and Nose Pierce, or Pierced Nose, Indians to our place to inquire of the white man how he ascertains the will of the Great Spirit, has excited much interest in their behalf among the benevolent in different parts of the United States, and well it may, when we consider the distance they traveled, and the countless hardships they endured to learn by what means we have access into this grace wherein we stand, and rejoice in the hope of the resurrection of the dead and the glory of God. Interrogatories have been proposed in reference to the tribe or band of Flat Heads, who sent the deputation to this city to wait on General Clark, and in answering the question as to their number, Mr. Campbell confines his answer to that particular band, and states the number at about two hundred and eighty. This statement, though strictly true and fully covering the inquiry proposed, might induce many not otherwise informed to suppose that the Flat Heads constitute a mere handful of people buried in the deep recesses of the stony mountains, near three thousand miles from the abodes of civilized man, and are scarcely worth looking after. This is not the fact: the deputation was from the Cho-pun-ish tribe, residing on Lewis River, and a small band of Flat Heads who live with them. The Cho-pun-ish or Pierce Nose Indians are about seven thousand in number, according to General Clark's account.

The Indians residing on the tide water of the Oregon and below the great falls are about eight thousand in number. Those residing on the northwest of the Oregon, on the coast of the Pacific, number about six thousand. Those on the southwest on the same coast number about ten thousand two hundred; all these Indians are Flat Heads except one Tribe—the Cook-koo-oose—living on the coast of the Pacific; these do not flatten the head, and are fairer in their complexion, and number about fifteen hundred. The Flat Heads living on Kilmox Bay speak the same language with the Lucktons, Ka-Kun-kle, Lick-a-wis, Yorich-cone, Neek-e-to, Ul-le-ah, You-itts, Shia Stuck-kle, and Kila-evats. The presumption is that it is the vernacular language of all those tribes living on the Oregon below the Great Falls and on the Pacific coast, northwest and southwest of the mouth of the Oregon. General Clark discovered on the waters of the Oregon and coast of the Pacific more than sixty tribes of Indians, numbering about eighty thousand souls. It is not, however, to be presumed that his account is complete. It is highly probable that the coast of the eastern Pacific is frequented by Indians from Behring's Straits to Upper California, and many tribes no doubt exist in the interior both south and north of the Oregon, which did not come to the knowledge of Messrs. Lewis and Clark.

How ominous this visit of the Cho-pun-ish and Flat Head Indians! How loud the call to the missionary spirit of the age! It calls to my mind a declaration made by Bishop Soule, when preaching at a camp in this country. Speaking of the missionary zeal of the Methodist preachers, of their extended field of labors, their untiring perseverance to compass the earth and spread Scriptural holiness through all the world: "We will not cease," said he, "until we shall have planted the standard of Christianity high on the summit of the Stony Mountains."

Already would it seem that a door is open, and the Indians from the lofty summit of the Rocky mountains look far east with burning desire to behold the coming of the messenger of God. Among the Cho-pun-ish and Flat Heads of Lewis river the work will commence; the honesty, hospitality, docility, and mildness of these Indians strongly recommended them first to the consideration of the civilian and Christian missionary; here the missionary may learn perhaps the language spoken by those of Kil-a-man Bay on the Pacific: this will give access to perhaps twenty or thirty thousand below the Great Falls and on the Pacific.

One word more and I shall close. Many of our fellow-citizens have gone from this country so diseased as to render it doubtful whether they could ever reach the mountains and have returned from thence with constitutions restored and health renewed, to the astonishment of all that knew them. If you think the information herein contained would serve the purposes of Christian benevolence, give it a place in your Journal.

Yours affectionately,
A. M'ALLISTER.

E

MISCELLANEOUS DATA RELATING TO THE FUR TRADE

State of the fur trade in 1831—General Ashley's method of moving parties through the Indian country—A fur hunter's business accounts.

STATE OF THE FUR TRADE IN 1831

(Letter from Thomas Forsyth to Lewis Cass, Secretary of War, Manuscript Department. State Historical Society of Wisconsin.)

St. Louis, October 24, 1831.

Sir:—In compliance with the request contained in your letter of the 9th ultimo, I have the honor to give the following as answers to your queries. I am sorry to say that these answers are not so complete as I would wish them to be, but it seems impossible to collect more detailed or comprehensive information in this country on the subject of the trade from this place to Mexico and to the base and west of the Rocky Mountains. Several persons with whom I have conversed, and who have decidedly the best knowledge of the subject, are unwilling to say anything about it, while others, who pretend to much knowledge of the business, are too ignorant to give even a plain common account, but tell so many wild stories and deal so much in the marvelous, that it appears unsafe to depend on anything they relate—

The Fur Trade on the Frontiers

The fur trade of the countries bordering on the Mississippi and Missouri rivers, as high up the former river as above the Falls of St. Anthony, and the latter as the Sioux establishment some distance above Council Bluffs, is carried on now in the same manner as it ever has been. This trade continues to be monopolized by the American Fur Company, who have divided the whole of the Indian country into departments as follows: Farnham & Davenport have all the country of the Sauk and Fox Indians, as high up the Mississippi River as Dubuque's mines (without including the Fox Indians who reside at that place) as also all the Winnebago and other Indians who reside on the lower parts of Rock River; also the Iowa Indians who live at or near the (Black) Snake Hills on the Missouri River. The division of Mr. Rolette includes all the Indians from Dubuque's mines to a point above the Falls of St. Anthony, and up the St. Peters (Minnesota) river to its source, as also all the Indians on the Wisconsin and upper parts of Rock river. Mr. Cabanne (who is a member of the American Fur Company) has in his division all the Indians on the Missouri as high as a point above the Council Bluffs, including the Pawnee Indians of the interior, in about a southwest direction from his establishment. Mr. Auguste P. Chouteau has within his department all the Indians of the Osage country and others who may visit his establishment, such as the Cherokees, Chickasaws, and other Indians. Messrs. McKenzie, Laidlaw & Lamont have in their limits the Sioux Indians of the Missouri, and as high up the river as they choose to send or go. The American Fur Company bring on their goods annually in the spring season to this city from New York, which are then sent up the Missouri river to the different posts in a small steamboat. At those places the furs are received on board and brought down to St. Louis, where they are opened, counted, weighed, repacked, and shipped by steamboats to New Orleans, thence on board of vessels to New York, where the furs are unpacked, made up into bales, and sent to the best markets in Europe, except some of the finest (particularly otter skins), which are sent to China.

Mr. Rolette procures his goods at Mackinaw, takes them on in Mackinaw boats to Prairie du Chien (by way of Green Bay, the Fox and Wisconsin rivers), where he assorts them. They are then forwarded, by clerks hired for the purpose, with the same boats and men, to the different trading posts. Farnham & Davenport take up their goods from this city to the Indian villages in keelboats, with their clerks and men. Mr. Cabanne and Mr. McKenzie & Company take up their goods in the American Fur Company steamboats as before stated. The goods of Mr. A. P. Chouteau are transported by water in keelboats, as high up the Osage River as the water will admit; from thence they are carried in wagons to his establishment in the interior of the country. In the spring of the year when the Arkansas is high Mr. Chouteau sends his furs down that river to New Orleans from whence they are shipped to New York. (1)

By the time that the Indians have gathered their corn, the traders are prepared with their goods to give them credits. The articles of merchandise which the traders take with them to the Indian country are as follows: viz., blankets 3 points, 2½, 2, 1½, 1; common blue stroud; ditto red; blue cloth; scarlet do; calicoes; domestic cottons; rifles and shot guns, gunpowder, flints, and lead; knives of different kinds; looking glasses; vermilion and verdigris; copper, brass, and tin kettles; beaver and muskrat traps; fine and common bridles and spurs; silverworks; needles and thread; wampum; horses; tomahawks and half axes, etc. All traders at the present day give credit to the Indians in the same manner as has been the case for the last sixty or eighty years. That is to say, the articles which are passed on credit are given at very high prices. Formerly, when the opposition and competition in the Indian Trade were great, the traders would sell in the spring of the year, payment down, for less than one-half of the prices at which they charged the same articles to the same Indians on credit the preceding autumn. This was sometimes the occasion of broils and quarrels between the traders and the Indians, particularly when the latter made bad hunts.

The following are the prices charged for some articles given on credit to the Sauk and Fox Indians, whose present population exceeds six thousand souls and who are compelled to take goods, etc., of the traders at their very high prices, because they cannot do without them, for if the traders do not supply their necessary wants and enable them to support themselves, they would literally starve. An Indian takes on credit from a trader in the autumn—

A 3-point blanket at	$10.00
A rifle gun	30.00
A pound of gunpowder	4.00
	————
Total Indian dollars	$44.00

The 3-point blanket will cost in England, say 16 shillings per
    pair 1 blanket at 100 per cent is equal to   . . . . . . $ 3.52
A rifle gun costs in this place from $12 to 13.00
A pound of gunpowder 20

                                                          ————
                                                           $16.72
Add 25 per cent for expenses 4.18

                                                            ————
                                                           $20.90

Therefore, according to this calculation (which I know is correct), if the Indian pays all his debt, the traders is a gainer of more than than 100 per cent. But it must be here observed that the trader takes for a dollar a large buckskin, which may weigh six pounds, or two doeskins, four muskrats, four or five raccoons, or he allows the Indian three dollars for an otterskin, or two dollars a pound for beaver. And in my opinion the dollar which the trader receives of the Indian is not estimated too high at 125 cents, and perhaps in some instances at 150 cents.

In the spring the trader lowers his price on all goods, and will sell a 3-point blanket for five dollars, and other articles in proportion as he receives the furs down in payment, and as the Indians always reserve the finest and best furs for the spring trade. In the autumn of every year the trader carefully avoids giving credit to the Indians on any costly articles, such as silverworks, wampum, scarlet cloth, fine bridles, etc., unless it be to an Indian who he knows will pay all his debt; in which case he will allow the Indian on credit everything he wishes. Traders always prefer giving on credit gunpowder, flints, lead, knives, tomahawks, hoes, domestic cottons, etc., which they do at the rate of 300 or 400 per cent, and if one-fourth of the prices of those articles be paid, he is amply paid. After all the trade is over in the spring it is found that some of the Indians have paid all for which they were credited, others one-half, one-third, one-fourth, and some nothing at all; but taken altogether, the trader has received on an average one-half of the whole amount of Indian dollars for which he gave credit the preceding autumn, and calls it a tolerable business; that is, if the furs bear a good price the trader loses nothing, but if any fall in the price takes place he loses money.

The American Fur Company ought to be satisfied with the Indians, for they have monopolized all the trade, especially at the posts before mentioned. There is a man now in this city who receives annually a sum from that company on condition that he will not enter the Indian country. (2) They have also monopolized the whole trade on the frontiers together with the Indian annuities, and everything an Indian has to sell, yet they claim a large amount for debts due them for non-payment of credits given to the Indians at different periods.

Trade to and West of the Rocky Mountains

I visited this country as early as April, 1798, and in many conversations I had with the French people of this place, all that they could say on the subject of the Indian trade was that there were many Indian nations inhabiting the country bordering on the Missouri River who were exceedingly cruel to all the white people that went among them. The highest point then known up the Missouri river was Cedar Island, which is somewhere in the Arikara country. The Arikara, Mandan, Blackfeet, Crow, Arapahoe, Assiniboin, and other Indians were well known in those days (1800) to the Hudson Bay and Northwest Companies. Clerks belonging to those companies with their men would visit the Missouri annually at different places for the purpose of trading with the Indians.

After the arrival of Lewis and Clark from the Pacific, a company was organized at this place for the purpose of trading with the Indians up the Missouri river to its forks and higher if necessary. That company did not exist long, as it appeared they were deficient in management and understanding of their new business. After their dissolution a Mr. Manuel Lisa carried on a trade with the nations as high up as the Sioux Indians. He afterwards with others formed a company who extended their trade up the Missouri river to the Mandan villages. Mr. Manuel Lisa appeared quite sanguine of success, having the sole management of this company, and it is supposed by some people that if he had been well assisted by his partners, he might have done something; but all his endeavors fell to the ground, and he died some years ago, insolvent. Mr. Manuel Lisa and his partners followed the custom of employing men to hunt in the Indian country.

After the war with Great Britain commenced our Indian trade almost ceased to exist, except where it was continued by some few hunters who got up among the Indians and would, in the spring season, bring down a few furs; yet the Hudson Bay and the Northwest companies at the same time extended their trade, and sent hunting parties to different points on the Missouri river as also to the Rocky Mountains. This kind of trade or business of hunting was conducted on a small scale until General Ashley took it in hand about the year 1821 or 2, when he took a number of hunters up towards the mountains as also some goods to trade with the Indians.

In 1823 General Ashley was attacked by the Arikaras. He then descended the Missouri river to Council Bluffs when Colonel Leavenworth went up (General Ashley and party being in company) and severely punished the Indians for their audacity. After this General Ashley took more men as hunters and more goods up towards the base of the Rocky mountains. About this time (say 1824–5) General Ashley was nearly one hundred thousand dollars in debt, as I have been informed, since which he has paid off all his debts and has now an independent fortune.

Some years back General Ashley extended his trade and hunting excursions west of the mountains, but he has since sold out to Messrs. Sublette, Jackson & Smith and now has nothing more to do with the business either of hunting or trading about the mountains. He brings on goods &c. from the eastward to this city and furnishes Sublette, Jackson & Smith with all they require and receives annually from them their furs in payment. Sublette & Co. transport their goods by water from this place up the Missouri to the Little Platte, thence in wagons to a given point on the Missouri River east of the mountains, as also round a spur of the mountains to the waters of Columbia. From what I can learn, there is but little trading done on either side of the Rocky mountains by Sublette, Jackson & Smith. It is altogether by hunting that they collect so many furs.

In the Hudson Bay establishments on Red river there are many half-breeds who are altogether brought up to hunting. They were formerly provided with an outfit to hunt by some of the Hudson Bay trading establishments, so that they became well acquainted with all the country on each side of the Rocky mountains. From them the Hudson Bay Company collected much fur. But General Ashley (as I have been told) has had the address to gain over many of those half-breeds to the American concern, by which means the returns of fur to the Hudson Bay establishments have been much curtailed.

Messrs, McKenzie, Laidlaw and Lamont are three young Scotchmen, of whom the two former were once in the employ of the Hudson Bay Company. But when that company and the Northwest Company joined their concerns together, about nine hundred clerks and men were dismissed that service. McKenzie and Laidlaw were among that number, and coming to St. Louis, they formed a concern with Lamont and others, calling themselves the Columbia Fur Company and trading under that firm. They were unsuccessful at the commencement and at one time were forty or fifty thousand dollars in debt, but one fortunate season of trade enabled them to pay off all their debts, leaving much money for themselves. After this they made arrangements with the American Fur Company for goods, and have been doing a good business ever since, so as to be now wealthy. Messrs. McKenzie & Co. send goods and hunters up the Missouri river from their establishments, toward the mountains, and from the knowledge McKenzie and Laidlaw obtained (during their employment in the Hudson Bay Company) of the country and Indians, they now trade with the Blackfeet and other Indians who always heretofore were in favour of the Hudson Bay Company. Perhaps it would not be exceeding the truth to say that half a million of dollars in furs are now annually brought down the Missouri river that formerly went to Hudson Bay, and it is the enterprising spirit of General Ashley which has occasioned the change of this channel of trade.

All traders procure as much wild meat as possible from the Indians, but where this article is scarce they have the precaution to take provisions with them in the fall of the year as they go into the Indian country. I am informed that Mr. A. P. Chouteau has a very large farming establishment in the Osage country, where he raises every article of necessary food and in greater abundance than is necessary for himself, his very numerous family and followers. Messrs. McKenzie & Co. have some domestic animals at their establishments; but the buffalo, elk, bear and deer (particularly the buffalo)-are so numerous that they are never in want of provisions of the meat kind. Their corn they can obtain in abundance from the Arikara and Mandan Indians and they can be supplied with a little flour from St. Louis so that they can never be in want. It is said that Sublette, Jackson and Smith take with them some horned cattle, which they drive with their wagons and which serve for provisions until they reach the buffalo country.

It is impossible for me to ascertain the number of lives that have been lost on the routes to and from the Rocky Mountains or Mexico. In the Indian country bordering on the frontiers no lives have been lost, according to my present recollection for the last fifteen years, except Findley and two others on Lake Pepin in the summer of 1824, and two men by the Winnebagos near Prairie du Chien in the summer of 1828. Smith (the partner of Sublette and Jackson) was killed this past summer on his way to Santa Fe, having gone that way with some goods.

I have no doubt that in most of the misunderstandings which take place between the whites and Indians in the interior of the Indian country, the fault is with the white people, except among the Comanches, or Hietans, as some call them. They are a roving, plundering, murdering nation.

The following are the names of the different nations of Indians who inhabit the country between this and the Rocky Mountains and west of the Mississippi, viz., Sauks, Foxes, Sioux, Otoes, Iowas, Mahas, Pawnees, Paducas, Snakes, Shoshones, Delawares, Peorias and Kickapoos, and there may be others that I have never heard of, or having heard of, have forgotten.

TRADE TO MEXICO

The trade to Mexico from this country is carried on by individuals. Sometimes two, three, or more individuals will join their small adventures together, either at St. Louis or on the route, and sell them to the best advantage at Santa Fe or other places in Mexico, during the winter months. Those people who are inclined to go to Mexico, prepare by purchasing goods, wagons, mules, and horses and hiring of men. The whole cavalcade rendezvous at Independence, Jackson county, in this state, about the month of May. They then move off together after having formed such regulations among themselves as are deemed beneficial to the whole, which regulations continue in force on the whole route from this state to Santa Fe.

From what I can learn there is little or no danger between this and the supposed line dividing Mexico and the United States, unless the cavalcade fall in with a war party of Pawnees or Paducas on their way to war against the Comanches or Hietans (as some call them), and then if the party of whites have in number say 100 or 150 men, the Indians will not attack them, but will try every stratagem to steal their horses and mules, because those Indians know that when they have once got the horses and mules, the white people cannot get their wagons away, but will abandon them, whereby the Indians will get much booty. By this mode they have succeeded in more than one instance, and after carrying away what they can they destroy the balance of the goods and wagons.

In May last upwards of two hundred men left Independence for Santa Fe and from what I am informed they did not meet with any difficulty either in going or returning. This was told me by a few who have returned. It appears that after the line above mentioned is crossed (in going outwards) the white people are more apt to fall in with the Hietans who follow the buffalo near the base of the mountains to the northward during the spring and summer months, and to the southward during the autumn.

Parties from this place on their arrival in the mountains, hide their goods and then they go into the settlements to make the necessary arrangements, after which, by means of bribes, their goods are smuggled in. They then sell them so as to be here again about this time (October) or ensuing month with the returns, whatever they may be. I cannot form any idea, neither can I gain any information as to the amount of goods taken, or the number of men employed, in the annual trade of Mexico, and I am equally uninformed as to the amount of returns from that place. In August last Mr. Charles Bent set out from St. Louis with a number of wagons loaded with goods for Santa Fe and drawn by oxen. His party consisted of from thirty to forty men, and if he succeeds with his ox wagons the oxen will answer the triple purpose: 1st, drawing the wagons; 2nd, the Indians will not steal them as they would horses and mules; and 3rdly, in cases of necessity part of the oxen will answer for provisions.

Observations Respecting our Relations with the Indian Nations

It is lamentable indeed for any one who has the least knowledge of Indians to observe that not only those who visit this place, but also those who have never been at any of the military posts, should have so little respect for the American people. In March, 1818, when I was at the city of Washington, I had several long conversations with Mr. Calhoun (then Secretary of War) on Indian affairs. I told him that it must appear strange to many people to perceive that we, as Americans, speaking the same language with the British, whose manners and customs were the same, exceeding them perhaps in our Indian expenditures, and having all the Indians residing within our own territories, still had not the same influence over them that the British had. Therefore (said I) there must be a fault somewhere. To this Mr. Calhoun replied, that I ought not to point out an evil without showing a remedy for it. I answered by saying that we ought to follow the same policy (so far as possible) towards the Indians that the British pursued with such success. The British government have a well-regulated Indian Department. No person is eligible for an Indian agency under that government unless he can speak some one of the Indian languages; for it is natural to suppose that a man understands at least the general manners and customs of all Indians if he has been among them long enough to learn any one of their languages, and they (the British) have brought their Indian affairs to a perfect system. But our government appoints young men to Indian agencies, generally from the interior of the United States, who, in all probability, have never seen more than three or four Indians together in the course of their lives, and those Indians perhaps civilized. When the old chiefs and warriors hear of the arrival of their new father (as they term the new agent) they call at the agency to see him, but the agent does not know what to say or do to them and perhaps does not give them a pipe of tobacco, or even a good or bad word. The Indians then go away dissatisfied, and consequently in cases of this kind, everything depends on the interpreter. If the interpreter is an honest man he may teach the agent something in the course of years; but on the contrary, if he is a designing man, and wishes that no one should share his influence, he will keep the agent and the Indians in continual broils and quarrels, and nothing being rightly done, the public service must suffer. Instead of trying to heal the old sores that have existed for the last fifty or sixty years between the American people and the Indians, the breach is made wider and fuel is added to the flame. I have been told that a young man who was appointed an Indian agent on the Missouri river cut off the ears of a half-breed who resided among the Sioux Indians because, being in a state of intoxication, he made use of some extravagant language disrespectful of the American people. Another agent on the Mississippi turned out of the guard-house an innocent Indian to other Indians, his enemies, who shot him down and butchered him in a horrid manner, in the presence of an American garrison of soldiers. Another Indian agent also invited some chiefs to a council, when a number of their enemies arrived at the agency, organized themselves, descended the Mississippi River, attacked the chiefs and others who were invited, and on their way to the council, killed nine and wounded three out of sixteen persons. In my intercourse with the Indians for the last forty years I never found that coercive measures ever had any good effect with them but that conciliatory measures always tended to produce every purpose required.

I am, &c.,

THOMAS FORSYTH.

The Honorable Lewis Cass,
    Secretary of War, Wash-
        ington City.

(Thomas Forsyth's Letter Book, 1822-33. Mss. Dept. State Historical Society of Wisconsin.)

GENERAL ASHLEY'S METHOD OF MOVING PARTIES THROUGH THE
INDIAN COUNTRY

In compliance with your request in relation to my manner of equipping and moving parties of men through the Indian country in the course of my general excursions to the Rocky Mountains, I will observe that, as mules are much the best animals for packing heavy burthens, each man has charge of two of them for that purpose, and one horse to ride. The equipage of each horse or mule consists of two halters, one saddle, one saddle blanket, one bear skin for covering the pack or saddle, and one pack strap for the purpose of binding on the pack, and a bridle for the riding horse. One of the halters should be made light for common use, of beef hide, dressed soft; the other should be made of hide dressed in the same way, or tarred rope, sufficiently strong to hold the horse under any circumstances, and so constructed as to give pain to the jaws when drawn very tight. The rein of each halter should not be less than sixteen feet long. A stake made of tough, hard wood, about two inches in diameter, and two feet long, with an iron socket, pointed at one end to penetrate the earth, and at the other end a band of iron to prevent its splitting, should be provided, to be used when in the prairies, with the halter last described. This stake, when well set in the ground, will hold any horse.

In the organization of a party of, say from 60 to 80 men, four of the most confidential and experienced of the number are selected to aid in the command; the rest are divided in messes of eight or ten. A suitable man is also appointed at the head of each mess, whose duty it is to make known the wants of his mess, receive supplies for them, make distributions, watch over their conduct, enforce order, etc., etc.

The party thus organized, each man receives the horses and mules allotted to him, their equipage, and the packs which his mules are to carry; every article so disposed of is entered in a book kept for that purpose. When the party reaches the Indian country, great order and vigilance in the discharge of their duty are required of every man. A variety of circumstances confines our march very often to the borders of large water courses; when that is the case, it is found convenient and safe, when the ground will admit, to locate our camps (which are generally laid off in a square) so as to make the river form one line and include as much ground in it as may be sufficient for the whole number of horses, allowing for each a range of thirty feet in diameter. On the arrival of the party at their camping ground, the position of each mess is pointed out, where their packs, saddles, etc., are taken off, and with them a breastwork immediately put up, to cover them from a night attack by Indians; the horses are then watered and delivered to the horse guard, who keeps them on the best grass outside and near the encampment, where they graze until sunset; then each man brings his horse within the limits of the camp, exchanges the light halter for the other more substantial, sets his stakes, which are placed at the distance of thirty feet from each other, and secures his horses to them. This range of thirty feet, in addition to the grass the horse has collected outside the camp, will be all-sufficient for him during the night. After these regulations, the proceedings of the night are pretty much the same as are practiced in military camps. At daylight (when in dangerous parts of the country) two or more men are mounted on horseback, and sent to examine ravines, woods, hills, and other places within striking distance of the camp, where Indians might secrete themselves, before the men are allowed to leave their breastworks to make the necessary morning arrangements before marching. When these spies report favorably, the horses are then taken outside the camp, delivered to the horse guard, and allowed to graze until the party has breakfasted, and are ready for saddling. In the line of march, each mess march together, and take their choice of positions in the line according to their activity in making themselves ready to move, viz,: the mess first ready to march moves up in the rear of an officer, who marches in the front of the party, and takes choice of a position in the line, and so they all proceed until the line is formed; and in that way they march the whole of that day. Spies are sent several miles ahead to examine the country in the vicinity of the route, and others are kept at the distance of a half mile or more from the party, as the situation of the ground seems to require, in front, rear, and on the flanks. In making discoveries of Indians, they communicate the same by signal or otherwise to the commanding officer with the party, who makes his arrangements accordingly. In this way I have marched parties of men the whole way from St. Louis to the vicinity of the Grand Lake, which is situated about one hundred and fifty miles down the waters of the Pacific Ocean, in 78 days. In the month of March, 1827, I fitted out a party of 60 men, mounted a piece of artillery (a four pounder) on a carriage which was drawn by two mules; the party marched to or near the Grand Salt Lake beyond the Rocky Mountains, remained there one month, stopped on the way back fifteen days, and returned to Lexington, in the western part of Missouri, in September, where the party was met with everything necessary for another outfit, and did return (using the same horses and mules) to the mountains by the last of November, in the same year.

A FREE HUNTER'S BUSINESS ACCOUNTS

The following seven exhibits, taken from many hundreds still among the Chouteau papers, will convey a good idea of the business transactions of the wilderness, and will show to what an extent the methods of business in the older and settled portions of the country obtained even in these remote sections where civilized man was yet almost an entire stranger. The particular person, whose accounts are here exhibited appears now and then in the narratives of that period and is believed to be the one for whom Gardiner river in the Yellowstone National Park is named:

COPY OF A FREE HUNTER'S CONTRACT

Articles of agreement made and entered into at Fort Union, Upper Missouri, on the fifth day of July, one thousand eight hundred and thirty-two, by and between Kenneth MacKenzie, agent of the American Fur Company, and Johnson Gardner, citizen of the United States and free hunter in the Indian country—

The said Johnson Gardner hereby agrees to sell, and the said Kenneth MacKenzie agrees to purchase, all his stock of beaver skins now en cache on the Yellowstone River, at and for the price per pound net weight of four dollars twelve and a half cents, to be delivered by the said Johnson Gardner to the agent or servants of the said Kenneth MacKenzie on the spot where it is cached, the weight thereof to be regulated and adjusted by Francis A. Chardon and James A. Hamilton on its arrival at Fort Union, the number of skins being . . . and the weight now considered to be . . . . The said Johnson Gardner further agrees to sell, and the said Kenneth MacKenzie agrees to purchase, all his stock of castorum at and for the price per pound of three dollars, the weight thereof to be adjusted by the parties aforesaid. The said Kenneth MacKenzie hereby further agrees to and with the said Johnson Gardner to furnish and supply and equip two men to hunt and trap beaver for the fall and spring seasons next ensuing, at the entire charge and cost of the said Kenneth MacKenzie, to hunt and trap under the direction of the said

Johnson Gardner; and the said Kenneth MacKenzie further agrees to furnish a third man, and at his cost and charge to supply a moiety or one-half of the requisite, necessary and usual equipment for a beaver hunter, and the said John Gardner hereby agrees to supply the said third man with the other moiety or half part of the needful equipment usual for a beaver hunter, and it is hereby agreed by and between the said Kenneth MacKenzie and the said Johnson Gardner that an entire moiety or half part of the beaver skins and castorum killed, taken and secured by the united skill and exertions of the said Johnson Gardner and the said three men to be furnished as aforesaid shall be the just and lawful share of the said Kenneth MacKenzie, the other moiety or half part to be the just and lawful share of the said Johnson Gardner, and it is further agreed that the said moiety or half part which shall become the property of the said Johnson Gardner shall be purchased of him by the said Kenneth MacKenzie at and for the price of three dollars fifty cents per pound for beaver skins taken and secured in the fall approaching, and four dollars per pound for beaver skins taken and secured in the spring following, and three dollars per pound for castorum. Signed, sealed and delivered by the said Kenneth MacKenzie and said Johnson Gardner at Fort Union the day and year first above written.

In the presence of   KENNETH MACKENZIE,
    J. A. Hamilton.   Agt. U. M. O.
                              his
               JOHNSON X. GARDNER
                          mark

Copy of an Account Current Between Johnson Gardner and the American Fur Company

"Mr. Johnson Gardner in account with the American Fur Company, U. M. O.

	Dr.			Cr.	
1820-1833	To Sundries advanced as per account A	$4,034.70	1831 July 12.	By 53 Beaver Skins at $6.50........	$ 344.50
				" 1 Otter skin, ...	2.50
			1832, July 21.	" 206 Beaver skins —278 Lbs. at $4½, ...	1,146.75
				" 1 Otter skin, ...	2.00
				" 27¼ lbs. Beaver skin (at Fort Cass) at 3 50-100	95.37
				" Note on Smith, Sublette & Co.	1,371.48
			1833 June 30.	" 16 Beaver Traps left at Fort Pierre,.........	192.00
				" Balance carried down,.........	930.10
		$4,034.70			$4,034.70
1833, June 30.	To balance,.....	$930.10			

For Am. Fur Company,
J. Archdale Hamilton
Fort Union, Sept. 12, 1833.

Copy of receipt for note referred to in above account current: "$1371.48.

Received of Johnson Gardner a note on Messrs. Smith, Sublette, and Jackson for thirteen hundred and seventy-one dollars forty-eight cents, which he wishes me to collect for him and be placed to his credit at 5 per cent interest, which I will endeavor to do if no unavoidable accident will happen to me or the note.

(Signed)   K. Mackenzie.

The above is a true copy of the receipt:
                          Witness: S. P. Winter."

Copy of weigh-bill of beaver mentioned in above account current.

"FORT UNION, August 6, 1832.

We, Francis A. Chardon and J. Archdale Hamilton, hereby certify that we have carefully weighed two hundred and six beaver skins purchased by the American Fur Company of Johnson Gardner and declare the weight thereof to be two hundred and seventy-eight pounds, as witness our hands the day and year first above written.

(Signed)   F. A. CHARDON.

J. ARCHDALE HAMILTON."

Extract from Account "A" referred to in above account current.

"1832.

June 28	Your share of advances to Tullock & Co.		$ 12.00
	Liquor 8.00, Feast 4.00 . . . . $12.00		
29	Ditto 4.00	4.00	
30	Shirts 8.00, Pantaloons 5.90	13.00	
	Liquor 11.00, Feast 2.00	13.00	
July 1	Ditto 6.00, Suit of clothes 70.00	76.00	
	Knives 4.00, Powder .75, Shoeing horse		
	3.00	7.75	
July 2	Tobacco .75, Cow skin 1.00	1.75	
5	Liquor	3.00	
6	Ditto	12.00	
7	Ditto 10.00, Tea 2.00, Pork 2.00 . . .	14.00	
	Blanket 12.00, Vinegar 1.00, Axe 6.00 .	19.00	
	Sugar 1.00	1.00	
8	Thread 1.00, Biscuit 8.50	9.50	
	Salt 6.00, Pepper 4.00, Handkfs 4.00 . .	14.00	
	Coffee 18.00, Tea 8.00, Sugar 24.00 . .	50.00	
	File 1.50, Tin Pans 2.00, Kettle 5.00 . .	8.50	
	Tin cups 2.00, Knives 4.00, Awls 1.50 .	7.50	
	Tobacco 15.00, Sirsingles 6.00	21.00	
	Liquor 14.00	14.00	
9	Rice 4.00, Knife 2.00, Liquor and Keg 27.00	33.00	$334.00
	Total		$346.00"

This amount seems to have been spent by Gardner while at Fort Union between spring and fall hunt. It is worth note that of this amount $109, or about one-third, is for liquor and feasting.

Copy of Gardner's Shipping Bill

"Shipped in good order per bull boat *Antoine* four pactons of beaver fur marked and weighing as follows:

No. 1 56 skins weighing 73 lbs. marked J G
 "   2 50   "   "   81 "   "   "
 "   3 50   "   "   76 "   "   "
 "   4 50   "   "   74 "   "   "

Total 206   304   N. B. 1 Otter Skin.
                                     Crossings of the Yellowstone,
                                          July 18, 1832.

The above boat is bound for Fort Union."

Copy of Bill for an Equipment for Fall Hunt

"Equipment for hunt, July 9th, 1832, viz.:

16	Traps 12.00	$192.00
5	Horses 60.00	300.00
1	Horse in January, 1833	60.00
5	Saddles and apichemons	25.00
8	Trap springs 16.00, Flints 1.00	17.00
	Powder 9.00, Balls 12.00, File 1.50	22.50
	Knives 7.50, Kettle 5.00, Axe 3.00	15.50
	Wages of 3 men.	750.00 $1382.00"

Copy of a Trader's Engagement

'Before the subscribing witness personally appeared the under-signed Colin Campbell, who voluntarily binds and by these presents does engage himself to Pierre D. Papin, agent of Pratte, Chouteau & Co., for Sioux outfit on the following terms and conditions to say— The said Campbell engages himself to said Papin, agent for said Sioux outfit, for and during the term of two and half years from the first of June one thousand eight hundred and thirty-nine.

"The said Papin, agent as aforesaid, for services faithfully rendered, promises to pay the said Campbell the sum of three thousand six hundred and sixteen dollars lawful money of the United States. The said Campbell on his part binds himself to serve, obey and execute with fidelity the orders or known wishes of his employers or any other persons entrusted with their business, to keep their secrets, make them acquainted with any thing which may come to his knowledge affecting their interest, and to do all such things as are usually done or ought to be done by a good and faithful clerk and trader.

In testimony whereof we have hereunto set our hand and seals this eighth day of November one thousand eight hundred and thirty-six.

C. CAMPBELL, (Seal)"
(No Signature.) (Seal)

Witness: JACOB HALSEY.

AUTHOR'S NOTES

(1) The reader will remember that the two principal divisions of the American Fur Company's field of operations were the Northern Department, headquarters at Michilimackinac, and the Western Department, headquarters at St.Louis. What the writer here calls departments were really sub-departments of these two. Rolette belonged to the Northern Department, Farnham and Davenport to the Western Department, as of course did the Missouri traders. Whether Auguste P. Chouteau, who controlled the trade with the Osage Indians, was connected with the American Fur Company, or wholly independent of it, is not very clear from the records.

(2) It is difficult to imagine who this individual was, if not General William H. Ashley, the founder of the Rocky Mountain Fur Company.

F

LIST OF TRADING POSTS

List of trading posts in the country west of St. Louis during the period from 1807 to 1843, with a few belonging to the periods before and after, and also a few military posts—The total number of posts referred to in this list is about one hundred and forty.

MISSOURI RIVER POSTS

Fort Orleans. This was the first fort ever built on the Missouri River. In 1720 the Spanish sent an expedition of two hundred men to the Missouri to destroy the tribe of the Missouris who were friendly to the French. Their plan was to join the Pawnees, who were at war with the Missouris. They unfortunately lost their way and came first to the latter tribe. Supposing them to be Pawnees, the Spanish unfolded their scheme directly to their intended victims. The astonished Missouris did not acquaint them with their mistake, but made instant preparations, took the Spaniards by surprise, and destroyed the entire party.

As a result of this expedition the Louisiana government ordered the erection of a fort on the Missouri. The work was entrusted to M. Bourgemont, who built Fort Orleans, in 1722, on an island in the Missouri, some two hundred and fifty miles above its mouth. The actual location was about five miles below the mouth of Grand River, opposite the old village of the Missouris. The fort was the scene of considerable activity for several years, and from it M. de Bourgemont made an important expedition to the country of the Paducas in 1724. There is a tradition that when Bourgemont left the fort a year or two later to do down to New Orleans, the Indians attacked it and massacred every inmate. De Margry says that "en 1726 la Campagnie des Indes supprima cette poste" (1).

In the valley of the Osage River, and for the accommodation of the Osage Indians, there were several posts, but they are scarcely ever mentioned in the annals of the time. They played a quite insignificant part in the history of the trade. Among these may be mentioned Forts Carondelet, Marais de Cygnes, and Pomme de Terre.

Fort Osage, or Fort Clark, stood near the site of Sibley, Missouri, about forty miles below the mouth of the Kansas. General William Clark passed this point in 1808 with a troop of cavalry on his way to make a treaty with the Osages. He selected the site for a post on his return. Lewis and Clark, June 23, 1804, had noted it as a good site for a fort. The post was occupied off and on until 1827, but not continuously with a regular garrison. It was permanently abandoned on the founding of Fort Leavenworth. It was here that was located the only government trading factory west of the Mississippi. (See further, Part III, Chapter VI.)

Chouteau's Post, or the Kansas Post. This was first established by Francis G. Chouteau on an island three miles below the mouth of the Kansas River for the trade of the Kansas Indians. The great flood of 1826 washed it into the river, and

Chouteau then went about ten miles up the Kansas River, where he would be safe from a similar calamity in the future, and built a post on the right bank of the river. It was maintained for many years.

French Fort. This post is noted by Lewis and Clark in 1804, and by Doctor James in 1819 as being in ruins. It was on the Kansas shore, opposite the upper end of Kickapoo Island, back of the bluffs and in rear of an old village of the Kansas Indians. Whether built as a trading post or a military fort is unknown. Bogy in his history of Missouri says that "the French government had a regular post and officer at (near?) the mouth of the Kansas River."

Camp Martin was a name given to a winter cantonment of United States troops at Isle a la Vache during the winter of 1818-19. The troops were a part of the Yellowstone Expedition and were commanded by a Captain Martin.

Leavenworth Fort. For circumstances of early history of this post see Part II, Chapter VI.

Blacksnake Hills, a post established by Joseph Robidoux where the city of St. Joseph now stands. Audubon in 1843 uttered the following prediction concerning the situation: "I was delighted to see this truly beautiful site for a town or city, as will be, no doubt, some fifty years hence."

Nishnabotna. In 1819 Robidoux, Papin, Chouteau, and Berthold, trading with a capital of $12,000, had their principal establishment near the mouth of this stream. Name variously spelled.

Council Bluffs. This name, though not specifically applied to any post, denoted a locality where many trading posts have been built. It was one of the most important points on the whole course of the Missouri and was resorted to by traders from the very commencement of the fur trade on the upper river. The meeting of the two great valleys, the Missouri and the Platte, which was in this vicinity, had something to do with the importance of the place. The particular situation always known in those early years as Council Bluffs was twenty-five miles above the modern city of that name, and on the opposite side of the river about where the little town of Calhoun is now located. On the 3rd of August,

1804, Lewis and Clark held a council there with the Oto and Missouri Indians and gave the name from this circumstance. In the course of the next fifty years there were probably not fewer than twenty posts established between this point and the mouth of the Platte, but all are now swallowed up in the great cities that have taken their places on both sides of the river. It is impossible now to recover the names of all or the locations of some whose names are known. Even those which are best known it is difficult to locate precisely.

Crooks and McLellan's post in 1810 was on the west bank of the river a little above the mouth of Papillon Creek and therefore near the later site of Bellevue. It was broken up in the spring of 1811 when its proprietors entered the service of the Pacific Fur Company.

Bellevue. This was an important place during most of the fur-trading era and promised at one time to be the progenitor of the future city which was bound to arise in that vicinity. The early history of Bellevue is exceedingly obscure. Some authorities say that Lisa built the first post there in 1805 and gave it its present name. This is a mistake. Crooks and Mc-Lellan seem to have been the first to locate near there. The next occupant was the Missouri Fur Company under Joshua Pilcher, who must have moved down there soon after Lisa's death. Fontenelle and Drips apparently bought Pilcher's post and established it in their own name, which it retained for many years. At a date between 1830 and 1840, which is not exactly known, the American Fur Company moved to Bellevue from Cabanne's post some distance above, and established a new post there under the management of P. A. Sarpy. The Indian agency of John Dougherty was also located near there at about the same time. The agency was at Côte à Quesnelle just above the American Fur Company post.

Fort Croghan, a military post of temporary character which stood a little above the present Union Pacific bridge in Omaha. When it was established is uncertain, but it was abandoned in the fall of 1843.

Cabanne's Post was located near the old site of Rockport, nine or ten miles (by land) above the Union Pacific bridge in Omaha and six or seven miles below Fort Calhoun. It was established between 1822 and 1826 for the American Fur Company by J. P. Cabanne, who remained in charge until 1833, when he had to leave the country on account of the Leclerc affair. Pilcher succeeded him, and the post was later moved down to Bellevue. The Columbia Fur Company also had a post near here which was absorbed by Cabanne's establishment in 1827.

Fort Lisa was located about a mile above Cabanne's post and five or six miles below old Council Bluffs. It was founded by Manuel Lisa as early as 1812 and it continued to be occupied as late as 1823. During this period it was the most important post on the Missouri River. It commanded the trade of the Omahas, Pawnees, Otoes, and other tribes.

Engineer Cantonment, "about half a mile above Fort Lisa, five miles below Council Bluffs, and three miles above the mouth of Boyer River" (James), was the winter encampment of Major Long's scientific party in 1819-20.

Camp Missouri was the winter encampment of the troops attached to the Yellowstone expedition of 1819-20. It was located at the old Council Bluffs and on or near its site was built the post which for several years after was known as

Fort Atkinson. It was abandoned in the spring of 1827. The post formed a quadrangle with the usual bastions or block houses at two opposite corners.

Fort Calhoun is the name which has succeeded to that of Fort Atkinson in the history of this locality and survives in the name of a little village near by. How it came to be applied to this post is not very well understood (A).

Cruzatte's Post, an early trading establishment two miles above old Council Bluffs, built in 1802. (Lewis and Clark.)

Fort Charles was an old trading post which stood about six miles below the present Omadi, Nebraska (B). It was occupied in 1795-96 by a Mr. McKay. (Lewis and Clark.)

Pratte and Vasquez, in 1819, had a trading post at the Omaha village a considerable distance above Council Bluffs, possibly at the old village above Blackbird Hill nearly opposite the modern town of Onawa, Iowa. The exact location is nowhere stated.

Big Sioux Post, an American Fur Company post at one time maintained near the mouth of the Big Sioux River by one Laframboise.

Vermillion Post was an important trading post for the convenience of the lower Sioux tribes. It was located just below the mouth of the Vermillion River about on the present line between Clay and Union counties, South Dakota. Another Vermillion fort of earlier date and sometimes called

Dickson's Post stood on the north bank of the river about halfway between the Vermillion and the James. The Columbia Fur Company also had a post there.

Riviére à Jacques. The Columbia and American Fur Companies had establishments at this point for the trade of the Yankton band of the Sioux.

Ponca Post was established for the trade of the Indians of this name. It was just below the mouth of the Niobrara. The Columbia Fur Company also had a post here.

Fort Mitchell. This post was established in 1833 by Narcisse Le Clerc and named for D. D. Mitchell. It was abandoned four years later, and for several years furnished excellent fuel for steamboats until the old palisades were all used up.

Handy's Post was situated on the west bank of the Missouri where Fort Randall later stood. Very little is known of its history.

Trudeau's House, also called Pawnee House, was an establishment occupied by one Trudeau in the years 1796–97 (C). It was on the left bank of the river a little above and opposite the site where Fort Randall later stood.

Fort Recovery was located at the lower end of American or Cedar Island a mile below the modern city of Chamberlain, South Dakota. This post was established in 1822 by the Missouri Fur Company which then included the prominent traders, Pilcher, Charles Bent, Fontenelle, and Drips. It was also called Cedar Fort and may have been first so named. This may have been the site of the old Missouri Fur Company post which burned in 1810 and the fact of its reestablishment may have given it its name. Leavenworth in 1823 refers to it as a post "called by the Indian traders Fort Recovery and sometimes Cedar Fort."

"Fort Brasseaux" was located in this vicinity, or possibly ten or twenty miles above. The only reference to it that has fallen under the author's notice is in a letter by Gen. Ashley dated at this post July 19, 1823, written to Major O'Fallon, Indian agent, in regard to the Aricara campaign then in progress.

Fort Lookout was a post of the Columbia Fur Company and must have been built as early as 1822. Near it was

Fort Kiowa, belonging to the American Fur Company and also built as early as 1822, or immediately after the Western Department went to St. Louis. The sites were so close together that early references confused the two more or less. They were situated on the right bank of the Missouri some ten miles above where Chamberlain, South Dakota, now stands. The journal of the Yellowstone expedition of 1825 says of the American Fur Company post: "Fort Kiowa consists of a range of log buildings containing four rooms, a log house and a storehouse forming a right angle, leaving a space of some thirty feet. At the south corner of the work is erected a block-house near which stands a smith's shop. At the north corner is erected a small wooden tower. The whole work is enclosed by cottonwood pickets. The sides or curtains of the work are 140 feet each." Referring to Fort Lookout in 1833, when it was used as an Indian agency, Maximilian says that it "is a square of about sixty paces surrounded by pickets twenty or thirty feet high (!) made of square trunks of trees placed close together." The buildings consisted of three block-houses.

Sublette and Campbell had a house near here in 1834.

Fort Defiance was built by Harvey, Primeau and Company about 1845-46. They were ex-clerks of the American Fur Company, bold and energetic men, who had set up an opposition on their own account in defiance of the American Fur Company. The location is on the right bank of the Missouri about six miles above the upper end of the Great Bend, near the mouth of Medicine Creek. This was also called Fort Bouis from one of the firm (D).

Cedar Fort, or Fort aux Cèdres, is a name which was applied to at least two different posts on as many Cedar Islands in the Missouri River. Their history is confused and uncertain. We have noted one already. The oldest one was at one time known as

Loisell's Post and was probably the first trading establishment built in the Sioux country along the Missouri River. It was about thirty-five miles below Fort Pierre. Loisell was in possession in 1803-04. The post was 65 to 70 feet square, with the usual bastions. The pickets were about 14 feet high. There was a building inside 45 x 32 feet divided into four equal rooms. This was probably the real Fort aux Cèdres which is so known in the narratives of the times. Several authorities speak of it as an old Missouri Fur Company trading post, but if so it was possibly the one which burned in the spring of 1810, for no such post is mentioned by Bradbury or Brackenridge in 1811, or by Leavenworth in 1823.

Fort George, a post belonging to Fox, Livingston and Company, 21 miles below Fort Pierre, on the right bank of the Missouri. It was built by Ebbetts and Cutting, agents of the firm, in 1842. The post was probably not occupied more than three or four years, for Fox, Livingston and Company did not remain long in the country.

Teton River posts. The mouth of the Teton River (first called Little Missouri and now Bad River) was the most important locality in the Sioux country. At this point the Missouri River, after a long southerly course, turns abruptly east and continues in this direction for many miles, gradually bearing off to the southeast. This bend was nearest of any point on the river to the Black Hills and the Upper Platte country. It therefore became a natural shipping point for all the region round about. The local situation was ideal. A fine bottom about a mile wide and six miles long lay along the right bank of the Missouri River immediately above the Teton. The treeless bluffs were so far back that hostile bands of Indians could not approach the fort unobserved. The bottoms were fertile and afforded a camping ground for Indians and grazing for stock.

Who built the first post here is not known, but very likely it was the original Missouri Fur Company. It is hardly probable that they would have overlooked so important a situation. The earliest definite record is that of

Fort Tecumseh, which stood two or three miles above the mouth of the Teton. It was the principal establishment of the Columbia Fur Company upon the Missouri and was probably established in 1822. It was turned over to the American Fur Company December 5, 1827, with an inventory of property amounting to $14,453. It retained its name for five years after this event and was managed by William Laidlaw, one of the old Columbia Fur Company men. In the course of time the river began to cut into the bottom where the fort stood and necessitated the rebuilding of it in a less exposed situation. The new site was 3 miles above the mouth of the Teton and back about a quarter of a mile from the Missouri. Work was begun in 1831 and a large part of the lumber was manufactured during the following winter. The erection was so far completed in the spring of 1832 that on the 15th of April Mr. Laidlaw and Mr. Halsey, the clerk, moved into it (E). Work was continued on it during the summer and the full change was not accomplished before the end of the season. On the occasion of the visit of the steamboat *Yellowstone* between May 31 and June 5, 1832, with Mr. Pierre Chouteau on board, the new post was christened.

Fort Pierre, in honor of the distinguished visitor and representative of the house at St. Louis. The new post was 325 by 340 feet and contained about two and a half acres of ground. It was one of the finest on the river and was the most important establishment except Fort Union.

The Navy Yard or Chantier of Fort Pierre was located some distance above, probably near Chantier Creek. It was here that boats and lumber for the post were manufactured.

Teton Post is a name which may be used to designate a post belonging to the firm of P. D. Papin & Co., which Maximilian calls the French Fur Company. The members of the company were Papin, the Cerre brothers and Honore Picotte. The post was probably built about 1828 or 1829. It stood just below the mouth of the Teton. The firm sold out to the American Fur Company and entered its service October 14, 1830, and the property was at once moved up to Fort Tecumseh.

Sublette and Campbell commenced erecting an opposition post a "little below old Fort Tecumseh" October 17, 1833. The post continued to do business only a year when it was sold to the American Fur Company.

Scattered through the Sioux country on both sides of the Missouri there were many subordinate posts or houses of the American Fur Company dependent upon Fort Pierre. There were no fewer than three in the valley of James River (Rivière à Jacques). There was one at the forks of the Cheyenne, another at its mouth, one at the Aricara villages and others on Cherry, White and Niobrara Rivers, and among the Brulé, Ogallala and other bands of the Sioux. In fact wherever there was an inducement to trade these temporary houses were erected.

Old Fort George was below but near the mouth of the Cheyenne River. Nothing further is known of it.

Aricara Post. Manuel Lisa had a post in this vicinity, but its exact location or particular name is not known.

Fort Manuel was on the west bank of the river—just above latitude 46° N (F).

The Mandan Villages were another important locality and the site of several posts. The course of the river here changed from a general easterly direction to one nearly due south. It was the point nearest the Red River settlements, and was the home of the Mandan and Minnetaree Indians.

Fort Mandan, the first structure built here, was the winter quarters of Lewis and Clark in 1804-05. It stood on the left bank of the Missouri 7 or 8 miles below the mouth of Big Knife River and opposite, though a little above, the site where Fort Clark later stood.

Lisa's Fort was the next one built in this locality. It was situated on the right or south bank of the river some ten or twelve miles above the mouth of the Big Knife near where the names Emanuel Rock and Emanuel Creek now are. The post was abandoned upon the breaking out of the War of 1812, but was occupied by Pilcher in 1822 or 1823 under the name of Fort Vanderburgh.

Sublette and Campbell had a post in 1833 a little below this point.

Tilton's Fort was built by James Kipp in 1822 for the Columbia Fur Company. It was on the opposite side of the river from the Mandan Villages and a little above the site of Fort Clark. Being driven from this position in 1823 by the Aricaras he crossed and established a house in the Mandan Villages. In the winter of 1825-26 Kipp went to the mouth of White Earth River, 140 miles above, and built a post for the Assiniboine trade. This post passed into the hands of the American Fur Company in 1827 with the rest of the Columbia Fur Company posts. In 1830 McKenzie ordered the erection of a new post for the Mandan trade and Kipp was put in charge of the work. It was built in the spring of 1831 and was named

Fort Clark, for General William Clark. It was on a bluff in an angle of the river and on its right bank, 55 miles above the N. P. R. R. bridge at Bismarck, N. D. The post was 132 by 147 feet, on the typical plan, and was a substantial structure. It ranked as one of the most important posts on the river.

The Mouth of the Yellowstone was the next important point above the Mandans and several posts sprang up here during the fur trade. It does not appear that the Missouri Fur Company ever established a post here, although it is not easy to understand why they did not. The first post was built by

Ashley and Henry in 1822 on the tongue of land between the two rivers about a mile above the junction and next to the Missouri. It was abandoned in the fall of 1823. In 1825 three sides of the stockade and a part of the buildings were still standing.

No other attempts were made to establish a post in this vicinity until 1828, when Kenneth McKenzie, then the leading partner in the "U. M. O." sent a party to the mouth of the Yellowstone to build a post. They probably commenced work about October 1 of that year. This post seems to have been named

Fort Floyd, while the name

Fort Union was applied to another post two hundred miles farther up. The name Union was, however, soon transferred to the mouth of the Yellowstone, and the advanced post was abandoned. Maximilian says that Union was begun in 1829.

There is some confusion in regard to the establishment of the important post of Fort Union, and to enable the reader to draw his own conclusions the correspondence of the American Fur Company relating to the subject will be reproduced here. McKenzie wrote to Chouteau from the Vermillion River October 2, 1828, that he had just returned with Indian Agent Sanford from the Mandans; that four days before he left, the keelboat *Otter* had left for the Yellowstone to establish a post for the Assiniboine trade. And in a letter from Fort Tecumseh December 26, 1828, he said: "The *Otter* arrived at the Yellowstone in sufficient time to build a fort and have all necessary preparations made for security." This establishes the fact that a post was built at the Yellowstone in 1828 and fixes October 1st as pretty close to the actual date of commencement.

In a letter written at Fort Tecumseh March 15, 1829, McKenzie says: "Your favor of the 5th of December reached me on the 25th ult., the date of my arrival from Fort Floyd near the Yellowstone"; and again in the same letter, "Old Glass came to Fort Floyd last fall." In a letter to W. B. Astor April 19, 1830, Pierre Chouteau, Jr., says: "A mon arrivee ici (St. Louis) le 16, j'ai trouve des lettre de Mr. McKenzie du 28 December, 1829, et de 2 et 20 Janvier, 200 miles au dessus de la Roche Jaune. Les chasseurs des montagnes n'avaient pas aussi bien reussi dans la chasse d'automne qu'il esperait, mais il esperait un meilleur succes pour le printemps. Il est d'opinion qu'il fera beaucoup plus de robes cette annee que de coutume; c'est a dire dans les trois posts d'en haut, chez les Mandans, a l'embouchure de la Roche Jaune, et Fort Union 200 miles audessus, et il dit que le pays du haut est tres rich en castors et robes." Taken as they read these extracts mean that there were three posts on the upper river in 1829, the Mandan post, Fort Floyd and Fort Union 200 miles farther up.

The only clue to the origin of the name "Union" that has come to our notice is in a letter from McKenzie in which he discusses the trade situation and his desire to fix upon some point at which he can unite all the routes of trade. "Keeping in view a union at some convenient point above with the free hunters," he thought that he could control the trade both of the rivers and of the mountains.

Fort Union was the best built post on the Missouri, and with the possible exception of Bent's Fort on the Arkansas, the best in the entire West. It was 240 by 220 feet, the shorter side facing the river, and was surrounded by a palisade of square hewn pickets about a foot thick and twenty feet high. The bastions were at the southwest and northeast corners, and consisted of square houses 24 feet on a side and 30 feet high, built entirely of stone and surmounted with pyramidal roofs. There were two stories; the lower one was pierced for cannon and the upper had a balcony for better observation. The usual banquette extended around the inner wall of the fort. The entrance was large and was secured with a powerful gate which in 1837 was changed to a double gate on account of the dangerous disposition of the Indians owing to the small-pox scourge. On the opposite side of the square from the entrance was the house of the bourgeois, a well-built, commodious two-story structure, with glass windows, fire-place and other "modern conveniences." Around the square were the barracks for the employes, the store houses, work shops, stables, a cut stone powder magazine capable of holding 50,000 pounds, and a reception room for the Indians. In the center of the court was a tall flag staff around which were the leathern tents of half-breeds in the service of the company. Near the flag staff stood one or two cannon trained upon the entrance to the fort. Somewhere in the enclosure was the famous distillery of 1833-34. All of the buildings were of cottonwood lumber and everything was of an unusually elaborate character. Nathaniel J. Wyeth, when he visited Union in 1833, declared that he had seen no British post that could compare with it.

Fort Union always had a large complement of clerks, artisans, and engagés about and was the most extensively equipped of any of the posts.

It has the honor of entertaining numerous distinguished visitors, among whom were Catlin in 1832, Maximilian in 1833, and Audubon in 1843. (For a very elaborate and detailed description of the fort see Audubon and His Journals, vol. II., pp. 180.)

Fort William was a fort belonging to Sublette and Campbell and was named for the former. It was located on the left bank of the Missouri opposite the mouth of the Yellowstone and on the site where Fort Buford was afterwards built. It was commenced August 29, 1833, and was abandoned when Sublette sold out to the American Fur Company a year afterward.

Fort Mortimer was Fort William resurrected under a new firm, Fox, Livingston & Co., of New York. This event took place in 1842 and the post succumbed to the American Fur Company three years later.

Fort Assiniboine was a temporary post at a point some distance above Union where the steamer *Assiniboine* was caught by low water in the summer of 1834 and compelled to spend the winter. The intention probably was to make it an outpost of Union. It was 100 feet square and the buildings ranged round the interior were in all 134 feet long and 18 feet deep. The post was abandoned April 2, 1835, and Lamont, who was in charge, brought the property back to Union. It is not known how far above Union this post was located, but wherever it was it marks the first advance of steamboats beyond the mouth of the Yellowstone.

Fort Jackson was built by C. A. Chardon (G) in December, 1833, at the mouth of Poplar River (Rivière aux Trembles). Chardon had a force of twenty men with a strong equipment and built a post fifty feet square. The name was probably given for Andrew Jackson, for in a letter from this point Chardon says, "We are all Jackson men." McKenzie thus states the purpose of the establishment: "I consider it desirable to establish a wintering post west of this, partly for the convenience of the Indians who frequent that section, but principally with a view of compelling our opponents (Sublette and Campbell) to divide their forces, for the principle of divide and conquer has often been verified."

The next important point above the mouth of the Yellowstone was the Blackfoot country near the mouth of the Marias. Prior to 1831 no post had been successfully established in the country of these Indians. About October 1st of that year

James Kipp commenced one on the left bank of the Missouri just above the Marias and called it

Fort Piegan in honor of the Piegan band of Blackfeet. The post was occupied only during the winter, when it was abandoned by Kipp, who went down the river with the returns. It was then burned by the Indians. In the spring of 1832 D. D. Mitchell went up the river and built a new post about six miles above the mouth of the Marias on the left bank of the river and called it

Fort McKenzie. It stood 120 yards back from the river. It was 140 feet square and was built on the regular plan, but with an exceptionally strong gate provided with double doors.

In 1833 Alexander Culbertson selected a new site for a post on the right bank of the Missouri at the mouth of the Shonkin, but it does not appear that a post was actually built here.

Fort McKenzie was occupied as late as 1843, for there is extant a letter from William Laidlaw written at Fort Union December 5, 1843, in which the writer says that he has "lately heard from Mr. Chardon, who is in charge of Fort McKenzie at the Blackfeet;" and he adds that "the Blackfeet are getting more and more troublesome in consequence of certain retrenchments of liquor heretofore given them in their ceremonies, the discontinuation of which had become absolutely necessary for the better regulation of that post. They, however, are so much dissatisfied that Mr. Chardon says that he can not get out at the gate more than once a week." Tradition says that the hostile feeling of the Blackfeet was due to the wanton massacre of some of their number by Chardon and Harvey the winter before. In any event Chardon was compelled to move down stream into a different neighborhood and build a new fort. After he left, the Indians burned Fort McKenzie and the post was often referred to afterwards as Fort Brulé. The site is known to this day as Brulé Bottom. (For a more complete description of this post see Audubon and His Journals, vol. II., p. 188; also the works of Maximilian, Prince of Wied.)

Fort Chardon was the name of the new post at the mouth of the Judith. It was probably built in the fall of 1843—not before that. It was occupied only for a short time when Alexander Culbertson moved the establishment to a point on the right bank of the Missouri opposite Pablois Island, about 18 miles above where the Fort Benton bridge now crosses the river. This event probably took place in 1845, and the new post was called

Fort Lewis, in honor of the explorer, Captain Meriwether Lewis. The situation proving unfavorable to the trade, the post was torn down in 1846 and rebuilt in a more favorable location farther down stream and on the left bank. The name Lewis was retained for several years. In 1850 the post was rebuilt of adobe and was dedicated amid grand festivities on Christmas day of that year. At the same time it was rechristened by Mr. Culbertson

Fort Benton, in honor of Thomas H. Benton, who had so often rescued the company from disaster. This noted post, situated at the head of navigation on the Missouri River, belongs to a later period than that covered by this work.

The Three Forks of the Missouri. The Missouri Fur Company built a large post here early in the year 1810. According to Lieutenant James H. Bradley, who visited the site of the post in 1870, and could still make out enough from the ruins to trace the general outline, "it was a double stockade of logs set three deep, enclosing an area of about three hundred feet square, situated upon the tongue of land (at that point only half a mile wide) between the Jefferson and Madison rivers, about two miles from their confluence, upon the south bank of the channel of the former stream called Jefferson Slough." (Transactions of the Montana Historical Society, vol. II.) The site was at that time mostly washed away by the river and is believed to be now entirely gone (H). The post was abandoned in the fall of 1810 owing to the persistent attacks of the Blackfeet. An anvil was left behind and remained on the site for upwards of forty years afterward and may now be in the bed of the river. With the lapse of years and the partial oblivion which overtook those early events, tradition linked this post with the expedition of Lewis and Clark, and it was the popular belief that these explorers passed a winter there. The post came to be known locally as "Lewis and Clark's

Fort." The only relic of this post still in existence is a letter written on the spot in the spring of 1810. It is reproduced elsewhere in this work. (Appendix A.)

This completes the list of posts on the Missouri proper, but there were several important ones on the Yellowstone which were directly dependent uoon Fort Union.

Braseau's Houses were on the left Bank of the Yellowstone about 50 miles above the mouth. They were built by a well-known trader who flourished upon the upper river in the early years of the trade.

The Crow country was favored with numerous trading posts, the principal situation being at the mouth of the Big-horn River. The first post built here, and the first known to have been built above old Fort aux Cèdres on the Missouri was

Fort Manuel, Manuel's Fort, or Fort Lisa, built by Manuel Lisa in 1807. It was situated on the right bank of both rivers. In 1809 it passed into the hands of the Missouri Fur Company and was probably abandoned in the summer of 1811 when Henry came down the river after the abandonment of his post on the Snake.

Fort Benton was the second post built here, but whether upon the same site as Fort Manuel is uncertain. It was built by the Missouri Fur Company under Joshua Pilcher in 1822 and was abandoned in the following year.

Ashley and Henry built a post in this locality in the fall of 1823. It was abandoned probably in 1824.

Fort Cass. This was the first American Fur Company post in the Crow country. Its establishment is duly referred to in the American Fur Company correspondence. The following extracts from Wyeth's Journal of August 17 and 18, 1833, give the essential facts relating to it: "About 3 miles below the mouth of the Bighorn we found Fort Cass"; it "is situated on the east (right) bank of the Yellowstone River, is about 130 feet square, made of sapling cottonwood pickets with two bastions at the extreme corners, and was erected in the fall of 1832." It was built by Samuel Tulloch and was often known as Tulloch's Fort. It was abandoned in 1835.

Fort Van Buren was the second American Fur Company post on the Yellowstone. It was built in the fall of 1835 and named for the Vice President of the United States and was abandoned in 1843. It was on the right bank of the Yellowstone near the mouth of Tongue River.

Fort Alexander, the third Crow post of the American Fur Company, was built as early as 1839. Larpenteur says that it was built by himself in 1842, but it is mentioned in the company's license for 1839. The post was on the left bank of the Yellowstone opposite the mouth of the Rosebud. It was abandoned in 1850.

Fort Sarpy was the last of the Crow posts of the American Fur Company and was not built until after 1843. Its date was 1850; its name was for John B. Sarpy: it stood on the right bank of the Yellowstone about twenty-five miles below the mouth of the Bighorn, and it was abandoned between September, 1859, and September, 1860. The post was 100 feet square, with pickets 15 feet high, but no flanking arrangements.

Fox, Livingston & Company built a post, probably in 1843, on the Bighorn River at the mouth of the Little Bighorn. It was soon abandoned.

There were many posts in the Missouri Valley whose location is not known. Forts Volcano, Lucien and Madison are of the number, the last being in the vicinity of the Mandans.

In the letter books of the American Fur Company may still be seen applications for licenses to trade on the upper river, and from these we may form some idea of the development and gradual decline of its trade.

The posts received from the Columbia Fur Company in 1827 were Council Bluffs, Vermillion, Rivière à Jacques, Ponca, Tecumseh, and the Mandans.

In 1831 the "U. M. O." licenses were for Vermillion, Rivière à Jacques, Ponca, Lookout, Forks White River, Tecumseh, Hollowood on Teton, Mouth Cheyenne, Little Cheyenne, Aricara Village, Heart River, Mandans, Mouth Yellowstone, Mouth Marias. It will be noted that Union, Clark and Piegan are not yet mentioned by name. Fort Cass was first mentioned in 1833.

In 1839 the list included Vermillion, Sioux, Lucien, Pierre, John, Clark, Union, Alexander, Van Buren and McKenzie. The name Lucien has not elsewhere come to our notice. It was doubtless given in honor of Lucien Fontenelle to some post ordinarily mentioned by locality only. Fort John was the post on the Laramie to be described farther on.

In 1851 the company maintained Vermillion, John, Pierre, Clark, Berthold, Union, Alexander, and Benton.

In 1859 there were Pierre, Clark, Berthold, Union, Sarpy, and Benton.

Cis-Montane Posts

Under this heading will be considered those posts along the eastern base of the Rocky Mountains which were not immediately dependent upon the Missouri River at their line of communication with St. Louis.

The Portuguese Houses stood very near the junction of the North and South Forks of Powder River, near where the military post of Fort Reno later stood. All we know of them is from the following extract from the report of Captain W. F. Raynolds, who explored the country around the sources of the Yellowstone in 1859 and 1860, and visited the site of these houses on the 26th of September, 1859. "After a ride of about 15 miles we came to the ruins of some old trading posts, known as the 'Portuguese Houses,' from the fact that many years ago they were erected by a Portuguese trader named Antonio Mateo. They are now badly dilapidated, and only one side of the pickets remains standing. These, however, are of hewn logs, and from their character it is evident that the structures were originally very strongly built. Bridger recounted a tradition that at one time this post was besieged by the Sioux for forty days, resisting successfully to the last alike the strength and the ingenuity of their assaults, and the appearance of the ruins renders the story not only credible but probable" (I).

Fort William, named for William L. Sublette, was the first trading establishment ever built at what later became an important situation—the confluence of the North Platte and Laramie rivers. The work was begun with thirteen men about June 1, 1834. (Wyeth.) "William L. Sublette has built such a fort as Fort Clark (Mandans) on Laramie Fork of the River Platte and can make it a central place for the Sioux and Cheyenne trade." (Fontenelle, Sept. 17, 1834.) "Fort Laramie was

built in 1835 (1834) by Robert Campbell and was called Fort
William." (Wislizenus, 1839.) The post was located on the left
bank of the Laramie about a mile above its mouth. Sublette
sold it to Fitzpatrick, Sublette and Bridger in 1835, and these
gentlemen entered into relations with Fontenelle the same
year, thus virtually turning the post over to the American
Fur Company. The post was then, or soon after, rechristened

Fort John, for Mr. John B. Sarpy. Its early history is exceedingly obscure. In 1839 it was noted by Wislizenus as being
rectangular in shape, 80 by 100 feet, surrounded by a palisade
of cottonwood pickets 15 feet high, with flanking towers on
three sides and a very strong gate. At this time the name
Laramie was coming into popular use and gradually replaced
"Fort John" in common usage, but the latter name alone was
used in the business transactions of the American Fur Company.

Before 1846 another post was built about a mile farther
up stream and to this the name

Fort Laramie was given. Fort John is said to have been
demolished soon after. About 1849 the American Fur Company
sold out to the government and moved some distance down
the river. The famous military post of Fort Laramie then
began its career and was for many years a principal base of
operations against the hostile Indians.

Fort Platte was situated on the right bank of the Platte
in the tongue of land between the Platte and the Laramie and
about three-fourths of a mile above the junction. It was built
about 1840, for it receives no notice from Wislizenus in 1839,
but was visited by Sage in 1841. Fremont in 1842 noted it as
belonging to Sybille Adams & Company, but in 1843 it belonged to Pratte, Cabanne & Company. It probably lasted
only a few years.

La Bonte was a temporary trading house on the Platte at
the mouth of La Bonte Creek. It was in operation in 1841.

In the valley of the South Platte, some thirty or forty
miles below where Denver now stands, were several trading
establishments whose history it is impossible to make
out satisfactorily.

Fort Lupton stood on the right bank of the river about

ten miles above the mouth of the St. Vrain. It was an adobe structure, the ruins of which are still visible.

Fort Lancaster was noted by Fremont in 1843 as being "the trading establishment of Mr. Lupton" and was apparently identical with Fort Lupton.

Fort St. Vrain was also on the right bank of the river and about opposite the mouth of the St. Vrain. It belonged to Bent and St. Vrain. This post was also known as

Fort George, and was in charge of Marcellus St. Vrain in 1841.

Between Lupton and St. Vrain there were two other posts at some indefinite time before 1842. Sage noted them in that year and Fremont two years later, and both speak of one of them as having been abandoned for a long time and the other as only recently abandoned. It appears that the lower of these two posts, which was about six miles above Fort St. Vrain, belonged to two traders by the names of

Locke and Randolph. They failed in their enterprise and abandoned their post in May, 1842.

The other post belonged to

Vasquez and Sublette. It was occupied in 1839 when Wislizenus passed it.

The valley of the Arkansas below the mountains was always an important one in the fur trade, and there were many posts or houses, mostly of a temporary character, located here. The first habitation ever built here, so far as we have any knowledge, dates from some time prior to 1763, when a trader visited the Arkansas and built a temporary fort on its upper course near the foot of the mountains. The fact is recorded by Amos Stoddard in his Sketches of Louisiana.

In 1806 Lieutenant Pike built a small temporary redoubt on the south bank of the Arkansas, a little above the mouth of Fountain Creek.

In all probability Chouteau and De Munn had a temporary house in this locality during their three years' stay there in 1815–17, but there is no record of it.

In the winter of 1821–22 Jacob Fowler built a log house on the modern site of Pueblo, Colorado, and occupied it for upwards of a month.

Gant and Blackwell built a post on the Upper Arkansas, about six miles above Fountain Creek, in 1832. Captain Gant is said to have been the first hunter to form friendly relations with the Arapahoes.

In 1842 a trading post was built at the mouth of Fountain Creek. James P. Beckwourth claims that it was built under his direction in October of that year. Sage confirms the date of 1842, but simply says that it was built by "independent traders." He adds that it was called the "Pueblo." Other authorities mention George Simpson and his associates as builders of the post. By whomever built, the date seems clearly to have been 1842.

Wislizenus in 1839 found a small post called Fort Pueblo four miles above Bent's Fort, "inhabited principally by Mexicans and Frenchmen." Farnham mentions the same post and calls it El Pueblo. He locates it five miles above Bent's Fort on the north bank of the river.

There were in 1843 two posts in this locality, one on American soil and one on Mexican, from which smuggling operations, particularly in liquor, were carried on extensively from Santa Fe to the trading posts farther north.

From these obscure and unsatisfactory references it is clear that there were, all through the period of the fur trade, small and transient trading houses in the valley of the Arkansas from Bent's Fort to the mountains. None of them amounted to anything of note. The one post of importance in this entire section was the celebrated

Bent's Fort, or Fort William, which stood on the left bank of the river about half way between the present towns of La Junta and Las Animas, Colorado. The Bent brothers first built a stockade near the mouth of Fountain Creek, but afterward moved down stream where they would be more in line with the trade between the United States and Taos on the mountain branch of the Santa Fe Trail. The fort was thus in touch with the trade of Santa Fe and that of the mountains. It was founded in 1829 and became a very important post. It was 150 by 100 feet in size, the longer sides extending north and south. The walls were adobe, about six feet thick at the base and 17 feet high. The entrance was through a large gate on the east side. At the northwest and southwest corners were cylindrical bastions or towers ten feet inside diameter and 30 feet high, loopholed for musketry and cannon. The interior was divided into two parts, one of which was devoted to the buildings and the other to corrals, wagon sheds and material and stock generally. The buildings had clay floors and gravel roofs. In 1839 the fort had in its employ from 80 to 100 men. It was in full operation in 1843. In 1852 it was destroyed by Colonel William Bent, for whom it had received its name, Fort William.

Glenn's Post was a temporary trading house in the Osage country on the Verdigris River about a mile above its mouth. It was built by Hugh Glenn and was apparently abandoned in 1821, when Glenn joined Jacob Fowler in an expedition to Santa Fe.

Tra-Montane Posts

On the western side of the Continental Divide there were few American posts, and fewer still of any permanence or importance.

Robidoux's Post on the Gunnison stood on the left bank of that stream a short distance below the mouth of the Uncompahgre River.

Fort Uintah, built by the same Robidoux who built the post on the Gunnison, stood on the banks of the Uintah River some distance above the mouth of the Du Chesne and in the foot hills of the Uintah Mountains. These were early posts although the dates of their establishment are not known. Robidoux was in the country as early as 1825. Fremont, who passed Fort Uintah in June, 1844, records that the fort was attacked shortly afterward by the Utah Indians and all its garrison massacred except Robidoux, who happened to be absent. If this is a correct report, it is the only instance of a successful attack by the Indians upon a trading post of the West.

Fraeb's Post, built by Henry Fraeb and James Bridger, stood on St. Vrain's Fork of Elkhead River, itself a branch of Yampah River, Colorado. Fraeb was killed in the latter part of August, 1841, in a battle between his own party of sixty men and a war party of Sioux. The whites lost five men and the Indians ten. The post was probably abandoned soon after.

Fort Davy Crockett was an inferior trading post located in the beautiful valley of Brown's Hole on Green River and stood upon the left bank of the stream. Very little is known of it. As seen by Wislizenus in 1839 it was a low one-story building with three wings and was built of lumber and adobe. It was not surrounded with pickets. According to Farnham, who also saw it in 1839, it was a "hollow square of one story log cabins with roofs and floors of mud, constructed in the same manner as those of Fort William," on the Arkansas. It belonged at this time to three Americans by the names of Thompson, Craig and St. Clair. In the closing years of the fur trade, just before the founding of Fort Bridger, it was a favorite rendezvous and wintering ground for the free trappers. The situation, however, despite the sublime natural environment, was wretched in the extreme, and the post was familiarly known among the trappers as "Fort de Misère."

Fort Bridger, which stood in the beautiful valley of Black's Fork of Green River, was one of the famous posts of the West. Its history, however, belongs to the emigration period and it was founded in the very year which has been designated as the dividing line between this period and that of the fur trade. It has the further distinction of being founded by one of the most noted characters which either period produced. Fortunately we have the founder's own account of the establishment of the post (Letter from James Bridger to Pierre Chouteau, Jr., Dec. 10, 1843). It is as follows: "I have established a small fort with a blacksmith shop and a supply of iron in the road of the emigrants on Black's Fork of Green River which promises fairly. They, in coming out, are generally well supplied with money, but by the time they get there are in want of all kinds of supplies. Horses, provisions, smith work, etc., bring ready cash from them, and should I receive the goods hereby ordered will do a considerable business in that way with them. The same establishment trades with the Indians in the neighborhood, who have mostly a good number of beaver among them."

There is no more important landmark in the history of the West than the event thus described.

Fort Bonneville or Bonneville's Fort are names applied to a rude stockade which Captain Bonneville built on the right bank of Green River, five miles above the mouth of Horse Creek, early in August, 1832. Though apparently commenced with a view of making it a trading post it was abandoned as soon as built and was never of any consequence whatever in the trade. The trappers called it "Fort Nonsense," or "Bonneville's Folly."

We are fortunate in having a detailed description of this establishment from the pen of one who saw it during construction and the year following. It is from *Life in the Rocky Mountains*, by W. A. Ferris: "This establishment was doubtless intended for a permanent trading post by its projector, who has, however, since changed his mind and quite abandoned it. From the circumstances of a great deal of labor having been expended in its construction, and the works shortly after their completion deserted, it is frequently called 'Fort Nonsense.' It is situated in a fine open plain, on a rising spot of ground, about three hundred yards from Green River on the west side, commanding a view of the plains for several miles up and down that stream. On the opposite side of the fort, about two miles distant, there is a fine willowed creek, called Horse Creek, flowing parallel with Green River, and emptying into it about five miles below the fortification. The view from the fort in one direction is terminated by a bold hill rising to a height of several hundred feet on the opposite side of the creek, and extending in a line parallel with it. Again on the east side of the river, an abrupt bank appears rising from the water's edge, and extends several miles above and below, till the hills, jutting in on the opposite side of the river, finally conceal it from sight. The fort presents a square enclosure, surrounded by posts or pickets of a foot or more in diameter firmly set in the ground close to each other and about fifteen feet in length. At two of the corners diagonally opposite to each other block houses of unhewn logs are so constructed and situated as to defend the square outside of the pickets and hinder the approach of an enemy from any quarter.

The prairie in the vicinity of the fort is covered with fine grass, and the whole together seems well calculated for the security both of men and horses."

Ashley's Fort was a temporary trading house, said to have been built in 1825, on the west shore of Utah Lake near where Provo, Utah, now stands. It was to this point that Ashley is supposed to have hauled his wheeled cannon in 1826.

Fort Hall was built by Nathaniel J. Wyeth in the year 1834 on the left bank of the Snake River, a little above the mouth of the Portneuf. The circumstances of its founding have been fully outlined in the chapters on Wyeth's enterprise in Part II of this work. Its history as a trading post is almost entirely associated with the Hudson Bay Company, to whom Wyeth sold it in 1836. It was an exceedingly important point during the emigration period, and later became a military post of considerable note.

Fort Henry was built by Andrew Henry in the fall of 1810 on Henry Fork of Snake River, near the mouth of the Teton, and probably near where the village of Egin, Idaho, now stands. It was abandoned by Henry in the spring of 1811, and was occupied for ten days by Hunt and the overland Astorians in October of that year. Nothing is known of it after this time. It consisted only of two or three log houses.

Camp Defiance "on the supposed waters of the Bonaventura" is the description of a trading locality mentioned by William L. Sublette in his application for a trading license for the year 1832.

Astoria was the Pacific Fur Company post on the Columbia River. For its history see the chapters on Astoria, Part II.

Fort William was a post established by Nathaniel J. Wyeth on the upper end of Wappatoo Island, at the mouth of the Willamette River, in the winter of 1834-35. It was occupied only for a short time. See chapter on Wyeth's enterprise, Part II.

This list will not describe the Hudson Bay Company posts which were located within what is now United States territory, for the reason that their history, except as related to the Astorian enterprise, is not a part of this work. There were nine of these posts besides Fort Hall— Vancouver,

Nisqually, Simcoe, Walla Walla, Okanagan, Spokane, Flathead, Owen, Boisé, and possibly one or two others. Of these Okanagan, Spokane, and the Flathead post were founded by the Astorians.

AUTHOR'S NOTE

(1) "There was a French post for some time on an island a few leagues in length over against the Missouris. The French settled in this fort at the east point (of the island) and called it Fort Orleans." —Du Pratz.

EDITOR'S NOTES

(A) Since Calhoun was a former Secretary of State, the post was probably named for him.

This note and others relating to the list of posts, except where otherwise noted, were furnished to the editor by Lawrence K. Fox.

(B) At the time Chittenden wrote, there was not and had not been for many years any such place as Omadi. This had long since been washed away by the river.

(C) This date should be 1794-1795.

(D) Bouis was an American Fur Company post.

(E) This is an error for April 5 is shown by the entry for that date in Appendix G.

(F) Fort Manuel is now believed to have been just below the 46th degree. See Luttig, Journal of a Trapper, page 68.

(G) It should be F. A. Chardon, not C. A. Chardon.

(H) Edward Burnett of Buffalo, Wyoming, writes the editor that traces of the old stockade were found by him on a visit in 1933, and that he has arranged for the Montana Historical Society to put a marker on the site.

(I) Mr. Burnett has himself placed a handsome marker on the site of Mateo's Fort.

G

THE FORT TECUMSEH AND PIERRE JOURNAL

Below are some extracts from the daily journal kept at Fort Tecumseh and its successor, Fort Pierre, which give as clear a picture as can now be had of the kind of life led at a fur trading post of the better class. The year is 1832.

"Saturday, (March) 3rd. Fair, Pleasant weather. Mr. Laidlaw and the Indians went out to surround (hunt buffalo). They returned at 1 p.m., having killed meat enough to load their horses.

"Sunday, 4th. Moderate and cloudy with rain at intervals. Gabriel V. Fipe and five Indians arrived from White River post with seven horses and mules and two hundred buffalo tongues.

Wednesday, 7th. Weather continues the same as yesterday. Several Indians of Gens de Poches band arrived on a begging visit. The Blackfeet Indians (Sioux band) who arrived yesterday left us today. One of them stole a kettle; we fortunately missed it before the fellow had proceeded far. Mr. Laidlaw and some Indians went out after them and succeeded in recovering the kettle. The Gens de Poches, who arrived today, say that Baptiste Dorion has been lately killed by a Sawon Indian; but we have reason to suppose the story to be fictitious. . . .

"Friday, 9th. A continuation of fair, pleasant weather. Five more lodges Yanctons arrived and camped. There is now about three feet of water on top of the Missouri ice. Two men arrived from Cedar Island. They were obliged to leave their plank (for new fort) and trains on the way—the ice being so bad that they could not travel on it. . . .

"Tuesday, 13th. Still continue strong gales from the north and colder, but the weather is now clear and the Indians are crossing on the ice in great numbers with robes to trade (Gens de Poches). . . .

"Friday, 16th. Strong north winds, cold and cloudy, with snow at intervals. Baptiste Defond arrived last evening from the Sawon post with horses and mules. . . .

"Sunday, 18th. Moderate and clear. Two Indians arrived from White River post with a letter from Mr. Papin, the commandant.

"Monday, 19th. Mild and clear throughout the day. Nothing new. Finished duplicate ledger.

"Tuesday, 20th. Still mild and pleasant weather. Employes making packs and pressing them. . . .

"Friday, 23rd. Still continues fine weather. Most of the lodges left us today. They have gone up the Little Missouri (Teton). The Missouri ice broke up at this place today. . . .

"Wednesday, 28th. Same weather as yesterday. Ice still drifting a little. Missouri four feet above low water mark. Mr. Picotte and a voyageur arrived from the Navy Yard in a canoe. . . .

"Friday, 30th. Fine weather. Ice commenced drifting at 9 p.m., and the water rose about four feet from sunrise to sunset. In the morning Baptiste Defond departed down stream to meet the steamboat *Yellowstone*. . . .

"Tuesday (April), 3rd. Moderate and pleasant. Missouri still rising. It is now eight and one-half feet above low water mark. Last evening J. Jewett arrived here from the Ogallala post with horses and mules, in all sixteen.

"Wednesday, 4th. A continuation of fine, pleasant weather.

"Thursday, 5th. Same weather as yesterday. Messrs. Laidlaw and Halsey moved up with their baggage to the new fort (Pierre).

"Friday, 6th. Still fine and pleasant. Hands employed variously. Two men arrived from the Yankton post with three horses. They report the arrival of Mr. P. D. Papin at the mouth of the White River with two skin canoes laden with buffalo robes.

"Saturday, 7th. Mr. William Dickson arrived from Rivière à Jacques with twelve packs furs.

"Sunday, 8th. Two men arrived from the Navy Yard with the news that the Indians had stolen all the company's horses at that place.

"Monday, 9th. Clear and moderate with north wind. Missouri falling fast. On the 6th inst. the water was so high that the old fort was nearly surrounded with water. Employed variously hauling property from the old fort, etc., etc. At 11 a.m. five skin canoes loaded with buffalo robes under charge of Colin Campbell arrived from the Ogallala post on Cheyenne River. They bring news of the murder of Francois Querrel (A) by Frederick Laboue, the company's trader at Cherry River. Laboue arrived in the canoes. . . .

"Wednesday, 11th. Moderate north winds and pleasant.

Several Sawons arrived last evening. The Missouri rising. . . .

"Friday, 13th. Strong northerly winds and pleasant. Mr. Dickson left for Rivière à Jacques. . . .

"Friday, 20th. We had a shower of rain in the morning. At 10 a.m. it cleared off. Hands employed variously. At 3 p.m. four men arrived from the Navy Yard. Buffalo in sight from the houses. Mr. Laidlaw and some Indians went out and they returned at 4 p.m., having killed four cows.

"Saturday, 21st. Calm and cloudy. Sent off Campbell and twenty-two men to Cherry River to bring down the peltries at that place.

"Sunday, 22nd. Clear and moderate winds from the northwest.

"Monday, 23rd. Fair, pleasant weather.

"Tuesday, 24th. Same weather as yesterday.

"Wednesday, 25th. A continuation of fine, pleasant weather. Nothing new.

"Thursday, 26th. Still fine, pleasant weather.

"Friday, 27th. Weather same as yesterday. At five o'clock p.m. Messrs. McKenzie, Kipp, and Bird with nine Blackfeet (Sihasapa) Indians arrived in a bateau from Fort Union. McKenzie brought down one hundred and eleven packs of beaver skins. . . .

"Wednesday, (May) 2nd. Cloudy with rain at intervals. Mr. Cerre arrived yesterday from the Yanctonnais with ninety odd packs of robes. Hands employed marking and pressing them.

"Thursday, 3rd. Clear and pleasant. Nothing new. Hands employed pressing packs, etc., etc. The Indians are now coming in every day to trade.

"Friday, 4th. Moderate and clear. Mr. Bird and the Indians returned from the Sawon camp. . . .

"Monday, 7th. Moderate winds and disagreeable rainy weather. Colin Campbell, with eleven skin canoes laden with buffalo robes, arrived from Cherry River. Mr. Campbell, while at Cherry River, disinterred the body of the deceased F. Querrel; and, as seven wounds were found in the body, Frederick Laboue was put in irons immediately on the arrival of the canoes. . . .

"Friday, 11th. Fair, pleasant weather. Sent off two men

to the Rees with goods for the trade of those Indians. Pierre Ortubize and two men left in a skiff in search of the steamboat. Hands employed in making and pressing packs. . . .

"Monday, 14th. Clear and pleasant. Crossed sixty-four horses to the other side of the Missouri. At 4 p.m. had a thunder shower. Indians coming in from every quarter to trade. . . .

"Thursday, 17th. Clear and fine. Employed crossing horses for Fort Union, etc., etc. . . .

"Saturday, 19th. Still continues clear and pleasant weather. But no news of consequence. At 4 p.m. two men arrived. Halsey's child was born. . . .

"Monday, 21st. Clear and pleasant. Sent off twenty men to the Navy Yard to cut timber and bring it down on rafts.

"Tuesday, 22nd. Fine, pleasant weather. Mr. Fontenelle, with twenty men and a number of horses, arrived here from St. Louis. They bring news of the steamboat *Yellowstone*. She is now between this place and the Poncas.

"Wednesday, 23rd. Cloudy with rain at intervals. Eighteen men arrived from steamboat *Yellowstone*. She is stopped for want of water about sixty miles below White River. William Dickson and family arrived from Rivière à Jacques.

"Friday, 25th. Clear and Fine. Baptiste Defond arrived from the steamboat at the Big Bend. Messrs. McKenzie, Fontenelle, and others left here in a keelboat to meet her. . . .

"Thursday, 31st. Same weather as yesterday. Missouri still rising. Four men arrived from White River post with horses, robes, etc. Steamboat *Yellowstone* arrived at 5 p.m. . . .

"Tuesday, (June) 5th. Fine and pleasant weather. Steamboat *Yellowstone* left here for Ft. Union. Water falling.

"Wednesday, 6th. Fine and pleasant weather. Mr. Fontenelle left here with forty odd men for Ft. Union and one hundred and ten or fifteen horses. Water rising. . . .

"Monday, 11th. Fine weather with south winds. Keelboat *Flora* left here for Fort Union with a cargo of merchandise, etc. Keelboat *Male Twin* left here for the Navy Yard to bring down timber.

"Friday, 15th. Hot and sultry the first part of the day. Keelboat *Male Twin* arrived from the Navy Yard. Latter part of the day we had a fine, refreshing shower. I forgot to say that four bateaux also arrived from the Navy Yard today. They, as well as the *Male Twin*, were loaded with pickets for the fort. . . .

"Sunday, 17th. Keelboat *Male Twin* and four bateaux conducted by Mr. Honore Picotte left here for St. Louis loaded with 1,410 packs buffalo robes.

"Wednesday, 20th. Fine, pleasant weather with moderate southerly winds. The Missouri still rising. It is now nearly over the bank. Joseph Jewett, who left here on the 10th, arrived today from the Ogallalas with dry meat, lodges, etc. 480 lbs. dry meat was left here in the spring, but the wolves broke into the house and ate it all except about 20 pieces. . . .

"Sunday, 24th. Steamboat *Yellowstone* arrived from Ft. Union. Sent down 600 packs robes on board of her.

"Monday, 25th. Steamboat *Yellowstone* left us for St. Louis with a cargo of 1,300 packs robes and beaver. Mr. Laidlaw went on board. He is to go down as far as Sioux agency and return by land. Ortubize has got a keg of whiskey and is continually drunk himself and he tries to make as many of the men drunk as will drink with him. . . .

"Sunday, (July) 1st. Messrs. Laidlaw and Dickson left us for Lac Traverse in quest of some Canadian Pork Eaters expected here this summer. Castorigi sick and off duty. . . .

"Sunday, 8th. Same weather as yesterday, with the exception of a light shower in the morning. At 2 p.m. Messrs. Brown, Durand, and two Americans (all beaver trappers) arrived with about a pack of beaver.

"Monday, 9th. Fine weather; at 6 a.m. Henry Hart arrived from Ft. Union with three bateaux loaded with robes, etc. Loaded one boat with 120 packs beaver and other skins and put on board of another 30 packs of robes. She is to take on 120 or 130 packs at Yancton post.

"Tuesday, 10th. Strong gales from the north. Four bateaux ready to start for St. Louis, but they were detained here all day by the wind.

"Wednesday, 11th. Four bateaux laden with 355 packs buffalo robes and 10,230 lbs. beaver skins left here for St. Louis. They will take in 120 or 130 packs robes at Yancton post. Water rising fast. It is now five feet above low water mark. . . .

"Thursday, 19th. Jewett and Ortubize returned from hunting, having killed two bulls. On their arrival on this side of the river, we discovered two more bulls on the opposite side, when we immediately recrossed them. At night they returned, having killed one more bull.

"Friday, 20th. Cloudy, and hot, sultry weather. Vasseau and two men belonging to Le Clerc Company arrived at the mouth of Teton River for the purpose of building and establishing a trdaing house there. Leclaire and a few men arrived here from Fort Lookout. . . .

"Sunday, 29th. Pleasant weather and light northerly winds. At 10 a.m., Mr. Laidlaw arrived on the other side from the east with 36 Pork Eaters. He lost two on the road. Employed the greatest part of the day crossing the men and their baggage. At 12 m. Cardinal Grant arrived from the Yancton post. . . .

"Thursday, August 2nd. Calm and pleasant. Plenty of buffalo. Mr. Laidlaw went out to hunt them and killed three. . . .

"Saturday, 4th. Four Brulé Indians arrived in search of a trader. They are encamped five days' march from this. . . .

"Monday, 6th. Baptiste Dorion, Charles Primeau, and Hipolite Neissel left here this morning with four Indians, who arrived on the 4th with Mdse., to trade meat, etc., etc. Sent up Ortubize to the Navy Yard (or shanty) (Chantier) to hunt for our men at work there. . . .

"Tuesday, 14th. Messrs. Catlin and Bogart arrived from Ft. Union on their way to St. Louis.

"Wednesday, 15th. A fine pleasant day. Baptiste Dorion and G. P. Cerre arrived from the Brulé camps, with dry meat, robes, etc.

"Thursday, 16th. Light southerly winds. Mr. Catlin left us for St. Louis, accompanied by Mr. Bogart, in a skiff.

"Friday, 17th, A fine, pleasant day, with a refreshing shower in the evening. In the early part of the day news was brought in of a band of buffalo not being far from the fort. Consequently a party went out to hunt them. Baptiste Dorion was one of the party; they all returned without killing any buffalo; but Dorion fell in with a Stiaago (?) Indian riding off with one of the Company horses. After a little scuffle he killed the Indian and we got back the horse. We suppose he was a Ree. Dorion did not fire at the Indian till he had fired two arrows at him.

"Saturday, 18th. Hot, sultry weather. Hands employed variously. Finished hay-making and have five mud chimneys under way. Brown arrived from the lumber yards, also two rafts of timber. . . .

"Tuesday, 21st. Weather as yesterday. At 11 a.m. Mr. Brown arrived from the lumber yards. Two of the men there, Louis Turcot and James Durant, having stolen a canoe and deserted last evening. Mr. Brown, with one man, left here in a canoe at 12 m. in pursuit of them. Several lodges, Yanctons and Esontis (?) arrived on the other side the Missouri and camped there.

"Thursday, 23rd. Fine weather. Mr. Brown arrived with the two deserters, Turcot and Durant. He caught them in the middle of the Big Bend.

"Friday, 24th. A continuation of fine, pleasant weather. Twelve or thirteen lodges Indians crossed the river and camped alongside of us. Commenced planting the pickets of the fort. . . .

"Sunday, Sept. 9th. Southerly winds and pleasant weather. The prairies are on fire in every direction. G. P. Cerré arrived from the Sawon Camp. . . .

"Monday, 24th. Laidlaw, Halsey, Campbell, Demaney, and an Indian left for Sioux agency, near Fort Lookout, and on

"Sunday, the 30th, they returned, accompanied by Dr. Martin, who visits this place for the purpose of vaccinating the Indians. Messrs. McKenzie and Fontenelle, with several others, arrived from Ft. Union in a bateau, having on board about 6,000 lbs. beaver skins. In the evening Wm. Dickson arrived from River Bois Blanc in quest of Mdse. for the trade there."

EDITOR'S NOTE

(A) This should probably be Quenel, according to Lawrence H. Fox.

H

JOURNAL OF A STEAMBOAT VOYAGE FROM ST. LOUIS TO FORT UNION

The journal which follows, like that which has just been given, affords a better idea of one of the peculiar features of fur trade life than can be had in any other way. The navigation of the Missouri River was a science *sui generis*. The reader will note especially the hourly presence of serious obstacles, such as sand bars and snags; the great annoyance from winds and storms; and the overshadowing importance of the wood question. He will also note how few of the old river names still survive, and how many "forts" or trading houses were then in existence whose very names are now utterly forgotten.

The following statistics show the rate of speed made by the vessels whose annual voyages are recorded in the Sire Journal. The distance from St. Louis to Fort Union was about 1,760 miles:

In 1841 the trip up consumed 80 days and the trip down 21 days.
In 1842 the trip up consumed 76 days and the trip down 22 days.
In 1843 the trip up consumed 49 days and the trip down 15 days.
In 1844 the trip up consumed 54 days and the trip down 16 days.
In 1845 the trip up consumed 42 days and the trip down 15 days.
In 1846 the trip up consumed 44 days and the trip down 31 days.
In 1847 the trip up consumed 40 days and the trip down 14 days.

The trip of 1847 was the shortest both ways of those here given. The average daily speed up was 44 miles; down, 123 miles.

THE STEAMBOAT "OMEGA"

LOG OF STEAMBOAT OMEGA, from St. Louis to Fort Union, 1843.

JOSEPH A. SIRE, Master
JOSEPH LA BARGE, Pilot

Among the passengers were the Naturalist Audubon and party.

(Translated from the original French.)

April 25. Tuesday. Left St. Louis at 11 a.m. Water high but falling slightly. Current strong. We make slow progress. Reach St. Charles at 4 o'clock next morning, when we put Sarpy on shore, who returns to St. Louis.

April 26. Wednesday. Set out at 6 a.m. Current still strong. Took wood twice. The steamboat *Rowena* passed us at the entrance to the channel along Bonhomme Island. Met the *Troja* at Leve Cul. Camped at South Point at 8:30 p.m. The river is undoubtedly in fine condition for night running; but it is dark and the weather threatening. Moreover, we have too much to lose to risk our cargo for the sake of gaining a little time.

April 27. Thursday. Set out rather late. At times our progress was very slow. It was 9 p.m. when we passed Portland. As the weather is clear we run all night. Passed the mouth of the Osage at day-break.

April 28. Friday. The current still strong and the river rising. Passed Jefferson City, where we met the *Mary Tompkins* and the *Weston* going to St. Louis. Wooded at 11 a.m., 9 miles above Jefferson City. Much difficulty in finding wood. We found some by chance, 4½ cords, below the large island 4 miles below Rocheport. We tried in vain to stem the current along the bluffs (*de monter les côtes*). At 10 p.m. I decided to put to shore on a little island in order not to consume our wood to no purpose. We had the good fortune to find some poles (perches) and I had 300 brought on board.

April 29. Saturday. Set out as soon as it was light, which enabled us to take some advantage of the current. We succeeded in ascending. Wood still scarce and poor. Stopped at Boonville to take on Brooker, a mulatto. Passed Glasgow at 7 o'clock. Great difficulty in doubling the point opposite the mouth of the Chariton. Camped on the island below Old Jefferson at 9:15 p.m. I send the yawl to look for some poles.

April 30. Sunday. Set out at 4 a.m. Current still strong, and to cap the climax the wind rises with incredible force. It is useless to try to keep on and we put to shore 4 miles from our last camp, where, most fortunately, we find poles and dry mulberry, which permits us to fill the boat. At 1 p.m. the wind seems to moderate. We set out, and thanks to the wood which we had chopped and the poles we had taken, we get along very well. As the night is fine we continue our voyage, and at break of day are at the "Coupe du Petits O." Took 5 cords of wood at Fine's. Passed Lexington at the dinner hour, where we were overtaken by the *John Auld*, which pushed along by.

May 1. Monday. Current still strong. Overtook the *John Auld* at camp, where we took 6 cords of wood and then lay-to for the night at the head of the chute.

May 2. Tuesday. Set out before day. It seems that we are making better progress. In fact, since the water is falling the current is less strong. Stop at Owen's, where I take 12 barrels flour for Richardson. Stopped at Liberty Landing for dispatches from Mr. Laidlaw, and at Madame Chouteau's, where I find everything abandoned. Passed the bad place at the mouth of the Kansas River after sunset. The weather was so fine that I decided to run all night. At 6 a.m. we reached Leavenworth.

May 3. Wednesday. Set out at 8 a.m. We got along well, although often slowly. At 4 p.m. we reached the little island below village 24. In order to avoid a bad chute on the right we took the left hand channel and had the misfortune to run aground. We got ourselves clear once, but had the misfortune to get fast crosswise the channel. It rained and blew in a frightful manner. We were compelled to stay where we were for the night in the hope of extricating ourselves in the morning.

May 4. Monday. We get clear, but by a false maneuver of the pilot we get aground again. Broke our large cable. Finally succeeded in getting off by shoving the stern around. The wind blows with incredible force, and we have to pass a place very dangerous on account of snags. We remain at the bank until 6 p.m., and finally camp at the wood yard above village 24.

May 5. Friday. Set out at day-break. Took 9 cords of wood 400 yards farther on. The strong wind annoys us much. Arrived at Robidoux (Blacksnake Hills or St. Joseph) at 1 p.m. and remained there an hour taking 5 cords of wood, 10 barrels lard, and some provisions. The wind increases. We enter the Nadowa chute. We have hard work to overcome the wind at Nadowa Island, and it is with difficulty that we arrive opposite our last year's encampment at 8 p.m.

May 6. Friday. The wind blows frightfully all night, with such violence that it seems as though the smoke-stacks would be blown down. It moderates a little at sunrise and we set out. We do not go far before it blows as strong as it did before. We land to cut some axe helves and get a little wood. It is one o'clock when we resume our journey, and in spite of wind and current we arrive at the Iowas at sunset, where I discharge the freight for the agent. We go on to Jeffrey's Point, where I take 10 cords of wood for which I give an order upon the House for $20.

May 7. Sunday. We set out at day-break. Good wood, calm weather, and good progress. Passed the Grand Nemaha (Tapon Glaire) and stopped at Brown's at Nishnabotana, where I take 5 cords of wood that I do not pay for. (I forgot to say that we chopped some wood at the point above Tapon Glaire.) Passed the Little Nemaha, where we were obliged *de muler pour prendre à droite.* We lost fully an hour. Finally we camped at a point on the left in view of Long Island.

May 8. Monday. We made good progress as far as to Beau Soleil Island, where we tried in vain to pass to the right along the prairie. It was necessary to take the old channel. Took 8½ cords of wood at Hank Roberts. We found everything carried off by water at Akays (?). Passed to the left *de l'Isle de l'Etroit;* passed the *Grand déboulis.* A little farther all the houses are demolished by the flood. Passed Table River. Stopped at McPherson's, where we bought and cut some wood, and finally went into camp opposite the mouth of the Weeping Water.

May 9. Tuesday. Passed Trudeau Island, Five Barrels Island, la Purre a Calument, L Oeil de fer. I find no wood. I decide to have some cut a little further on. Tried the left hand channel, where the steamboat *Pirate* was lost, but could not get through. Tried the right hand, but it was shallow, *bouleversé* and full of sand bars. Found 5 cords of wood at Baptiste Le Clair's, which we took. Crossed to Abbadie's, where we put off his freight. Went on to *L'Issue,* where I put off freight for the sutler and for Captain Brugwin. Set out at

7 p.m. and camped above the bad sand bar near the marsh at Hart's cut-off at 9 p.m.

May 10. Wednesday. We progressed finely as far as Hart's Bluffs (côtes à Hart), where, at 7 a.m., we were summoned by an officer and four dragoons to land. I received a polite note from Captain Burgwin, informing me that his duty obliged him to to make an inspection of the boat. We put ourselves to work immediately, while Mr. Audubon goes to call upon the Captain. They return in about two hours. I compel, as it were (*en quelque sort*), the officer to make the strictest possible inspection, but on the condition that he would do the same with the other traders. I have the men chop 15 cords of *liard vert* for the return trip. Heaven knows if it will be there when I get back. Resumed our journey at noon. Passed the house of Mr. Cabanne, Boyer River, Fort Manuel, and stopped for the night at the head of Four-house Cut-off in the hope of finding wood there. I was cruelly disappointed. There is nothing but some elms there, which will be very difficult to split. I dread to use drift wood, but we shall have to come to it and will use rosin to make it burn.

May 11. Thursday. We soon find some drift wood, which we proceed to cut, since there is no other kind in this country. As I expected, it will burn only by the aid of rosin. Passed Soldier River. Proceeded slowly on account of the wood. Cut some more wood, which was worse than the other. It is almost impossible to keep going. We camp at 8:30 p.m. Tomorrow I hope to find some ash at Little Sioux River. The water rose 5 feet last night.

May 12. Friday. Scarcely had we started when we were obliged to lay-to on account of the fog. Started again half an hour later. Found the difficult chute of the Little River of the Sioux stopped up, and the channel passing through the mud bars. Stopped at the end of the long straight stretch and chopped some ash. It is a good place for this kind of wood. Passed Pratt Cut-off, Wood's Bluffs, and camped at Blackbird. The water rose last night 2½ feet.

May 13. Saturday. Just as we were on the point of starting a fog arose, which compelled us to remain in camp until 6.30 a.m. During this time I had some ash cut. Came on in good shape. Passed McClellan's Bluffs, where a cut-off has formed on the opposite side, which saves two or three miles. Chopped some *liard sec* below the prairie, where the Omaha village stands. Passed this prairie. Chopped some more wood about 3 miles below Sergeant's Bluffs. There is enough here for several years. Passed Setting Sun Bluffs. Camped at the mouth of the Big Sioux. It is wretched weather, rainy and windy. Last night the river stopped rising.

May 14. Sunday. We depart before day break by moonlight. The weather is uncertain all the morning. At 11.30 a.m. we stopped at the point where we arrested 4 deserters two years ago, and loaded the boat with dry wood. We push on at 1.30 p.m., but the wind, which had risen with incredible force, and the strength of the current (for the water commenced to rise again last night) made us give it up. I had the boat put to shore and set the men to cutting wood for the return trip. Instead of subsiding the wind increases. It is rather a hurricane. I am momentarily in fear that the smoke stacks will fall down. If this wind continues it will be a sleepless night (*nuit blanche*) for me.

May 15. Monday. The wind continues to blow as hard as yesterday. I set the men to cutting *bois de liard* again. At about 3 p.m. the wind seems to soften. In case it continues (to fall?) I will have the boilers pumped up so that we may be ready if it falls enough. We set out, but Great Heaven, how slow we go! Often we drift backward by the force of the current. We come as far as to the foot of the bluffs of Little Iowa River. Last night the river rose 14 inches, and I think that it is still rising. The *Omega* does all she can, but she is too heavily loaded to continue against a strong current like this, and the wind of this country, which is almost always strong.

May 16. Tuesday. The river rose 11 inches last night, and consequently we have a h——l of a current (*un courant d'enfers*). It is 11.30 a.m. when we reach the Vermillion houses. We set out again at 12.30, after having taken on some wood which I left there last year; but scarcely had we doubled the point of the island when the engineer announced the sad news that one of our boilers had burned out. We have to tie up, and I much fear that we shall be here a part of tomorrow. I set the men to cutting green *liard*, which will be of use, if not for the return trip, then for next year.

May 17. Wednesday. We remain here longer than I thought we should, for at the hour of this writing we have not finished (the repairs). I have more wood cut and we have 50 to 60 cords. The water, which had risen last night, has commenced falling since dinner. May it so continue until we reach Fort Pierre.

May 18. Thursday. It takes us another day to complete our repairs. This is due to the difficulty of introducing rivets between the flues and the wall of the boiler. The water continues to fall rapidly—3 feet since yesterday noon. Messrs. Laidlaw and Drips passed down at 8 o'clock with 4 Machinaw boats. I write to the house and Mr. Audubon sends his dispatches.

May 19. Friday. We push on at daybreak. We find the current still strong in spite of the fall of water. Lost considerable time in passing the mouth of the Vermillion. It is necessary to sound, and we find only 4½ feet. Cut 8 or 10 cords of wood at the first point on the left above the Vermillion. We find the channel which follows the bluffs below the *Petit Arc* extremely bad (there is considerable ash at this place). We cut some more dry *liard* at the beginning of the point below the *Perkin's woods*. We went into camp at the said woods.

May 20. Saturday. The water fell only 2½ inches last night. We set out at break of day in spite of wind and rain, which hinder us a great deal. We arrive at noon at the ash point on the right going up, below Bonhomme Island. It is useless to try to chop any: the water has flooded everything. I am seriously embarrassed; when opposite the entrance to the Bonhomme channel we find enough dry *liard* to fill the boat. It is half past three. All day long the wind blows as it only can on the Upper Missouri. Often we scarcely move at all. We pass to the left of the island. The water is shallow and swift. Finally we come to the first prairie to the right, where there is a good quantity of drift. Camped at 8.30.

May 21. Sunday. Set out at 3.15 a.m. The wind blew all night and is blowing still. We still see a good deal of drift wood, but we are not in need of any. Passed Manuel River and

Bazille River. A little below we saw a band of cows (buffalo), something that has not been seen here for many years. At 10 a.m. we arrive at Fort Mitchell, where we cut dry wood from the pickets, houses and fences. If the Indians or other do not burn this establishment, there will be enough dry wood there for two or three years. Resumed our voyage at 11 a.m., but the wind, which increases, retards us considerably. Passed Chouteau River. There the wind becomes almost irresistible. Nevertheless we enter the channel of Ponca Island, but at the head of the island, where the bluffs rise directly from the water (*trempent a l'eau*) we are forced to stop. I land on the island and go to cutting green wood which will be of use on the return trip or next year. It is 3 p.m. Finally, toward 6 o'clock, the wind seems to moderate. We set out and follow those interminable bluffs, which *trempent a l'eau*, and go into camp on the opposite shore at the commencement of the prairie at 8.30 p.m. Last night the water fell only an inch and a half.

May 22. Monday. We push out at 3 a.m. Passed the town at 4.30. All along the bluffs (*côtes*), where it is shallow, we move slowly. Cut more wood at 6 a.m., some miles below Handy's. It is necessary to take wood wherever one can find it. In passing Handy's point a party of savages fired a volley at us, two shots of which passed through the men's cabin. Fortunately no one was hit. It is probably those rascally Santees; no one else would be capable of such an attack. We had much difficulty in passing the point of oaks opposite the River Pratte. We had to sound, and found only 4 feet large. During this time I had some oak wood cut, poor fuel for steam. Finally we lay-to at 8 p.m. at Little Cedar Island. It will be necessary to chop some wood in the morning, notwithstanding that we have commenced this evening.

May 23. Tuesday. After cutting some wood we set out at 5.30 a.m. Cedar Island is no longer worth the trouble of stopping there, since it is impracticable to land where the best wood is. Took the same route as last year; passed to the right of Snag Island (*Isle aux Chicots*). Took on board the hunters whom I sent out last night. Passed the Three Islands safely, but opposite the Bijoux Hills at Desire Island I plunge into the sand bars and soon we are aground athwart the current. Our spars break and it is dark before Durack returns with others. We will begin again tomorow morning. The heat has been unsupportable all day. Thermometer 92°.

May 24. Wednesday. We find the boat in the morning pretty much in the same situation. We set at work immediately and are just about to get afloat again when one of the spars breaks, and we are obliged to send 2 miles to look for another on an island where they are very scarce. It is 10 a.m. and the yawl has not yet returned. We met La Charite, who is descending the river in a skin canoe with goods for the Poncas and brings me a letter from Mr. Honore Picotte. The yawl returns at last and we succeed in extricating ourselves, but we go aground again, again get off, and after having sounded again find only one passage and that a doubtful one. We lurch and break one of our rudders, but 10 minutes afterward we are afloat. We put to shore to mend the rudder, and meanwhile I have some wood cut from drift. At 6 p.m. we resume our journey and come to the head of the Bijoux Hills before night, where I send out men to chop a little wood. The river continues to fall slowly. The wind has changed to the N.W., and it has turned cold.

May 25. Thursday. We did not get off until 6 a.m. because I had a full load of dry wood taken on. The wind rises with rain and the weather is frightful. We are obliged to stop and sound before we reach John's Bluffs. We run with difficulty on 4 feet of water. The river has fallen considerably and in many places we find no more water than we have to have. Passed White River. At American River (*Rivière des Americans*) we spend a good deal of time in sounding. At the head of the channel at Cedar Island we find no way out. Nevertheless, Desire, whom I send to sound, reports 4.4 feet. We shall try it tomorrow morning.

May 26. Friday. We are a little late in starting, for it is very necessary to see clearly before leaving the channel. Sent out the yawl. Found the same depth again, 4 ft. 4 inches. Passed through. Stopped at the foot of the bluffs below Fort Lookout, where we cut more cedar, which we have to go a good way for. We had much trouble at two places in passing

Fort Lookout Point. We passed to the right of Deslaurier's Island for the first time. I believe that the (good) water was that way last year, but it did not suit Francis (pilot) to try it, and I was compelled to lighten the boat of her whole cargo. At the head of the chute we had to sound, and found just enough water to pass. If we drew 4 inches more we should frequently have had to lighten half the cargo. Much trouble in passing along the bluffs below the Great Bend. Put ashore Mr. Audubon, his companions, and 3 men, who will camp on the other side of the bend and wait for us there. Chopped more drift wood and camped at 8.15 at the first bluffs on the right going up. I forgot to say that I have sent 3 men express to Fort Pierre with papers for that establishment.

May 27. Saturday. Scarcely have we set out when we consumed two hours making a crossing. A little farther it looks for a moment as if we should be obliged to lighten the cargo a half (it was raining in torrents), but we have the good luck to get through. Passed the chain of rocks at dinner time, and at 3 p.m. arrived at the head of the Great Bend, where I have some wood cut, and Mr. Audubon and companions return on board. We try in vain to pass to the right of the island below the mouth of Medicine River. We have to return and take the small channel to the left. There is a good deal of good cedar wood at the entrance and if the channel remains there it will be a good place to get wood. Camped near the head of the channel at 8.30 p.m.

May 28. Sunday. As far as to the mouth of the Medicine River there is good wood. We have much difficulty to the point where we broke our rudder last year. We get along very well after that. I do not cut any wood at the bluffs below the Grand Cedar Island, because I expect to find some where I cut some last year opposite La Chapelle Island. But a large sand bar has formed there. I am compelled to stop in sight of Simeneau Island at 1.30 p.m. to cut some poor wood. Resumed our voyage at 2.15. We got along well to Ebbitt's house, where I take on 30 packs of robes and Major Hamilton. At the head of Simeneau Island there is not enough water, only 3 feet large. To take off half the cargo will not be enough. I therefore decide to await until tomorrow morning. Perhaps some changes will take place.

May 29. Monday. I send out to sound the channel. No more water than yesterday, but appearances are more favorable. Where there was no water yesterday we find 3 feet 6 inches. The gentlemen from Fort George pay us a visit and take dinner with us.

May 30. Tuesday. In one place we find 4 feet. In the other 3 feet 10 inches. We set to work and it is 5 p.m. before we have passed those two cursed bars. We are obliged to send the yawl for wood. Messrs, Picotte, Chardon, and several others arrive from the fort (Pierre). Camped at 8 p.m. opposite Fleury Island, where we loaded up with dry wood. Fleury, who came on board, tells me that the river has risen 7 inches since noon.

May 31. Wednesday. It seems that we may not be able to reach the fort (Pierre), for we shall not be able to pass along the small island below the fort. We resolve to try the small channel to the left, but after a long trial we are convinced that it is impossible. I send to the fort for the ferry boat and a Mackinaw boat, and having transferred some lead and tobacco we are able to pass up the right of the island. We reach the fort at 3 p.m. The unloading of the freight for this post is finished at sundown.

June 1. Thursday. I remain at the fort a part of the forenoon on account of business. Write to the House and to Durack with my instructions concerning the *Trapper*. Crossed at 11 a.m. Took on some articles I had need of. Gave some provisions to Durack for his journey. Cut 2 cords of drift wood and stopped for the night above old Fort George at 9.30 p.m. (There is a good deal of drift wood at the old dirt village.)

June 2. Friday. We set out at 3 a.m. Passed the Big Cheyenne, the island at Ash Point, to the left of Assiniboine Island, where we could not land and consequently could not take on the wood which I left there last year. Stopped five times to take on drift wood. Passed to the left of Little Cheyenne Island and camped about 2 miles below the Little Cheyenne at 8.45 p.m.

June 3. Saturday. The wind blows violently all night and

has not stopped when we set out. We try to pass to the left of Touchon Kaksah, but are obliged to go back about 2 miles and take the right hand channel, and we pass to the head of a small willow island. We come along very well, although there some bad places. It is not suprising for we are today in the worst part of the Missouri. Stopped at the willow island below the mouth of the Moreau at 10 a.m. and took on some very poor drift wood, but there is no other. We try the right hand of Prele Island, where we went down last year, but we find no way out. We go back and take the left hand channel, where we lost 2 days last year, and find good water. Passed Grand River, where I thought I could land and cut up an old house for wood, but we could not get in there. Passed the rampart and landed opposite the little island below the old Aricara village. The weather is threatening, and I believe a bad storm is on. I have scarcely a cord of wood for the start tomorrow morning, but I hope I have enough to reach the ash point below the old village. It is 8.30 p.m.

June 4. Sunday. We got a late start on account of our bad wood. Stopped a little farther on at Ash Point below the old Aricara village. Stopped again at La Chapelle Point where we take in the remains of the Primeau houses. Passed *La Bourbeuse*, Fort Manuel, and camped at Primeau's Fort a little below Beaver River, where we load up with cord wood, leaving some for the return trip. I note that this side of the *Bourbeuse*, and even below there is a good deal of drift wood. All day we have had a north wind which has delayed us a good deal. But for that we should have made a much better day.

June 5. Monday. We have just enough water at the second Beaver River crossing. Passed Cannon Ball River, Mitchell's wintering house, Bouis' wintering house, where we fill the boat with worthless wood, which makes me curse all the rest of the day. It is only by the aid of rosin that we can raise barely enough steam to keep us moving very slowly. I have left several cords of the same wood for the down trip. Passed Apple River, the place where the *Assiniboine* burned, and finally went into camp at 9.20 p.m., at the beginning of Heart River Point. We have passed today a good deal of drift wood between and considerable below Bouis' wintering ground. If the water does not carry it off between now and next year it will be very easy to get. The water seems to be rising rapidly all day. It rose two inches last night.

I forgot to say that we were not able to land opposite the mouth of the *Rivière au Berchet*, where I had chopped some oak wood last year. It is necessary therefore to go there again, although the report is that the Indians have burned a part of it.

June 6. Tuesday. We set out at day break. We lose a good deal of time in finding the channel a little above the mouth of Heart River. It is 9 a.m. when we get clear. We meet Kipp with four barges at the Square Buttes. He joins us. I write to St. Louis by the barges, care Mr. Burguiere. Passed the Square Buttes, where we cut some ash wood. Camp at the point where the Assiniboines met us two years ago. Filled the boat with poor ash wood, which Mr. Chardon had cut for us. All day the weather has been miserable, rain and an east wind.

July 7 [evidently an error for June 7]. Wednesday. Bad weather continues all night. We reach Fort Clark early. We are much delayed in getting the freight ashore, for it rains continually. The wind rises with such force that I decide to remain here all day. Give a feast to the Aricaras and get everything ready to start at daybreak tomorrow.

June 8. Thursday. We are off at 2.45 a.m. We pass safely the Grosventre bar because the water is up; otherwise I think we should have had a hard time of it there. Stopped with these Indians and lose an hour being polite to them. Passed the Great Rock. Passed the wintering ground of the Aricaras last year, which is situated a little below Dancing Bear, where there are three wagons which I must take to Fort Clark on my way down. At the same time we can cut some wood from the lodges and houses. Camped a little above the wintering ground at 8 p.m. I have the boat loaded with ash and dry *liard*. Three times today we have cut *bois de bature*. The river continues to rise. It is high enough for a good down trip.

June 9. Friday. We set out again at the same hour. Passed Dancing Bear an hour later. This point has *deboulée* a good deal and it will be of use to cut wood there for the down trip. Passed without difficulty the place which used to be so bad. The channel has improved greatly. Passed the mouth of the

Little Missouri and all the bad places below and above the river without difficulty. Stopped at the prairie a little below the foot of the Great Bend to pack our cylinder. During this time we kill a cow. We pass to the left of the little island. In passing the chute our yawl is considerably damaged. We land for a moment to put it on deck and during this time I have *bois de bature* cut. We get ourselves entangled in a channel *tout le long de terre*, which has no outlet. We have to back out and follow the island. We do not go far along the bluffs *qui trempent à l'eau*, when we run into the same difficulty and have to withdraw. We lie-to finally at 10.30 p.m. at the place where we cut wood every year. I will have the boat loaded tomorrow morning.

June 10. Saturday. We cut wood until 4.30 a.m. Stopped a moment and killed two bulls. Passed the Little Knife River at 12 o'clock. A little farther we cut some dry *liard*. Passed the chain all right. Met four lodges of Assiniboines at the beginning of White River Point. Again we cut a good lot of dry *liard*, little more than we cut last year, at the upper end of the point. Met the same Indians again at 7 p.m. Camped near the Butte au Cure at 8.45 p.m. Strong wind and rain.

June 11. Sunday. We start a little late on account of bad weather. Cut some ash wood at 9.30. Continued our journey at 11 o'clock. It blows strong all day and at times we scarcely move. Do our best we cannot reach the Muddy. We camp at 9 p.m. at the foot of the bluffs below that river. The water has fallen a little since day before yesterday.

June 12. Monday. The water fell last night about three inches. We set out at 3.15 a.m. and soon pass the Muddy. Stopped to cut a little dry wood. We have no more. Stopped again at 11 a.m. at the place where we usually cut wood. We fill the boat with dry *liard*. I am indeed afraid that we shall not reach (the fort) this evening. Wind strong and frequent rain. Finally we start at 12.45. We make but slow progress on account of wind and current. Passed Fort Mortimer opposite the mouth of the Yellowstone, and reached Fort Union at sunset. The water continues to fall.

June 13. Tuesday. We discharged the freight for the fort

in a short time, made some repairs, and spent the rest of the day at the fort. The water is still falling, but not fast.

June 14. Wednesday. It was after breakfast when we set out (on the return trip). Stopped a little way down and took on enough wood, if we do not run aground, to carry us to Fort Clark. It is 9.30 a.m. when we pass the mouth of the Yellowstone. Made good progress the rest of the day. Stopped for the night at 8.15 a little below the mouth of Knife River. The water continued to fall last night.

June 15. Thursday. As I anticipated we had a good deal of trouble at the head of the island at Little Knife River. Run aground, worked a long while, and did not get off till noon. We ran the Great Bend without difficulty until we reached the island at the foot, where we ran hard aground again and did not get off until sunset. Camped eight or ten miles farther down. Tomorrow will be another bad day. I forgot to say that at midnight there came on board a band of Assiniboines who, in my inmost soul, I would like to send to the devil. I had to pass the rest of the night with them, and to take ten of them along with us as far as to the Grosventres.

June 16. Friday. Contrary to my expectations we did not ground at the mouth of the Little Missouri. Stopped opposite Dancing Bear, where I took on several wagons for Fort Clark and also some good dry wood from Chardon's houses. Farther down we stopped at an old village where there was some more good wood. A little farther down we had to cast anchor because of a break of a valve stem. We came slowly to the bank and resumed our voyage at 5 p.m. Put off the Assiniboines at the Grosventres. We soon came to the bad sand bar. We looked for a channel a long while without finding a sure one. It being already late and a prospect of bad weather, I put to shore a little below the mouth of Knife River. Tomorrow morning we must sound. River stationary last night.

June 17. Saturday. We sound the channel—scarcely enough water, but by aid of the spars we force ourselves over the bar. We are soon at the Mandans, where I take on board 500 odd packs. Set out at 2.30, make good progress. Took the rest of the wood that Chardon had had cut; passed Heart River after sunset; struck the bar but had the good luck to back off.

Camped at the same place where we camped on our way up on the 5th. River stationary.

June 18. Sunday. Started a little late. Passed Cannon Ball River. Killed a cow and a bull. Wooded at Beaver River. I left four cords which were too far to go after, and we have enough anyway, and the heat is insupportable. In backing up we scuttled our yawl. Ran aground at the same place, but got off soon. Put to the bunk a moment. After that we got along all right. Camped a little above Prele Island, where we remained two days last year waiting for the channel to cut out. The river is still stationary.

June 19. Monday. This has been a day of running aground and of fatigue, but we expected it. We find all the channels changed. Passed the Moreau and ran aground a little below. Aground again opposite Touchon Kaksa. Stopped at the bluffs opposite the Little Cheyenne, where we cut a little cedar, but set out again three-quarters of an hour later. Stopped at Assiniboine Island at 6.30 p.m., where I have the yawl fetch the wood which I left there last year. The heat is extremely oppressive today. The water does not fall any yet. As I am writing a hurricane rises accompanied with thunder and rain, lasting much of the night. It already commences to turn cold.

June 20. Tuesday. It is still blowing too hard this morning to set out, but at 5 a.m. the wind seems to fall a little. I have the fire lighted. As nearly as I can judge by the water marks the river has risen four inches. Passed the island at Ash Point. where there is a bad place. We soon reach the Big Cheyenne. We have trouble at the crossing and more at the place where we generally cut cedar. The weather is so bad that I stop and go to cutting wood. I send and have the channel sounded, which takes a long while on account of the wind. Finally we get by. Stopped at 7 p.m. a little above the dirt village, where we gathered all the drift wood we could find. Finished work at 8.30. All day we have had wind and rain. The river still seems to be rising.

June 21. Wednesday. We soon reach the fort (Pierre). I learn with pleasure that the *Trapper* left nine days ago. The water rose last night and is still rising. I therefore wait all day at the fort. It is frightful weather all day.

June 22. Thursday. Set out a little late. Arrived at the farm, where we take on wood which is all soaked. It is not surprising, for it has rained and blown ever since we left Fort Clark. Resumed our voyage at 8 o'clock. A little trouble below the farm and a little above Lachappelle Island (always a bad place) passed Frederick with six barges and camped at foot of the bluffs below White River. The wind is still high. The river stopped rising last night.

June 23. Friday. A little late in starting again. But that is on account of the gloomy weather which we have had for some time. Today it has turned out pleasant. Made good progress all day. We take more of the cut wood on Ponca Island. It is too far to carry it. We stop below Manuel River, where we cut up some good drift wood. There is a good deal of it from the head of Bonhomme Island to Manuel River, and it will be a good resource for next year. Camped at the point above Vermillion. I would much have preferred to have reached the place where we cut some wood on the way up, but it is too late and here we are in the land of snags. The river rose an inch last night.

June 24. Saturday. We reach a wood pile in a little while. Wooded quickly. Stopped at the Vermillion houses where the channel is so full of snags that we cannot get to the bank. I land with the yawl. As Paschal has not the means of sending the packs to me—all his horses having been stolen and one man killed by those brigand Santes, probably the same who fired on us on our way up—I bring four packs in the yawl and at 10 a.m. we set out. I do not stop where we have some wood cut below Little Iowa River, because we have enough to take us to Hart's Bluffs. We came along finely and camped at Little Sioux River where the mosquitoes eat us up. The weather threatens wind and rain.

June 25. Sunday. We came along very well. Stopped at the cut-off at Hart's Bluffs, where we take on the rest of the wood that we cut on our way up. Stopped at Hardin's and at Sarpy's, where we met the *Oceana*. We remained some time and put off 11 barrels of lard and two of biscuit. Took some wood from opposite Baptiste Leclair's. Stop again at Arcot's, where we take three cords that I do not pay for. We came along very well until in sight of the narrows, when our packing blows out. We can scarcely reach the bank, being in a place full of snags. It is dark when we stop.

June 26. Monday. We have a good deal of trouble in extricating ourselves from the obstructions in which our wheels are buried. It is necessary to repair the arms. The sun is already high when we set out. Stopped at Brown's and took five cords of wood which I do not pay for. Stopped at Robidoux, where I take on six cords more, which I do not pay for *non plus à* $1.50. Finally we camped at Leavenworth. Met the steamboat *Admiral* at Weston.

June 27. Tuesday. Set out as usual. Stopped at Madame Chouteau's. Took wood at Sharp's; also at the chute of Mammy's wood yard. Camp at Old Jefferson, where we take three cords of wood to fill the boat.

June 28. Wednesday. In spite of wind and rain we make good progress. Took five cords at Bear River. Continued our journey and camped at night opposite St. Charles where we took four cords of wood at Chauvain's.

June 29. Thursday. Reached St. Louis in time for breakfast.

I

THE FUR TRADE OF THE SOUTH WEST
By the Editor

As General Chittenden states, he does not consider the fur trade of the Southwest as within the limits set by him as the scope of his work, and accordingly he says little of activities in that field, except as incidental to the matters of which he treats. It has been deemed desirable however, to round out the history of the fur trade by an outline sketch of the American fur trade in that region. (A)

For the most part, the sources of information are scattered and scanty. There is good reason for this. The visits of the traders and trappers were almost always in violation of the laws forbidding the activities of foreigners. In the South therefore, they generally came and went secretly and in small parties and frequently no records were made. To the North, on the contrary, the Spanish, later Mexican, power was ineffective and the authorities were ignored. In New Mexico, Arizona and California there was always the risk of imprisonment, fine or confiscation, tempered by bribery. So the expeditions to the Southwest were generally more or less surreptitious, and few details have come down to us. Yet it is certain that there was a fairly steady infiltration of trappers to the Southwest.

Gregg wrote of a time which was the Golden Age of the Santa Fe trade, from 1831 on, and he devotes little attention to the fur traders and trappers, for this trade as such had by that time dwindled to comparative insignificance. Some of the earlier expeditions have been treated in the text and notes in the chapters on the Santa Fe Trail. These include Clamorgan, De Munn and Chouteau, Philibert, Glenn and Fowler, and McLanahan. Nor need more than mention be made of the expeditions of J. S. Smith and J. R. Walker as these have been adequately treated.

Chittenden says in note 14, Part II, Chapter 28, under date of 1826, that according to Inman, Ceran St. Vrain left for Santa Fe in September of that year and that with him was the runaway Kit Carson. In note 2 to Part II, Chapter 30, he says Carson joined Charles Bent at this time. It could not have been St. Vrain, as he had been to Santa Fe earlier that year and had already left for Gila.

This Gila expedition of 1826 has been described by T. M. Marshall in the Southwestern Historical Society *Quarterly*, Volume XIX, page 251, in which are set forth Mexican official documents throwing much light on the expedition.

In August, 1826, Narbona, the Governor of New Mexico, issued a passport to St. Vrain (there called Seran Sambrano) and S. W. Williams to trap. The expedition split into four parties in which one under Miguel (Michel) Robidoux was almost exterminated on the Gila by the Indians. This is the group with which Pattie was connected. Others trapped on the San Francisco and the Colorado. Ewing Young, called Joachin-Joon in the records, led one of the parties. According to Honorable Bontwell Dunlap as recorded by Charles L.

Camp in the California Historical Society *Quarterly*, Volume II, Part 1, S. W. Williams was probably none other than Old Bill Williams.

Reports from nervous Mexican officials are on record showing that members of the expedition were approaching Tucson, Zuni and other villages. A touch of comedy is given by the violent protest that "foreigners" were poaching on the preserves of loyal New Mexican citizens. The protestant was that same James Baird, one of McKnight's party, but now an enthusiastic New Mexican citizen, who had himself spent nine years in jail as a foreigner. As a result, diplomatic representations were made to the American Minister who promised to investigate; but so far as is known, nothing effectual had been done up to the time of the Mexican War.

St. Vrain had begun his activities in the southwest in 1824. He and his brother Marcelline were for many years partners with the Bents both in Bent's Fort on the Arkansas and the later Fort St. Vrain, which was erected on the South Platte near the mouth of the St. Vrain River.

George C. Yount was with this expedition to the Gila in 1826 and probably in Young's division. The following year in 1828 he also trapped on the Gila. In 1830 he went with Wolfskill to California over what is now called the Old Spanish Trail. His reminiscences are set forth in the California Historical *Quarterly* just cited. An interesting item is his belief that Jedediah S. Smith discovered gold in California in 1828 and intended to go back there to work the deposits.

Ewing Young went to Santa Fe with Becknell and Wolfskill in 1822, the first time wagons were used on the Santa Fe Trail. In 1824 he trapped at Juan with Wolfskill. He made another journey to California in 1831 in the course of which he trapped on the Gila and arrived in Los Angeles in April of 1832. Most of the party under David E. Jackson returned with horses and mules, while Young and several of the men remained to trap in California. Young lived there for several years and ultimately went to Oregon where he died.

James Ohio Pattie has left us his colorful *Personal Narrative*, edited by Timothy Flint and published in Cincinnati in 1831. A mere boy, he with his father, Sylvester Pattie, left

Council Bluffs in July 1824. Arrived at Santa Fe, he was engaged in several trapping expeditions on the Gila in 1825 and 1826 and also worked at the copper mines. They were with the St. Vrain expedition to the Gila of 1826 and young Pattie at least was apparently with the detachment of Michel Robidoux. In 1827 the two Patties and six men split off from Yount's expedition to the Gila, went down the Colorado and across lower California to San Diego. They endured terrible hardships, including imprisonment in the end, during the course of which Sylvester Pattie died. Most of the survivors became permanent residents of Colorado. Doubts had long been entertained of the entire truthfulness of the *Narrative* largely because of young Pattie's vagueness as to his companions. It would seem that he deliberately suppressed the names of the leaders of the expeditions in order to magnify his own importance. Joseph J. Hill of the Bancroft Library of California, in the Southwestern Historical *Quarterly*, XXV, page 243, and Charles L. Camp in his editing of Yount, have given us a clue. It would seem that his expeditions were those of St. Vrain, Ewing Young and Yount.

Kit Carson was a member of Ewing Young's 1829-1830 trapping expedition to California. This was the first of Carson's six journeys to California. In Volume I, No. 2 of the *Quarterly* of the California Historical Society, Charles L. Camp has given a complete history of all of these. Only the first need concern us, for his next visit was with Fremont in 1844.

The party left Taos in August, 1829. To deceive the Mexican authorities, they pretended to be bound for the Green River, but after traveling fifty miles to the north, they turned southwest and proceeded through the country of the Navahoes to the Zuni village, then to Salt River, where they had a battle with the Indians and killed many of them. They trapped on the San Francisco River and the party then divided, some returning to Taos, and eighteen under Young, including Carson, started for California. Enduring great suffering from hunger and thirst, they crossed Colorado "below the Grand Cañon," probably near Camp Mohave or at the Needles, traversed the Mohave Desert, went up the dry bed of the Mohave River for two days until water was reached, then proceeded through the Cajon Pass to San Gabriel Mission. They then began to trap down the San Joaquin. Here they found signs of trappers ahead of them and a few days later overtook a party of sixty under Ogden, who had been sent into that country by the Hudson's Bay Company after learning of Jedediah Smith's California expedition of the previous year. The two parties kept more or less in touch as they trapped down the San Joaquin to the Sacramento, at which point Ogden left and proceeded up the Sacramento on his way to the Columbia.

At San Raphael, which Camp thinks might possibly be a mistake for San José, they ingratiated themselves with the Mission Fathers by attacking an Indian village to compel the return of some runaways from the mission. At this point they sold their furs to the captain of a trading schooner who was at the mission.

On the return journey they were not so fortunate in keeping on good terms with the Californians, and escaped arrest at Los Angeles only by over-awing the authorities. Arriving again at the Colorado, they trapped down its northern bank to Tidewater, then up the other side to the San Pedro. From there they went to the mines on the Gila and left their furs with Robert McKnight. Young and Carson went alone to Santa Fe and secured a license to trade with the Indians on the Gila; sent for the secreted beaver skins, and on their arrival at Santa Fe astonished the local authorities with the magnificent result of such quick and successful "trading."

Besides that with St. Vrain in 1826, Bill Williams is known to have been on many trapping expeditions in the southwest until he was killed by the Utes in Colorado in 1849. The account of his death in Ruxton is necessarily purely fanciful as Ruxton had died the preceeding year.

Little is known of Williams' trapping activities in the southwest. He flits in and out of the old narratives as mysteriously as a ghost. In his long and largely solitary career, he ranged from Oregon to old Mexico and from the villages of the Osage Indians to those living at the mouth of the Colorado. A city, a river and a mountain in Arizona still bear his name. Yount tells us of a certain "Williams, an American" among the Hopis in 1827. It probably was Old Bill for the account is entirely consonant with his eccentric character. Among these Indians he participated in their own religious rites and conducted elaborate Christian ceremonies before them. He succeeded in making a great impression upon them, and when the next year they had phenomenal crops they attributed it to the great medicine of the now absent Williams and almost deified his memory. (B)

Fort William, known as Bent's Fort, founded in 1829 on the Arkansas, was long an important post. Here off and on for years Kit Carson worked as a buffalo hunter. Ruxton's description of the fort is given in a note to Part I, Chapter 6.

Antoine Robidoux; a brother of Michel of the 1826 Gila party, of Joseph, the founder of St. Joseph, Missouri, and of Louis, the founder of Riverside, California, played an important part in the southwestern fur trade. In 1824 he left Fort Atkinson, going to Santa Fe and then to Green River to trap. On this journey occurred the attack on his party and that of Huddert (Heddest) referred to in Part II, Chapter 27. In October, 1833 Kit Carson found him trapping on the Uintah where, then or a little later, he established the well known Robidoux Fort on the Uintah. He also had a fort on the Gunnison, near the mouth of the Uncompaghre. Robidoux made frequent expeditions down the Colorado, to the Gunnison and to Santa Fe. After the political troubles of 1837 in New Mexico, Robidoux' fort on the Uintah was the chief base for such fur trapping as was done in the southwest.

EDITOR'S NOTES

(A) There is in press a history of the fur trade of the southwest by Joseph J. Hill of the Bancroft Library.

(B) Frederic C. Voelker is preparing a life of Old Bill Williams.

BIBLIOGRAPHY

Out of the vast number of authorities, some only of the more representative and important have been listed. Of these a rough classification has been attempted. Through these, references can generally be had to the more limited or obscure sources. Of course, the periods and subject often overlap.

MAPS

Useful maps, showing the growth of geographical knowledge and the routes of the fur traders and others, will be found in:

Bancroft, H. H., Histories (various dates).
Gilbert, E. W., Exploration of Western America (1933).
Merk, Frederick, Fur Trade and Empire, (1931).
Richman, Irving B., California Under Spain and Mexico (1911).

ASTORIA

Coues, Elliott, New Light; the Henry-Thompson Journals (1897).
Cox, Ross, Adventures on the Columbia (1832).
Franchere, Gabriel, Narrative (1854).
Irving, Washington, Astoria (1841)
Ross, Alexander, Adventures on the Oregon and Columbia (1849).

EARLY FUR TRADE

Bancroft, H. H., Histories (various dates).
Brackenridge, H. M., Views of Louisiana (1814).
Bradbury, John, Travels in the Interior of America (1819).
Coues, Elliott, New Light; Henry-Thompson Journals (1897).
Dale, Harrison Clifford, Ashley-Smith Explorations (1918).
Douglas, W. B., Manuel Lisa; Missouri Historical Society Collections, Vol. III.
Drumm, Stella, Luttig's Journal of a Trapper (1920).
Elliott, T. C., Peter Skene Ogden; Oregon Historical Society *Quarterly* Vols. X and XI.
Alexander Ross, Journals; Oregon Historical Society *Quarterly* Vol. XIV.

James, Thomas, Three Years Among the Indians and Mexicans (2nd edition 1916).

Merk, Frederick, Fur Trade and Empire (Simpson's Journal, 1824–1825) (1931).

Ross, Alexander, Fur Hunters of the Far West (1855).

Sulliuan, Maurice S., The Travels of Jedediah Smith (1934).

Thwaites, R. G., Original Journals of Lewis and Clark (1904, 1905).

Truteau, Jean Baptiste, Journal; American Historical *Review*, Vol. XIX.

Missouri Historical Society Collections, Vol. V.

Wheeler, O. D., On the Trail of Lewis and Clark (1904).

Work, John, Journals, Portions in Washington Historical *Quarterly* III, V, VI, XI.

Journal of John Work, 1831–1832, XIII, Ed. W. S. Lewis and Paul C. Phillips (1923).

PERIOD OF GREAT ACTIVITY

Alter, Cecil B., James Bridger (1925).

Bonner, T. D., Life and Adventures of James P. Beckwourth (1856).

Camp, Charles L., James Clyman, Frontiersman (1928).

Chittenden and Richardson, De Smet (1846).

Chittenden, H. M., Early Steamboat Navigation of the Missouri River (1903).

Coues, Elliott, Forty Years a Fur Trader (Larpenteur) (1898).

Farnham, T. J., Travels in the Great Western Prairies (1843).

Grinnell, G. B., Bent's Old Fort (1923).

Hafen and Ghent, Broken Hand (Fitzpatrick) (1931).

Irving, Washington, Rocky Mountain Sketches (Bonneville) (1837).

Maximilian, Prince of Wied, Travels in the Interior of America (1843).

Parker, Samuel, Journal of an Exploring Tour (1846).

Ruxton, George F., Adventures in Mexico and Rocky Mountains (1847).

Life in the Far West (1846).

Sage, R. B., Rocky Mountain Life (1860).

Victor, Frances Fuller, River of the West (Meek) (1870).

Wagner, W. F., Narrative of Zenas Leonard (1904).

Watson, Douglas S., West Wind, The Life Story of Joseph Reddeford Walker (1934).

Wislezenus, F. A., A Journey to the Rocky Mountains (1912).

Wyeth, Nathaniel J., Sources of the History of Oregon (Letters and Journals) (1899).

Santa Fe and Southwest

Bancroft, H. H., Histories (various dates).

Camp, Charles L., Chronicles of George C. Yount, California Historical Society *Quarterly* 2-1.

Kit Carson in California, California Historical Society *Quarterly* 1-2.

Conard, H. L., Uncle Dick Wooten (1890).

Coues, Elliott, Jacob Fowler (1898).

Pike (1895).

Duffus, R. L., Santa Fe Trail (1930).

Garrard, L. H., Wah-To-Yah and the Taos Trail (1850).

Gregg, Josiah, Commerce of the Prairies (1842).

James, Thomas, Three Years (2nd edition 1916).

Marshal, T. M., St. Vrain's Gila Expedition Southwest Historical Society 1-4.

Pattie, J. O., Personal Narrative (1831).

Robidoux, O. M., Memorial of the Robidoux Brothers (1924).

Sabin, Kit Carson Days (1919).

INDEX

sion. The move was, in his own words, "providential confirmation of my desire to write a history of the fur trade."[3]

That desire was realized in six years of research and writing sandwiched between service assignments that took him away from St. Louis during the Spanish-American War. In hindsight, what emerged in print in 1902 is a testament to Chittenden's diligence, discipline, and efficiency as well as a tribute to his broad vision and analytical skills. Completion of the two-volume history was a monumental undertaking and one that few "professional" historians could have accomplished in the same time period.

Chittenden the historian bridged several worlds. As Gordon B. Dodds, his primary biographer has noted, Chittenden's "philosophy of history partook both of the older, romantic histories, in the mode of Parkman, Irving, and Theodore Roosevelt, and of the newer scientific approach of Beard and Turner."[4] To read Chittenden is to indulge in the last of the sweeping, loosely documented romantic histories of nineteenth-century America. Yet Chittenden's writing also benefited from the new Progressive historians' approach, for he forced upon himself the burden of evidence and scrutinized his sources for proof. As in his engineering reports, he used formulas and raw data, weaving together the bits and fibers of evidence as they surfaced in his research. The result was a work that has stood the test of time as the most important and most comprehensive narrative history produced to date on the white-directed trade in the trans-Mississippi West from approximately 1807 to 1843.[5]

The project was a success for several reasons beyond Chittenden's abilities and his devotion to the task. Once in St. Louis, Chittenden gained open, uncensored access to the papers of the American Fur Company through the courtesy of the Chouteau family, whose ancestors were at the financial and organizational

FOREWORD
By William R. Swagerty

The publishing career of Hiram M. Chittenden began in 1890 and ended with his death in 1917 at age fifty-nine. During those twenty-seven years, this remarkably energetic amateur historian produced three major interpretive histories as well as a multivolume edited work and a dozen articles and technical reports. Today, Chittenden is best remembered for two acclaimed classics: *The American Fur Trade of the Far West* (1902) and *Life, Letters and Travels of Father Pierre-Jean De Smet, S.J., 1801–1873,* collected and edited in collaboration with Alfred Talbot Richardson in 1905.[1] Since their publication, collectors of Western Americana, students of the Far West, and professional librarians have fondled the weighty and now rare first editions of Chittenden's histories. Until the release of this Bison Book edition of *The American Fur Trade of the Far West,* only Chittenden's study of Yellowstone National Park was widely available in paperback to audiences other than academics and collectors.[2]

Chittenden was proud of his study of the fur trade, considering it a truly "professional" work, in contrast to his Yellowstone book, which was, by his own admission, "somewhat amateurish." The fur trade study was something of an accident—an offshoot of the technical reclamation reports and "ordinary literary work" demanded of a War Department engineer with a budding interest in scientific historical writing. Shortly before his death, Chittenden reflected that the most important transition in his life came in 1896 when he was transferred to St. Louis to supervise the Army Corp of Engineers' Missouri River Commis-

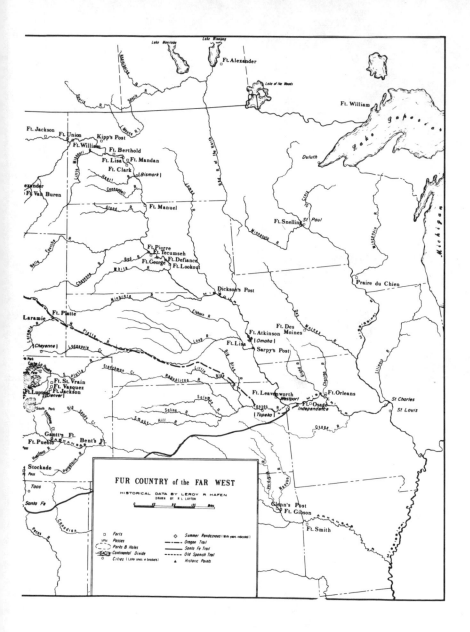

FUR COUNTRY of the FAR WEST

HISTORICAL DATA BY LEROY R HAFEN
DRAWN BY R L LAYTON

Forts
Passes
Parks & Holes
Continental Divide
Cities (Later ones in brackets)

Summer Rendezvous (with years indicated)
Oregon Trail
Santa Fe Trail
Old Spanish Trail
Historic Points